The Visual World in Memory

Current Issues in Memory
Series Editor: Robert Logie
Professor of Human Cognitive Neuroscience, University of Edinburgh, UK

Current Issues in Memory is a series of edited books that reflect the state of the art in areas of current and emerging interest in the psychological study of memory. Each volume is tightly focused on a particular topic and consists of seven to ten chapters contributed by international experts. The editors of individual volumes are leading figures in their areas and provide an introductory overview. Example topics include: binding in working memory, prospective memory, memory and ageing, autobiographical memory, visual memory, implicit memory, amnesia, retrieval, memory development.

The Visual World in Memory

Edited by
James R. Brockmole

 Psychology Press
Taylor & Francis Group

HOVE AND NEW YORK

First published 2009 by Psychology Press
27 Church Road, Hove, East Sussex, BN3 2FA

Simultaneously published in the USA and Canada
by Routledge
270 Madison Avenue, New York, NY 10016

*Psychology Press is an imprint of the Taylor & Francis Group,
an Informa business*

© 2009 Psychology Press

Typeset in Times New Roman by
Communication Crafts, East Grinstead
Printed and bound in Great Britain by
TJ International Ltd, Padstow, Cornwall
Cover design by Lisa Dynan

British Library Cataloguing in Publication Data
A catalogue record for this book is available from the British Library

Library of Congress Cataloging-in-Publication Data
The visual world in memory / [edited by] James R. Brockmole.
   p. cm.
 Includes bibliographical references and index.
 ISBN 978-1-84169-684-3 (hardcover)
 1. Memory. 2. Visual perception. 3. Vision. I. Brockmole, James R., 1977–
BF371.V58 2009
153.1'32—dc22

2008012565

ISBN 978-1-84169-684-3

Contents

List of contributors

James R. Brockmole, Department of Psychology, University of Edinburgh, 7 George Square, Edinburgh, EH8 9JZ, UK

Vicki Bruce, School of Psychology, Newcastle University, Ridley Building, Newcastle upon Tyne, NE1 7RU, UK

Deborah Davis, Department of Psychology/296, University of Nevada, Reno, Reno, NV 89557, USA

Giorgio Ganis, Department of Radiology, Harvard Medical School, 149 Thirteenth Street, Charlestown, MA 02129, USA

Mary M. Hayhoe, Department of Psychology, The University of Texas at Austin, 1 University Station A8000, Austin, Texas 78712–0187, USA

Andrew Hollingworth, Department of Psychology, The University of Iowa, 11 Seashore Hall E, Iowa City, IA 52242–1407, USA

Yuhong V. Jiang, Department of Psychology, University of Minnesota, 75 East River Road, S251 Elliott Hall, Minneapolis, MN 55455, USA

Stephen M. Kosslyn, Department of Psychology, Harvard University, 830 William James Hall, 33 Kirkland St, Cambridge MA 02138, USA

Elizabeth F. Loftus, Department of Psychology and Social Behavior, University of California, Irvine, 2393 Social Ecology II, Irvine, CA 92697-7085, USA

Robert H. Logie, Department of Psychology, University of Edinburgh, 7 George Square, Edinburgh, EH8 9JZ, UK

Tal Makovski, Department of Psychology, University of Minnesota, 75 East River Road, N504 Elliott Hall, Minneapolis, MN 55455, USA

Amy L. Shelton, Department of Psychological and Brain Sciences, Johns Hopkins University, 223 Ames Hall, 3400 North Charles Street, Baltimore, MD 21218, USA

Won Mok Shim, McGovern Institute for Brain Research, Building 46–3160, Massachusetts Institute of Technology, 77 Massachusetts Ave., Cambridge, MA 02139, USA

William L. Thompson, Department of Psychology, Harvard University, 844 William James Hall, 33 Kirkland Street, Cambridge MA 02138, USA

Marian van der Meulen, University of Edinburgh, 7 George Square, Edinburgh, EH8 9JZ, UK (now at Department of Neuroscience, University of Geneva Medical Center, 1 rue Michel-Servet, 1211 Geneva, Switzerland)

Naohide Yamamoto, Department of Psychology, George Washington University, 2125 G Street, NW, Washington, DC 20052, USA

Preface

Every morning at the same time (give or take 15 minutes depending on the speed with which my 2- and 5-year-olds decide to eat their cereal), I head off on a one-mile walk to the Psychology Department at the University of Edinburgh. The windswept Scottish rain aside, I thoroughly enjoy this walk—first among the eighteenth-century Georgian townhouses, then down the sixteenth-century streets, with the rocky crags of Holyrood Park and the majesty of Edinburgh Castle all the while framing my path (how could one not be in awe?). It was on these walks that the idea for this book slowly developed. I'd occasionally discover new and interesting *objects* in shop windows or aspects of the panoramic *scenes* I hadn't noticed before while standing on the bridges and hilltops overlooking the city. I started to realize that I was passing the same *faces* every morning coming down the hill from the city centre as I climbed up. When a traffic accident blocked my normal route home, I found that I was able to *navigate* home along a completely novel path (happily discovering quaint hidden pubs along the way). I'd come home and tell my wife about the interesting street performances and other *events* that I'd stumbled across. I constantly found myself captivated by the city's ancient buildings and tried to create *mental images* of what the city must have looked like centuries ago. In short, it struck me just how much of what I thoroughly enjoy about my walk to work depends on my ability to represent the visual world around me in memory. This book, in some sense, then, is a story of a one-mile stroll through Edinburgh and the amazing, striking, and at times desperately limited nature of memory for our visually based experiences, from simple patterns to highly complex, dynamic, and emotion-inspiring events.

How is the visual world represented in memory? The question has literally been asked for centuries, but the past decade has witnessed an explosion in scientific research on the question. With a recent PsycInfo search, I found 1,605 peer-reviewed journal articles that included "visual memory" as a key concept or major index term, dating as far back as 1897. Strikingly, 1,056 of these articles (66%) have been published in the last 10 years. It seemed, then, that the time was right to produce a volume that surveys the current issues confronting visual memory research and previews the challenges for researchers in the years ahead.

Although terms like "visual memory" sound as though they might be addressed by a unitary line of scientific enquiry, research on visual representation varies tremendously across the timescales, stimuli, and scenarios of interest. As will be apparent in this book, while some researchers are interested in memory for events in the distant past, other researchers' investigations are restricted to memory for visual experiences that occurred no longer than a second ago. While some examine memory for simple visual features such as color or shape, others consider memory for entire scenes. While some are interested in memory for specific objects, places, or events, others are interested in how memory for those objects, places, and events can be mentally manipulated to support future action and reasoning. While some are interested in the veridicality of memory, others are interested in the susceptibility of memory to various errors and distortions.

Although all of these areas of study combine to characterize our visually based experiences and memories, because of these disparate interests, research in the field of visual representation is in practice rather compartmentalized and as such is disseminated across a range of nonoverlapping literatures. The purpose of this book, therefore, was to collect a series of chapters written by leaders in the field that concisely present the state-of-the-science in all the aforementioned areas of memory research. The chapters are written by researchers who have made influential and lasting contributions to the study of memory mechanisms involved in representing the visual world; when taken together, these contributions provide a single source of information that uniquely bridges the field.

In the first chapter, "Fragmenting and Integrating Visuospatial Working Memory," Robert H. Logie and Marian van der Meulen introduce the concepts of visual and spatial working memory and analyze the major theories regarding working memory for visual information. They consider the question of whether a unique memory system exists for visual information, and, if so, how many visually and spatially based systems exist. The relationship between visual working memory and executive control, developmental aspects, and computational modeling of visuospatial working memory are also discussed.

The next three chapters are written by experts in the fields of object, face, and scene processing who have made highly influential and lasting contributions to the study of memory mechanisms involved in the processing of these stimuli. In their chapter, "Visual Memory for Features, Conjunctions, Objects, and Locations," Yuhong V. Jiang, Tal Makovski, and Won Mok Shim pick up on the distinction between visual and spatial working memory outlined in chapter 1 and review the evidence for whether the neural division of labor for the perception of objects and their locations extends to working memory. Turning to a behavioral analysis, they then consider the determinants of the limits of visual working memory, including those related to capacity, resolution, and executive control. Finally, they consider the relationship between short- and long-term memory for objects and their locations by considering how each is used to coordinate visually guided behaviours such as visual search. In chapter 3, "Remembering Faces," Vicki Bruce considers theories and models of face recognition including the role of visual and visually derived semantic codes in face memory. In describing the factors that affect face recognition, she contrasts the known properties of face memory with those of object memory. In this discussion she reflects on the configural or holistic processes involved in face recognition and on how the methods used in the expertise and neuro-science literatures have been used recently to critically assess whether face memory is a special class of object memory. Also considered is the role that dynamic information, such as head movement while making expressions or while speaking, plays in facial memory and the recognition of faces, especially when other information is impoverished. In chapter 4, "Memory for Real-World Scenes," Andrew Hollingworth analyzes the structure of scene repre-sentations and how elaborate those representations are. While considering how scene memory is constructed as participants view a natural scene and how both short- and long-term scene memory reciprocally influence scene percep-tion, he considers the nature of change blindness, the spatial and schematic structure in scene memory, the influence of gist and context in scene percep-tion, the effects of scene memory on object recognition, and the relationship between visual memory and conscious awareness.

Chapters 5–7 are written by very well-known researchers who consider the role of memory in natural real-world tasks in which the observer is an active player. These chapters discuss, in turn, the memory mechanisms involved in the motor planning and coordination of body movements, navigation, and witnessed events. In her chapter, "Visual Memory in Motor Planning and Action," Mary M. Hayhoe addresses how memory representations are involved in the coordination of natural tasks such as making a sandwich, batting a ball, or driving. While previous chapters have considered visual memory in a single brief exposure or trial, here the focus is on the sequence of different visual operations, the selec-tion and timing of which are controlled by the observer. With an analysis of eye, hand, and body movements in both real and virtual environments, she asks to what extent a current visual operation depends on memory for the output of a previous operation and what information from the world is actually needed in order to perform natural tasks. Next, Amy L. Shelton and Naohide Yamamoto consider the relationships between "Visual Memory, Spatial Representation, and Navigation." They point out that memory for space and spatial relationships draws heavily, but not exclusively, on vision and discuss how auditory informa-tion and textual descriptions also lead to spatial representation. They further outline the nature of the memory representations by considering the importance of viewpoint, observer orientation, and landmarks on both the recognition of, and navigation through, the visual world. They describe how a veritable menagerie of spatial representations available to humans and animals—including egocentric and allocentric representations, cognitive maps, eidetic memory, and memory for movement velocity, acceleration, and optic flow—give rise to remarkable spatial reasoning abilities. Deborah Davis and Elizabeth F. Loftus round off this set of chapters with a discussion of "Expectancies, Emotion, and Memory Reports of Visual Events." Drawing on their extensive research on the accuracy of eyewitness testimony, they consider the quality of memory for objects and faces when they must be interpreted and remembered in the context of real-life events. They discuss the malleability of memory for visual events at all stages of memory generation, from what is originally encoded in memory to the multiple efforts to retrieve and report on the original events. These authors also consider how factors such as emotion and stress influence our memory of witnessed events and how this requires a reinterpretation of current theory regarding memory for visual events.

In the final chapter, "Visual Mental Imagery: More Than 'Seeing with the Mind's Eye'," Giorgio Ganis, William L. Thompson, and Stephen M. Kosslyn discuss recent advances in the study and characterization of visual imagery. As many readers will be aware, an extensive debate surrounding the nature of imagery ensued in the late 1970s and 1980s without coming to any clear resolution. These authors turn to recent advances in noninvasive neuroimaging and neuropsychology in an effort to finally answer the question: How tightly linked are visual imagery and visual perception? Their focus in this discussion is on whether, and to what extent, visual mental imagery and visual perception recruit the same neural resources and whether there are different types of visual imagery, each relying on nonoverlapping brain networks. Although the authors argue that the study of mental imagery with these approaches is still in its early stages, the result of their analysis is the most up-to-date review of visual mental imagery available.

Throughout the chapters, readers will discover that many psychological constructs and research methods appear and reappear in discussion of wide-ranging lines of psychological investigation. For example, the building blocks of memory for objects constrain memory for scenes (collections of objects), which in turn influence memory for events (collections of dynamically changing scenes). Extensive cross-referencing of concepts among the chapters will highlight the myriad connections that exist between multiple lines of research. Readers will also see how advances in technology, including eyetracking, virtual reality, and neuroimaging, have caused a revolution in the research questions that can be addressed. With regard to the growing ubiquity of neural considerations in psychological research, all chapters include discussion of neuropsychology and/or neuroimaging findings.

In closing this short introduction, I would like to take the opportunity to thank the people that made this volume possible. First, of course, I would like to offer my sincere thanks to all of the authors whose outstanding chapters are presented here. Second, many thanks are owed to Lucy Kennedy, Tara Stebnicky, and Rebekah Waldron at Psychology Press for guiding this book from concept to reality. Third, I thank Chris Moulin and those anonymous reviewers who were kind enough to comment on previous drafts of this work; through their efforts this work has certainly been strengthened. Finally, I would like to thank my teachers and colleagues, especially Laura Carlson, John Henderson, David Irwin, and Frances Wang, who have stimulated my interest in visual cognition over the past 10 years and whose influences are apparent in the way I think about the field. For my part, I would like to offer this work for Ellen and Owen, and all those who marvel at the visual world around them. I hope that the rigorous discussion and analysis included in each chapter will appeal to established researchers and that the breadth of the book will make it a useful companion for students learning about memory.

James R. Brockmole
Edinburgh, September 2008

1 Fragmenting and integrating visuospatial working memory

Robert H. Logie and Marian van der Meulen
University of Edinburgh

1. INTRODUCTION

Remembering what we have just seen and retrieving visual details of past experiences underlies our every waking moment as well as being crucial for successful performance of a vast range of everyday tasks. The capacity for doing so is often attributed to temporary memory functions that can retain recently presented features of objects, where those objects are in relation to each other and to ourselves, and the movement sequences and trajectories for dynamic visual arrays. These same temporary memory functions are considered to support the manipulation of the information that they hold as well as to act as vehicles for the formation of integrated representations and mental images derived from stored knowledge and from clusters of stimulus features. Inevitably, cognitive psychology hosts a range of conceptual models devised to account for this temporary visual memory (for reviews see, e.g., Conway, Jarrold, Kane, Miyake, & Towse, 2007; Logie & D'Esposito, 2007; Miyake & Shah, 1999; Osaka, Logie, & D'Esposito, 2007; Shah & Miyake, 2005). In this chapter, we focus on a conceptual model that views visual and spatial temporary memory functions as being supported by a combination of domain-specific and general-purpose resources within a multi-component working memory system as originally proposed by Baddeley and Hitch (1974) and subsequently modified by Baddeley and Logie (1999; Logie, 1995, 2003). A schematic diagram of the Logie (1995, 2003) framework for visuospatial working memory that will serve as the basis for discussion in this chapter is shown in Figure 1.1.

The original Baddeley and Hitch (1974) proposal was that visual temporary memory reflected the operation of a visuospatial sketchpad (VSSP), which was thought to store the visual appearance of stimulus input and to support visual imagery tasks (i.e., the mental manipulation of visual input). The VSSP was complemented by the phonological loop, which was thought to serve a similar function for retaining verbal material, and both memory systems were controlled by a central executive. Over the last three decades, experimental investigation of visuospatial working memory in healthy adults and children and in brain-damaged adults has led to the concept becoming more complex (reviews in Baddeley,

1

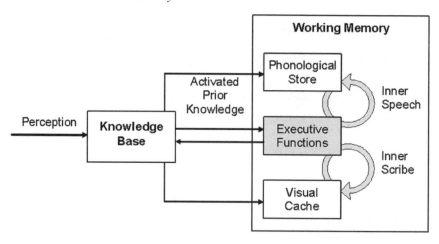

Figure 1.1. Working memory as a multiple component cognitive system with contents derived from activated prior knowledge. Adapted from Logie (2003; van der Meulen, 2008).

2007; Logie, 1995, 2003; Logie & Della Sala, 2005). Initially the focus was on identifying separable components that support, for example, dynamic functions such as remembering movements and pathways between objects, retaining the spatial location of objects, or retaining the visual appearance of individual objects such as their colour, shape or texture. However, the identification of these separable components has given rise to the problem of how a working-memory system might support integrated representations, and the relationship between stored representations and phenomenal mental experiences of images. A second challenge has been the interaction between working memory and stored knowledge traditionally attributed to a long-term memory: typically immediate memory for meaningful material greatly exceeds that for non-meaningful material, indicating a major role for prior knowledge in immediate memory tasks.

In this chapter we draw on experimental evidence from both healthy and brain-damaged adults, first to address possible dissociations in the infrastructure of visuospatial working memory, and then to address how the components of that infrastructure might act in concert to support phenomenal experience and temporary visual memory.

2. FRAGMENTING THE INFRASTRUCTURE OF VISUOSPATIAL WORKING MEMORY

The dissociation between verbal and visuospatial short-term storage is clear from single case reports of selective impairments in individuals with focal brain damage. A number of patients have been described who appear to have severe impairments in visual temporary memory in the absence of any peripheral deficits in visual perception, temporary verbal memory, or access to long-term stored knowledge (e.g., Beyn & Knyazeva, 1962; De Renzi & Nichelli, 1975; Warrington & Rabin, 1971). Moreover, patients with verbal short-term memory deficits (and again intact long-term memory) such as KF (Shallice & Warrington, 1970), IL (Saffran & Marin, 1975), or PV (Basso, Spinnler, Vallar, & Zanobio, 1982) have pathologically poor recall of aurally presented verbal sequences, yet they show a much higher verbal memory span when the sequences are presented visually. Their visual digit span is similar to that found for healthy participants with visual presentation under articulatory suppression. We shall return later to evidence for the use of visual codes in retaining verbal material, but the evidence above appears to suggest that visual temporary memory and auditory-verbal temporary memory can be impaired independently, pointing to separate, modality-specific systems. In the sections below, we consider the degree to which visual and spatial information is also maintained by separable memory systems.

2.1. Dissociating memory for visual and spatial properties of objects

One major approach to the study of visuospatial working memory has been to use selective dual-task techniques in which a primary memory load is accompanied by performance of a secondary task such as tapping in a set pattern (e.g., Farmer, Berman, & Fletcher, 1986; Quinn & Ralston, 1986), following a moving target with arm or eye movements (e.g., Baddeley & Lieberman, 1980; Pearson & Sahraie, 2003; Postle et al., 2006), or watching irrelevant pictures or abstract patterns (Logie, 1986; Quinn & McConnell, 1996, 2006) (see chapter 2 for extensive discussion of other approaches). These kinds of experiments led to the suggestion that visual and spatial as well as verbal temporary memory might be served by different components of the cognitive system. For example, Quinn and Ralston (1986) asked participants to retain an imagined pathway around a square matrix array (cf. Brooks, 1968) or to remember a verbal sequence while either concurrently tapping a pattern on the table or concurrent vocalization of an irrelevant word (articulatory suppression; Murray, 1965). They reported that tapping disrupted the ability of participants to retain an imagined pathway but did not disrupt retention of a verbal sequence. In contrast, concurrent vocalization disrupted retention of a verbal sequence but had no impact on remembering an imagined pathway. In complementary experiments, Logie (1986) demonstrated that concurrent displays of unrelated line drawings of objects disrupted the use of a visual imagery mnemonic (the peg-word mnemonic—see, e.g., Paivio, 1971) to remember aurally presented word lists. The same manipulation does not disrupt use of rote rehearsal for word-list recall. Irrelevant speech has the opposite effect, in that it disrupts use of rote rehearsal but not the imagery mnemonic. Consistent findings were reported by Quinn and McConnell (e.g., 1996, 2006) who developed a technique known as dynamic visual noise, which is a robust method for disrupting use of an imagery mnemonic while not affecting memory based on verbal rehearsal. We shall return to the technique of irrelevant visual input when discussing the relationship between visual short-term memory and the phenomenal experience of visual imagery.

Brain imaging studies of healthy adults also highlight a spatial/visual distinction. For example, using positron emission tomography (PET) functional imaging Jonides et al. (1993) tested two groups of participants on visual and location immediate-memory tasks using a change detection paradigm. In the location task, volunteers were shown dots at random positions. After a short retention interval they were shown a visual cue and had to indicate whether or not the cue identified the location of one of the previously presented dots. In the visual task, an unfamiliar shape was displayed followed, after a retention interval, by a second shape for comparison, and shapes were different from trial to trial. Both tasks were performed in a memory condition as described above, as well as in a perceptual condition, in which the target locations or shapes remained on the screen while the comparison took place. There were clearly different neuroanatomical networks associated with memory (rather than perception) for object shape, primarily in the left hemisphere, and memory for object location, primarily in the right hemisphere. Jonides and colleagues (e.g., see Smith & Jonides, 1995) interpreted these different activation patterns as reflecting different components of working memory and with the operation of the "what" and "where" pathways, previously identified in non-human primates by Ungerleider and Mishkin (1982). A similar dissociation has been identified using electrophysiological techniques (Ruchkin, Johnson, Grafman, Canoune, & Ritter, 1997). More recently, a network focused on dorsolateral prefrontal cortex (for detailed discussion, see chapter 2, section 2.2.1) and the mediodorsal thalamic nucleus have been associated with spatial working memory (e.g., Funahashi, Takeda, & Watanabe, 2004), while the posterior parietal cortex is associated with visual temporary memory (e.g., Todd & Marois, 2004, 2005). This, together with the dissociation between verbal and both visual and spatial working memory, appears to be consistent across a range of brain imaging studies, as shown in a formal meta-analysis of this literature reported by Wager and Smith (2003).

2.2. Dissociating memory for static patterns versus movement sequences

The evidence outlined above indicated a clear separation between the resources that support verbal temporary memory and those that support temporary memory for visual and spatial material, as well as a clear separation between a short-term and a long-term memory system. A similar approach has indicated that temporary memory for primarily static visual configurations appears to be distinct from memory for pathways and movement sequences. For example, Logie and Pearson (1997) showed that memory for visual matrix patterns appears to develop in children much more quickly than does memory for a sequence of movements between targets arranged in a random array—often referred to as the Corsi blocks task (Corsi, 1972; Milner, 1971). That same study demonstrated that matrix memory and Corsi block sequence memory are poorly correlated within each age group. A similar dissociation in children has been reported by Pickering, Gathercole, Hall, and Lloyd (2001), who demonstrated that memory for a pathway through a maze had a different developmental trajectory from memory for a static pattern. Furthermore, Della Sala, Gray, Baddeley, Allamano, and Wilson (1999; see also Logie & Marchetti, 1991) reported that memory for visual matrix patterns appears to be disrupted by presenting irrelevant pictures (abstract art) but not by concurrent spatial tapping, while memory for Corsi block sequences is sensitive to the converse pattern of interference.

Visual and location/movement-based working memory appear to be impaired differentially following brain damage. For example, Farah, Hammond, Levine, and Calvanio (1988) reported patient LH who suffered damage in both temporal/occipital areas, in the right temporal lobe, and in the right inferior frontal lobe. He performed well on tasks concerned with memory for locations and for pathways, such as letter rotation, 3-D form rotation, mental scanning, and recalling a recently described pathway but was severely impaired in his ability to remember colours and to recall the relative size of objects and shapes of states in a map of the United States. Wilson, Baddeley, and Young (1999) reported a similar patient, LE, a professional sculptress, who after suffering diffuse damage to both the cortex and white matter, was unable to generate visual images of possible sculptures and had a severe visual short-term memory deficit—for example, in retention of visual matrix patterns. However, she could draw complex figures that did not rely on memory, and she performed within the low normal range for Corsi block sequence recall. A contrasting case was reported by Carlesimo, Perri, Turriziani, Tomaiuolo, and Caltagirone (2001), who had damage in the right dorsolateral frontal cortex. The patient performed within the normal range on judging from memory the shapes, colours, and sizes of objects and animals, but had pathologically poor performance on mental rotation tasks, on Corsi block span, and on immediate memory for an imagined path around a matrix.

2.3. Dissociations of executive involvement in visuospatial working memory

These findings from healthy and brain-damaged adults led to suggested distinctions between visual and spatial (the "visual cache" and the "inner scribe"— Logie, 1995, 2003), static and dynamic (Pickering et al., 2001), and passive and active (Cornoldi & Vecchi, 2003) forms of visuospatial working memory. However, the position was complicated by demonstrations that memory for sequences of spatial locations appears to be sensitive to general attentional load and is disrupted by detecting the spatial location of tones (Smyth & Scholey, 1994) or even by pitch discrimination in which tones originate from the same location (Klauer & Stegmaier, 1997). Corsi block type movement sequences or pathways are remembered less well when the memory task is accompanied by movement of attention and by movement of the eyes (Pearson & Sahraie, 2003; Postle et al., 2006), as well as by arm movement and tapping shown in the earlier studies. Therefore, the retention of serially presented spatial material appears to involve central-executive or general attentional resources to a greater extent than had previously been suggested in the literature. This kind of evidence did not fit with the original proposal for the VSSP as a system for supporting mental imagery and visual short-term memory that was quite separate from the central-executive component of working memory (Baddeley & Hitch, 1974).

The theme of executive resources supporting spatial working memory is paralleled in the brain imaging literature. Fletcher and Henson (2001), among others (e.g., Collette & Van der Linden, 2002; Courtney, Roth, & Sala, 2007; Funahashi, 2007), have implicated the dorsolateral areas of the prefrontal cortex (DLPFC) in executive functioning, including information updating, attention shifting, and the inhibition of inappropriate responses. Zarahn, Aguirre, and D'Esposito (2000) and Leung, Gore, and Goldman-Rakic (2002) both found increased activation in the DLPFC during the maintenance of the relative location of sequentially presented spatial stimuli.

Further evidence for executive involvement in memory for spatial sequences arose from the use of random generation as a secondary task. This involves participants generating a continuous stream of items from a well-learned set, such as the alphabet or the numbers 1–9, but to do so in as random a fashion as possible. Random generation is thought to require inhibition of well-learned sequences such as "1–2–3–4" as well as keeping track of the frequency with which items have been generated previously (Baddeley, 1966; Evans, 1978; Salway, 1991; Vandierendonck, De Vooght, & Van der Goten, 1998). Inhibition has been identified as one of several executive functions (e.g., Miyake et al., 2000). Moreover, Jahanshahi, Dirnberger, Fuller, and Frith (2000) found that performance of random generation is associated with increased activity in the left dorsolateral prefrontal cortex.

Random generation was adopted as a secondary task by Salway and Logie (1995), who showed that both memory for mental pathways and memory for verbal sequences (from Brooks, 1968) were dramatically disrupted when participants were required to generate random sequences of numbers during stimulus presentation. Consistent with previous studies, memory for pathways was disrupted by concurrent pattern tapping but not by concurrent articulatory suppression, while the converse was true for remembering a verbal sequence. Therefore, there appeared to be a major role for general attentional resources in remembering spatial and verbal sequences in addition to any modality-specific resources. Fisk and Sharp (2003) reported disruption of spatial serial recall by random-letter generation, even when relatively short sequences of spatial locations were presented, while Vandierendonck, Kemps, Fastame, and Szmalec (2004) reported interference with Corsi block sequence memory from random-interval generation that has no verbal, visual, or spatial component. More recently, Rudkin, Pearson, and Logie (2007) showed that memory for sequentially presented spatial locations is sensitive to concurrent random-interval tapping (Vandierendonck et al., 1998, 2004), while memory for simultaneously presented spatial locations shows no such sensitivity to this kind of general attentional or executive load (see also

Darling, Della Sala, & Logie, 2007). Finally, using structural equation modelling Miyake, Friedman, Rettinger, Shah, and Hegarty (2001) found equal loading on a latent variable linked with executive functioning for tasks that require memory for sequential spatial information (e.g., Corsi blocks).

2.4. Summary

The conclusion from these dual-task studies, neuropsychological case reports, and brain imaging investigations with healthy adults appears to be that memory for dynamic information such as a movement sequence is reliant on different resources from those that support memory for a static array, and that both rely on different resources than does temporary memory for verbal sequences. However, memory for movement sequences also draws heavily on executive functions.

3. VISUAL WORKING MEMORY AND VISUAL IMAGERY

A different kind of dissociation has arisen when considering visuospatial memory function, compared with visuospatial mental imagery and the phenomenal experience of visual imagery. Phenomenal experiences of images are often assessed by self-ratings using instruments such as the Vividness of Visual Imagery Questionnaire (VVIQ) developed by Marks (1973). For the VVIQ, individuals rate the vividness of their mental experiences when recollecting a sunrise, a close relative or friend, and a familiar shop or landscape. This questionnaire has been used very widely and is known to generate a spread of scores in the normal population, to be reliable on test-retest with the same individuals, and to correlate with other measures of visual imagery experience (see McKelvie, 1995 for a review). However, it does not correlate highly with objective performance measures of visual working memory (e.g., Dean & Morris, 2003; McKelvie, 1995). Moreover, these self-ratings appear to be affected by personal beliefs: Reisberg, Pearson, and Kosslyn (2003) reported that researchers who rated themselves as having highly vivid imagery also were more likely than low-scoring researchers to feel that research on mental imagery was an important phenomenon and worth pursuing. This was true for the VVIQ and also for a new rating scale that Reisberg et al. devised, the Subjective Use of Imagery Scale (SUIS). Other studies showed strong correlations between subjectively rated mental imagery and social desirability (reviewed in McKelvie, 1995). These, and other results, point to the suggestion that phenomenal conscious experience of mental imagery and the functioning of the visual temporary memory system might not be as closely entwined as has been widely assumed.

A possible reason for the lack of a relationship between rated conscious experience of an image and memory performance is the problem of inter-rater calibration of subjective ratings: one person might rate a particular conscious experience as being highly vivid, but a similar experience might be rated as less vivid by someone else. As such, rating scales for visual mental images might be poor measures of individual differences in the phenomena being rated, even if they are robust and reliable measures within one individual tested on different occasions.

One approach to this problem is to examine how subjective ratings of mental images within the same individuals are affected by experimental manipulations, and a clear example of this approach was reported by Baddeley and Andrade (2000). They asked participants to generate and rate the vividness of mental visual or auditory images and to remember visually presented or aurally presented material while they performed another task, such as tapping the keys on a 4 × 3 keypad, counting aloud, or watching irrelevant random dot patterns (similar to dynamic visual noise—Quinn & McConnell, 1996). Both memory performance and rated vividness of visual images were reduced by concurrent tapping, but only vividness ratings were affected by watching random dot patterns, while the effect of counting varied between experiments, most likely dependent on the amount of verbal coding that accompanied task performance.

The disruptive effects of the secondary tasks on rated vividness of imagery were more evident for imaging novel patterns and tone sequences (using working memory) than they were for familiar scenes such as cows grazing, a game of tennis, or a sleeping baby (using long-term memory). This points towards a more positive link between working memory and conscious experience, and because each participant is being compared with him/herself, there is not a problem of differences between individuals in the criteria that they use for their vividness rating. However, because rated vividness was affected by random dots and tapping, but memory was only affected by tapping, there might not be a complete overlap between visual memory and subjective experience of visual imagery.

There are several cases of brain-damaged individuals who report an inability to experience visual images, but these patients often have other cognitive deficits such as an inability to recognize familiar faces (prosopagnosia), visual memory deficits, or inability to remember routes around cities and buildings that they have experienced many times (topographical amnesia). This combination of impairments is known as Charcot–Wilbrand syndrome (Charcot & Bernard, 1883; Wilbrand, 1887; for discussions see Logie & Della Sala, 2005; Solms, Kaplan-Solms, & Brown, 1996). However, Botez, Olivier, Vézina, Botez, and Kaufman (1985) described a single case of a 38-year-old teacher who reported an inability to experience visual images, and it appeared that he had never been able to do so. Despite this, his immediate and delayed visual memory was intact, and he had no difficulty in recognizing objects physically or from drawings, no problems in spatial orientation, driving, or in recognizing faces, and his verbal and other cognitive abilities were in the normal range. The CT scan available at the time was inconclusive about the site or extent of any structural abnormalities in the brain. It appeared that visual memory could function in the absence of a phenomenal experience of visual imagery.

A related case has been examined in our own laboratory recently (Zeman et al., 2007, 2008). This is an individual (MX—not the real initials), age 65 at the commencement of testing, who had a sudden loss of visual imagery that appeared to follow angioplasty, but with no detectable structural abnormality from a magnetic resonance imaging (MRI) brain scan. Like the Botez et al. (1985) case, MX had normal visual and verbal short- and long-term memory and executive function. However, unlike the earlier case described by Botez et al. (1985), prior to the reported problem MX had very vivid imagery ability, which he had used on a regular basis in his profession as a building surveyor prior to his recent retirement, as well as in all other aspects of his daily life. He found that he could no longer imagine the faces of friends and family or the characters in books that he was reading. Despite performing in the normal range on a wide range of tests of cognitive function and having an IQ of 136, he rated himself on the VVIQ and on the SUIS at the lowest possible points on each scale. The only hint of objective evidence for a deficit arose from a mental rotation task using the Shepard and Metzler (1971) figures, in which he showed a less steep slope between angle of rotation and decision time than a group of age- and occupation-matched controls.

Clearer evidence for MX's reported problem came from a functional MRI (fMRI) study in which he was asked to view famous faces (perceptual condition) or to look at the names of famous people and try to imagine what the people looked like (imagery condition). These two conditions were compared with a perceptual control in which grey-scale abstract patterns were shown and with an imagery control condition in which strings of random letters were shown. The paradigm was based on an fMRI study of healthy adults reported by Ishai, Haxby, and Ungerleider (2002). MX showed exactly the same pattern of activation as the controls when the perception condition was contrasted with the perceptual control, including expected activation of the fusiform gyrus that is often associated with face processing (e.g., Haxby, Hoffman, & Gobbini, 2000; for detailed discussion of the fusiform gyrus and other neural substrates underlying face memory, see also chapter 3, section 3.4). When the imagery condition was contrasted with the imagery control, the control patients showed the expected activation in the fusiform area that had also been found by Ishai et al. (2002). However, MX showed, if anything, decreased activation in the fusiform and related areas linked with face processing, but showed greater activation than controls in predominantly anterior regions including bilateral anterior cingulate, bilateral inferior frontal gyri, and the precunei. It appeared that the imagery condition resulted in a very different pattern of brain activation in MX than in controls, pointing to some functional difference in the patient that was not readily detectable by behavioural measures. However, the functional difference could be detected through fMRI techniques and was evident to the patient through his phenomenal mental experience. That is, there appeared to be intact visual perception and intact visual memory but an impaired ability to use the neuroanatomical networks associated with visual imagery. MX appeared to be attempting to use more prefrontal areas in imagery tasks, possibly to develop and implement an alternative strategy for task performance that did not require imagery. We have yet to examine the patterns of activation associated with visual short-term memory rather than visual imagery tasks.

4. MODELLING VISUAL IMAGERY

Kosslyn (e.g., 1980, 1994, 2005) has developed an influential computational model for visual perception, object recognition, and visual imagery. This has been driven by evidence that imaging and perceiving appear to share a number of functional properties (thorough discussion is provided in chapter 8). For example, when asked to scan across a mental image, rotate it, or zoom in (to inspect detail) or zoom out (to make gross comparisons), participants' response times are similar to those obtained when inspecting a physical display (e.g., Kosslyn, 1980; Laeng & Teodorescu, 2002). Neuroimaging experiments have demonstrated that the same brain regions are active during perception and during imagery (e.g., Farah, Peronnet, Weisberg, & Monheit, 1989; Kosslyn & Thompson, 2003; Mellet et al., 2000). For example, Kosslyn et al. (1993) found that the primary visual cortex (Brodmann Area 17 or Area V1) was active during visual imagery and, moreover, that regions activated during perception of objects also were activated when imagining those objects. These results are consistent with other studies that have found similar activation patterns for perception tasks and imagery tasks (reviewed in Kosslyn & Thomson, 2003). A diagram of Kosslyn's model is shown in Figure 1.2.

The key structure in Kosslyn's model is the *visual buffer*, thought to be involved in both perception and conscious visual imagery. The visual buffer holds visual images that are topographically organized within primary visual

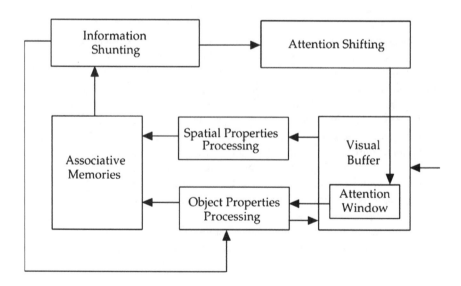

Figure 1.2. Kosslyn's model of visual imagery. Originally published as Figure 1 in Kosslyn, S. M. (2005). Mental images and the brain. *Cognitive Neuropsychology,* *22*(3/4), 333–347. Taylor & Francis Ltd. Reproduced with permission of the publisher and author.

cortex, broadly isomorphic with the visual array from the outside world. The capacity of the visual buffer is limited, and an attention window selects material that is projected through afferent connections to other parts of the cognitive system for additional processing. An object is recognized if the perceptual input (or visual-buffer output) matches a stored visual memory. Visual memories are stored long-term in the pattern activation subsystem (PAS) or "associative memory". This structure is the store of long-term memory representations, containing visual, spatial, semantic, and other properties. Input to the visual buffer also can come from efferent connections that are driven by high-level cognition and from knowledge stored in long-term associative memory. In other words, the visual buffer acts as a form of gateway through which visual input is passed on to other parts of the cognitive system, but the buffer can also receive input from the cognitive system. These characteristics then point to the visual buffer as being the primary focus for forming visual mental images either as memories of recently perceived scenes, or as images generated from prior knowledge with or without the inclusion of recently perceived material (e.g., Kosslyn, Thompson, Sukel, & Alpert, 2005).

The visual buffer has some of the characteristics of the concept of the visuospatial sketchpad in the Baddeley and Hitch (1974) multi-component model of working memory, in that both are thought to hold images derived directly from perception, or through direct retrieval from long-term memory. However, there are some important differences, and some of the data from studies of visuospatial working memory and from brain imaging of visual imagery tasks offer a challenge to the assumed overlap between perception and visual imagery and to the assumed role of the visual buffer as an input gateway between perception and the cognitive system.

From the brain imaging studies it appears that activation of primary visual cortex is not present when spatial (remembering a set of directions) rather than object imagery is involved (e.g., Mellet et al., 1996). Also, when the control condition involves participants being required to "imagine blackness" and with no ambient light in the experimental environment, there is no additional activation detected in V1 when the control condition is compared with a requirement to image objects, also in the absence of ambient light (e.g., Mellet, Tzourio, Denis, & Mazoyer, 1995; Roland & Gulyas, 1994). Kosslyn (2005) suggests that the activation of V1 might depend essentially on the demands of the task, and that V1 might be activated when a high-resolution image is formed (e.g., Mellet et al., 2000). However, he also suggests that the lack of increased activation in V1 when compared with an "imagine blackness" control might be due to the use of V1 to imagine blackness as well as to imagine the items in the experimental condition. It seems difficult to argue that imagining blackness would require a high-resolution image, so it appears difficult to use this approach to account for both kinds of anomalous results reported by Mellet and colleagues and by Roland and Gulyas.

Earlier in the chapter, we mentioned that the use of visual imagery such as in the peg-word mnemonic appears to be disrupted when items to-be-remembered are presented aurally but presentation is accompanied by irrelevant visual input such as unrelated pictures (Logie, 1986) or randomly changing dots, referred to as dynamic visual noise (Quinn & McConnell, 1996, 2006). This finding is consistent with Kosslyn's view that visual perceptual input and visual mental imagery rely on largely overlapping parts of the cognitive system. An obvious interpretation is that the irrelevant visual input is swamping the visual buffer, making it difficult to form an image from stored knowledge of the to-be-remembered words. However, this interpretation is complicated by the finding that dynamic visual noise does not appear to disrupt visual memory performance. For example, memory for square-matrix patterns or unfamiliar Chinese characters is unimpaired if dynamic visual noise is presented during a retention interval between presentation and test of the visual memory items (e.g., Andrade, Kemps, Werniers, May, & Szmalec, 2002; Avons & Sestieri, 2005; Zimmer & Speiser, 2002; Zimmer, Speiser, & Seidler, 2003). Other studies have indicated that dynamic visual noise appears to affect the use of the peg-word mnemonic only during presentation of the words for recall or during the recall period. There is no impact on performance if the irrelevant visual input occurs during a retention interval (Quinn & McConnell, 2006). Zimmer and Speiser (2002; Zimmer et al., 2003) also had difficulty in finding an impact of irrelevant visual input on the peg-word mnemonic during encoding. However, in those experiments it was striking that performance levels in the control (no interference) conditions were in the range 35–45%. This is extremely low compared with performance levels of around 65–75% found by Logie (1986) and by Quinn and McConnell (1996, 2006). Zimmer and colleagues also note that several of their participants had difficulty forming images using their version of the peg-word mnemonic. Moreover, the Zimmer et al. experiments did not include a rote rehearsal condition to check whether the peg-word mnemonic was showing the typical mnemonic advantage (reviewed in Paivio, 1971). Therefore, it is possible that participants in the Zimmer et al. studies were not actually using visual imagery, and this is the reason that they failed to replicate the effect of irrelevant visual input during encoding.

   In sum, it appears that irrelevant visual input disrupts the process of generating images, either for encoding or for retrieval, but does not affect the temporary retention of visual information, nor the retention of images when using the peg-word mnemonic. We could account for the peg-word results within Kosslyn's model by suggesting that the generation of images in the visual buffer occurs during encoding and retrieval of images, and these generation processes and Kosslyn's attention window are therefore vulnerable to disruption by additional, irrelevant visual input to the visual buffer. However, the use of this mnemonic strategy requires a different image to be generated and stored for each item on the list of to-be-remembered items on each trial, and therefore a limited capacity, and a topographically organized visual buffer is unlikely to be able to store the seven or so bizarre interactive images that are required. Kosslyn's PAS or associative memory would therefore be a good candidate for holding the set of images for each trial, and this system might be insensitive to additional, irrelevant visual input. This interpretation is consistent with a view expressed in Logie (2003) in which a visual imagery generation process might be vulnerable to irrelevant pictures or to dynamic visual noise, but storage in long-term associative memory would not be. Quinn and McConnell (2006; McConnell & Quinn, 2004) discuss this possible interpretation and argue that Kosslyn's mechanisms for the generation of visual imagery—the attention window together with the contents of the visual buffer—would be disrupted by dynamic visual noise.

Whether image generation is seen primarily as a process or as the operation of specific constructs such as an attention window and a visual buffer, this approach deals only with the results from experiments with the peg-word mnemonic. We are still left with the question as to what kind of system might retain the random, meaningless square-matrix patterns or Chinese characters used, for example, in the Andrade et al. (2002) experiments. The visual buffer is unlikely to be the host for this memory function, given that there is no impact of irrelevant visual input. It also seems unlikely that a PAS could support memory retention, because these patterns are chosen to be unfamiliar and non-meaningful. Therefore, a pattern activation system might be activated when the stimuli are presented, but any matches would be poor or partial at best and would be ill suited to retain novel patterns that have few, if any, prior associations in long-term memory. Logie (2003) suggested that the visual cache offers a memory function that might deal with novel material, but that is thought to hold the products of any initial processing of perceptual input rather than being directly accessible from visual input. So the information it holds could be partially processed in the sense of being characterized as "a Chinese character" or "similar to a letter shape" but would also hold elements of the stimulus that were approximations to the original physical characteristics. This visual cache also can retain visual characteristics of scenes or objects that have been verbally described (e.g., Denis, Beschin, Logie, & Della Sala, 2002; Deyzac, Logie, & Denis, 2006; Logie, Beschin, Della Sala, & Denis, 2005). At a neuroanatomical level, its characteristics are similar to those associated with the temporary visual memory linked with posterior parietal activation described earlier (Todd & Marois, 2004, 2005). Therefore, the visual cache is quite separate from, and quite different from, a buffer for visual input that Kosslyn associates with visual perception and as a medium for experiencing visual mental imagery. This is a distinction that also fits with the data from patient MX (described above) who appeared to have intact visual memory but severely impaired ability to generate visual mental images.

Some recent evidence from our own lab (van der Meulen, 2008; van der Meulen, Logie, & Della Sala, 2008) speaks to this dissociation between visual temporary memory and visual imagery. These contrasting cognitive functions were compared directly with respect to their sensitivity to disruption by a selective distracter. For visual temporary memory, participants were asked to remember a series of letters shown as a mixture of upper and lower case, one after the other, in the centre of a computer screen—for example h-Q-r-D or M-H-r-q. Following a retention interval of 15 s, participants were to write down the letters in the order of presentation and in the case in which they were presented. Previously published studies have shown that this task uses visual codes, particularly for retention of letter case (Logie, Della Sala, Wynn, & Baddeley, 2000). During the retention interval, participants were asked to simply remember the letters, or to watch a series of irrelevant and unrelated line drawings, or to tap their hand (unseen) in a figure-of-eight pattern. If a visual buffer is used to hold the visually presented letters, we might expect recall to be impaired by irrelevant pictures, which involves direct visual input into the visual buffer, but not by tapping, which involves no visual input. If instead a visual temporary memory system such as a visual cache is holding the letters, we might expect no disruption from irrelevant visual input, but we might expect disruption from tapping because of the requirement to simultaneously maintain a representation of the unseen tapping pattern to be followed. For mental imagery, participants were asked to respond to a series of aurally presented letters by generating a visual image of each and making a judgement about its visual characteristics—for example, whether the letter had an enclosed area, or curved lines. This kind of task has been used in a range of previous studies of visual imagery (e.g., Kosslyn et al., 1993; Weber & Castleman, 1970). The series of imaged letter-appearance judgements for each trial were made over a period of 15 s in a control condition and with each of the same secondary-task conditions as for the visual memory task. In the case of image generation, the two contrasting theoretical positions assume that broadly the same cognitive function is involved and therefore make the same prediction, namely that generating visual images of letters would be disrupted by irrelevant pictures because of the overlap between visual input and the image-generation process, but not by tapping, which involves no visual input and little, if any image generation.

A third, alternative theoretical perspective assumes that temporary memory is simply the temporary activation of long-term memory representations coupled with a limited-capacity attentional focus (e.g., Cowan, 2005; Postle, 2007; Ruchkin, Grafman, Cameron, & Berndt, 2003). According to this view, any secondary-task disruption is the result of the general cognitive demands of performing two concurrent tasks. In this case, imagery and temporary memory should both involve the same process of temporary activation of stored visual representations, and whichever secondary task is the most demanding should result in the greatest amount of interference regardless of the nature of the main task. However, there is no clear expectation in advance of the experiment as to which of the two distracters is likely to be the more demanding of the two, which highlights a certain circularity in this particular approach.

Summary results are illustrated in Figure 1.3. They were clear in showing disruption of visual imagery by concurrent irrelevant pictures but not by tapping, and, conversely, disruption of visual temporary memory by concurrent tapping but not by irrelevant pictures. This double dissociation or differential pattern of interference between memory and imagery cannot be explained by the overall demands of dealing with a secondary distracter as assumed by the last theoretical perspective considered above (for further evidence and discussion challenging this perspective, see Cocchini, Logie, Della Sala, & MacPherson, 2002; Logie, Cocchini, Della Sala, & Baddeley, 2004). The results are consistent with those

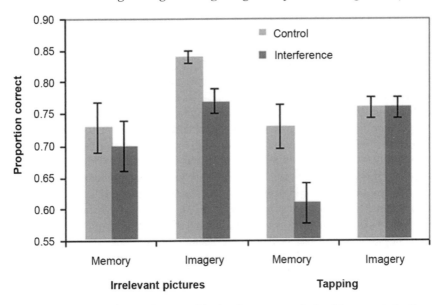

Figure 1.3. Differential interference with visual memory and visual imagery tasks from irrelevant pictures and from unseen pattern tapping. Results from van der Meulen (2007).

reported by Andrade et al. (2002) and Avons and Sestieri (2005) in showing an impact of irrelevant visual input on visual imagery but not on visual short-term memory tasks. If the visual buffer was being used for memory and for imagery, we would expect that the visual input from irrelevant pictures would disrupt both and that tapping would affect neither: tapping involves no visual input and is primarily a spatial/movement-based task that, as Kosslyn (2005) has argued, would not involve the visual buffer. If the letter-memory performance is supported by a PAS based on associative memory, it is difficult to see why this would be disrupted by repetitive motor output. The results are more readily explained by the same model that we have used to account for results from previous experiments on the use of irrelevant visual input—that is, we assume that visual temporary memory is supported by a visual cache that provides temporary memory and that is separate from the system that is involved in generating visual imagery or in buffering visual input.

A related argument has been made by Pearson (2001; Pearson, Logie, & Gilhooly, 1999), who argued that a visual buffer, like Kosslyn's visual buffer, is needed to subserve conscious visual imagery and that the visual cache acts as a temporary back-up store for non-conscious visual representations. Pearson describes the visual buffer as a structure that holds conscious mental images, "generated either from representations stored in long-term visual memory, or loaded directly from the perceptual systems in the form of visual traces" (Pearson, 2001, p. 51).

5. CONTENT AND CAPACITY OF THE VISUAL CACHE

The argument thus far has focused on the identification of a separate temporary visual memory system to which we have referred as the visual cache. However, apart from the argument that it is separate from visual perceptual processing and the visual imagery system, we have not as yet discussed what kind of memory codes might be used in such a system or what its capacity limits might be. We have referred briefly to the use of codes based on the visual appearance of letters when discussing the selection of task materials for the van der Meulen (2008) study. There is a broader body of literature consistent with the use of such visual codes in temporary memory tasks, and key experiments on this topic have focused on the manipulation of visual similarity among the materials to be remembered. If visual codes are being used to store the materials, then items that are visually similar to one another should give rise to confusions and consequent poorer recall than items that are visually distinct (e.g., Avons & Mason, 1999; Hitch, Halliday, Schaafstal, & Schraagen, 1988; Logie et al., 2000; Smyth, Hay, Hitch, & Horton, 2005; Walker, Hitch, & Duroe, 1993). Estimates of the capacity of a visual short-term memory system have varied from a single item (Broadbent & Broadbent, 1981; Phillips & Christie, 1977a, 1977b; Walker et al., 1993) to four or more items (Avons, 1998; Avons & Mason, 1999; Logie et al., 2000), although in the latter case, there is a debate in the literature (for detailed discussion, see chapter 2, section 2.3) as to whether this refers to four integrated objects (Luck & Vogel, 1997) or to the number of individual features that should be retained (Treisman, 2006; Wheeler & Treisman, 2002). We first address the studies of visual similarity and then move on to discussion of capacity limits.

5.1. Visual similarity in serial recall

Immediate serial recall of words, digits, or letters is widely used in the study of human memory, and a key finding has been the disruptive impact of phonological similarity on recall performance, even when the materials are presented visually (e.g., Conrad, 1964; for reviews see Baddeley, 1997; Baddeley & Logie, 1999). However, there is evidence that visual codes may also be used in these tasks. For example, articulatory suppression has a very substantial disruptive effect on verbal serial recall, but the impact is much less with visual than with aural presentation of the to-be-remembered sequence. Moreover, as mentioned earlier, patients with selective deficits of digit span can typically recall more items when these are presented visually than when they are presented aurally (reviewed in Caplan & Waters, 1990), suggesting that visual features of the digits can support serial recall performance despite the impairment of a phonologically based memory system.

More direct evidence for the use of visual codes in immediate, verbal serial recall tasks was reported by Logie et al. (2000). Across two experiments, they demonstrated that participants performed more poorly when recalling sequences drawn from sets of items that were visually similar (e.g., FLY PLY CRY DRY

TRY SHY), compared with sequences that were visually dissimilar (e.g., GUY THAI SIGH LIE PI RYE). The influence of phonological similarity was controlled by having both sets comprise phonologically similar items, and the use of phonological codes was controlled by using articulatory suppression. This effect of visual similarity for serial-ordered recall of verbal materials was replicated in that same paper in a further two experiments using recall of letter sequences. Lists were presented with a mixture of upper- and lower-case letters shown one after the other in the centre of a screen—for example, K-w-c-Y or g-B-h-Q—with written serial-ordered recall of the letters in the correct case. Letter sequences for which upper- and lower-case versions of the letters were visually similar (e.g., Ww Cc Kk etc.) were recalled less well than sequences for which the upper- and lower-case versions look quite different (e.g., Gg Bb Qq). The visual-similarity effect appeared both with and without articulatory suppression. Moreover, the visual-similarity effect appeared across serial positions. This suggests the operation of a visual short-term memory system that supports the retention of serial order.

Using a serial reconstruction technique, Avons (1998; Avons & Mason, 1999) has shown that serial recall of sequences of matrix patterns is disrupted by visual similarity of the material with performance following a bowed serial position curve. Here, participants select items in the correct serial order from a larger array of target and non-target items. Using a similar serial reconstruction technique, Smyth et al. (2005) reported an analogous pattern of visual similarity and bowed serial position curve with sequences of faces.

Visual-similarity effects do provide support for a memory system that relies on visual coding. However, whether this system can also retain serial order remains a topic of debate. One feature of the Logie et al. (2000) study was that the materials allowed the systematic investigation of the effects of visual similarity while attempting to control for phonological similarity. However, it was not possible to manipulate phonological as well as visual similarity within the same materials. As a result, it is unclear just how independent is the system for retaining visual serial order from the system that retains phonologically based serial order. This is important because one model that has gathered significant momentum in recent years assumes a single mechanism for retaining serial order for visual or for verbal codes, namely the Object-Oriented Episodic Record Model proposed by Jones and colleagues (e.g., Jones, 1993; Jones, Macken, & Nicholls, 2004). Similarly, Avons (1998), Avons and Mason (1999), and Smyth et al. (2005) have raised the possibility that a single mechanism might support retention of serial order regardless of whether the material is visual or phonological. An alternative view, also raised by Smyth et al. (2005), is that any system supporting memory for serial order might show characteristic serial position curves and effects of within-list item similarity even if there are separate, modality-specific temporary memory systems, each of which can retain both order and item information.

The Jones model has been developed principally to account for the impairment in serial verbal recall caused by irrelevant sounds. He suggests that sensory stimuli from various modalities are combined and retained as integrated objects.

Irrelevant fluctuating sounds disrupt serial order cues. He reports some analogous effects in visuospatial recall (e.g., Farrand & Jones, 1996) and argues for a common mechanism for retaining serial order of integrated objects. He argues further that any changing state material, such as irrelevant speech or articulatory suppression, will disrupt the codes retaining serial order regardless of the modality. Presumably in the case of the Logie et al. (2000) results, this model would argue that the objects incorporate a combination of visual and phonological codes, leading to the effects on recall performance of both phonological similarity and visual similarity. The suggestion that the visual and phonological codes are combined in these represented objects would seem to predict that when phonological and visual similarity are manipulated in the same materials, we might expect the effects to interact rather than to appear independently. We might also expect that both would be affected by concurrent articulatory suppression. Therefore, a systematic investigation in which phonological and visual similarity are manipulated within the same set of materials should be highly informative. While this kind of manipulation is very difficult to achieve with Roman letters and English words, it is possible with alternative writing systems that rely on ideographic characters such as Chinese or Japanese.

Zhang and Simon (1985) reported that Chinese speakers could retain sequences of items comprising characters (Chinese radicals) that have no specific phonological association, and they concluded that either a visual or a semantic code was being used for these materials. Hue and Ericsson (1988) found visual-similarity effects in immediate retrieval of Chinese characters. However, that study involved English-speaking participants for whom the phonological codes associated with each character would have been unfamiliar. Yik (1978) also used Chinese characters in an immediate recall task, but with readers for whom the characters were familiar. Yik observed both phonologically based and visually based confusions, suggesting the use of both forms of code with this kind of material and subject sample. Some of our own recent experiments (Saito, Logie, Morita, & Law, 2008) examined in groups of native Japanese speakers written immediate serial recall of visually presented Japanese Kanji characters, with factorial manipulation of phonological and visual similarity. An example of a pair of visually dissimilar characters would be "家" and "空", while visually similar characters share one radical—for example, "坂" and "板".

Results from three experiments were very similar, and the results from one of these experiments are shown in Figure 1.4. There were main effects of phonological similarity and of visual similarity, but these effects did not interact, indicating that both phonological and visual codes were being used independently to support memory. Across experiments, it was clear that the visual-similarity effect appeared across all serial positions, and also appeared when phonological coding was inhibited by using articulatory suppression.

A question here might be how the visual code for the materials supports performance of verbal immediate serial recall. In other words, what kind of mechanism might lead to a visual-similarity effect in immediate serial recall? One possibility might be that visual features could only act as supplementary

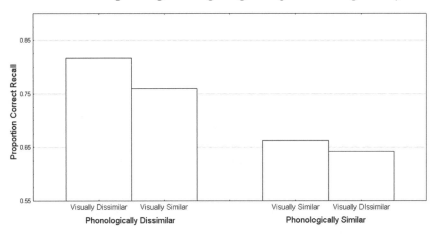

Figure 1.4. Immediate and serial recall of sequences of Japanese Kanji characters varying in phonological and visual similarity. Data from Saito et al. (2008), Experiment 3.

information to discriminate among the verbal items presented. In one version of this account, it might be possible to assume that only a phonological code can retain serial order information, but that visual as well as phonological codes could be used in the process of redintegration at recall. Although visual redintegration might have occurred, it was clear from the Saito et al. data and from Logie et al. (2000) that the visual code itself can maintain serial order. Also, as discussed earlier, evidence from Smyth et al. (2005) demonstrated that serial order memory for faces showed serial position curves similar to those found for verbal materials, and it seems more likely that a visual, rather than a phonological, code played a major role in retaining faces.

The second possibility could be that, as Avons (1998; Avons & Mason, 1999) and Smyth et al. (2005) indicated, the same mechanism might support retention of serial order regardless of whether the material is visual or phonological. In the strongest version of this view, it could be argued that a common mechanism could be used for retaining serial order of both visual and phonological memory materials (e.g., Farrand & Jones, 1996). However, here we might expect that manipulations affecting phonological similarity should also affect visual similarity in the same manner. One of the Saito et al. (in press) experiments showed that articulatory suppression completely eliminated the phonological similarity effect in the visually dissimilar condition at all serial positions, but had no impact on the visual-similarity effect. Thus, visual and phonological codes do not appear to involve a common retention system for serial order information.

An alternative hypothesis suggested by Smyth et al. (2005) could be that a retention system for visual serial order information is domain-specific, but that it functions in a similar manner to that for phonological serial order information. In principle, then, any memory system might function in a similar manner when given the task of retaining serial order. In this case, we could assume that patterns of memory performance for visual and phonological materials might be very similar, but that experimental manipulations might differentially affect memory performance for different sets of materials. This last interpretation appears to offer the best account of the Logie et al. (2000) and the Saito et al. (2008) experiments. However, it is clear from these experiments that recall of visually presented verbal sequences can be supported by the use of both phonological and visual codes. Although these codes appear to be handled by separable memory systems, they can nevertheless both be brought to bear on performing a recall task. They may also offer redundancy in the system, allowing for graceful degradation in the face of competing demands or localized damaged—for example, visual codes can support memory when phonological codes cannot, and vice versa. There are separable components of working memory, but these components may act in concert to support cognitive task performance.

5.2. Capacity of visual temporary memory

In addition to similarity of visual codes and retention of serial order, a major question remains as to what other factors might limit the capacity of a visual temporary memory system. Early experiments on this topic presented participants with sequences of random square-matrix patterns (Phillips & Christie, 1977a, 1977b; Walker et al., 1993) or abstract line drawings (Broadbent & Broadbent, 1981) and reported one-item recency effects with very poor performance. This led to the conclusion that the capacity of a visual short-term memory system might be just one item. However, Avons (1998; Avons & Mason, 1999) has shown that the one-item recency effect with visual patterns appears to arise only when assessing item memory using probe recognition techniques. These, and other studies reviewed earlier, demonstrated that multiple items can be retained, even when presented sequentially, and Logie et al. (2000) suggested a capacity limit of 3–4 items.

A range of studies over the last decade has shown that capacity limits of around 3–4 items also appear when using a variation of probe recognition often referred to as change detection. In these kinds of studies, an array of several stimulus items is shown briefly followed by a retention interval and then a test array. On half of the trials, one item in the test array is changed from the original, and the task is to decide whether a change has or has not occurred. Because participants are not forewarned of which item will change, they have to remember the entire array for accurate change detection. In many of these studies, each item is defined by two or more features, such as colour, shape, or location, and change trials comprise swapping features between items. Therefore participants also have to remember the particular combinations or "bindings" of features for each item. In one widely cited study using this kind of paradigm, Luck and Vogel (1997) varied the number of items shown in each stimulus array and also varied the number of features that defined each object (colour, orientation, size, or the presence of a gap). They found that participants could accurately detect changes with arrays of up to 3 or 4 items, with performance deteriorating for larger array sizes. However, performance did not appear to be affected by the number of features that defined each object, leading to the suggestion that visual short-term memory is limited by the number of integrated objects, and not by the total number of features depicted.

There has been a considerable debate in the area, in that a number of studies have shown a clear impact on change detection performance of the number of features as well as the number of objects (e.g., Wheeler & Treisman, 2002). Treisman (e.g., 2006) has argued that both individual features and object files comprising integrated features are represented in memory. She argues further that the bindings require attention for maintenance in a limited-capacity visual working memory. This temporary memory system has a capacity of 2–4 items, is vulnerable to disruption, and is quite distinct from long-term memory. The debate as to whether only integrated objects or both object files and features are retained in memory is reviewed thoroughly in chapter 2, so will not be presented in detail here. However, we do explore in this final section whether the literature on feature binding can speak to some of the major themes discussed thus far.

Clearly, Treisman's view that visual working memory is not simply activated long-term memory fits with our arguments on this issue in the earlier sections of this chapter. More controversial from our perspective are her claims about the role of attention in the maintenance of bindings and the assumed direct association with visual perception. For example, Allen, Baddeley, and Hitch (2006) showed that a demanding secondary task, such as random generation, is not any more disruptive of memory for bindings than it is of memory for individual features. Likewise, Gajewski and Brockmole (2006) showed that a visual distracter presented between the target and the test array appears to have no particular impact on memory for binding. These findings suggest that attention might not be crucial for maintaining bindings that are held in visual working memory after the stimulus array has been removed.

An obvious question is how immediate memory for bindings might be explained in the context of the framework for visual working memory that we have presented. The stimulus items in these experiments tend to comprise arbitrary combinations of visual features such as colour, shape, orientation, and location that are unlikely to match any pre-existing representation in long-term memory. Moreover, the combinations of features change from trial to trial: so on one trial, participants might see a large green triangle in the top left corner, and a small blue square on the right of the screen. On the next trial they might see a small blue triangle in the top right corner and a large green circle in the middle of the screen. Task performance relies on there being no trace of feature combinations presented on previous trials. So, whatever memory system holds the bound features on a given trial must be vulnerable to displacement by different feature combinations in a new stimulus array.

Preliminary evidence for the vulnerability of the binding representations has come from a reanalysis of some of the Gajewski and Brockmole (2006) data (Brockmole, personal communication) to examine whether there is any evidence of a build-up of proactive interference across trials. There appeared to be no change in the levels of performance on later trials compared with earlier trials, indicating no evidence of learning. Treisman (2006) reports an experiment in which particular combinations of colour and shape were presented on up to 80% of trials in a change detection paradigm, although the location of the items changed across trials. There was no evidence of improvement in detecting changes in the repeated colour–shape combinations, although in a surprise post-experimental test, participants appeared to have learned these associations. Clearly, even when learning took place it provided no benefit for change detection performance. A similar finding has been reported by Colzato, Raffone, and Hommel (2006). Some recent work in our own lab, in collaboration with Brockmole and Vandenbroucke, has indicated that even when the same target array of colour, shape, and location bindings is repeated on every third trial, there is no evidence of any improvement for the repeated array compared with arrays that are unique across trials (Logie, Brockmole, & Vandenbroucke, in press).

This lack of an impact of learning of repeated arrays offers further evidence for the idea that the memory system involved in these feature-binding experiments is a specific, temporary memory system. This makes it an unlikely candidate for the use of an image generation system such as that described by Kosslyn (2005) and colleagues. The observation that the storage of bound features is unperturbed by an exogenous, distracting visual cue immediately after stimulus offset (Gajewski & Brockmole, 2006) makes it unlikely that memory for the arrays is reliant on a visual buffer that lies between visual perceptual input and associative memory. Moreover, for many of these experiments, participants are required to suppress articulation throughout the task, making it extremely unlikely that verbal coding supports memory performance.

Research on binding in working memory has largely grown out of a well-established literature on feature binding in perception (e.g., Treisman & Gelade, 1980). From that literature, visual attention appeared to be crucial for detecting and orienting towards the location of a stimulus as well as to form perceptually based bindings. So, for example, attempting to process a stimulus display with a pink T and a blue X under an additional load on attention made it more likely that participants would generate illusory conjunctions and would recall having seen a blue T and a pink X. However, this situation is very different from the case in which a representation has already been formed of the conjunctions of features, and the task is to retain that representation after stimulus offset for the duration of a trial. Earlier in the chapter, we discussed in some detail the extent to which a temporary visual memory can be dissociated from visual perception. The Gajewski and Brockmole (2006) finding that visual short-term memory for bindings is insensitive to irrelevant visual input following stimulus offset bears a striking similarity to the findings that retention in visual short-term memory is insensitive to the effects of dynamic visual noise (Andrade et al., 2002). This leads to some possible predictions that retention of feature bindings would be insensitive to dynamic visual noise, but might be disrupted by visual memory preloads and by unseen pattern tapping. These are experiments that have yet to be done. However, there is one set of data that point in this direction. Treisman and Zhang (2006, Experiment 5) presented an array of items in a change detection task, but for one condition, in between presentation and test, all of the locations of the items in the stimulus array were changed. This was compared with a condition in which the locations were identical between presentation and test. The task was to detect changes in the bindings of shapes and colours and to ignore location. Results from this experiment are shown in Figure 1.5. What Treisman and Zhang found was that when the delay between presentation and test was 0.1 s or 0.9 s then changing location resulted in a substantial disruption of performance compared with no location change. However, for longer delays of 3 or 6 s, this disruptive effect was removed, and performance for the location change condition improved to the level that was obtained with the no location change condition.

In a series of experiments carried out in collaboration with Jaswal and Brockmole in our own lab (Logie, Brockmole, & Jaswal, under review), we have found very similar results to those reported in the Treisman and Zhang (2006) experiment, except that the performance improvement in the location change condition occurs after about 1.5 s, and the result generalizes to experiments in which colour changes randomly between presentation and test, and participants have to remember shape–location bindings. Further experiments show a very similar result when shape changes randomly between presentation and test, and the task is to remember colour–location bindings. In other words, the disruption caused by an irrelevant feature changing between presentation and test appears to affect processing of the stimuli immediately after stimulus offset. In this sense,

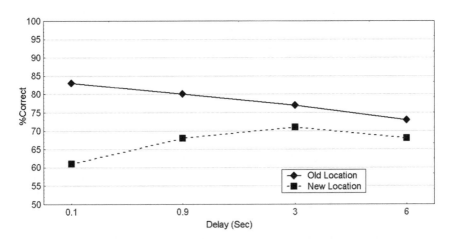

Figure 1.5. Change detection performance with location consistent (Old Location) or randomized (New Location) between presentation and test at different delays from stimulus offset. Data from Figure 8 in Treisman, A., & Zhang, W. (2006). Location and binding in visual working memory. *Memory and Cognition, 34*(8), 1704–1719. The Psychonomic Society. Reproduced with permission from the publisher and author.

the changing feature acts to capture visual attention. However, the binding of task-relevant features can be held in, and reported from, working memory with no apparent impact of the post-stimulus visual attentional disruption. Moreover, the memory representation is the outcome of selecting from among features in the display only those features that are relevant to the current task. In other words, the contents of the memory store have been subject to high-level strategic selection and driven by task goals; the selection of these contents has not been driven by stimulus input.

These kinds of results offer a way to bring together theoretical discussion in the field of visuospatial working memory and in the area of memory for feature bindings, pointing to a role for the visual cache described earlier in this chapter.

6. FRAGMENTATION OR INTEGRATION OF VISUOSPATIAL WORKING MEMORY?

Much of this chapter, and much of the literature in working memory, has attempted to identify components of the working memory system and to specify the characteristics of those components. This has followed the general framework for a multi-component working memory system, and, as we have argued earlier in the chapter, this framework has been extremely successful in accounting for the wide range of neuropsychological dissociations, and double dissociations, found in dual-task studies with healthy adults. However, in doing so, there is a danger of losing sight of the fact that if there are components of working memory, then clearly these must function in an integrated fashion. Working memory is often described as temporary memory and online processing in the service of everyday cognition. The slightly speculative argument in the previous section points to the visual-cache component being able to store integrated visual representations. This fits comfortably with the concept of the visual cache as a temporary memory store for representations of material that has completed the processes of initial visual perception, is not directly linked with visual perceptual input or visual imagery, and may incorporate additional interpretation or selection of material. This leaves open a range of questions as to how these representations are integrated with verbal and other semantic information. Baddeley (2000) suggested that a temporary amodal memory system—the episodic buffer—might serve this function. However, the episodic buffer is thought to require attentional control to form and maintain integrated, multi-modal representations, and the recently published experiments on memory for feature binding (Allen et al., 2006) decry the need for general attentional resources, at least for this kind of binding. Dismantling complex systems can help us understand how components of the system work, and how such systems respond to localized damage. Putting the multiple components of working memory back together again remains a challenge, but addressing how integrated representations are formed and maintained offers a promising means to meet that challenge.

7. REFERENCES

Allen, R. J., Baddeley, A. D., & Hitch, G. J. (2006). Is the binding of visual features in working memory resource-demanding? *Journal of Experimental Psychology: General, 135*, 298–313.

Andrade, J., Kemps, E., Werniers, Y., May, J., & Szmalec, A. (2002). Insensitivity of visual short-term memory to irrelevant visual information. *Quarterly Journal of Experimental Psychology, 55A*(3), 753–774.

Avons, S. E. (1998). Serial report and item recognition of novel visual patterns. *British Journal of Psychology, 89*, 285–308.

Avons, S. E., & Mason, A. (1999). Effects of visual similarity on serial report and item recognition. *Quarterly Journal of Experimental Psychology, 52A*, 217–240.

Avons, S., & Sestieri, C. (2005). Dynamic visual noise: No interference with visual short-term memory or the construction of visual images. *European Journal of Cognitive Psychology, 17*(3), 405–424

Baddeley, A. D. (1966). The capacity for generating information by randomization. *Quarterly Journal of Experimental Psychology, 18*, 119–130.

Baddeley, A. D. (1997*). Human memory: Theory and practice* (Revised ed.). Hove, UK: Psychology Press.

Baddeley, A. D. (2000). The episodic buffer: A new component of working memory? *Trends in Cognitive Sciences, 4*, 417–423.

Baddeley, A. D. (2007). *Working memory, thought and action.* Oxford, U.K.: Oxford University Press.

Baddeley, A. D., & Andrade, J. (2000). Working memory and vividness of imagery. *Journal of Experimental Psychology: General, 129*, 126–145.

Baddeley, A. D., & Hitch, G. J. (1974). Working memory. In G. Bower (Ed.), *The psychology of learning and motivation* (Vol. 8, pp. 47–90). New York: Academic Press.

Baddeley, A. D., & Lieberman, K. (1980). Spatial working memory. In R. S. Nickerson (Ed.), *Attention and performance VIII* (pp. 521–539). Hillsdale, NJ: Lawrence Erlbaum Associates.

Baddeley, A. D., & Logie, R. H. (1999). Working memory: The multiple component model. In A. Miyake & P. Shah (Eds.), *Models of working memory* (pp. 28–61). New York: Cambridge University Press.

Basso, A., Spinnler, H., Vallar, G., & Zanobio, E. (1982). Left hemisphere damage and selective impairment of auditory verbal short-term memory: A case study. *Neuropsychologia, 20*, 263–274.

Beyn, E. S., & Knyazeva, G. R. (1962). The problem of protoagnosia. *Journal of Neurology, Neurosurgery and Psychiatry, 25*, 154–158.

Botez, M. I., Olivier, M., Vézina, J.-L., Botez, T., & Kaufman, B. (1985). Defective revisualization: Dissociation between cognitive and imagistic thought [Case report and short review of the literature]. *Cortex*, 21, 375–389.

Broadbent, D. E., & Broadbent, M. H. P. (1981). Recency effects in visual memory. *Quarterly Journal of Experimental Psychology, 33A*, 1–15.

Brooks, L. R. (1968). Spatial and verbal components in the act of recall. *Canadian Journal of Psychology, 22*, 349–368.

Caplan, D., & Waters, G. S. (1990). Short-term memory and language comprehension: A critical review of the neuropsychological literature. In G. Vallar & T. Shallice (Eds.), *Neuropsychological impairments of short-term memory* (pp. 337–389). Cambridge, UK: Cambridge University Press.

Carlesimo, G., Perri, R., Turriziani, P., Tomaiuolo, F., & Caltagirone, C. (2001). Remembering what but not where: Independence of spatial and visual working memory. *Cortex, 36,* 519–534.

Charcot, J.-M., & Bernard, D. (1883). Un cas de suppression brusque et isolée de la vision mentale des signes et des objects (formes et couleurs). *Le Progrès Médicale, 11,* 568–571.

Cocchini, G., Logie, R. H., Della Sala, S., & MacPherson, S. E. (2002). Concurrent performance of two memory tasks: Evidence for domain specific working memory systems. *Memory and Cognition, 30,* 1086–1095.

Collette, F., & Van der Linden, M. (2002). Brain imaging of the central executive component of working memory. *Neuroscience and Behavioral Reviews, 26*(2), 105–125.

Colzato, L. S., Raffone, A., & Hommel, B. (2006). What do we learn from binding features? Evidence for multilevel feature integration. *Journal of Experimental Psychology: Human Perception and Performance, 32,* 705–716.

Conrad, R. (1964). Acoustic confusions in immediate memory. *British Journal of Psychology, 55,* 75–84.

Conway, A. R. A., Jarrold, C., Kane, M. J., Miyake, A., & Towse, J. N. (Eds.). (2007). *Variation in working memory.* New York: Oxford University Press.

Cornoldi, C., & Vecchi, T. (2003). *Visuo-spatial working memory and individual differences.* Hove, UK: Psychology Press

Corsi, P. M. (1972). *Human memory and the medial temporal region of the brain.* Unpublished thesis, McGill University, Montreal.

Courtney, S. M., Roth, J. K., & Sala, J. B. (2007). A hierarchical biased-competition model of domain-dependent working memory maintenance and executive control. In N. Osaka, R. H. Logie, & M. D'Esposito (Eds.), *The cognitive neuroscience of working memory* (pp. 369–383). Oxford, UK: Oxford University Press.

Cowan, N. (2005). *Working memory capacity.* New York: Psychology Press.

Darling, S., Della Sala, S., & Logie, R. H. (2007). Behavioural evidence for separating components of visuo-spatial working memory. *Cognitive Processing, 8,* 175–181.

Dean, G. M., & Morris, P. E. (2003). The relationship between self reports of imagery and spatial ability. *British Journal of Psychology, 94,* 245–273.

Della Sala, S., Gray, C., Baddeley, A., Allamano, N., & Wilson, L. (1999). Pattern span: A tool for unwielding visuo-spatial memory. *Neuropsychologica, 37*(10), 1189–1199.

Denis, M., Beschin, N., Logie, R. H., & Della Sala, S. (2002). Visual perception and verbal descriptions as sources for generating mental representations: Evidence from representational neglect. *Cognitive Neuropsychology, 19*(2), 97–112.

De Renzi, E., & Nichelli, P. (1975). Verbal and non-verbal short-term memory impairment following hemispheric damage. *Cortex, 11,* 341–353.

Deyzac, E., Logie, R. H., & Denis, M. (2006). Visuospatial working memory and the processing of spatial descriptions. *British Journal of Psychology, 97,* 217–243.

Evans, F. J. (1978). Monitoring attention deployment by random number generation: An index to measure subjective randomness. *Bulletin of the Psychonomic Society, 12,* 35–38.

Farah, M. J., Hammond, K. M., Levine, D. N., & Calvanio, R. (1988). Visual and spatial mental imagery: Dissociable systems of representation. *Cognitive Psychology, 20,* 439–462.

Farah, M. J., Peronnet, F., Weisberg, L. L., & Monheit, M. A. (1989). Brain activity underlying mental imagery: Event-related potentials during image generation. *Journal of Cognitive Neuroscience, 1,* 302–316.

Farmer, E., Berman, I., & Fletcher, Y. (1986). Evidence for a visuo-spatial scratch-pad in working memory. *Quarterly Journal of Experimental Psychology, 38A*, 675–688.

Farrand, P., & Jones, D. M. (1996). Direction of report in spatial and verbal short-term memory. *Quarterly Journal of Experimental Psychology, 49A*, 140–158.

Fisk, J. E., & Sharp, C. A. (2003). The role of the executive system in visuo-spatial memory functioning. *Brain and Cognition, 52*(3), 364–381.

Fletcher, P. C., & Henson, R. N. A. (2001). Frontal lobes and human memory: Insights from functional brain imaging. *Brain, 124*, 849–881.

Funahashi, S. (2007). The general-purpose working memory system and functions of the dorso-lateral pre-frontal cortex. In N. Osaka, R. H. Logie, & M. D'Esposito (Eds.), *The cognitive neuroscience of working memory* (pp. 213–229). Oxford, UK: Oxford University Press.

Funahashi, S., Takeda, K., & Watanabe, Y. (2004). Neural mechanisms of spatial working memory: Contributions of the dorsolateral prefrontal cortex and the thalamic nucleus. *Cognitive, Affective, and Behavioral Neuroscience, 4*, 409–420.

Gajewski, D. A., & Brockmole, J. R. (2006). Feature bindings endure without attention: Evidence from an explicit recall task. *Psychonomic Bulletin & Review, 13*, 581–587.

Haxby, J. V., Hoffman, E. A., & Gobbini, M. I. (2000). The distributed human neural system for face perception. *Trends in Cognitive Science, 4*, 223–233.

Hitch, G. J., Halliday, M. S., Schaafstal, A. M., & Schraagen, J. M. C. (1988). Visual working memory in young children. *Memory & Cognition, 16*, 120–132.

Hue, C., & Ericsson, J. R. (1988). Short-term memory for Chinese characters and radicals. *Memory and Cognition, 16*, 196–205.

Ishai, A., Haxby, J. V., & Ungerleider, L. G. (2002). Visual imagery of famous faces: Effects of memory and attention revealed by fMRI. *NeuroImage, 17*, 1729–1741.

Jahanshahi, M., Dirnberger, G., Fuller, R., & Frith, C. D. (2000). The role of the dorso-lateral prefrontal cortex in random number generation: A study with positron emission tomography. *NeuroImage, 12*(6), 713–725.

Jones, D. (1993). Objects, threads and streams of auditory attention. In A. D. Baddeley & L. Weiskrantz (Eds.), *Attention: Selection, awareness and control* (pp. 87–104). Oxford, UK: Clarendon Press.

Jones, D. M., Macken, W. J., & Nicholls, A. P. (2004). The phonological store of working memory: Is it phonological and is it a store? *Journal of Experimental Psychology: Learning, Memory, and Cognition, 30*, 656–674.

Jonides, J., Smith, E. E., Koeppe, R. A., Awh, E., Minoshima, S., & Mintun, M. A. (1993). Spatial working memory in humans as revealed by PET. *Nature, 363*, 623–625.

Klauer, K. C., & Stegmaier, R. (1997). Interference in immediate spatial memory: Shifts of spatial attention or central-executive involvement? *Quarterly Journal of Experimental Psychology, 50A*(1), 79–99.

Kosslyn, S. M. (1980). *Image and mind*. Cambridge, MA: Harvard University Press.

Kosslyn, S. M. (1994). *Image and brain: The resolution of the imagery debate*. Cambridge, MA: MIT Press.

Kosslyn, S. M. (2005). Mental images and the brain. *Cognitive Neuropsychology, 22*(3/4), 333–347.

Kosslyn, S. M., Alpert, N. M., Thompson, W. L., Maljkovic, V., Weise, S. B., Chabris, C. F., et al. (1993). Visual mental imagery activates topographically organized visual cortex: PET investigations. *Journal of Cognitive Neuroscience, 5*, 263–287.

Kosslyn, S. M., & Thompson, W. L. (2003). When is early visual cortex activated during visual mental imagery? *Psychological Bulletin, 129*, 723–746.

Kosslyn, S. M., Thompson, W. L., Sukel, K. E., & Alpert, N. M. (2005). Two types of image generation: Evidence from PET. *Cognitive, Affective and Behavioral Neuroscience, 5*, 41–53.

Laeng, B., & Teodorescu, D.-S. (2002). Eye scanpaths during visual imagery reenact those of perception of the same visual scene. *Cognitive Science, 26*(2), 207–231.

Leung, H. C., Gore, J. C., & Goldman-Rakic, P. S. (2002). Sustained mnemonic response in the human middle frontal gyrus during online storage of spatial memoranda. *Journal of Cognitive Neuroscience, 14*(4), 659–671.

Logie, R. H. (1986). Visuo-spatial processing in working memory. *Quarterly Journal of Experimental Psychology, 38A*(2), 229–247.

Logie, R. H. (1995). *Visuo-spatial working memory*. Hove, UK: Lawrence Erlbaum Associates.

Logie, R. H. (2003). Spatial and visual working memory: A mental workspace. In D. Irwin & B. Ross (Eds.), *Cognitive vision: The psychology of learning and motivation* (Vol. 42, pp. 37–78). New York: Elsevier Science.

Logie, R. H., Beschin, N., Della Sala, S., & Denis, M. (2005). Dissociating mental transformations and visuo-spatial storage in working memory: Evidence from representational neglect. *Memory, 13*, 430–434.

Logie, R. H., Brockmole, J., & Jaswal, S. (under review). *Feature binding in visual working memory is unaffected by task-irrelevant changes of location, shape and color*.

Logie, R. H., Brockmole, J. R., & Vandenbroucke, A. (in press). Bound feature combinations in visual short-term memory are fragile but influence long-term learning. *Visual Cognition*.

Logie, R. H., Cocchini, G., Della Sala, S., & Baddeley, A. D. (2004). Is there a specific executive capacity for dual task co-ordination? Evidence from Alzheimer's disease. *Neuropsychology, 18*, 504–513.

Logie, R. H., & Della Sala, S. (2005). Disorders of visuo-spatial working memory. In A. Miyake & P. Shah (Eds.), *Handbook of visuospatial thinking* (pp. 81–120). New York: Cambridge University Press.

Logie, R. H., Della Sala, S., Wynn, V., & Baddeley, A. D. (2000). Visual similarity effects in immediate verbal serial recall. *Quarterly Journal of Experimental Psychology, 53A*(3), 626–646.

Logie, R. H., & D'Esposito, M. (Eds.). (2007). The neuropsychology of working memory [Special issue]. *Cortex, 43*(1).

Logie, R. H., & Marchetti, C. (1991). Visuo-spatial working memory: Visual, spatial, or central executive? In R. H. Logie & M. Denis (Eds.), *Mental images in human cognition* (pp. 105–115). Amsterdam: North-Holland.

Logie, R. H., & Pearson, D. G. (1997). The inner eye and the inner scribe of visuo-spatial working memory: Evidence from developmental fractionation. *European Journal of Cognitive Psychology, 9*, 241–257.

Luck, S. J., & Vogel, E. W. (1997). The capacity of visual working memory for features and conjunctions. *Nature, 390*, 279–281.

Marks, D. F. (1973). Visual imagery differences in the recall of pictures. *British Journal of Psychology, 64*, 17–24.

McConnell, J., & Quinn, J. G. (2004). Cognitive mechanisms of visual memories and visual images. *Imagination, Cognition and Personality, 23*, 201–207.

McKelvie, S. J. (1995). The VVIQ as a psychometric test of individual differences in visual imagery vividness: A critical quantitative review and a plea for direction. *Journal of Mental Imagery, 19*(3&4), 1–106.

Mellet, E., Tzourio, N., Crivello, F., Joliot, M., Denis, M., & Mazoyer, B. (1996). Functional anatomy of spatial imagery generated from verbal instructions. *Journal of Neuroscience, 16*, 6504–6512.

Mellet, E., Tzourio, N., Denis, M., & Mazoyer, B. (1995). A positron emission tomography study of visual and mental spatial exploration. *Journal of Cognitive Neuroscience, 7*, 433–445.

Mellet, E., Tzourio-Mazoyer, N., Bricogne, S., Mazoyer, B., Kosslyn, S. M., & Denis, M. (2000). Functional anatomy of high-resolution visual mental imagery. *Journal of Cognitive Neuroscience, 12*(1), 98–109.

Milner, B. (1971). Interhemispheric differences in the localization of psychological processes in man. *British Medical Bulletin, 27*, 272–277.

Miyake, A., Friedman, N. P., Emerson, M. J., Witzki, A. H., Howerter, A., & Wager, T. D. (2000). The unity and diversity of executive functions and their contributions to complex "frontal lobe" tasks: A latent variable analysis. *Cognitive Psychology, 41*, 49–100.

Miyake, A., Friedman, N. P., Rettinger, D. A., Shah, P., & Hegarty, M. (2001). How are visuospatial working memory, executive functioning, and spatial abilities related? A latent variable analysis. *Journal of Experimental Psychology: General, 130*, 621–640.

Miyake, A., & Shah, P. (Eds.). (1999). *Models of working memory: Mechanisms of active maintenance and executive control.* New York: Cambridge University Press.

Murray, D. (1965). Vocalization-at-presentation, with varying presentation rates. *Quarterly Journal of Experimental Psychology, 17*, 47–56.

Osaka, N., Logie, R. H., & D'Esposito, M. (Eds.). (2007). *The cognitive neuroscience of working memory.* Oxford, UK: Oxford University Press.

Paivio, A. (1971). *Imagery and verbal processes.* New York: Holt, Rinehart & Winston.

Pearson, D. G. (2001). Imagery and the visuo-spatial sketchpad. In J. Andrade (Ed.), *Working memory in perspective* (pp. 33–59). Hove, UK: Psychology Press.

Pearson, D. G., Logie, R. H., & Gilhooly, K. J. (1999). Verbal representations and spatial manipulation during mental synthesis. *European Journal of Cognitive Psychology, 11*(3), 295–314.

Pearson, D. G., & Sahraie, A. (2003). Oculomotor control and the maintenance of spatially and temporally distributed events in visuo-spatial working memory. *Quarterly Journal of Experimental Psychology, 56A*(7), 1089–1111.

Phillips, W. A., & Christie, D. F. M. (1977a). Components of visual memory. *Quarterly Journal of Experimental Psychology, 29*, 117–133.

Phillips, W. A., & Christie, D. F. M. (1977b). Interference with visualization. *Quarterly Journal of Experimental Psychology, 29*, 637–650.

Pickering, S. J., Gathercole, S. E., Hall, S., & Lloyd, S. (2001). Development of memory for pattern and path: Further evidence for the fractionation of visual and spatial short-term memory. *Quarterly Journal of Experimental Psychology, 54A*, 397–420.

Postle, B. R. (2007). Activated long-term memory? The basis of representation in working memory. In N. Osaka, R. H. Logie, & M. D'Esposito (Eds.), *The cognitive neuroscience of working memory* (pp. 333–349). Oxford, UK: Oxford University Press.

Postle, B. R., Idzikowski, C., Della Sala, S., Logie, R. H., & Baddeley, A. D. (2006). The selective disruption of spatial working memory by eye movements. *Quarterly Journal of Experimental Psychology, 59*, 100–120.

Quinn, J. G., & McConnell, J. (1996). Irrelevant pictures in visual working memory. *Quarterly Journal of Experimental Psychology, 49A*, 200–215.

Quinn, J. G., & McConnell, J. (2006). The interval for interference in conscious visual imagery. *Memory, 14*, 241–252.

Quinn, J. G., & Ralston, G. E. (1986), Movement and attention in visual working memory. *Quarterly Journal of Experimental Psychology, 38A*, 689–703.

Reisberg, D., Pearson, D. G., & Kosslyn, S. M. (2003). Intuitions and introspections about imagery: The role of imagery experience in shaping an investigator's theoretical views. *Applied Cognitive Psychology, 17*, 147–160.

Roland, P. E., & Gulyas, B. (1994). Visual imagery and visual representation. *Trends in Neurosciences, 17*, 281–296.

Ruchkin, D. S., Grafman, J., Cameron, K., & Berndt, R. S. (2003). Working memory retention systems: A state of activated long-term memory. *Behavioral and Brain Sciences, 26*, 709–777.

Ruchkin, D. S., Johnson, R., Grafman, J., Canoune, H., & Ritter, W. (1997). Multiple visuo-spatial working memory buffers: Evidence from spatio-temporal patterns of brain activity. *Neuropsychologia, 35*, 195–209.

Rudkin, S., Pearson, D. G., & Logie, R. H. (2007). Executive processes in visual and spatial working memory tasks. *Quarterly Journal of Experimental Psychology, 60*, 79–100.

Saffran, E. M., & Marin, O. S. M. (1975). Immediate memory for word lists and sentences in a patient with deficient auditory short-term memory. *Brain and Language, 2*, 420–433.

Saito, S., Logie, R. H., Morita, A., & Law, A. (2008). Visual and phonological similarity effects in verbal immediate serial recall: A test with kanji materials. *Journal of Memory and Language, 59*, 1–17.

Salway, A. F. S. (1991). *Random generation in the working memory dual-task paradigm.* Unpublished doctoral thesis, University of Aberdeen, UK.

Salway, A. F. S., & Logie, R. H. (1995). Visuo-spatial working memory, movement control and executive demands. *British Journal of Psychology, 86*, 253–269.

Shah, P., & Miyake, A. (Eds.). (2005). *The Cambridge handbook of visuospatial thinking.* New York: Cambridge University Press.

Shallice, T., & Warrington, E. K. (1970). Independent functioning of verbal memory stores: A neuropsychological study. *Quarterly Journal of Experimental Psychology, 22*, 261–273.

Shepard, R. N., & Metzler, J. (1971). Mental rotation of three-dimensional objects. *Science, 171*, 701–703.

Smith, E. E., & Jonides, J. (1995). Working memory in humans: Neuropsychological evidence. In M. S. Gazzaniga (Ed.), *The cognitive neurosciences* (pp. 1009–1020). Cambridge, MA: MIT Press.

Smyth, M. M., Hay, D. C., Hitch, G. J., & Horton, N. J. (2005). Serial position memory in the visuo-spatial domain: Reconstructing sequences of unfamiliar faces. *Quarterly Journal of Experimental Psychology, 58A*, 909–930.

Smyth, M. M., & Scholey, K. A. (1994). Interference in immediate spatial memory. *Memory and Cognition, 22*, 1–13.

Solms, M., Kaplan-Solms, K., & Brown, J. W. (1996). Wilbrand's case of "mind-blindness". In C. Code, C.-W. Wallesch, Y. Joanette, & A. R. Lecours (Eds.), *Classic cases in neuropsychology* (pp. 89–110). Hove, UK: Psychology Press.

Todd, J. J., & Marois, R. (2004). Capacity limit of visual short-term memory in the human posterior parietal cortex. *Nature, 428*, 751–754.

Todd, J. J., & Marois, R. (2005). Posterior parietal cortex activity predicts individual differences in visual short-term memory capacity. *Cognitive, Affective, and Behavioral Neuroscience, 5*, 144–155.

Treisman, A. (2006). Object tokens, binding, and visual memory. In H. D. Zimmer, A. Mecklinger, & U. Lindenberger (Eds.), *Handbook of binding and memory: Perspectives from cognitive neuroscience* (pp. 315–338). Oxford, UK: Oxford University Press.

Treisman, A., & Gelade, G. (1980). A feature integration theory of attention. *Cognitive Psychology, 12*, 97–136.

Treisman, A., & Zhang, W. (2006). Location and binding in visual working memory. *Memory and Cognition, 34*(8), 1704–1719.

Ungerleider, L. G., & Mishkin, M. (1982). Two cortical visual systems. In D. J. Ingle, R. J. W. Mansfield, & M. S. Goodale (Eds.), *The analysis of visual behavior* (pp. 549–586). Cambridge, MA: MIT Press.

van der Meulen, M. (2008). *Exploring the interaction between working memory and long-term memory: Evidence for the workspace model.* Unpublished doctoral thesis, University of Edinburgh, UK.

van der Meulen, M., Logie, R. H., & Della Sala, S. (2008). *Selective interference with visual working memory: Evidence for the workspace model.* Manuscript submitted for publication.

Vandierendonck, A., De Vooght, G., & Van der Goten, K. V. (1998). Interfering with the central executive by means of a random interval repetition task. *Quarterly Journal of Experimental Psychology, 51A,* 197–218.

Vandierendonck, A., Kemps, E., Fastame, M. C., & Szmalec, A. (2004). Working memory components of the Corsi blocks task. *British Journal of Psychology, 95,* 57–79.

Wager, T. D., & Smith E. E. (2003). Neuroimaging studies of working memory: A meta-analysis. *Cognitive, Affective, and Behavioral Neuroscience, 3,* 255–274.

Walker, P., Hitch, G. J., & Duroe, A. (1993). The effect of visual similarity on short-term memory for spatial location: Implications for the capacity of visual short-term memory. *Acta Psychologica, 83,* 203–224.

Warrington, E. K., & Rabin, P. (1971). Visual span of apprehension in patients with unilateral cerebral lesions. *Quarterly Journal of Experimental Psychology, 23,* 423–431.

Weber, R. J., & Castleman, J. (1970). The time it takes to imagine. *Perception and Psychophysics, 8,* 165–168.

Wheeler, M. E., & Treisman, A. M. (2002). Binding in short-term visual memory. *Journal of Experimental Psychology, General, 131,* 48–64.

Wilbrand, H. (1887). *Sie Seelenblindheit als Herderscheinung und ihre Beziehung zur Alexie und Agraphie.* Wiesbaden, Germany: Begmann.

Wilson, B., Baddeley, A. D., & Young, A. W. (1999). LE, a person who lost her "mind's eye". *Neurocase, 5,* 119–127.

Yik, W. F. (1978). The effect of visual and acoustic similarity on short-term memory for Chinese words. *Quarterly Journal of Experimental Psychology, 30,* 487–494.

Zarahn, E., Aguirre, G., & D'Esposito, M. (2000). Replication and further studies of neural mechanisms of spatial mnemonic processing in humans. *Cognitive Brain Research, 9*(1), 1–17.

Zeman, A., McGonigle, D., Gountouna, E., Torrens, L., Della Sala, S., & Logie, R. (2007). Blind imagination: Brain activation after loss of the mind's eye. *Journal of Neurology, Neurosurgery and Psychiatry, 78*: 209.

Zeman, A., Torrens, L., Gountouna, E., Della Sala, S., McGonigle, D., & Logie, R. H. (2008). *Loss of imagery phenomenology with intact visual imagery performance.* Manuscript submitted for publication.

Zhang, G., & Simon, H. A. (1985). STM capacity for Chinese words and idioms: Chunking and acoustical loop hypothesis. *Memory and Cognition, 13*, 193–201.

Zimmer, H. D., & Speiser, H. R. (2002). The irrelevant picture effect in visuo-spatial working memory: Fact or fiction? *Psychologische Beiträge, 44*, 223–247.

Zimmer, H. D., Speiser, H. R., & Seidler, B. (2003). Spatio-temporal working-memory and short-term object-location tasks use different memory mechanisms. *Acta Psychologica, 114*(1), 41–65.

2 Visual memory for features, conjunctions, objects, and locations

Yuhong V. Jiang and Tal Makovski
University of Minnesota

Won Mok Shim
Massachusetts Institute of Technology

1. INTRODUCTION

In her Multiple-Entry, Modular Memory (MEM) model on human cognition, Marcia Johnson differentiated perceptual subsystems that interact directly with the external environment and reflective subsystems that operate in the absence of external input (Johnson, 1992). Visual memory is an example of processes that are situated at the border between these two. Short-term visual memory directly bridges visual perception with conceptual representation. It is abstracted from visual perception yet operates on perceptual input and retains many properties of visual objects including size, color, orientation, number, and spatial layout. Short-term visual memory can result from active encoding and retention of information in visual working memory (Phillips, 1974), or as a by-product of perceptual analysis of a previous trial event (Maljkovic & Nakayama, 1994, 1996). In either case, content previously stored in short-term memory may remain in long-term visual memory (Hollingworth, 2005), and both short-term and long-term visual memory can be used explicitly or implicitly to guide future visual processing (Brockmole & Henderson, 2006a, 2006b; Chun & Jiang, 1998; Downing, 2000; Vickery, King, & Jiang, 2005). The goal of this chapter is to provide a synthesis of visual memory for different visual attributes.

2. VISUAL WORKING MEMORY

When people view a briefly presented visual display, they first acquire a veridical, high-fidelity memory of the display, known as iconic memory (Averbach & Sperling, 1961; Neisser, 1967; Sperling, 1960). This memory is short-lived, typically lasting for less than half a second, and is easily erased by new visual input (Phillips, 1974). Iconic memory may be considered a lingering form of visual sensory processing, and it is useful for integrating input separated by very short intervals (Di Lollo, 1984; see also chapter 4, section 2.1). At longer delay intervals, visual information is stored in visual working memory (VWM). This memory can last for several seconds and is more resistant to interference from new visual input (Phillips, 1974).

Visual working memory is important for many cognitive activities. When crossing a busy street, we must look left and right and remember what is on each side before deciding to cross. In team sports, players often need to be aware of the whereabouts of their team mates and opponents. Even in social interactions, we must encode who are around us to direct proper conversations to the right individual. Visual working memory was extensively studied both in neurophysiology and behavioral research. Neurophysiological studies have focused primarily on the domain specificity of the prefrontal cortex in spatial and nonspatial working memory tasks. They are guided by the influential working-memory model of Baddeley and Hitch (1974; Baddeley, 1986), where working memory is divided into a central executive process and multiple slavery systems including the phonological loop, the visuospatial sketchpad, and the episodic buffer (Baddeley, 2000). In behavioral studies, VWM research has followed two traditions: the Baddeley tradition of using interference tasks to subdivide VWM into different domain-specific components (e.g., Logie, 1995), and a change detection tradition that links VWM with visual perception and visual attention. Chapter 1 extensively considered the domain specificity of VWM. Our review of VWM will primarily follow the change detection tradition.

2.1. Testing VWM

To probe VWM, researchers have devised two tasks that, by now, are operational definitions of VWM: the change detection task, and a delayed match-to-sample task. Figure 2.1 shows a schematic illustration of the tasks. In the change detection task (Rensink, 2002), a visual display is briefly presented for observers to remember. After a short interval of between one and several seconds, a test display is presented. The test display is either the same as the initial memory display or is changed in some manner. Observers are asked to decide whether a change is present or absent (Figure 2.1, left). To fulfill this task, observers must encode the initial display into VWM, keep it there during the retention interval, and compare it with the test display. By varying VWM load (i.e., the amount of information presented on the first display) and measuring change detection accuracy of different VWM loads, it is possible to estimate the capacity of VWM for various types of visual input, such as spatial locations and object features (Cowan, 2001; Pashler, 1988).

In addition to the change detection task, a delayed match-to-sample task is also frequently used to assess VWM (Figure 2.1, right). This task is used most often in nonhuman primate research (e.g., Davachi & Goldman-Rakic, 2001; Miller, Erickson, & Desimone, 1996). In this task, a sample—usually a single object or a single location—is presented, followed by a sequence of test stimuli. Subjects must decide whether each test stimulus matches the original sample. The delayed match-to-sample task is procedurally similar to the change detection task. However, presentation of successive test stimuli places a high demand on the main-

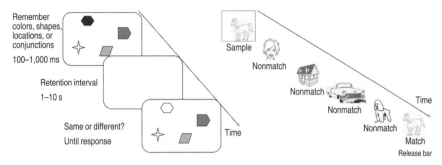

Figure 2.1. A schematic illustration of the change detection task (left) and delayed match-to-sample task (right). Each item is typically presented for 500 ms; interstimulus interval is usually 1 s.

tenance of the original sample's memory across filled-delay intervals of other stimuli and tasks. Adding new visual input and new cognitive tasks during the delay interval interferes significantly with the maintenance of sample memory (Fougnie & Marois, 2006; Makovski, Shim, & Jiang, 2006). As a result, filled-delays are usually avoided in human VWM tasks, and a change detection task with a blank retention interval has become the standard paradigm to test VWM (however, for challenges to this paradigm, see Hollingworth, 2003; Landman, Spekreijse, & Lamme, 2003; Makovski & Jiang, 2007; see also chapter 4).

2.2. Spatial versus object VWM

2.2.1. *Neuroscience evidence*

One of the most important questions in cognitive research is the division of labor for different cognitive processes. In vision, perception of object identity is considered separate from perception of object location or visually guided motor processing (Goodale & Milner, 1995; Sagi & Julesz, 1985; Ungerleider & Mishkin, 1982). In the primate brain, object vision and spatial vision (or visuomotor action) map roughly onto the occipitotemporal ventral stream and the occipitoparietal dorsal stream. The division is not absolute, with extensive crosstalk between brain regions in the ventral and dorsal streams (Felleman & Van Essen, 1991), but functions subserved by the two streams are characteristically different and can exist independently of each other.

Is the functional division between object and spatial processing confined to visual perception, or does it also extend to visual working memory? If yes, can we continue to identify a dorsal system for spatial VWM and a ventral system for object VWM? These are important questions because they pertain to the degree of domain specificity in high-level cognitive processes. The widely accepted model of working memory by Baddeley (1986) proposes that an important element of working memory is the central executive, whose work is augmented by several slave systems. Because working memory is so closely related to central-executive processes such as attention (Awh & Jonides, 2001; see also chapter 1, section 2.3), its processes may be largely domain-general and applicable to memory for all kinds of materials. On the other hand, the existence of slave storage systems may result in some degree of domain specificity.

Studies on visual imagery have provided evidence that some degree of domain specificity is retained for internally generated visual representations. Brain-damaged patients with color perception deficits also have difficulty imagining the canonical color of everyday objects. They may be able to answer metaphorical questions about color, such as "what color is associated with envy?", but not real-world questions about color, such as "what color is a peach?" (De Renzi & Spinnler, 1967). In addition, patients with damage to the occipitotemporal lobe are able to imagine spatial locations such as the triads of states within the United States, but they have difficulty imagining object properties such as whether George Washington had a beard. Patients with damage to the occipitoparietal lobe often show the opposite deficits: an impairment at imagining spatial locations but no impairment at imagining object identities (Farah, 1988; Levine, Warach, & Farah, 1985). These studies suggest that, like perception, visual imagery may also be divided into ventral and dorsal streams (an issue considered at length in chapter 8, section 2.2). However, because these studies involve visual imagery rather than visual working memory, they may not directly inform us about the division of labor in VWM (but see chapter 1, sections 3 and 4). An important difference between visual imagery and VWM is that visual imagery is often derived from long-term memory and, as such, can be less veridical than the kind of memory formed from immediate perception (Olson & Jiang, 2004).

Neurophysiologists have approached the division of labor in VWM using the delayed match-to-sample task (Fuster, 1990). Their interest focuses on the function of the prefrontal cortex (PFC), which has extensive connections with both the parietal lobe and the temporal lobe (Goldman-Rakic, 1990). Empirical evidence on the functional division of the PFC has been mixed. On the basis of monkey neurophysiology data, Goldman-Rakic and colleagues propose that dorsolateral PFC underlies spatial VWM whereas ventrolateral PFC underlies object VWM—that is, the functional division in the prefrontal cortex parallels that in the posterior cortex (Wilson, Scalaidhe, & Goldman-Rakic, 1993).

However, the segregation of spatial and object VWM in dorsal and ventral lateral PFC has not been universally confirmed. Rao, Rainer, and Miller (1997) found that PFC neurons that carry memory for spatial properties of an object can also carry memory for nonspatial properties of that object. In their task, monkeys were trained to first remember the shape of a sample object. After a delay interval, an array of several test items was shown. Monkeys must localize the test item that matched the sample object and remember its location. After another delay interval, monkeys saccaded to the matched test location to obtain a reward. Rao et al. (1997) found that the same PFC neurons can be activated both during the first, object VWM delay and during the second, spatial VWM delay. In addition, Rainer, Asaad, and Miller (1998) trained monkeys to remember both an object's identity and its location in a VWM task. They mapped out the receptive fields of PFC neurons and found that using traditional spatial VWM and object VWM tasks, the same neurons in PFC can convey both spatial and nonspatial information.

In light of the mixed results, an alternative theory is proposed to characterize PFC functional segregation. Petrides and colleagues argue that the PFC is not organized around the type of visual input (spatial or nonspatial), but around the type of cognitive processes necessitated by the VWM task (for a recent review, see Petrides, 2005). Specifically, merely maintaining something over time engages the dorsolateral PFC, but further manipulation and operation on that input (e.g., mentally rotating the object) engages the ventrolateral PFC. Whether PFC is divided along the content of VWM or along cognitive operations necessitated by a VWM task remains to be determined.

The same controversy exists in human functional neuroimaging studies on VWM. Using positron emission tomography (PET), Courtney, Ungerleider, Keil, and Haxby (1996) scanned normal subjects while they engaged in a spatial VWM task or an object VWM task. In these tasks, subjects had to remember either the location or identity of a single face among 23 gray squares. Courtney et al. (1996) found that the inferior frontal regions were more involved in object VWM tasks than spatial VWM tasks and that the superior frontal regions showed the reverse pattern. Dissociation between spatial and object VWM was also seen in other studies using functional magnetic resonance imaging (fMRI) (Courtney, Petit, Maisog, Ungerleider, & Haxby, 1998; McCarthy et al., 1996; Ungerleider, Courtney, & Haxby, 1998). These results, however, are not representative of all neuroimaging studies on human VWM, as many studies failed to find convincing dissociations between spatial VWM and nonspatial VWM tasks in the PFC (Dade, Zatorre, Evans, & Jones-Gotman, 2001; D'Esposito et al., 1998; Owen et al., 1998; Postle & D'Esposito, 1999).

The failure to cleanly separate spatial VWM and nonspatial VWM in the human brain does not necessarily mean that spatial VWM and object VWM must also be inseparable at the functional level. The mapping between cognitive functions and brain anatomy is that of many-to-many. Two processes can both activate the same brain regions yet still be separable at the functional level. Behavioral studies on VWM thus provide unique insight into the relationship between spatial VWM and object VWM.

2.2.2. *Behavioral evidence*

In this discussion, it is necessary to clarify two terms: "spatial" and "object". In human behavioral studies of spatial VWM, at least two types of spatial memory have been tested: memory for spatial locations of an array of objects, and memory for spatial locations of a single object or a sequence of dot locations. Some researchers consider the former—spatial locations of an array of objects—a form of object memory or pattern memory (Logie, 1995; Phillips, 1974), as subjects seem to remember the entire pattern or spatial configuration of the array rather than individual item locations (Jiang, Olson, & Chun, 2000; Santa, 1977). In the following discussion we consider both types of spatial VWM.

The term "object" also requires clarification. By contrasting "spatial VWM" with "object VWM", we do not intend to discuss whether VWM is space-based or object-based, an issue familiar to visual attention researchers (Scholl, 2001). Here, object VWM simply refers to VWM for properties of an object that are not its location. Object VWM would include such things as color, size, orientation, shape, and so on.

Empirically testing spatial VWM and object VWM is simple: show observers an array of items (or a sequence of items) and instruct them to remember locations or object identities and measure VWM performance. If the two types of VWM are not separable, then one might expect that: (1) both types of VWM are interfered with to similar degrees by various kinds of secondary tasks, and (2) VWM for spatial locations is contingent on VWM for object identities, such that a change in object identity from initial memory to later testing would impair memory retrieval of spatial locations, and vice versa. Conversely, dissociation of dual-task interference on spatial and object VWM tasks, and separable encoding of spatial location and object identity information would indicate a dissociation between the two. So, to what degree is spatial VWM separable from object VWM in behavior?

2.2.2.1. *Dual-task interference*

Studies using dual-task interference as a means to separate object and spatial memory are extensively reviewed in chapter 1 (see section 2), but the approach is worth briefly recapping here. In interference studies, spatial VWM is usually tested using the Corsi block task, in which an experimenter taps a sequence of blocks presented on the table and the observer then has to imitate that tapping sequence. Object VWM, in contrast, is usually tested with a pattern matrix. After being shown a grid of squares, some of which are filled in, observers are tasked to replicate what they have seen on a blank grid. Della Sala, Gray, Baddeley, Allamano, and Wilson (1999) found that adding additional spatial tasks such as following the sequence of pegs haptically interfered more with the Corsi task than the pattern matrix task, while adding visual tasks such as viewing irrelevant pictures during the delay interval interfered more with the pattern matrix task than with the Corsi task. Thus, the two types of spatial VWM—VWM for spatial sequence and VWM for a static pattern—can be separated (see also Klauer & Zhao, 2004).

Can spatial VWM for a static pattern be distinguished from object VWM for shapes? The answer seems to be "no". A study that tested recall for static matrix patterns and recognition of Chinese characters found that both types of memory are insensitive to dynamic visual noise (Andrade, Kemps, Werniers, May, & Szmalec, 2002). In addition, both spatial VWM for an array of dots and nonspatial VWM for colors or scenes are significantly impaired by filled delay tasks, including those of an auditory-choice reaction time task (Makovski et al., 2006).

Thus, the two types of spatial VWM are separable, but object VWM and spatial VWM for an array of items are not easily dissociated. The latter finding may seem surprising, given that the VWM capacity for remembering objects appears to be much lower than that for remembering locations of an array of items (Jiang et al., 2000; Rensink, 2000; Simons, 1996). However, the disparity in capacity may not be a good measure of different systems, given that it is much easier to chunk individual locations into a bigger pattern than to chunk features of multiple objects. One may still find greater capacity for array locations than identities even if the same system is used to remember these two types of stimuli. Woodman, Vogel, and Luck (2001) found results consistent with this proposal: visual search was unimpaired when observers held several colors or shapes in VWM, yet it was impaired when they held the locations of two sequentially presented dots in spatial VWM (Woodman & Luck, 2004).

2.2.2.2. *Separable encoding of spatial and nonspatial properties*

Although interference studies fail to dissociate object VWM from spatial VWM for static patterns, there is strong evidence that the two types of information are not always coregistered in VWM. Remembering the identity of an object obligatorily puts the location of the object into VWM (Jiang, et al., 2000; Olson & Marshuetz, 2005; Tsal & Lamy, 2000), but remembering the locations of an array of items usually does not put the identities of these items in VWM (Jiang et al., 2000). These findings were obtained from change detection tasks that manipulated the consistency between test array properties and memory array properties (see Figure 2.2). When observers must perform a change detection task on object identities such as color or shape, their performance is significantly affected by whether the test array contains a change in item locations, even though location is a task-irrelevant dimension (Jiang et al., 2000). Interestingly, a change in location impairs performance only if the change has perturbed the relative configuration of element locations, but not if the change has resulted in no change in overall configuration (e.g., the change involves an expansion, con-traction, or shifting of the original display). These results suggest that the spatial layout of an array of objects is obligatorily encoded, even when the task does not explicitly require location memory. The configuration, or spatial pattern, of an array of items allows VWM to use topographic representation of the display: identities are bound to locations, and locations are bound to an imaginary con-figuration. Finally, even with single-item arrays, the identity of the object seems to obligatorily encode the object's spatial location into VWM, which enables faster change detection at the object's location (Olson & Marshuetz, 2005).

The relationship between spatial and nonspatial encoding is asymmetric (Fig-ure 2.2). When observers must remember dot locations for a change detection task, changing the shape or color of the array items has negligible effects on loca-tion change detection (Jiang et al., 2000). This finding suggests that nonspatial

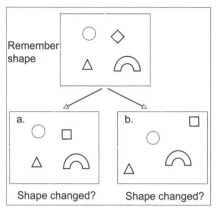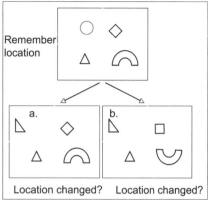

Figure 2.2. Effects of change in an irrelevant dimension on visual working memory accuracy of a relevant dimension. Left: Detection of a shape change is easier if
the locations of items do not change (a) than if they do (b). Right: Detection
of a location change is unaffected by whether the items change shapes (b) or
not (a).

properties are easily discarded during spatial VWM tasks, even when the change
in nonspatial properties is highly salient. However, there is an exception to this
independence, primarily in cases when items occupying the original memory
array are elongated: memory for these items' center locations is significantly
impaired if the individual items change orientation, which results in a change
in the perceived grouping of elements (Delvenne & Bruyer, 2006; Jiang, Chun,
& Olson, 2004).

   Taken together, behavioral studies on the relationship between spatial VWM
and object VWM have indicated their close relationship as well as possible dissociations. In spatial VWM, memory for an array of elements appears to be dissociable from memory for a single element or for a sequence of single-dot locations.
Dual-task interference tasks reveal this dissociation, which possibly reflects two
different mechanisms involved in registering space: a relational, object-based
mechanism, and an environment-based or viewer-based mechanism. Interference
studies have not reliably shown differences between spatial VWM for an array
of items and object VWM for that array. In this case, remembering objects usually leads to memory for these objects' locations, but the reverse is typically not
true. The complexity of the functional relationship between spatial VWM and
object VWM may partly explain why neuroscientists have so far not succeeded
at isolating the neural dissociation between the two.

2.3. The building blocks of VWM: Objects versus features

One of the most influential studies in VWM was the demonstration by Luck and
Vogel (1997) that VWM was limited by the number of objects rather than the
number of features per object. In their study, Luck and Vogel first tested VWM

for simple objects with a single feature, such as colored disks or tilted lines. They found that observers could remember about 4 different colors simultaneously, or about 4 different tilted lines simultaneously. They then tested observers on VWM of compound objects of multiple features, such as tilted lines of different colors. The results were clear: when color and orientation conjoined to form a single object, observers could remember about 4 of these compound objects, a total of 8 features. Indeed, there was no apparent limit to the number of features one could potentially remember, as long as they belong to a single object. Four compound objects containing 4 features each, including color, size, orientation, and the presence of a gap, could be easily remembered. These results were reminiscent of the object-based attention findings (Duncan, 1984; Egly, Driver, & Rafal, 1994; Lamy & Egeth, 2002), where visual attention operates upon all dimensions of a single object, allowing multiple features of a single object to be attended to simultaneously without any cost.

Although the equivalent performance between compound objects and single-dimension features has been used to argue for an object-based VWM account, this finding is also consistent with a feature-based VWM account that assumes separate storage limits for different dimensions. This alternative view, known as the multiple-pools of memory resources view, receives some support from studies on compound objects formed from a single dimension. Although Luck and Vogel (1997) reported that a compound object created by the juxtaposition of two colors was remembered as well as a simple object of just one color, this finding seemed specific to the highly saturated colors used in that study. Several groups found that color–color compound objects were as hard to remember as two simple color objects, finding no benefit for conjoining two features of the same dimension (Olson & Jiang, 2002; Wheeler & Treisman, 2002; Xu, 2002). However, the strongest version of the multiple-resources view—that conjoining features into objects plays no role in VWM—was also not supported by empirical data. When observers were presented with 4 colors and 4 orientations on a single display, they performed better if these features formed 4 colored-oriented bars than if they formed 8 objects, half of which were colored disks and half were tilted bars (Olson & Jiang, 2002). Thus, conjoining features of different dimensions into a single object enhanced VWM performance. Interestingly, observers tended to do better when a display contained simple feature objects that were heterogeneous, such as 4 colored disks and 4 tilted lines, than if the display contained simple feature objects that were homogeneous, such as 8 colored disks or 8 tilted lines. Thus, there is truth both to an object-based account and a multiple-pools of resource account of VWM (Olson & Jiang, 2002).

Why does the formation of a single object enhance VWM of multiple features? Is it simply because these features share the same location and thus are easier to remember? Lee and Chun (2001) directly contrasted the object-based account with a space-based account by using overlapping objects. Their results were consistent with the object-based account, finding no effects of the number of spatial locations on VWM performance. However, Xu (2006) provided the most comprehensive data on this debate and found that spatial proximity as well as connectivity between parts (to form a single object) contribute to VWM performance.

Although more features are remembered when they form compound objects than when they are multiple, single-feature objects (Luck & Vogel, 1997), these data do not provide direct evidence that the proper conjunction between different features is entirely resource-independent. In most studies on object- versus feature-based VWM discussed above, a change-present trial usually consists of replacing an old property with a new property not shown on the initial memory array. Thus, a red vertical line may change into a blue vertical line, with none of the initial memory items being blue. To correctly perform the task, observers only need to remember which features are present; correct conjunction between red and vertical and their spatial locations is not strictly required. To test whether features-conjunction in VWM comes for free, Wheeler and Treisman (2002) compared two types of change trials: a change involving a new feature value not presented on the initial memory array, and a change involving an old feature value presented at a location occupied by a different object. They found that performance was worse on the latter type of "feature-swapping" trials, suggesting that memory for proper conjunction of features was imperfect. In addition, whether multiple features of a single object are stored in VWM depends on task requirements. In visually guided motor tasks such as picking up a blue block and placing it at a designated location, observers usually acquire one relevant feature at a time, rather than storing all features of an object simultaneously (Droll & Hayhoe, 2007; Droll, Hayhoe, Triesch, & Sullivan, 2005).

The imperfect memory for conjunction, however, does not necessarily mean that VWM for feature conjunction demands more attention than VWM for single features. Gajewski and Brockmole (2006) asked observers to remember the color and shape of several objects. During the retention interval, attention was directed to a subset of the objects with an exogenous cue. Recall performance was enhanced for the cued positions. Interestingly, the uncued objects were also remembered as an integrated whole, as participants often recalled both features or neither of the two features of an object. In interference studies, Johnson, Hollingworth, and Luck (2008) found that a secondary task presented during the filled-delay interval interfered with feature VWM to the same degree as it did with conjunction VWM (see also Allen, Baddeley, & Hitch, 2006). These results are understandable given that feature–location conjunction appears to be obligatory (Jiang et al., 2000; Olson & Marshuetz, 2005). Thus, conjunction is an important element for VWM for feature–location binding as well as for multiple-feature conjunctions.

2.4. VWM capacity limit

Much of VWM research has been devoted to characterizing its capacity limit. Two separate questions on this issue have been raised (Figure 2.3 [in color plate section]). First, is the capacity limit of VWM influenced by the complexity of visual features? That is, do complex features fill up the VWM space more quickly than do simple features? Second, should this limit be thought of as limited in the number of slots, or should it be conceptualized as limited in resolution in a slot-less space? Much progress has been made to answer these questions, but no clear conclusions have been reached.

2.4.1. *Does feature complexity matter?*

Is the number of items one can hold in VWM fixed for different visual attributes, or is it variable, such that VWM can hold more simple objects (e.g., colors) than complex objects? The empirical data are clear: complexity matters in change detection tasks. For example, Alvarez and Cavanagh (2004) showed that when observers must remember several colors for a color change detection task, they can remember about 4 colors. But when they must remember several random polygons for a shape change detection task, they can only remember about 2 polygons. These results have led Alvarez and Cavanagh to propose a "flexible-slot" model of VWM, where the number of slots in VWM varies with object complexity. Complex attributes such as random polygons, cubes of different lightness shadings, and unfamiliar faces fill up VWM space more quickly than do simple attributes such as colors.

To provide an independent index of complexity, Alvarez and Cavanagh (2004) calculated the "informational load" of each object by measuring the slope of visual search RT as a function of the number of elements on a display. Thus, colors have low informational load because searching for a color among other colors results in a shallow slope. Unfamiliar faces have high informational load because searching for an unfamiliar face among other unfamiliar faces results in a steep slope. These empirical data are highly replicable (Curby & Gauthier, 2007; Eng, Chen, & Jiang, 2005; Olsson & Poom, 2005), but their interpretation is far from straightforward.

Do these data uniquely support the flexible-slot model? Advocates for the fixed-slot model have quickly pointed out that there may indeed be a fixed number of slots in VWM, but one complex shape can occupy more than one fixed slot (Zhang & Luck, 2003). A random polygon, for example, has definable parts and may take up two or more slots. Regardless of whether one adopts the "flexible-slots" or the "fixed-slots" view, what seems clear is that complexity of an object matters. But why does complexity matter? Is it because complex objects are truly harder to remember in VWM, or is it because the change from one complex object to another complex object results in a smaller change signal?

Unfortunately, this question is not easily answered. The informational load used to index complexity is essentially a similarity measure: faces are considered more complex than colors because the unfamiliar faces are more similar to one another than simple colors are to one another, as reflected by less efficient visual search for faces among faces than for colors among colors (Duncan & Humphreys, 1989). However, because faces always change into other faces and colors always change into other colors, not only are items on the memory display more "complex" for face trials, but the memory items are also more similar to a changed test item on those trials. In other words, to detect a face changing into another face, observers are operating on the detection of a relatively small change signal. It is only logical that performance on face change trials will be lower than that on color change trials, even if the number of VWM slots for faces is equivalent to that for colors (or even if the resolution for faces is comparable to that for colors). (For additional discussion of the impact of visual similarity on memory and how such effects have been used to test assumptions regarding the contents and capacity of VWM, see chapter 1, section 5.1.)

Because the "complexity" measure used in preceding studies directly affects the size of the change signal, reduced performance for remembering complex items can be accounted for at the output change detection stage, without considering any influence of complexity on intrinsic memory capacity. Indeed, in a recent study, Awh, Barton, and Vogel (2007) made a simple manipulation: they changed polygons into Chinese characters or vice versa and found that performance on between-category change trials was much better than performance on within-category change trials. These results underscore the inadequacy of disregarding output limitations in change detection. That similarity at the output-comparison stage matters, however, does not refute the possibility that complexity at the memory-input stage could also matter. The latter must be tested while controlling for the size of change signal for different visual attributes. This work remains to be done.

2.4.2. *Neuroimaging evidence for VWM of locations, simple features, and complex features*

Recent neuroimaging studies on human VWM have shown that the posterior parietal cortex correlates with increasing VWM load (Linden et al., 2003; Todd & Marois, 2004). Its activation increases as the number of colors to be remembered increases from 1 to about 4. As the capacity of VWM is reached, parietal activity also asymptotes, showing no further increase as memory load increases from 4 to 7 (Todd & Marois, 2004). But what aspects of the VWM task is the posterior parietal cortex (PPC) reflecting? Is it the number of locations (or objects) that must be monitored? Is it memory for identities? Or is it both spatial monitoring and VWM for object identities?

If PPC is involved primarily in monitoring space (or objects; Culham, Cavanagh, & Kanwisher, 2001; Jovicich et al., 2001), then its activity should be sensitive to the number of items in VWM but not to the complexity of these items. Thus, PPC activation should be comparable when observers must remember colors (a simple attribute) and shapes (a complex attribute). Alternatively, if PPC is involved primarily in memorizing the identity of objects, then its activation should be modulated by the aspect of the object that is relevant to the memory task. Remembering colors exerts a lower load on VWM than remembering shapes (Alvarez & Cavanagh, 2004), so PPC activity should be lower for remembering 1 color than remembering 1 shape. Furthermore, given that it takes about 4 colors to fill up VWM space and about 2 shapes to fill up VWM space, PPC activity should reach asymptote when memory load exceeds 4 colors or 2 shapes. Figure 2.4 [in color plate section] shows different predictions of the two models.

Empirical evidence has provided some support for both models (Song & Jiang, 2006). When observers are presented with colored polygons and must remember either color or shape on separate trial blocks, PPC activity was higher for remembering one shape than for remembering one color, suggesting that PPC was sensitive to what must be remembered. However, activity in PPC increased when the number of memory objects increased and asymptoted at 4 objects for both the color task and the shape task, even though behavioral capacity reached asymptote at 4 for color and only 2 for shape. Thus, the asymptote of PPC activity was sensitive only to the number of objects and not to their identity. PPC appears to be involved both in monitoring spatial locations (or individual objects) and in memory of specific object attributes.

The coding of spatial properties and object attributes can be separated to some degree to different parts of the posterior parietal cortex (Xu & Chun, 2006). Activation in the inferior segment of the intraparietal sulcus correlated with the number of objects regardless of object complexity, whereas activity in the superior segment of the intraparietal sulcus and the lateral occipital complex was modulated by complexity. Xu and Chun suggest that the inferior intraparietal sulcus represents the number of locations occupied by objects while the superior intraparietal sulcus and the lateral occipital complex encode the total amount of visual information.

2.4.3. *How is VWM limited: storage slots, resolution, or central executive?*

Why is VWM limited? At least two possibilities exist. First, VWM may be limited because central-executive limits prevent us from encoding more items into VWM. Second, VWM is limited in terms of the amount of information one can store. This storage limit can be revealed in one of two ways: as limited slots or limited resolution. When the storage information is capped at some level, adding more items can overflow in a limited-slot model, or it can result in each item being stored with low fidelity (in a limited-resolution model). These possibilities are not mutually exclusive, although different researchers have emphasized different aspects of the capacity limit.

2.4.3.1. *Is VWM limited in storage space or in resolution?*

Although no serious researcher would deny that resolution must be limited in VWM, many have endorsed a somewhat different conception of VWM's capacity limit—namely, that of limited slots in a metaphorical storage locker. There are historical reasons why slot models are so heavily preferred over the alternative conception of a "resolution limit". Visual WM studies were preceded by many years of research on verbal WM, and the capacity limit of verbal WM was conceptualized in slot models: there are 7 plus or minus 2 chunks in verbal WM (Miller, 1956), with this magical number being modulated by an individual's articulatory speed and the phonological word-length effect (Baddeley, 1986). Naturally, when researchers approach visual WM, the first question to ask is: how many slots does VWM contain?

The answer can sometimes be surprising. Using the change detection task, Pashler (1988) suggested that the capacity of VWM for upright letters was approximately four. He also found that the capacity was not significantly influenced by familiarity: upright letters did not result in a higher capacity than inverted letters. That the capacity of VWM was somewhat insensitive to familiarity was also confirmed in other studies using unnameable stimuli (Chen, Eng, & Jiang, 2006). As more studies were conducted, the magical number four started to emerge as the approximate capacity limit for a wide range of visual stimuli, including colors, line orientations, letters, and compound objects created by conjunction of colors and orientations (Cowan, 2001; Irwin & Andrews, 1996; Luck & Vogel, 1997). The magical number four is very attractive to researchers seeking parsimony across cognitive domains. "Four" is also the upper limit of independent objects that one can individuate simultaneously (Pylyshyn & Storm, 1988), and "four" is the transition between a small, exact number system and a large, approximate number system in animals, human infants, and adults (Dehaene, 1997). Indeed, the fact that this number concerns coherent objects rather than features making up those objects strengthens the link between VWM and other cognitive processes. It is probably no coincidence that objects seem to be the operating units for selective attention, enumeration, multiple-object tracking, and VWM.

However, the model of VWM as limited in four slots is challenged on two grounds. First, "four" fails to characterize the capacity limit for many properties of objects. Complex attributes, such as the shapes of random polygons or faces of unfamiliar individuals, have a much lower capacity limit than simple properties such as color (Alvarez & Cavanagh, 2004; Olsson & Poom, 2005). This challenge, although significant, does not fundamentally shake the conception of VWM as limited in slots. It places constraints on how the slots are used up by different visual attributes, something researchers are currently debating (see section 1.4.1). The more damaging challenge to slot models is the idea that VWM is an amorphous space limited not by the number of slots but by how veridical the representation is (Wilken & Ma, 2004).

Data discussed so far—that change detection declines as the number of items to be remembered increases—can be explained by both the limited-slot view and the limited-resolution view, as long as the latter assumes that resolution declines with increasing memory load. Thus, memory for a red color may be relatively veridical at lower set sizes, such that a correct change detection can be made when red turns into purple. But as load increases, memory for the red color may be less veridical, such that it fails to detect the red turning into purple, but the memory may be good enough to detect the red turning into green, a more dramatic change.

There are two major differences between the limited-slot and limited-resolution views: the source of performance limitation, and the fate of overflowing input. According to the limited-slot view, only four (or some other number of) objects can be encoded in VWM. Performance is thus limited by memory input load, and items overflowing the limited slots will not be retained in VWM. At high load, a random subset will be encoded in VWM and the rest will not be encoded. If the memorized subset is later tested, then performance should be perfect. But if the other subset is tested, then observers must make a random guess. This is essentially the assumption in Pashler's method of VWM capacity calculation (Pashler, 1988). The limited-resolution view makes very different assumptions about the source of performance limitation. In this view, all items are encoded in VWM to some degree, no matter how many are to be remembered. Memory load changes the veridicality of VWM. With a lower load, each item is represented with high fidelity, allowing a small change between the memory and the test stimuli to be detected. With a higher load, each item is represented with poorer fidelity, so correct detection requires a much bigger change signal between the memory and the test stimuli. The main source of performance limitation thus lies both at the level of memory input load (the higher the load, the lower the fidelity), and at the level of change detection output (the smaller the change signal, the lower the performance). In this view, there are no "overflowing" items: all items are retained in VWM to some degree. In addition, the decline in resolution across memory load is a gradual process. There is no cut-off of four, for example, below which the resolution is perfect and above which the resolution is very poor.

The limited-resolution view receives strong support from studies that systematically varied both memory load and size of the change signal between the original memory element and the testing stimulus (Jiang, Shim, & Makovski, in press; Wilken & Ma, 2004). Consistent with the limited-resolution view, it takes a larger change signal for performance to reach a constant threshold as memory load increases. There is no evidence for a cut-off at four or another number for remembering color, orientation, spatial frequency, or face identity. If we use the standard method to calculate capacity (Pashler, 1988), we would get very different estimates of the capacity depending on the size of the change signal. The limited-slot view must either revise its assumptions or allow the number of slots to be resizable depending on testing conditions.

Despite greater empirical support for the limited-resolution view, what still dominates VWM researchers' conception is the limited-slot view. Stronger advocates and additional empirical data may be needed to reverse this trend.

2.4.3.2. *Is VWM limited in storage or in central-executive control?*

So far we have considered VWM as limited in storage capacity, either in terms of the number of slots or in terms of resolution. However, recent event-related brain potential (ERP) studies by Vogel and colleagues have provided a new perspective, according to which the VWM capacity limitation is closely related to central-executive limits.

In Vogel's studies, colors or tilted lines served as memory items in a change detection task. These items were evenly displayed in the left and right hemifields, of which only one hemifield contained relevant memory items. At the beginning of each trial a cue signaled the relevant side for observers to remember. A sustained negative ERP signal during the change detection retention interval was found, and it was contralateral to the remembered hemifield. The ERP signal increased as VWM load increased and reached plateau when VWM capacity limit was reached. The increase in amplitude from 2 to 4 correlated with individual observers' memory capacity (Vogel & Machizawa, 2004), allowing Vogel and colleagues to use this ERP signal to probe VWM capacity limit.

This neurophysiological marker was used further to examine differences between groups of individuals who have high or low VWM capacity (Vogel, McCollough, & Machizawa, 2005). The relevant memory items (which varied in number as 2 or 4) were either presented alone, or intermixed with 2 irrelevant items that were distinguished from the relevant items by color (red vs. blue) or by locations (different visual quadrants). When the relevant memory items were presented without distractors, both low and high VWM capacity groups showed higher ERP signal as memory load increased from 2 to 4. Surprisingly, when the relevant memory items must be extracted from 2 other distractors, the ERP signal in the high-memory-capacity group reflected the number of relevant memory items, but the ERP signal in the low-memory-capacity group reflected the total number of items. These results show that high-capacity individuals are also efficient at filtering out unwanted information, but low-capacity individuals fail to protect VWM from being filled up with unwanted information. These results suggest that the capacity of VWM is closely related to an individual's ability to exclude irrelevant items from current tasks, an arguably important element of central-executive control. Vogel and colleagues' findings fit well with the Baddeley's working memory model, where the central-executive process is important for VWM. Consistent with these findings, recent studies that added filled-delay tasks during change detection showed that amodal, central attention is a necessary component of change detection (Makovski et al., 2006). Models of VWM capacity that focus exclusively on storage limit are thus unlikely to be adequate.

To summarize, behavioral and cognitive neuroscience research in the past decade has significantly enhanced our understanding of factors that influence performance in a short-term change detection task. However, this research has not unambiguously resolved several fundamental questions about VWM capacity, including whether VWM is limited by storage slots or by resolution, whether its storage space is limited by the complexity of to-be-remembered visual attributes, and whether the "magical number four" plays any role in VWM capacity limitation.

3. SHORT-TERM VERSUS LONG-TERM VISUAL MEMORY

Human memory is historically divided into short-term and long-term stores which are considered somewhat separable, at least when memory for verbal materials is considered (Atkinson & Shiffrin, 1968). Evidence for the separation includes (1) different effects on the serial position curve, (2) different types of encoding (phonological vs. semantic) (3) capacity (limited versus unlimited) (Miller, 1956; Nickerson & Adams, 1979), and (4) dissociation in neural correlates, where the hippocampus is considered critical for transforming short-term memory (STM) into long-term memory (LTM) (Scoville & Milner, 1957).

There is some evidence that visual STM and visual LTM may also be separable. Short-term memory for visual materials is highly limited in capacity, but long-term memory for visual stimuli has no clear capacity limit. After viewing 600 photographs of scenes and events, each for 2 s, subjects recognized 92% of images when tested one day later, and 63% of images when tested one year later (Nickerson, 1965; see also additional discussion in chapter 4, section 2.3). Such dramatic differences in capacity are vividly depicted in the titles of two widely cited articles, "Learning 10,000 Pictures" (Standing, 1973), and "The Magical Number 4 in Short-term Memory" (Cowan, 2001). However, increasing evidence has shown that the separation between visual STM and visual LTM may not be the most natural way to carve out visual memory systems.

The enormous capacity difference between visual STM and LTM may lead us to expect that if we can rely on visual LTM for a short-term change detection task, performance would improve. Thus, if we have already acquired familiarity with a visual display, change detection on that display can be supported by visual LTM and STM. Such "dual coding" may help alleviate the degree of failure to detect changes. This proposal, however, has not stood the test of several studies. Wolfe, Oliva, Butcher, and Arsenio (2002) and Oliva, Wolfe, & Arsenio (2004) found that change detection failed to improve on displays repeated for hundreds of trials, as long as the object that might change varied from one trial to another. Thus, the ability to detect a change in your own living-room is probably not better than detecting a change in someone else's living-room. Similarly, Olson and Jiang (2004) found that repeating the same exact memory display 30 times failed to improve change detection on those trials, even though subjects were able to recognize the repeated displays at the end of the experiment, suggesting that they acquired visual LTM for the displays. The only case in which visual LTM seemed to facilitate change detection was when the target that might change was always the same one on a repeated display. In this case, visual LTM informed observers which locations or objects were more important, allowing attention to be preferentially directed to that item (Olson, Jiang, & Moore, 2005).

The availability of visual LTM for scenes (Oliva et al., 2004), novel objects (Wolfe et al., 2002), and spatial locations (Olson & Jiang, 2004) does not contribute further to a short-term change detection task. The dramatic, previously observed capacity difference between visual LTM and visual STM perhaps reflects not so much the qualitative differences between the two stores as differences in the visual system's efficiency at encoding details versus encoding gist. Previous short-term tasks usually required people to detect minute differences between two similar images, while long-term tasks usually required people to differentiate qualitatively different images. When placed within the same testing context where the size of the change signal is controlled for, dual-coding of an image in both visual LTM and visual STM does not provide any advantage over coding of the image only in visual STM. This is not to deny a role of past experience in current processing. As will be reviewed in subsequent sections, experience modifies the allocation of spatial attention (Chun & Jiang, 1998; Olson et al., 2005). To the degree that important regions in past experience coincide with the target region in the current task, visual LTM can enhance performance by prioritizing the retention of that region in visual STM. But it does not, in itself, contain any further information that cannot be extracted online. The 10,000 pictures remembered in visual LTM (Standing, 1973) are simply not held at the same level of precision as the 4 images remembered in visual STM (Cowan, 2001).

Undeniably, there is more information available in visual LTM than what can be currently accessed. This kind of "capacity difference", however, does not constitute a qualitative difference between memory systems. Both visual STM and LTM can support detection of changes to visual details and semantic gist (Brockmole & Henderson, 2005; Hollingworth, 2005), and both rely on similar brain regions (Ranganath & Blumenfeld, 2005). Even medial temporal lobe-damaged patients, traditionally considered normal with short-term memory, have difficulty retaining information in visual STM (Olson, Page, Moore, Chatterjee, & Verfaellie, 2006). Together, these studies suggest that it is time to seek an alternative taxonomy for human visual memory, one that separates memory for gist versus details rather than memory in the long-term versus short-term.

4. EFFECTS OF VISUAL MEMORY ON SEARCH

Although we do not usually think of visual search as a memory task, several lines of research suggest that memory is accumulated from visual search tasks and is used to affect future search processes. Examples of memory influence on search include trial-sequence effects, contextual cueing, the preview effect, online search memory, and guidance from visual working memory. These different paradigms likely result from different mechanisms. We consider them separately here.

4.1. Trial-sequence effects

It has been known for decades that visual perception is strongly influenced by trial-sequence effects. For example, if the current trial's target happens to be the same as the preceding trial's target, response is facilitated, showing positive priming (Schacter & Buckner, 1998). Conversely, if the current trial's target happens to be the same as the preceding trial's distractor, response is delayed, showing negative priming (Neill, 1977; Tipper, 1985). These priming effects are usually stronger in the short-term and without intermittent trials. Additionally, they may be difficult to detect after 30 s or so, perhaps because new memory is formed from the intermittent trials, rendering the old memory less useful. However, intertrial priming effects can last for days or years and can survive the interference from hundreds of intermittent trials (DeSchepper & Treisman, 1996).

An example of an intertrial sequence effect is the "priming-of-popout", initially described by Maljkovic and Nakayama (1994, 1996; see also Kristjánsson & Nakayama, 2003). Maljkovic and Nakayama used a popout search task where subjects reported the shape of a red item among green items, or vice versa. The target on a given trial can either be red or green, so it was defined by a singleton rather than by particular feature values. Nonetheless, if the target was red on trial N and happened to be red again on trial $N + 1$, performance was faster than if the target color on trial $N + 1$ did not match that of trial N. This kind of priming occurred not only for target color but also for target location, even when neither was the target-defining feature. By varying the lag between repetitions, Maljkovic and Nakayama (1994) found that the priming effect decayed over time but was observable for up to 30 s. Interestingly, observers were generally unaware of the intertrial priming effect shown in this paradigm, distinguishing this kind of memory from visual working memory. The cross-trial priming effect has been extended to conjunction search tasks (Geyer, Muller, & Krummenacher, 2006; Kristjánsson, Wang, & Nakayama, 2002) and reflects both bottom-up and top-down biases toward repeated target properties (Hillstrom, 2000).

4.2. Contextual cueing

Humans process a visual display more quickly the second time it is presented. This kind of repetition effect has been systematically explored in a paradigm dubbed "contextual cueing" by Chun and Jiang (1998). Observers were asked to perform a standard visual search task for a letter T among Ls. Unknown to them, some of the search trials repeated occasionally in the experiment, such that over the course of an hour, observers had seen several hundred novel displays and a few repeated displays. Because the repetition was not immediate and was dispersed among many nonrepeating trials, observers typically were unaware of the repetition and could not recognize the repeated displays (Chun & Jiang, 1998, 2003). Even so, visual search speed on repeated displays became progressively faster than on nonrepeated displays (Figure 2.5). This facilitation was not simply due to learning of potential target locations (Miller, 1988), as Chun and Jiang controlled for the repetition of target locations for repeating and nonrepeating trials (i.e., the target locations were repeated on nonrepeating trials but the distractor locations were not). It was also not due to motor priming (Nissen & Bullemer, 1987), as the identity of the target was randomly assigned so the repeated displays were not associated with repeated motor responses. In addi-

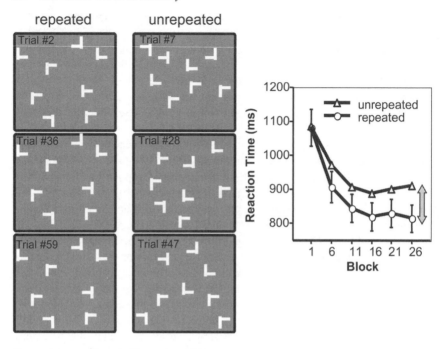

Figure 2.5. A schematic illustration of the contextual cueing paradigm and typical experimental results.

tion, the facilitation was not produced by perceptual familiarity with the entire configuration of a repeated trial, as the benefit was eliminated if all locations were repeated but the target's location was randomly swapped with distractors' locations (Chun & Jiang, 1998; Jiang, King, Shim, & Vickery, 2006; Wolfe, Klempen, & Dahlen, 2000). The improvement in RT observed in this paradigm thus reflects an implicit, associative learning mechanism, where the display configuration is associatively learned with the target location. When a repetition is detected, visual attention can be quickly directed to the associated target location, allowing search to be completed on the basis of "instance" memory (Logan, 1988). The benefit has been known as "contextual cueing", as if the search context surrounding the target is cueing attention toward the target's location (but see Kunar, Flusberg, Horowitz, & Wolfe, 2007, reviewed next).

What makes contextual cueing so intriguing as a form of visual memory is that although its content lacks semantic gist, it is very powerful and has high capacity. Because all displays are created essentially by random placement of T and Ls on the screen, they are visually similar and cannot be distinguished by semantic gist. Indeed, putting a natural scene in the background, such that the target location is consistently paired with a particular scene, usually results in explicit learning of the association (Brockmole & Henderson, 2006a; Jiang et al.,

2006). In the absence of semantic gist, learning is usually implicit and operates on completely abstract and homogeneous visual displays. It is thus surprising to see how robust contextual cueing is to various kinds of stressors. Observers have no difficulty learning 60 repeated displays among 1,800 novel displays, spread over 5 different search sessions, and learning from one day did not result in proactive or retroactive interference on learning from another day (Jiang, Song, & Rigas, 2005). Once acquired, memory for repeated displays lasts for at least 1 week, in that search remained faster on previously learned displays than on new ones (Chun & Jiang, 2003; Jiang et al., 2005). Simultaneously loading VWM up with colors, locations, or potential search targets does not at all impair learning (Vickery, Sussman, & Jiang, 2006). Even selectively tuning attention away from repeated elements does not eliminate learning (Jiang & Leung, 2005; Rausei, Makovski, & Jiang, 2007). Finally, learning transferred to displays that did not exactly match the original trained displays (Brady & Chun, 2007; Jiang & Wagner, 2004; Olson & Chun, 2001), and in some cases, a repetition of just 3 locations was sufficient for transfer (Song & Jiang, 2005). Contextual cueing is such a powerful effect that, at this point, conditions that lead to no learning (Jiang & Chun, 2001; Ono, Jiang, & Kawahara, 2005) seem more informative than conditions that result in learning!

The exact mechanism that leads to facilitation of search speed, however, remains controversial. The dominant view is an attentional guidance view, according to which repeated context guides attention to the target location. This memory-based search can be faster than the default, perception-based serial search. A simple prediction from the attentional guidance view is that contextual cueing should be stronger for visual search involving a larger number of elements, because the memory-based search will likely win more often if the default, serial search takes longer (as is the case on large set-size displays). However, repeated attempts to find an increase in cueing effect for larger set sizes have failed (Kunar et al., 2007). This led Kunar et al. to propose an alternative account, according to which search itself always proceeds via the default, perception-based serial search, even on repeated displays. Once the target is located, however, observers are faster at making a response on repeated trials, perhaps because they are more confident that the target is in that position.

Although the lack of modulation by set size is perplexing, it is not as damaging to the attentional guidance view as one might think. The prediction that cueing should be greater at higher set sizes rests on several assumptions, some of which are known to be false. One assumption is that the resultant memory trace is as strong on high set-size displays as on low set-size displays. But this may not be true. Indeed, Hodsoll and Humphreys (2005) found that contextual cueing was weaker for set size 20 than for set size 10, suggesting that the memory trace may be weaker at higher set sizes, perhaps because different displays become less distinctive as set size increases. In addition, many studies have shown that learning in the search task is local and that observers seem to rely on the nearest items to help search. If observers always learn to associate with the target the nearest four items (Brady & Chun, 2007; Olson & Chun, 2001), then learning will not be modulated by how many other elements are on the display. The idea that contextual cueing reflects only response-stage learning is also inconsistent with eye-tracking studies. Using real-world scenes as the learning context, Brockmole and Henderson (2006b) found that fewer eye movements were required to find the target on repeated displays, with direct orienting of gaze to the target once learning is complete. Thus, repeated search context can guide attention, at least when the context involves real-world scenes.

Regardless of whether one endorses the attentional guidance view or a response bias view, it is clear that research on visual context learning has gone beyond demonstrating that humans are capable of various types of statistical learning under various conditions.

Research on this topic, however, faces significant challenges. Despite the robustness of contextual cueing to many stressors, researchers have not yet sorted out all factors that modulate the size of the learning. As a result, one cannot always predict whether contextual cueing will be reliably found in a given situation. Indeed, contextual cueing is sometimes not found, even though a priori one may expect a learning effect. For example, Junge, Scholl, and Chun (2007) found that contextual cueing was absent if observers first searched through all nonrepeating displays and then were introduced to some repeating displays. It was as if the initial phase of no-repetition tuned the system out of a repetition detection mode. Lleras and Von Muhlenen (2004) found that cueing was seen only when observers were told to adopt a more passive strategy for search; if observers were told to devote an active effort to find the target, contextual cueing was not found. Hodsoll and Humphreys (2005) obtained a very weak contextual cueing effect when the display contained 20 elements, even though there was no a priori reason why cueing would not occur there. The quirks of visual implicit learning remain to be fully sorted out.

4.3. Preview effect

Watson and Humphreys (1997) systematically explored a preview effect in visual search first reported by Kahneman, Treisman, and Burkell (1983). Instead of presenting all items simultaneously for observers to search, Watson and Humphreys (1997) presented a subset of the distractor first for about 1 second before adding the remaining distractors and the target. They found that previewing the distractors and keeping them on the search display resulted in efficient rejection of the previewed items. The preview effect was initially given the term of "visual marking," reflecting the hypothesis that previewed items were "marked" or inhibited from future search.

The inhibition account was challenged by alternative views that placed more emphasis on the new, rather than the previewed, items (Donk & Theeuwes, 2001b, 2003; Jiang, Chun, & Marks, 2002). Donk and Theeuwes (2001b), for example, proposed that the preview effect simply reflected capture of attention by the abrupt onset of the newly added items. They showed that if the new items were isoluminant with the background and thus providing no abrupt onset, then the preview effect was much reduced or eliminated. However, more recent research by Humphreys and colleagues provide strong evidence for the existence of an active inhibition process for the previewed items (Braithwaite, Hulleman, Watson, & Humphreys, 2006; Braithwaite, Humphreys, Watson, & Hulleman, 2005; Kunar & Humphreys, 2006; Kunar, Humphreys, Smith, & Hulleman, 2003). It is fair to say that both inhibition and attentional capture contribute to the preview effect initially reported by Watson and Humphreys (1997) and Kahneman et al. (1983).

To be able to eliminate the previewed items from search, some kind of visual memory must be involved because the previewed items and new distractors are indistinguishable at the time when all items are presented. There are several candidates for this memory, including visual memory for the locations of the previewed items, visual memory for the locations of the new items, and visual memory for different temporal onsets of the two groups. A systematic exploration on this topic showed that the memory needed for the preview effect came primarily from the latter two sources, where observers held in visual memory the locations of the new items and the differential temporal onset between the two groups (Jiang & Wang, 2004). Inhibition of the old group and abrupt onset of the new group may contribute to the representation of different temporal groups and are thus part of visual memory used for the preview effect.

4.4. Online search memory

In many visual search tasks, serial (or partially serial) allocation of attention is needed. In this process, attention moves from one location to another or from one cluster to another. An online search memory about already visited locations is important, as an efficient serial search avoids visiting the same location multiple times. Several studies have provided evidence for the existence of a within-trial, online search memory. They compared visual search through unchanging displays and changing displays on which the target and distractors are relocated randomly every 100 ms or so. Despite earlier observations suggesting the opposite (Horowitz & Wolfe, 1998), later studies show that search is significantly disrupted in the relocation condition (Gibson, Li, Skow, Brown, & Cooke, 2000; Kristjánsson, 2000; Takeda, 2004), suggesting that previously visited locations are retained in memory for that search trial.

This kind of online search memory is quite durable but is not robust against disruption. If a search trial is interrupted by a blank interval before search is complete, observers can resume their search after the interval without any difficulty. Thus, performance on a continuous trial without blank interruption is comparable to performance on a paused trial with many blank interruptions (Shen & Jiang, 2006), even when the blank interval lasted for 6 s or more. The online search memory is also robust against interference from passively viewing additional visual displays. However, filling in the blank interval with other spatial tasks, such as additional search on a new display or an additional visual working memory task, significantly disrupted the search memory accumulated before the interruption. The online search memory may reflect both inhibition of return to already visited locations (Klein, 1988), and observers' deliberate intention not to revisit already searched locations.

4.5. Attentional guidance by contents in VWM

Although visual working memory and visual attention are characterized by two different terms, they are intimately related processes (see, e.g., Olivers, Meijer, & Theeuwes, 2006). Holding additional information in verbal or visual working memory significantly interferes with visual search performance (de Fockert, Rees, Frith, & Lavie, 2001; Woodman & Luck, 2004). In addition, the content of spatial and nonspatial working memory directly interacts with the allocation of attention to corresponding locations and features. For example, Awh, Jonides, and Reuter-Lorenz (1998) showed that shape discrimination of the target was facilitated when a target happened to land at a location held in VWM. Downing (2000) found that when observers held an object shape in VWM and subsequently performed a discrimination task on two other items, one of which matched the shape in VWM, discrimination was faster on the matched object than on the novel object. The content of VWM can facilitate not only overall response speed, but also the slope of the RT–set-size function. For example, Soto, Heinke, Humphreys and Blanco (2005) found that search efficiency was enhanced when the target was surrounded by an item matching what was currently in VWM (for a similar effect in a popout search task, see also Soto, Humphreys, & Heinke, 2006). Items that were recently viewed but not actively stored in VWM did not influence subsequent visual search, suggesting that active use of VWM was the primary source for facilitation of search.

The guidance of visual search by the content of VWM is consistent with several models of visual search, such as the Feature Integration Theory (Treisman, 1988), the Guided Model (Wolfe, 1994), and the Biased Competition Model (Desimone & Duncan, 1995). Visual working memory serves to exert top-down bias on the weighting of relevant target properties, facilitating visual search for those properties (Vickery et al., 2005).

The content of VWM, however, does not automatically bias visual search toward items matching VWM's content. If an item in VWM was never the target of search, search was not biased toward that item (Woodman & Luck, 2007). An active attentional set at using VWM content for search seems a necessary condition for their interaction, suggesting that the cognitive system is flexible at using VWM in current search.

5. CONCLUDING REMARKS

In an influential paper, O'Regan (1992) argued that visual memory never needs to be developed to an exquisite level because the external visual world is a proxy for internal representation. If we need to know what object is where, we can simply open our eyes and look! Indeed, studies by Hayhoe and colleagues (e.g., Ballard, Hayhoe, & Pelz, 1995; Droll & Hayhoe, 2007; Droll et al., 2005; Triesch, Ballard, Hayhoe, & Sullivan, 2003) showed that observers prefer to look back at an object they had looked at previously to extract additional perceptual properties about it rather than pushing all properties into VWM once and for all. Certainly, visual memory lacks the kind of details and richness provided by visual perception, and this lack of richness contributes to the surprisingly inefficient coding of detailed changes across cuts of visual scenes or social interactions (Levin & Simons, 1997; Simons & Chabris, 1999; Simons & Rensink, 2005). While we agree that visual memory cannot be used to substitute for visual perception, we have reviewed evidence that visual perception is constantly aided by visual memory, and visual memory is constantly accumulated from visual perception. Visual memory allows us to maintain spatiotemporal continuity in this constantly changing environment. It enables us to visualize without actually seeing, and it helps us see things we already experienced more efficiently.

6. ACKNOWLEDGMENTS

The authors were supported by funding from NIH MH071788, NSF 0733764, and ARO 46926-LS. We thank Kristine Liu for comments and suggestions. Correspondence should be sent to Yuhong Jiang, 75 East River Road, S251 Elliott Hall, Minneapolis, MN 55455. Email: jiang166@umn.edu.

7. REFERENCES

Allen, R. J., Baddeley, A. D., & Hitch, G. J. (2006). Is the binding of visual features in working memory resource-demanding? *Journal of Experimental Psychology: General, 135,* 298–313.

Alvarez, G. A., & Cavanagh, P. (2004). The capacity of visual short-term memory is set both by visual information load and by number of objects. *Psychological Science, 15,* 106–111.

Andrade, J., Kemps, E., Werniers, Y., May, J., & Szmalec, A. (2002). Insensitivity of visual short-term memory to irrelevant visual information. *Quarterly Journal of Experimental Psychology, 55A,* 753–774.

Atkinson, R. C., & Shiffrin, M. (1968). Human memory: A proposed system and its control processes. In K. W. Spence & J. T. Spence (Eds.), *The psychology of learning and motivation* (Vol. 2, pp. 89–195). New York: Academic Press.

Averbach, E., & Sperling, G. (1961). Short term storage of information in vision. In C. Cherry (Ed.), *Information theory* (pp. 196–211). London: Butterworth.

Awh, E., Barton, B., & Vogel, E. K. (2007). Visual working memory represents a fixed number of items regardless of complexity. *Psychological Science, 18,* 622–628.

Awh, E., & Jonides, J. (2001). Overlapping mechanisms of attention and spatial working memory. *Trends in Cognitive Sciences, 5,* 119–126.

Awh, E., Jonides, J., & Reuter-Lorenz, P. A. (1998). Rehearsal in spatial working memory. *Journal of Experimental Psychology: Human Perception and Performance, 24,* 780–790.

Baddeley, A. D. (1986). *Working memory.* Oxford, UK: Clarendon Press.

Baddeley, A. D. (2000). The episodic buffer: A new component of working memory? *Trends in Cognitive Science, 4,* 417–423.

Baddeley, A. D., & Hitch, G. (1974). Working memory. In G. H. Bower (Ed.), *The psychology of learning and motivation: Advances in research and theory* (Vol. 8, pp. 47–89). New York: Academic Press.

Ballard, D. H., Hayhoe, M. M., & Pelz, J. B. (1995). Memory representations in natural tasks. *Cognitive Neuroscience, 7,* 66–80.

Brady, T. F., & Chun, M. M. (2007). Spatial constraints on learning in visual search: Modelling contextual cueing. *Journal of Experimental Psychology: Human Perception and Performance, 33*(4), 798–815.

Braithwaite, J. J., Hulleman, J., Watson, D. G., & Humphreys, G. W. (2006). Is it impossible to inhibit isoluminant items, or does it simply take longer? Evidence from preview search. *Perception & Psychophysics, 68,* 290–300.

Braithwaite, J. J., Humphreys, J. W., Watson, D. G., & Hulleman, J. (2005). Revisiting preview search at isoluminance: New onsets are not necessary for the preview advantage. *Perception & Psychophysics, 67,* 1214–1228.

Brockmole, J., & Henderson, J. M. (2005). Prioritizing of new objects in real-world scenes: Evidence from eye movements. *Journal of Experimental Psychology: Human Perception and Performance, 31,* 857–868.

Brockmole, J., & Henderson, J. M. (2006a). Using real-world scenes as contextual cues during search. *Visual Cognition, 13,* 99–108.

Brockmole, J., & Henderson, J. M. (2006b). Recognition and attention guidance during contextual cueing in real-world scenes: Evidence from eye movements. *Quarterly Journal of Experimental Psychology, 59,* 1177–1187.

Chen, D., Eng, H. Y., & Jiang, Y. (2006). Visual working memory for trained and novel polygons. *Visual Cognition, 14,* 37–54.

Chun, M. M., & Jiang, Y. (1998). Contextual cueing: Implicit learning and memory of visual context guides spatial attention. *Cognitive Psychology, 36,* 28–71.

Chun, M. M., & Jiang, Y. (2003). Implicit, long-term spatial contextual memory. *Journal of Experimental Psychology: Learning, Memory, and Cognition, 29,* 224–234.

Courtney, S. M., Petit, L., Maisog, J. M., Ungerleider, L. G., & Haxby, J. V. (1998). An area specialized for spatial working memory in human frontal cortex. *Science, 279,* 1347–1351.

Courtney, S. M., Ungerleider, L. G., Keil, K., & Haxby, J. V. (1996). Object and spatial visual working memory activate separate neural systems in human cortex. *Cerebral Cortex, 6,* 39–49.

Cowan, N. (2001). The magical number 4 in short-term memory: A reconsideration of mental storage capacity. *Behavioral and Brain Sciences, 24,* 87–114.

Culham, J. C., Cavanagh, P., & Kanwisher, N. G. (2001). Attention response functions: Characterizing brain areas using fMRI activation during parametric variations of attentional load. *Neuron, 32,* 737–745.

Curby, K. M., & Gauthier, I. (2007). A visual short-term memory advantage for faces. *Psychonomic Bulletin & Review, 14*(4), 620–628.

Dade, L. A., Zatorre, R. J., Evans, A. C., & Jones-Gotman, M. (2001). Working memory in another dimension: Functional imaging of human olfactory working memory. *NeuroImage, 14,* 650–660.

Davachi, L., & Goldman-Rakic, P. S. (2001). Primate rhinal cortex participates in both visual recognition and working memory tasks: Functional mapping with 2-DG. *Journal of Neurophysiology, 85,* 2590–2601.

De Fockert, J. W., Rees, G., Frith, C. D., & Lavie, N. (2001). The role of working memory in visual selective attention. *Science, 291,* 1803–1806.

Dehaene, S. (1997). *The number sense: How the mind creates mathematics.* New York: Oxford University Press.

Della Sala, S., Gray, C., Baddeley, A. D., Allamano, N., & Wilson, L. (1999). Pattern span: A tool for unwelding visuo-spatial memory. *Neuropsychologia, 37,* 1189–1199.

Delvenne, J. F., & Bruyer, R. (2006). A configural effect in visual short-term memory for features from different parts of an object. *Quarterly Journal of Experimental Psychology, 59,* 1567–1580.

De Renzi, E., & Spinnler, H. (1967). Impaired performance on color tasks in patients with hemisphere lesions. *Cortex, 3,* 194–217.

DeSchepper, B., & Treisman, A. (1996). Visual memory for novel shapes: Implicit coding without attention. *Journal of Experimental Psychology: Learning, Memory, and Cognition, 22,* 27–47.

Desimone, R., & Duncan, J. (1995). Neural mechanisms of selective visual attention. *Annual Review of Neuroscience, 18,* 193–222.

D'Esposito, M., Aguirre, G. K., Zarahn, E., Ballard, D., Shin, R. K., & Lease, S. J. (1998). Functional MRI studies of spatial and nonspatial working memory. *Cognitive Brain Research, 7,* 1–13.

Di Lollo, V. (1984). On the relationship between stimulus intensity and duration of visible persistence. *Journal of Experimental Psychology: Human Perception and Performance, 10,* 144–151.

Donk, M., & Theeuwes, J. (2001a). Prioritizing selection of new elements: Bottom-up versus top-down control. *Perception & Psychophysics, 65,* 1231–1242.

Donk, M., & Theeuwes, J. (2001b). Visual marking beside the mark: Prioritizing selection by abrupt onsets. *Perception & Psychophysics, 63,* 891–900.

Donk, M., & Theeuwes, J. (2003). Prioritizing selection of new elements: Bottom-up versus top-down control. *Perception & Psychophysics, 65*(8), 1231–1242.

Downing, P. E. (2000). Interactions between visual working memory and selective attention. *Psychological Science, 11,* 467–473.

Droll, J. A., & Hayhoe, M. M. (2007). Trade-offs between gaze and working memory use. *Journal of Experimental Psychology: Human Perception and Performance, 33*(6), 1352–1365.

Droll, J. A., Hayhoe, M. M., Triesch, J., & Sullivan, B. T. (2005). Task demands control acquisition and storage of visual information. *Journal of Experimental Psychology: Human Perception and Performance, 31,* 1416–1438.

Duncan, J. (1984). Selective attention and the organization of visual information. *Journal of Experimental Psychology: General , 113,* 501–517.

Duncan, J., & Humphreys, G. W. (1989). Visual search and stimulus similarity. *Psychological Review, 96 ,* 433–458.

Egly, R., Driver, J., & Rafal, R. D. (1994). Shifting visual attention between objects and locations: Evidence from normal and parietal lesion subjects. *Journal of Experimental Psychology: General, 123*(2), 161–177.

Eng, H. Y., Chen, D., & Jiang, Y. (2005). Visual working memory for simple and complex visual stimuli. *Psychonomic Bulletin & Review, 12,* 1127–1133.

Farah, M. J. (1988). Is visual imagery really visual? Overlooked evidence from neuropsychology. *Psychological Review, 95,* 307–317.

Felleman, D. J., & Van Essen, D. C. (1991). Distributed hierarchical processing in the primate cerebral cortex. *Cerebral Cortex, 1,* 1–47.

Fougnie, D., & Marois, R. (2006). Distinct capacity limits for attention and working memory: Evidence from attentive tracking and visual working memory paradigms. *Psychological Science, 17,* 526–534.

Fuster, J. M. (1990). Behavioral electrophysiology of the prefrontal cortex of the primate. In H. B. M. Uylings, J. P. C. Van Eden, M. A. De Bruin, M.A. Corner, & M. G. P. Feenstra (Eds.), *Progress in Brain Research* (pp. 313–323). Amsterdam: Elsevier.

Gajewski, D. A., & Brockmole, J. R. (2006). Feature bindings endure without attention: Evidence from an explicit recall task. *Psychonomic Bulletin & Review, 13*(4), 581–587.

Geyer, T., Muller, H. J., & Krummenacher, J. (2006). Cross-trial priming in visual search for singleton conjunction targets: Role of repeated target and distractor features. *Perception & Psychophysics, 68,* 736–749.

Gibson, B. S., Li, L., Skow, E., Brown, K., & Cooke, L. (2000). Searching for one or two identical targets: When visual search has a memory. *Psychological Science, 11,* 324–327.

Goldman-Rakic, P. S. (1990). Cellular and circuit basis of working memory in prefrontal cortex of nonhuman primates. In H. B. M. Uylings, J. P. C. Van Eden, M. A. De Bruin, M.A. Corner, & M. G. P. Feenstra (Eds.), *Progress in Brain Research* (pp. 325–336). Amsterdam: Elsevier.

Goodale, M., & Milner, D. (1995). *The visual brain in action.* Oxford: Oxford University Press.

Hillstrom, A. P. (2000). Repetition effects in visual search. *Perception & Psychophysics, 62,* 800–817.

Hodsoll, J. P., & Humphreys, G. W. (2005). Preview search and contextual cuing. *Journal of Experimental Psychology: Human Perception and Performance, 31,* 1346–1358.

Hollingworth, A. (2003). Failures of retrieval and comparison constrain change detection in natural scenes. *Journal of Experimental Psychology: Human Perception and Performance, 29,* 388–403.

Hollingworth, A. (2005). The relationship between online visual representation of a scene and long-term scene memory. *Journal of Experimental Psychology: Learning, Memory, and Cognition, 31,* 396–411.

Horowitz, T. S., & Wolfe, J. M. (1998). Visual search has no memory. *Nature, 394,* 575–577.

Irwin, D. E., & Andrews, R. V. (1996). Integration and accumulation of information across saccadic eye movements. In T. Inui & J. L. McClelland (Eds.), *Attention and performance, XVI: Information integration in perception and communication* (pp. 125–155). Cambridge, MA: MIT Press.

Jiang, Y., & Chun, M. M. (2001). Selective attention modulates implicit learning. *Quarterly Journal of Experimental Psychology, 54A,* 1105–1124.

Jiang, Y., Chun, M. M., & Marks, L. E. (2002). Visual marking: Selective attention to asynchronous temporal groups. *Journal of Experimental Psychology: Human Perception and Performance, 28,* 717–730.

Jiang, Y., Chun, M. M., & Olson, I. R. (2004). Perceptual grouping in change detection. *Perception & Psychophysics, 66,* 446–453.

Jiang, Y., King, L. W., Shim, W. M., & Vickery, T. J. (2006, November). *Visual implicit learning overcomes limits in human attention.* Paper presented at the 25th Army Science Conference, Orlando, FL.

Jiang, Y., & Leung, A. W. (2005). Implicit learning of ignored visual context. *Psychonomic Bulletin & Review, 12,* 100–106.

Jiang, Y., Olson, I. R., & Chun, M. M. (2000). Organization of visual short-term memory. *Journal of Experimental Psychology: Learning, Memory, and Cognition, 26,* 683–702.

Jiang, Y. V., Shim, W. M., & Makovski, T. (in press). Visual working memory for line orientations and face identities. *Perception & Psychophysics.*

Jiang, Y., Song, J.-H., & Rigas, A. (2005). High-capacity spatial contextual memory. *Psychonomic Bulletin & Review, 12,* 524–529.

Jiang, Y., & Wagner, L. C. (2004). What is learned in spatial contextual cueing: Configuration or individual locations? *Perception & Psychophysics, 66,* 454–463.

Jiang, Y., & Wang, S. W. (2004). What kind of memory supports visual marking? *Journal of Experimental Psychology: Human Perception and Perception & Performance, 30,* 79–91.

Johnson, J. S., Hollingworth, A., & Luck, S. J. (2008). The role of attention in the maintenance of feature bindings in visual short-term memory. *Journal of Experimental Psychology: Human Perception and Performance, 34*(1), 41–55.

Johnson, M. K. (1992). MEM: Mechanisms of recollection. *Journal of Cognitive Neuroscience, 4,* 268–280.

Jovicich, J., Peters, R. J., Koch, C., Braun, J., Chang, L., & Ernst, T. (2001). Brain areas specific for attentional load in a motion-tracking task. *Journal of Cognitive Neuroscience, 13,* 1048–1058.

Junge, J. A., Scholl, B. J., & Chun, M. M. (2007). How is spatial context learning integrated over signal versus noise? A primacy effect in contextual cueing. *Visual Cognition, 15,* 1–11.

Kahneman, D., Treisman, A., & Burkell, J. (1983). The cost of visual filtering. *Experimental Psychology: Human Perception and Performance, 9,* 510–522.

Klauer, K. C., & Zhao, Z. (2004). Double dissociations in visual and spatial short-term memory. *Journal of Experimental Psychology: General, 133,* 355–381.

Klein, R. (1988). Inhibitory tagging system facilitates visual search. *Nature, 334,* 430–431.

Kristjánsson, A. (2000). In search of remembrance: Evidence for memory in visual search. *Psychological Science, 11,* 328–332.

Kristjánsson, A., & Nakayama, K. (2003). A primitive memory system for the deployment of transient attention. *Perception & Psychophysics, 65,* 711–724.

Kristjánsson, A., Wang, D., & Nakayama, K. (2002). The role of priming in conjunctive visual search. *Cognition, 85,* 37–52.

Kunar, M. A., Flusberg, S., Horowitz, T. S., & Wolfe, J. M. (2007). Does contextual cueing guide the deployment of attention? *Journal of Experimental Psychology: Human Perception and Performance, 33*(4), 816–828.

Kunar, M. A., & Humphreys, G. W. (2006). Object-based inhibitory priming in preview search: Evidence from the "top-up" procedure. *Memory & Cognition, 34,* 459–474.

Kunar, M. A., Humphreys, G. W., Smith, K. J., & Hulleman, J. (2003). What is "marked" in visual marking? Evidence for effects of configuration in preview search. *Perception & Psychophysics, 65,* 982–996

Lamy, D., & Egeth, H. (2002). Object-based selection: The role of attentional shifts. *Perception & Psychophysics, 64,* 52–66.

Landman, R., Spekreijse, H., & Lamme, V. A. (2003). Large capacity storage of integrated objects before change blindness. *Vision Research, 43,* 149–164.

Lee, D., & Chun, M. M. (2001). What are the units of visual short-term memory, objects or spatial locations? *Perception & Psychophysics, 63,* 253–257.

Levin, D. T., & Simons, D. J. (1997). Failure to detect changes to attended objects in motion pictures. *Psychonomic Bulletin & Review, 4,* 501–506.

Levine, D. N., Warach, J., & Farah, M. J. (1985). Two visual systems in mental imagery: Dissociation of "what" and "where" in imagery disorders due to bilateral posterior cerebral lesions. *Neurology, 35,* 1010–1018.

Linden, D. E. J., Bittner, R. A., Muckli, L., Waltz, J. A., Kriegeskorte, N., Goebel, R., et al. (2003). Cortical capacity constraints of visual working memory: Dissociation of fMRI load effects in the fronto-parietal network. *NeuroImage, 20,* 1518–1530.

Lleras, A., & Von Muhlenen, A. (2004). Spatial context and top-down strategies in visual search. *Spatial Vision, 17,* 465–482

Logan, G. D. (1988). Toward an instance theory of automatization. *Psychological Review, 95,* 492–527.

Logie, R. H. (1995). *Visuo-spatial working memory.* Hillsdale, NJ: Lawrence Erlbaum Associates.

Luck, S. J., & Vogel, E. (1997). The capacity of visual working memory for features and conjunctions. *Nature, 309,* 279–281.

Makovski, T., & Jiang, Y. V. (2007). Distributing versus focusing attention in visual short-term memory. *Psychonomic Bulletin & Review, 14*(6), 1072–1078.

Makovski, T., Shim, W. M., & Jiang, Y. V. (2006). Interference from filled delays on visual change detection. *Journal of Vision, 6,* 1459–1470.

Maljkovic, V., & Nakayama, K. (1994). Priming of pop-out: I. Role of features. *Memory & Cognition, 22,* 657–672.

Maljkovic, V., & Nakayama, K. (1996). Priming of pop-out: II. The role of position. *Perception & Psychophysics, 58,* 977–991.

McCarthy, G., Puce, A., Constable, R. T., Krystal, J. H., Gore, J. C., & Goldman-Rakic, P. (1996). Activation of human prefrontal cortex during spatial and nonspatial working memory tasks measured by functional MRI. *Cerebral Cortex, 6,* 600–611.

Miller, E. K., Erickson, C. A., & Desimone, R. (1996). Neural mechanisms of visual working memory in prefrontal cortex of the macaque. *Journal of Neuroscience, 16,* 5154–5167.

Miller, G. A. (1956). The magical number seven, plus or minus two: Some limits on our capacity for processing information. *Psychological Review, 63,* 81–97.

Miller, J. (1988). Components of the location probability effect in visual search tasks. *Journal of Experimental Psychology: Human Perception and Performance, 14,* 453–471.

Neill, W. T. (1977). Inhibitory and facilitatory processes in selective attention. *Journal of Experimental Psychology: Human Perception and Performance, 3,* 444–450

Neisser, U. (1967). *Cognition psychology.* New York: Appleton-Century-Crofts.

Nickerson, R. S. (1965). Short-term memory for complex meaningful visual configurations: A demonstration of capacity. *Canadian Journal of Psychology, 19,* 155–160.

Nickerson, R. S., & Adams, J. J. (1979). Long-term memory for a common object. *Cognitive Psychology,* 11, 287–307.

Nissen, M., & Bullemer, P. (1987). Attentional requirements of learning: Evidence from performance measures. *Cognitive Psychology, 19,* 1–32.

Oliva, A., Wolfe, J. M., & Arsenio, H. C. (2004). Panoramic search: The interaction of memory and vision in search through a familiar scene. *Journal of Experimental Psychology: Human Perception and Performance, 30,* 1132–1146.

Olivers, C. N. L., Meijer, F., & Theeuwes, J. (2006). Feature-based memory-driven attentional capture: Visual working memory content affects visual attention. *Journal of Experimental Psychology: Human Perception and Performance, 32,* 1243–1265.

Olson, I. R., & Chun, M. M. (2001). Perceptual constraints on implicit learning of spatial context. *Visual Cognition, 9,* 273–302.

Olson, I. R., & Jiang, Y. (2002). Is visual short-term memory object based? Rejection of the "strong-object" hypothesis. *Perception & Psychophysics, 64,* 1055–1067.

Olson, I. R., & Jiang, Y. (2004). Visual short-term memory is not improved by training. *Memory & Cognition, 32,* 1326–1332.

Olson, I. R., Jiang Y., & Moore, K. S. (2005). Associative learning improves visual working memory performance. *Journal of Experimental Psychology: Human Perception and Performance, 31,* 889–900.

Olson, I. R., & Marshuetz, C. (2005). Remembering "what" brings along "where" in visual working memory. *Perception & Psychophysics, 67,* 185–194.

Olson, I. R., Page, K., Moore, K. S., Chatterjee, A., & Verfaellie, M. (2006). Working memory for conjunctions relies on the medial temporal lobe. *Journal of Neuroscience, 26,* 4596–4601.

Olsson, H., & Poom, L. (2005). Visual memory needs categories. *Proceedings of the National Academy of Sciences, U.S.A., 102,* 8776–8780.

Ono, F., Jiang, Y., & Kawahara, J. (2005). Inter-trial temporal contextual cueing: Association across successive visual search trials guides spatial attention. *Journal of Experimental Psychology: Human Perception and Performance, 31,* 703–712.

O'Regan, J. K. (1992). Solving the "real" mysteries of visual perception: The world as an outside memory. *Canadian Journal of Psychology, 46,* 461–488.

Owen, A. M., Stern, C. E., Look, R. B., Tracey, I., Rosen, B. R., & Petrides, M. (1998). Functional organization of spatial and nonspatial working memory processing within the human lateral frontal cortex. *Proceedings of the National Academy of Sciences, U.S.A., 95,* 7721–7726.

Pashler, H. (1988). Familiarity and visual change detection. *Perception & Psychophysics, 44,* 369–378.

Petrides, M. (2005). Lateral prefrontal cortex: Architectonic and functional organization. *Philosophical Transaction of the Royal Society of London, B: Biological Sciences, 360,* 781–795.

Phillips, W. A. (1974). On the distinction between sensory storage and short-term visual memory. *Perception & Psychophysics, 16,* 283–290.

Postle, B. R., & D'Esposito, M. (1999). "What"—then—"where" in visual working memory: An event-related fMRI study. *Journal of Cognitive Neuroscience, 11,* 585–597.

Pylyshyn, Z. W., & Storm, R. W. (1988). Tracking multiple independent targets: Evidence for a parallel tracking mechanism. *Spatial Vision, 3,* 179–197.

Rainer, G., Asaad, W. F., & Miller, E. K. (1998). Memory fields of neurons in the primate prefrontal cortex. *Proceedings of the National Academy of Science, U.S.A., 5,* 15008–15013.

Ranganath, C., & Blumenfeld, R. S. (2005). Doubts about double dissociations between short- and long-term memory. *Trends in Cognitive Sciences, 9,* 374–380.

Rensink, R. A. (2000). Visual search for change: A probe into the nature of attentional processing. *Visual Cognition, 7,* 345–376.

Rensink, R. A. (2002). Change detection. *Annual Review of Psychology, 53,* 245–277.

Rao, S. C., Rainer, G., & Miller, E. K. (1997). Integration of what and where in the primate prefrontal cortex. *Science, 276,* 821–824.

Rausei, V., Makovski, T., & Jiang, Y. V. (2007). Attention dependency in implicit learning of repeated search context. *Quarterly Journal of Experimental Psychology, 60*(10), 1321–1328.

Sagi, D., & Julesz, B. (1985). "Where" and "what" in vision. *Science, 228,* 1217–1219.

Santa, J. L. (1977). Spatial transformations of words and pictures. *Journal of Experimental Psychology: Human Learning and Memory, 3,* 418–427.

Schacter, D. L., & Buckner, R. L. (1998). Priming and the brain. *Neuron, 20,* 185–195.

Scholl, B. J. (2001). Objects and attention: The state of the art. *Cognition, 80,* 1–46.

Scoville, W. B., & Milner, B. (1957). Loss of recent memory after bilateral hippocampal lesions. *Journal of Neurology, Neurosurgery and Psychiatry, 20,* 11–21.

Shen, Y., & Jiang, Y. V. (2006). Interrupted visual searches reveal volatile search memory. *Journal of Experimental Psychology: Human Perception and Performance, 32,* 1208–1220.

Simons, D. J. (1996). In sight, out of mind: When object representations fail. *Psychological Science, 7,* 301–305.

Simons, D. J., & Chabris, C. F. (1999). Gorillas in our midst: Sustained inattentional blindness for dynamic events. *Perception, 28,* 1059–1074.

Simons, D. J., & Rensink, R. A. (2005). Change blindness: Past, present, and future. *Trends in Cognitive Sciences, 9,* 16–20.

Song, J.-H., & Jiang, Y. (2005). Connecting the past with the present: How do humans match an incoming visual display with visual memory? *Journal of Vision, 5,* 322–330.

Song, J.-H., & Jiang, Y. (2006). Visual working memory for simple and complex features: An fMRI study. *NeuroImage, 30,* 963–972.

Soto, D., Heinke, D., Humphreys, G. W., & Blanco, M. J. (2005). Early, involuntary top-down guidance of attention from working memory. *Journal of Experimental Psychology: Human Perception and Performance, 31,* 248–261.

Soto, D., Humphreys, G. W., & Heinke, D. (2006). Working memory can guide pop-out search. *Vision Research, 46,* 1010–1018.

Sperling, G. (1960). The information available in brief visual presentations. *Psychological Monographs: General and Applied, 74*(11), 1–30.

Standing, L. (1973). Learning 10,000 pictures. *Quarterly Journal of Experimental Psychology, 25A,* 207–222.

Takeda, Y. (2004). Search for multiple targets: Evidence for memory-based control of attention. *Psychonomic Bulletin & Review, 11,* 71–76.

Tipper, S. P. (1985). The negative priming effect: Inhibitory priming by ignored objects. *Quarterly Journal of Experimental Psychology, 37A,* 571–590.

Todd, J. J., & Marois, R. (2004). Capacity limit of visual short-term memory in human posterior parietal cortex. *Nature, 428,* 751–754.

Treisman, A. (1988). Features and objects: The Fourteenth Bartlett Memorial Lecture. *Quarterly Journal of Experimental Psychology, 40A,* 201–237.

Triesch, J., Ballard, D. H., Hayhoe, M. M., & Sullivan, B. T. (2003). What you see is what you need. *Journal of Vision, 3,* 86–94.

Tsal, Y., & Lamy, D. (2000). Attending to an object's color entails attending to its location: Support for location-special views of visual attention. *Perception & Psychophysics, 62,* 960–968.

Ungerleider, L. G., Courtney, S. M., & Haxby, J. V. (1998). A neural system for human visual working memory. *Proceedings of the National Academy of Sciences, U.S.A., 95,* 883–890.

Ungerleider, L. G., & Mishkin, M. (1982). Two cortical visual systems. In D. J. Ingle, M. A. Goodale, & R. J. W. Mansfield (Eds.), *Analysis of visual behavior* (pp. 549–586). Cambridge, MA: MIT Press.

Vickery, T. J., King, L.-W., & Jiang, Y. (2005). Setting up the target template in visual search. *Journal of Vision, 5,* 81–92.

Vickery, T. J., Sussman, R. S., & Jiang, Y. (2006). Selective attention and general attentional resources in the learning of spatial context [Abstract]. *Journal of Vision, 6,* 844.

Vogel, E. K., & Machizawa, M. G. (2004). Neural activity predicts individual differences in visual working memory. *Nature, 15,* 748–751.

Vogel, E. K., McCollough, A. W., & Machizawa, M. G. (2005). Neural measures reveal individual differences in controlling access to visual working memory. *Nature, 438,* 500–503.

Watson, D. G., & Humphreys, G. W. (1997). Visual marking: Prioritizing selection for new objects by top-down attentional inhibition. *Psychological Review, 104,* 90–122.

Wheeler, M. E., & Treisman, A. M. (2002). Binding in short-term visual memory. *Journal of Experimental Psychology: General, 131,* 48–64.

Wilken, P., & Ma, W. J. (2004). A detection theory account of change detection. *Journal of Vision, 4,* 1120–1135.

Wilson, F. A., Scalaidhe, S. P., & Goldman-Rakic, P. S. (1993). Dissociation of object and spatial processing domains in primate prefrontal cortex. *Science, 260,* 1955–1958.

Wolfe, J. M. (1994). Guided search 2.0: A revised model of visual search. *Psychonomic Bulletin & Review, 1*(2), 202–238.

Wolfe, J. M., Klempen, N., & Dahlen, K. (2000). Postattentive vision. *Journal of Experimental Psychology: Human Perception and Performance, 26,* 693–716.

Wolfe, J. M., Oliva, A., Butcher, S. J., & Arsenio, H. C. (2002). An unbinding problem? The disintegration of visible, previously attended objects does not attract attention. *Journal of Vision, 2,* 256–271.

Woodman, G. F., & Luck, S. J. (2004). Visual search is slowed when visuospatial working memory is occupied. *Psychonomic Bulletin & Review, 11,* 269–274.

Woodman, G. F., & Luck, S. J. (2007). Do the contents of visual working memory automatically influence attentional selection during visual search? *Journal of Experimental Psychology: Human Perception and Performance, 33,* 363–377.

Woodman, G. F., Vogel, E. K., & Luck, S. J. (2001). Visual search remains efficient when visual working memory is full. *Psychological Science, 12,* 219–224.

Xu, Y. (2002). Encoding colour and shape from different parts of an object in visual short-term memory. *Perception & Psychophysics, 64,* 260–1280.

Xu, Y. (2006). Understanding the object benefit in visual short term memory: The roles of feature proximity and connectedness. *Perception & Psychophysics, 68,* 815–828.

Xu, Y., & Chun, M. M. (2006). Dissociable neural mechanisms supporting visual short-term memory for objects. *Nature, 440,* 91–95.

Zhang, W., & Luck, S. J. (2003). Slot-like versus continuous representations in visual working memory [Abstract]. *Journal of Vision, 3,* 681a.

3   Remembering faces

Vicki Bruce
Newcastle University

1. INTRODUCTION

The most important source of information that we use to identify someone in daily life is the face. Burton, Wilson, Cowan, and Bruce (1999) demonstrated this rather dramatically when they showed that students could accurately identify their lecturers from low-quality CCTV images, provided that the face was visible. Other information from clothing, gait, and body shape was much less important for recognition. In the modern world we are each familiar with literally thousands of faces—from home and from work, and through the media—politicians, actors, sports stars. Human faces are all very similar one to another, and so our visual memories for faces are in some ways rather remarkable. However, although visual memory for faces is remarkable, it is not infallible—and errors of person identification abound.

In 1969 Laszlo Virag was tried and initially convicted of being a person who had committed armed robberies in Liverpool and Bristol. He was convicted on the basis of testimony from several witnesses who picked him out of line-ups or identified him from photographs. One police witness claimed that "his face is imprinted on my brain". But it transpired that another person, known as George Payen, was responsible for these crimes—someone who bore a passing but not striking resemblance to Mr Virag. Mr Virag was pardoned in 1974, having been the victim of a miscarriage of justice based upon mistaken identity. Those witnesses to the incident who identified Virag undoubtedly had memories that were sufficient to say that Mr Virag was the person in the line-up or photo-spread who most resembled the man they saw commit the crime—but they should not have sworn it was that person (for a more detailed account of this case, see Wagenaar, 1988).

Later in this chapter I describe how our visual representations of unfamiliar faces make us particularly vulnerable to mistakes of this kind. But it is not just unfamiliar people who can give rise to mistaken identity. In 1548, Martin Guerre, a young French peasant, disappeared from his home village, leaving his wife of ten years and a newly born child. Eight years later, an impostor arrived in the village, claiming to be Martin, and proved sufficiently persuasive to his wife and other family members that he was accepted for several years before increasing suspicion and conflict over property led to a court case contesting his identity. At the eleventh hour, just as Martin appeared to have proved that he was who he claimed to be, the real Martin returned to claim his family and property, and the impostor was denounced and executed.

This tale is well-known to cinema-goers through two films (*The Return of Martin Guerre*, 1983; and an updated fictional variant based in the United States—*Somersby*, 1993). Other similar incidents have been reported more recently, too. Hadyn Ellis (1988) described the complex case of the "Tichborne Claimant", who claimed to be the long-lost missing heir to estates in southern England but did not win his claim. In this case there was some photographic record of the appearance of the lost person in 1853, and the "claimant" some thirteen years later. The resemblance seems no greater than that between Virag and Payen. Yet the mother of the missing person and several other members of the household believed it was he. But how likely is it that our knowledge of a highly familiar person could be so readily deceived by such an impostor?

Clearly there was much more to the issue than memory for the face. Madame Guerre and Lady Tichborne should have had other sources of information than the face of the missing husband/son to go by. The impostor in each case knew things about people and past events that he couldn't (or shouldn't) have known unless he was who he claimed to be. Moreover, the passage of time and other circumstances have their effects—people's appearances can change a good deal through diet, ageing, physical hardship or injury, as well as hairstyle and facial hair. No dental or DNA records could be used to help verify identity. Then there is the motivation—an abandoned wife with fatherless child has every reason to focus on the positive evidence that her husband has returned. Every mother would rather believe that her child is alive than has perished.

Thus, the cases of Martin Guerre and the Tichborne Claimant are ones where context, motivation, and uncertainty about changes in appearance worked together so that even the closest of kin could be deceived about identity. Stranger things still can happen when context is deliberately manipulated. Don Thomson (1986) arranged for the daughter of some friends of his to appear unexpectedly near their hotel abroad, but to walk past them without any sign of recognition when they approached. The parents did not pursue the daughter and demand an explanation—their initial signals of recognition went unacknowledged, and they simply assumed they had been mistaken.

When we talk about *visual memory* for faces, therefore, we must understand that the very difficult discriminations required to differentiate one human face from another probably render contextual factors more important in remembering faces than is generally recognized in theoretical models of face recognition. Nonetheless, for the remainder of this chapter, I shall mainly focus on the visual representation of faces in memory.

2. FACTORS AFFECTING FACE RECOGNITION

In marked contrast to the cases of mistaken identity described above, during the 1970s considerable attention was given to experiments appearing to suggest that memory for once-glimpsed unfamiliar faces was remarkably accurate. Shepard (1967) included faces among other kinds of pictures and showed that participants were over 90% accurate when asked to discriminate old from new items even three days after initial presentation. Goldstein and Chance (1971) used a much more difficult task where memory for highly similar patterns was tested—human faces, inkblot patterns, and snowflake patterns. At test, participants were asked to pick out the 14 old items from a total set of 80. Face patterns gave recognition rates of 71% on immediate testing (compared with 46% for inkblots and 33% for snowflakes—significantly above chance in this task), and there was little change over a 48-hour delay.

In other studies memory for faces was compared with memory for pictures drawn from other familiar categories of objects such as houses (Yin, 1969, 1970), canine faces (Scapinello & Yarmey, 1970), and teacups (Deregowski, Ellis, & Shepherd, 1973). While performance with faces was generally better than with other homogenous categories, this was not always found—presumably it was dependent on the inter-item similarity operating within each class of items. More importantly, the classic studies by Yin (1969, 1970) showed that while upright faces were better recognized than pictures of houses or schematic men in motion, when inverted, faces were recognized *less* well than the comparison materials. This *disproportionate* effect of inversion on face recognition ability is one of the hallmarks of expert adult face recognition performance, and I return to consider the nature of this expertise later in this chapter (section 3.1).

The experiments discussed above generally used identical pictures of faces at study and test. A minority of other studies conducted in the late 1970s found high recognition rates even when there was a change in picture between study and test (Davies, Ellis, & Shepherd, 1978a; Patterson & Baddeley, 1977), and this led to some claims that initial representations of faces in memory allowed good generalization to different views and expressions. Patterson and Baddeley's studies involved rather small sets of faces at study, combined with techniques encouraging attention to view-invariant characteristics. Davies et al.'s (1978a) finding of insensitivity of recognition memory to pose change was clear, though rather surprising, and now appears anomalous in the context of other studies before and since. For example, Bruce (1982) showed participants 24 unfamiliar male faces for 8 s each, and asked them to respond "old" or "new" to each of 48 faces (the 24 faces with an equal number of distractors) 15 min later. The targets could appear in same or changed pictures from those studied (and participants were forewarned that pictures might change and that they should be remembering the people not the pictures). Hit rates at test showed significant and substantial decline from 90% when faces were tested in identical pictures, to 76% when there was a change in pose or expression, to 61% when there was a change in pose and expression. The target set used were photographs of university teachers and researchers taken in the late 1970s, with a great variety of hairstyles, facial hair, and spectacles, making the set appear rather distinctive. Moreover, head-and-shoulders pictures revealed something of the clothing worn by these colleagues. Given that these features of hairstyle and clothing would be readily seen in changed views, the large effects of picture change were quite surprising in this study.

Although recognition rates for faces shown upright in *identical* study and test pictures are very high, even apparently superficial differences in the way these images are depicted can impede recognition. Faces studied in detailed line drawings obtained by tracing around all the major face features shown in the image, and then tested in photographs, are recognized much less accurately than when both study and test phases used photographs (Davies et al., 1978). Similarly, people presented in films in which full-face views were depicted for several seconds but then tested in full-face still photographs, or vice versa, were recognized substantially less well than when mode of testing matched that of study (Patterson, 1978), even though in this study participants learned each of only four items quite thoroughly.

An even more dramatic finding was that reported by Bruce et al. (1999), where participants were asked to match an image of a target face taken from video film against an array of still photographs of faces that might or might not include one of the target face, taken on the same day as the video. This task did not require any memory of the target face, only visual matching—and yet performance averaged only 70% correct, dropping still further if there was some variation in expression or pose between the target and array faces.

One of the main differences between the video images of the targets and the photo-images of the array faces in Bruce et al.'s (1999) study was in the lighting and the effects of that lighting on the appearance of the faces. In more controlled lighting conditions a number of studies have shown that matching faces is impaired when the two are shown with different directions of lighting (Braje, 2003; Hill & Bruce, 1996). In contrast to face matching, Hill and Bruce (1996) found that matching unfamiliar "amoeba" shapes was much less influenced by lighting changes than had been found with faces. Other reported effects of illumination change on non-face object matching (e.g., Tarr, Kersten, & Bülthoff, 1998) may be at least partly dependent on specific task demands (Nederhouser & Mangini, 2001), though Braje (2003) argues that faces and objects are affected similarly by lighting changes.

Faces are also extremely susceptible to contrast reversal in photographic negation (Galper, 1970). Even though a negative image of a face portrays the same spatial layout of luminance contrasts, the appearance of the face is rendered dramatically different. There are several possible explanations for why negation has such a damaging effect. It is possible that negating images of faces disrupts the processing of "configuration" of the face as inverting faces is held to do (see section 3.1). However, Bruce and Langton (1994) found that the effects of inversion and negation were additive, suggesting that these manipulations may affect different sources of information used for face perception and identification. Negative images also change the apparent three-dimensional shape of an object, on the assumption that lighting direction remains constant, so a positive image with light reflected from prominent cheekbones will appear in the negative with dark cheekbone areas instead. Negative images also reverse the surface pigmentation—a negative image of a light-skinned person with dark hair will appear dark-skinned with blonde hair. Bruce and Langton (1994) attempted to resolve which of these two potential sources of difficulty was the most important source of the negation effect by presenting three-dimensional reconstructions of laser-scanned faces that would be familiar to participants and seeing if negating these images affected their recognition. Recognition of such three-dimensional surface images was poor, but it was not further reduced by negation. Bruce and Langton argued that recognition was poor because the images lacked the pigmented features usually used for recognition, and that if negation had its principal effect via the reversal of pigmentation, then little further decline should be found following negation, as observed.

Russell, Sinha, Biederman, and Nederhouser (2006) confirmed and extended Bruce and Langton's findings. In two experiments they examined the effects of negation on a delayed match-to-sample task, where a decision had to be made on each trial of which of two items matched one presented for study a second earlier. Sets of faces were created that varied only in shape with constant pigmentation; or varied only in pigmentation, with constant shape; or varied both in shape and pigmentation. Negation only reduced matching performance significantly when the faces had variation in pigmentation, suggesting that the primary effect of negation is in the contrast reversal of pigmented surfaces rather than in the derivation of shape—whether two- or three-dimensional.

In some respects the effects of negation on face recognition are "disproportionate" compared with recognition of other kinds of objects. Subramaniam and Biederman (1997) reported that negation does not at all disrupt matching of pictures of chairs. However, Vuong, Peissig, Harrison, and Tarr (2005) showed that matching images of pigmented "Greeble" shapes (these are artificial three-dimensional shapes with the same overall configuration but varying features—see Figure 3.2 and section 3.2) was significantly disrupted by negation, though not as substantially as the disruption to pigmented face surfaces. Both faces and Greebles were more affected by negation when the surfaces shown were pigmented rather than non-pigmented, and this effect was quite striking given that the face images used had no visible hair—a most important pigmented component used extensively for matching of unfamiliar faces. However, there were some detrimental effects of negation even on the non-pigmented surfaces. Thus, while the pigmentation of surfaces clearly contributes significantly to the detrimental effects of negation, other factors may also contribute. Moreover, Vuong et al.'s study suggests that when stimulus structure and task demands are made more similar, the recognition and matching of objects other than faces can also be susceptible to contrast reversal.

Importantly, these effects of negation and mode suggest that representations that mediate face recognition reflect in a fundamental way the pattern of light and dark across the image of the face rather than being based primarily on some more abstract set of derived two- or three-dimensional-shape measurements. If abstract measurements formed the basis of our visual memories of faces, it is difficult to understand why a change in mode or lightness polarity that preserves two- or even three-dimensional shape should be so disruptive to matching and/or recognizing faces.

3. FACE MEMORY COMPARED WITH OBJECT MEMORY

I have already reviewed above experiments on recognition memory for faces compared with pictures of other kinds of objects. In a recognition memory task participants are typically shown a set of study items and later asked to decide which items of a test set were studied and which are novel. A sense of familiarity to items that are judged "old" could arise from different kinds of remembered information. There might be a match at the level of the specific pictorial details of the remembered item (termed "pictorial code" by Bruce, 1982; Bruce & Young, 1986), at a more abstract visual level (termed "structural code"), or at semantic or verbal (name) levels. These are also the kinds of levels of description that must be derived in order to fully recognize the item in question. Building on the discussion of object memory in chapters 1 and 2, here I discuss how "object" memory can be described at these different levels of abstraction or specificity and then enter into a discussion of visual memory for faces compared with objects—we need to compare like with like.

We can recognize a particular visual shape as a "dog" and later remember verbally that "dog" was among the items we were shown. This is the same level as recognizing and later remembering that we saw "a face". The visual representational level that allows us to tell, say, a dog from a cat, or a mug from a cup, lies at the level of major shape features that may even be perceived quite independently of viewpoint. Biederman's (1987) influential model of visual object recognition suggests that objects are recognized via a set of primitive shape elements called "geons", which can be derived from more or less any recognizable viewpoint of that object. In Biederman's model it is the geon structural descriptions (GSDs) and not metric variations that are critical for basic-level object recognition. However, at the level of GSDs all human faces are identical. Any finer level than "a face" requires analysis of metric variations and features of surface colouration.

Finer level discriminations within basic-level categories also allow us to recognize different types of basic objects—so we can recognize an Alsatian dog, a poodle dog, or a cairn terrier dog; or a steak knife, a carving knife, or a butter knife. This discrimination of different types of the same kind of object might be likened to our ability to categorize faces on semantically meaningful dimensions on the basis of their shape—so we can categorize faces as old or young, male or female, on the basis of relatively major variations in their appearance. We do not know in any detailed way what kinds of visual representational descriptions are used to make type discriminations within basic categories, but they are unlikely to be possible on the basis of GSDs alone. And when we turn to face classification, a task as apparently simple as deciding whether faces are male or female appears to rely on a very large set of different dimensions, some local—such as bushiness of eyebrows or coarseness of skin texture—and some much more configural—such as the protuberance of the nose/brow regions (Bruce et al., 1993; Burton, Bruce, & Dench, 1993).

A finer level of discrimination allows us to recognize individual members of the same type of object—our own suitcase at the airport, our own Labrador in the park. Farmers are able to distinguish between their different individual cows or sheep. Importantly, at the level of individual recognition, the mapping between visual form and semantics (identity) is arbitrary. Bruce and Young (1986) distinguished between *visually derived* semantic information for faces—such as sex, race, age—and *identity-specific semantics*. The latter describes a level of categorization achieved not from generic mapping of form to meaning but by specific personal knowledge. So, the visual form of an otherwise unfamiliar face allows us to categorize it as male or female, and the visual form of an unfamiliar dog allows us to assign it as German Shepherd or a Labrador. But it is only my acquired specific knowledge of the visual form of my sister's face that allows me to recognize her and know that this person is my sister and what she does for a living, and it is only my acquired specific knowledge of my dog's visual form that allows me to recognize Barney, *my* collie, and to tell him apart from lots of similar-looking collies we meet when we go out together.

The above discussion is important, because if we want to ask the question of whether the representational basis for face recognition differs from that of object recognition, or whether there is specialization of neural structures for face recognition compared with object recognition, it is really only legitimate to compare tasks of similar logic and complexity.

3.1. Configural processing and the inversion effect

As noted earlier, face recognition suffers disproportionately when faces are inverted. The effect of inversion appears to arise because we cannot decipher the "configuration" of the face when it is upside-down. This was dramatically illustrated when Peter Thompson (1980) first produced the "Thatcher illusion"; when faces are inverted, even major reorientation of features within the face becomes virtually invisible. An arrangement that looks grotesque when upright looks virtually identical to the original when shown upside down (see Fig 3.1, left panel).

Young, Hellawell, and Hay (1987) developed another novel means of demonstrating configural processing. They divided faces horizontally and paired top halves of faces with bottom halves of different identities. When the two halves were aligned, it was extremely difficult to correctly identify each half. When they were misaligned, it became much easier. The explanation was that the features

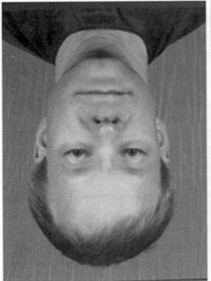

Figure 3.1. Demonstrations of configural processing of faces. Left panel: This image of my colleague Peter Hancock looks quite normal—until you turn the book upside down and see what he has done to himself. Right panel: It is difficult to recognize the identity of one half of a face when it is aligned with a different identity. How easy is it for you to recognize Tony Blair and George Bush in this composite? (These images were kindly provided by Peter Hancock at the University of Stirling.)

of one half of the face could not be processed independently of other features from the "wrong" half—because the two halves together yielded a configuration that did not match that stored for either of the original identities. Misalignment of the face halves "freed" each half from the configural influence of the other (see Figure 3.1, right panel).

Interestingly, when these composites were inverted it became relatively easy to identify the separate halves of the face, an inverted face "superiority" effect. So just as the relationship between the different features of a "Thatcherized" face is invisible when the face is inverted, so too does the influence of one part of the face on another become dramatically reduced by inversion.

Inversion does not, however, affect the capacity to process the individual parts of faces; it appears specifically to be their interrelationships that are distorted in this way. Leder and Bruce (1998) compared the rated and memorial distinctiveness of upright and inverted faces whose features were altered to be made more distinctive through local manipulations (e.g., bushier eyebrows) or configural manipulations (e.g., moving the eyes closer together). The relative distinctiveness of faces with local feature manipulations was maintained when they were inverted, while the effects of configural manipulations were completely lost.

The precise meaning of the term "configural" or "holistic" processing has been unclear in much of the literature (see Rakover, 2002). Some seem to imply that faces are processed holistically in the sense that the patterns are not decomposed at all; others imply that it is the details of the relationships between local parts, but that these configural relationships themselves involve analytic decomposition. It is actually extremely difficult to distinguish between these different sources of information since normally any change to part of the face affects local, configural/relational, and configural/holistic information. Leder and Bruce (2000) generated faces that could be identified either by unique combinations of local information (e.g., a specific eye colour plus hair colour) or by unique relational information (e.g., nose–mouth distance). The former showed no inversion effect, but the latter did. Since faces with unique combinations of purely local information differ "holistically", Leder and Bruce used this and similar results to argue that configural processing must involve the representation of the spatial relationships between local features rather than holistic pattern processing.

3.2. The expertise debate

One of the most heated (and to some extent futile) debates in the field of face perception has revolved around the question of whether face processing is "special" or not (for a recent review, see Liu & Chaudhuri, 2003). We have already reviewed above that representations subserving face recognition are different from those implicated in basic-level object recognition. But the demands of object recognition can be made more similar to face recognition—as we discussed above, in many everyday activities we want not just to recognize that an object is a dog, or even a collie dog, but that it is this particular collie (Barney) that lives in our house. Discriminating between individual members of a sub-category all sharing the same overall shape requires that we pay attention to subtle variations in shape and markings. However, we rarely become expert at such discriminations unless we have some professional reason or passionate interest in the area. Expertise in a sub-domain, however, appears to yield similarities to face processing. So Diamond and Carey (1986) compared expert dog perceivers (breed judges) and non-experts at face and dog recognition, and they found that the dog experts (but not the dog novices) suffered as much when pictures of dogs were inverted as they did when faces were inverted, suggesting that the experts had developed sensitivity to configural relationships, absent from non-expert dog recognizers (but for a failure to replicate this study, see McKone, Kanwisher, & Duchaine, 2007). Rhodes and McClean (1990) investigated configural processing using a different kind of method, recruiting participants with expertise in the perception of birds. Rhodes and McClean found that caricaturing outline drawings of these birds produced a stronger caricature advantage in the expert group, whereby outline drawings whose shape differences from the norm were exaggerated were recognized more quickly than the originals.

It is obviously difficult to recruit participants with specific expertise in non-face domains, but a series of studies by Gauthier, Tarr, and their colleagues have taken the approach of creating expertise in an artificial domain that shares some of the characteristics of face processing in order to explore similar kinds of questions.

The group developed families of shapes collectively termed "Greebles" (see Figure 3.2). Greebles are multi-component shapes that share a common configuration within which there is variation in the shape, orientation, and placement of parts. Greebles are designed to come from different "families" that differ in terms of the overall shape of the "body" parts; there are also two different types of Greeble—that is, "genders" ("ploks" and "glips")—which differ in terms of the orientation of their appendages. The remaining variations of the parts and their arrangements define the individual members of each family, and these can be given names to be learned by participants in experiments.

In a series of experiments, Gauthier, Tarr, and associates (Gauthier & Tarr, 1997; Gauthier, Williams, Tarr, & Tanaka, 1998; Vuong et al., 2005) have trained participants to become experts at identifying Greebles and have investigated the consequences of this expertise, sometimes comparing the resulting effects with those found in face recognition. While not all these explorations have yielded clear results, there are certainly some indications that, compared with "novices" in the Greeble domain, experts are more disadvantaged by a change in orientation (cf. the inversion effect), and more affected by contrast reversal (cf. the negation effect). When Greeble composites are composed of

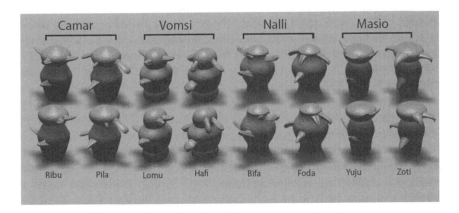

Figure 3.2. Examples of "Greebles". In the top row, four different "families" are represented. For each family, two members of different "genders" are shown (e.g., Ribu is one gender and Pila is the other; orientation of the appendages differs between genders). The two rows show images constructed using the same logic, but those in the top row are symmetrical in structure and those in the bottom row are asymmetric. Images provided courtesy of Michael J. Tarr (Brown University, Providence, RI) (see www.tarrlab.org).

the top half of one Greeble paired with the bottom half of a different one of the same gender, Greeble experts are better at identifying the halves when shown misaligned than aligned, similar to the face composite effect. So there is *some* converging evidence from a few experiments with real-world experts (dogs, etc.) and some rather variable evidence from experiments with artificial "Greeble" experts, suggesting that some of the hallmarks of expert adult face processing may arise when we become skilled at making discriminations between other classes of shape with similar characteristics. McKone, Kanwisher, and Duchaine (2007) disagree—they conclude from their review of the evidence that expertise in other domains does not give face-like sensitivity to inversion and other hallmarks of configural processing—but in their review they do not include the full range of candidate expertise effects such as those of negation and caricature.

My own conclusion is that some domains of expertise may give rise to some of the same types of processing that characterize skilled face recognition. Does it matter if face recognition shares characteristics of other skilled within-category object recognition? This issue becomes central once we turn from describing the functional characteristics of face representations to ask how these representations are implemented neurally.

3.3. Neuropsychology of face memory

Until recently, there was rather little direct evidence that face processing relied on face-specific neural machinery. Single-cell recordings from monkey inferotemporal lobe had revealed cells that seemed to respond better to faces than to any other complex, significant, or biological stimulus (Gross, Rocha-Miranda, & Bender, 1972; Perrett, Rolls, & Cann, 1982). These cells were generally found in a fold of brain known as the superior temporal sulcus (STS). While there were some suggestions that some cells seemed tuned to specific individual face identities (Perrett et al., 1984), in general the cells seemed to code particular head, gaze, and/or body directions and seem then generally to be implicated more in social attention processes than in identification ones. Heywood and Cowey (1992) reported a lesion study when, after ablation of STS, monkeys' major deficits were in processing gaze information, but not in recognizing faces.

In humans, brain damage following stroke or other injury occasionally leads to a dramatic impairment in face recognition called "prosopagnosia" (Bodamer, 1947—for an overview see Ellis & Young, 1989; Young, 1998). Patients fail to recognize famous faces from the media or personally familiar faces of friends and family, and even their own face in the mirror may seem unfamiliar to them. It is rare for brain damage arising from stroke to be confined to a very discrete area of brain, and so perhaps not surprisingly prosopagnosic patients usually have other deficits as well. Often they are agnosic for a range of other objects, or impaired in other kinds of perceptual abilities such as topographical memory or colour perception. Sometimes they complain about difficulties, particularly with other categories where they had previously been expert. For example, Bornstein

(1963) described a prosopagnosic amateur ornithologist who complained that she could no longer recognize different species of bird.

However, a small number of quite specific dissociations have been observed that have led people to claim that prosopagnosia must involve damage to a face-specific region of the brain. There have been a number of dissociations with the recognition of other kinds of animals. Bruyer et al. (1983) reported a prosopagnosic farmer who could still recognize his individual cows, and McNeil and Warrington (1993) described an intriguing case of a person who became a sheep farmer after an injury that left him prosopagnosic and who became highly skilled at recognizing his individual sheep. Conversely a farmer studied by Assal, Favre, and Anderes (1984) regained his powers of face recognition but remained unable to identify his individual animals. "Pure" cases of prosopagnosia without deficit in any other area are extremely rare, however (e.g., De Renzi, 1986), and even these may sometimes be criticized for insufficient methodological rigour. It is important to test face and non-face object processing using tasks of equivalent difficulty for control participants and using a range of measures including time as well as accuracy. For example, Gauthier, Behrmann, and Tarr (1999) made extensive tests of two prosopagnosic patients whose deficits appeared to be confined to faces if accuracy on matching tasks was the principal measure, but whose deficits in the processing of other objects including Greebles and snow-flake patterns could be revealed in latency measures or in sensitivity measures in other tasks.

As well as dissociations between faces and other objects, there are dissociations between abilities on different tasks of face processing, too. While some prosopagnosic patients find it difficult to extract any kind of meaning from faces (e.g., Campbell, Landis, & Regard's 1986 patient), some appear to perceive facial expressions and other facial gestures quite normally. Indeed, for some prosopagnosic patients, it is other people's visual expressions of recognition that helps them to understand that this must be someone who is known to them. Young, Newcombe, De Haan, Small, and Hay (1993) examined a large number of ex-servicemen with gunshot injuries in a careful study where two different tests of each ability (expression analysis, unfamiliar face matching, familiar face identification) were given and latency as well as accuracy scores recorded for each. There was a clear double dissociation among their participants, with a small group of mainly left-hemisphere-lesioned patients who were impaired only on expression analysis but normal on face recognition and matching, and others impaired on familiar or unfamiliar face matching but spared on expression processing.

While most cases of prosopagnosia arise as a result of brain damage to adults who were (presumably, through their own reports) originally "expert" face recognizers, in recent years there have been reports of a small number of people who appear to have been "blind" to faces from birth (for a recent review, see Behrmann & Avidan, 2005). Such individuals are typically able to recognize faces as faces and, like acquired prosopagnosics, show some variation in their abilities beyond this level. About half the reported cases can tell the sex of faces, and about half can decipher expressions.

There is, however, very strong evidence in all these people that they are poor at processing facial configurations. Behrmann, Avidan, Marotta, and Kimchi (2005) have studied five such participants in detail and report that all show some impairment in processing non-face objects too, particularly when the task requires discrimination at the individual level and thus is likely to require sensitivity to configural rather than local features (e.g., distinguishing between two different chairs or between two different Greebles from the same gender and family). Unlike control subjects, these five participants tend to be influenced more by local than global properties of compound items in selective attention and priming tasks.

3.4. The cognitive neuroscience of face memory

As indicated earlier, it has been known for some time that there are cells particularly responsive to faces in the superior temporal sulcus of the temporal lobe of monkey (Gross et al., 1972; Perrett et al., 1984), but it is now thought that this area is more engaged in social attention than in person/individual recognition, which is the focus of this chapter. A rather different area of the temporal lobe within the fusiform gyrus, now generally labelled the "fusiform face area" (FFA; Kanwisher, McDermott, & Chun, 1997), has attracted much more interest in recent years as the possible locus of face-specific processing in the human brain. Activation in the FFA is much stronger to faces than to other classes of object, often chosen carefully to share perceptual properties with faces (e.g., Rhodes, Byatt, Michie, & Puce, 2004), but the activation seems particularly strong for upright rather than inverted faces (Yovel & Kanwisher, 2005). Where prosopagnosic people have had brain scans that can locate their brain damage, the FFA seems to coincide with damaged areas in such individuals.

While there is no doubt that the FFA responds to faces, it is also clear that there are other kinds of objects that activate areas in or near the FFA. Haxby et al. (2001) showed that fine-scale activation patterns within FFA and the wider ventral temporal cortex surrounding it coded for both faces and non-face objects, leading them to posit a model of distributed coding of different object categories, including faces, in these areas. Other research has identified a "fusiform body area" (FBA) responding strongly to headless bodies rather than faces, partly overlapping with the FFA (Schwarzlose, Baker, & Kanwisher, 2005).

A related question that has been hotly debated is whether the FFA is really a "faces" area, or an area that is needed to make fine within-category discriminations within domains where we become expert. Gauthier and colleagues have reported that FFA is activated also by cars and birds in participants who have expertise with these categories (Gauthier, Skudlarski, Gore, & Anderson, 2000) or by Greebles in participants who have learned to become experts with these shapes (Gauthier et al., 1999). In contrast, Rhodes et al. (2004) found little evidence of activation of FFA by pictures of lepidoptera in participants with expertise in these insects (Rhodes et al., 2004), and several other studies have found either no effect of the objects of expertise in FFA or greater effects in immediately adjacent areas than in FFA itself (see McKone et al., 2007).

An extremely interesting observation in this context comes from Avidan, Hasson, Malach, and Behrmann (2005) from fMRI investigations with congenital prosopagnosics. Four such people, who have never gained any expertise with faces throughout their lifetimes, nonetheless showed normal patterns of fMRI activation in the FFA. Follow-up structural MRI investigations reported by Behrmann and Avidan (2005) suggest that the critical fusiform gyrus regions are physically smaller in these participants than in control subjects, but nonetheless are activated by faces in the normal way. Thus it appears that face-related activation in the FFA may not itself be sufficient to explain the processes of normal face identification, and that abnormalities in conformation of this region may either arise from deficient face processing or be the underlying reason for deficient face processing. Nonetheless, the activity of the FFA by faces in this group of inexpert face perceivers does suggest that the area has some intrinsic connection with faces rather than with expertise per se.

Even within normal face perceivers, other areas of the brain are also involved in face processing, and activation in FFA alone is far from sufficient to explain the full derivation of identity from a familiar face. James Haxby and colleagues have gone some way to describing the roles played by different regions, including the STS region first identified through single-cell recording in the monkey, in the overall skill of deciphering social signals from faces (Gobbini & Haxby, 2007; Haxby, Hoffman, & Gobbini, 2000).

3.5. Dynamic information in face memory

One way that faces differ from other kinds of objects is through the wealth of other social information carried by the face. We don't just identify people from their faces—we register their emotional states from momentary expressions, we use patterns of lip and tongue movements to help understand speech, and we use shifts in eye gaze and head direction to decipher what people are talking or thinking about. The face moves both rigidly when the head turns or nods, and non-rigidly when making expressions, chewing, or speaking. Recent evidence suggests that these dynamic patterns may themselves be remembered and help face recognition—at least when other information is impoverished.

Knight and Johnston (1997) showed that when famous faces were presented in photographic negatives, thus making them hard to recognize, identification was more often successful if the faces were shown moving rather than in still image. In a series of studies, Karen Lander and colleagues showed that the beneficial effects of movement were not an artefact of the additional information content of the frames from a movie (Lander & Bruce, 2000; Lander, Christie, & Bruce, 1999). When famous faces were made difficult to recognize, the benefits of seeing an animated presentation were much greater if the film was played at its original tempo than if the same frames were played more slowly or more quickly, or if their temporal order was changed. Slowing a film down or playing it backwards shows the same static information in the frame sequence, but clearly this was not the major reason for the benefit of animation. Lander and Bruce (2000) suggest that the benefits of motion may arise because, for familiar faces, characteristic patterns of motion are stored in memory and can help activate the appropriate person identity when the static visual form system is deficient.

There is much less clear evidence for beneficial effects of motion on representations for matching or remembering unfamiliar faces. Some studies have found that seeing faces in motion helps recognition memory for the faces seen later (Pike, Kemp, Towell, & Phillips, 1997; Pilz, Thornton, & Bülthoff, 2006). In other studies no advantages have been found (Bruce et al., 1999; Christie & Bruce, 1998). Suggestions that motion would help build a representation of three-dimensional structure would lead to the prediction that non-rigid motion of unfamiliar faces would be particularly beneficial, and would help generalization to novel viewpoints. This prediction has generally not been confirmed (Lander & Bruce, 2003). Where beneficial effects of motion of unfamiliar faces are found, these seem to arise as much from non-rigid, expressive and speaking movements, suggesting a different source for the influence of motion.

To sum up, the representations we store in memory that allow us to recognize faces are based around an analysis of surface features—patterns of light and dark—in which the inter-relationships between different parts of the pattern have become particularly important. Dynamic patterns of movement also form some part of the representation we use to remember familiar faces, and these movement patterns include non-rigid, expressive, and speech movements that are probably unique to faces.

4. RECALL OF FACES BY EYEWITNESSES

So far I have discussed the way in which our visual memories for faces may be organized to allow people to recognize the faces that we see. Sometimes, however, during a criminal investigation, we may want to try to help a witness recall a face in a form that allows us to build an image of the person that someone else might be able to recognize. Most people cannot draw well enough to attempt to recall a face directly by sketching, and so generally witnesses are invited to work with a police artist or with some kind of facial composite generator (usually also via a police operator) to "build" an image of how the face looks. Jacques Penry (1971) developed the Photofit system, in which parts and regions from actual photographs of faces were stored and the witnesses invited to search for the face parts/regions that matched their memory. A composite image of the face was built up from the selected parts. The Photofit system, and Identikit—a similar, US-based system originally based on line drawings but later developed in photographic form—were adopted by large numbers of police forces worldwide. However, attempts at evaluating the efficacy of these systems yielded very disappointing results.

During the late 1970s, a US-based team (e.g., Laughery & Fowler, 1980) and a team based at the University of Aberedeen (e.g., Davies, Ellis, & Shepherd, 1978b; Ellis, Davies, & Shepherd, 1978) evaluated Identikit and Photofit respectively and found very similar results. Both groups found that there was no significant difference in the quality of constructed composites produced from memory compared with those produced when the target face was in view and could be copied. This was because the quality of likenesses produced from view was poor and so was affected rather little by the additional problems created by remembering the face. In contrast, sketch-artist renditions (Laughery) or the witnesses own attempt to draw the face (Ellis) were both very much poorer when the face was not in view.

These days, computer-based systems such as E-Fit and PROfit allow face features to be moved and blended much more effectively, so that a skilled operator can produce a remarkably close likeness when trying to copy a face from view. The limitations of electronic composite systems no longer lie with the art-work. However, it is still very difficult to get witnesses to produce recognizable composites using such systems.

In two recent studies, Charlie Frowd and colleagues made a systematic comparison of all current composite systems, using the same methodology that resembles in some ways the task faced by an eyewitness (Frowd et al., 2005a, 2005b). In each study, each simulated "witness" viewed a photograph of a face unfamiliar to him or her and attempted to build a composite from memory. The composites were then shown to other participants who would be likely to recognize these targets, and naming rates and other measures of performance were used to assess the efficacy of the likenesses. The same set of targets were used for each of the different systems evaluated, and composites were built using the kinds of techniques used in a real interview—using cognitive interview techniques to encourage participant-witnesses to recall context that might help them to build the face composite. Frowd et al. (2005a) asked the simulated witnesses to build composites from memory about 3–4 hours after viewing each target face. Under these conditions, E-Fit and PROfit yielded 19% and 17% correct naming of the target faces respectively, and this performance was better than was found with artist sketches (9%) and Photofit (6%). However, in a related study, Frowd et al. (2005b) used a delay of 2 days between viewing the photograph and attempting to build the composite. Under these conditions, much closer to the conditions of a real criminal investigation, sketches produced the best performance; however, this was only 8% correctly named composites, and no other system evaluated exceeded 4% correct naming rates.

One reason why contemporary composite systems produce such poor likenesses may be found when we examine how well witnesses can remember different parts of the face (for discussion of the impact that expectations, beliefs, stereotypes, and emotions have on facial memory by eyewitnesses, see chapter 7, section 4.1.1). A witness is trying to recall a face that was unfamiliar to him or her at the time of the incident (or experiment). The external features of the face—particularly the hairstyle—dominate our memory for unfamiliar faces, while there is a better representation of the internal features in familiar faces (Ellis, Shepherd, & Davies, 1979). Frowd, Bruce, McIntyre, and Hancock (2007) have shown that both naming and sorting of the composites is conducted nearly as accurately if only the external features of the composites are displayed as when the full composite is displayed. In contrast, if just the internal features of composites are shown, then performance is very low. But the composites produced by witnesses are aimed at provoking recognition by people *familiar* with the faces—and here we know that the internal features of the faces are more important. If witnesses cannot create composites showing accurate internal features, then perhaps the poor performance at triggering recognition from their reconstructed images is unsurprising.

Given this rather bleak picture, are there other ways to obtain better likenesses from witnesses via composite systems? Bruce, Ness, Hancock, Newman, and Rarity (2002) reasoned that better likenesses might result if different independent witness composites were combined by averaging ("morphing") them together. The logic used was that there was no reason to suppose that different witnesses would make the same errors, so that errors should tend to cancel out while correct aspects should be reinforced in the morph. Two separate experiments confirmed this prediction. A morphed composite that combined the independent memories of four witnesses was rated as a better likeness than the average of the individual composites, and no worse than the best of these. In experiments simulating recognition of these composites, there was also evidence that the morphed composite could be recognized or matched with its corresponding target at least as accurately as the best of the individual composites.

Not all crimes will lend themselves to this combination of different independent memories, but where there is more than one witness, and it can be established that each is describing the same person, the supplementary rules of evidence applying here in the United Kingdom have now been modified to allow such an approach to be taken.

One problem with combining different witness composite faces together will be a tendency also to average out some of the more distinctive characteristics of a remembered face. Each of four independent witnesses might remember that the person had a large nose, but unless all remembered the large nose in a similar way, the morph of these impressions might be a more average-size nose than the most accurate nose remembered. This led us to speculate that applying a modest amount of positive caricaturing to a morphed composite might make it more recognizable still. There is some evidence for this in a recent study (Frowd, Bruce, Ross, McIntyre, & Hancock, 2007). Participants were given composites of particular, familiar people and asked to adjust the degree of caricature shown to maximize the likeness of each composite. Morphs were preferred at modest positive caricatures (+7%), while individual composites were preferred at modest degrees of anti-caricature (–11%). This study revealed very large individual differences in the degrees of caricature preferred by different participants and for different target faces. This meant it was difficult to set a specific level of caricature or anti-caricature that would produce consistent gains in an identification task. So Frowd reasoned that showing people dynamic caricatures of target faces that spanned the range from anti- to pro-caricature should ensure that the optimum level of caricature was displayed for recognition. Very significant gains in recognition were obtained by showing a range in this way.

A more fundamental problem with composite production lies in its require-ment that witnesses try to recall individual features of faces to build a composite. Earlier in this chapter I reviewed in some detail evidence that suggests that our representations of faces are based upon holistic or configural processes. Inter-rogating visual memories for faces in a feature-by-feature way is unnatural and extremely difficult. This has led my colleagues at the University of Stirling to develop a new form of composite system based on recognition of faces rather than recall of face features. In "EvoFIT" (Hancock & Frowd, 2002), faces are synthesized from holistic "dimensions" (principal components or "eigenfaces"; Hancock, 2000) rather than piecemeal features, and participants only ever see whole faces. A witness is shown a screen of faces and asked to select a small number of these faces that most closely resemble their memory of the target. The component dimensions of the selected faces are then used along with genetic algorithms to "breed" another set of faces on the screen, and the witness chooses again. Gradually the screen choices begin to converge on something that the witness will select as the final version of the target he or she is trying to remember. In some circumstances EvoFIT out-performs existing composite systems, and it has already been used successfully in one police investigation. However, the existing interface is quite demanding to use, and the numbers of faces shown probably too large to be optimal. It remains a promising tool for future development, however.

Will witness memory be made redundant by the use of cameras? The United Kingdom has more CCTV cameras per head of population than any other coun-try in the world, and the probability that a criminal will be captured on camera, as well as the quality of such captured images, is increasing. While there will always be crimes in which no camera images are likely to be available (e.g., assault on persons in their own home), there is an increasing temptation to use images on CCTV cameras to identify suspects, where these are available. How-ever, the possible use of apparent *resemblance* between an image and a suspect to assert identity raises similar problems reviewed at the start of this chapter when we considered cases where resemblance to a memory of a face led to mistaken conviction. CCTV images are best used to help the investigative stage, where release on TV programmes such as the UK's *Crimewatch* can generate new leads in an investigation (for discussion, see Bruce et al., 1999).

5. CONCLUSION

This chapter has reviewed what we know about visual memory for faces. Face memories are based upon relatively "raw" patterns of light and dark processed in a way that emphasizes their configuration. It is difficult for a witness to interrogate such a memory through recalling individual features. Visual recognition of faces involves some specialized neural machinery in, and beyond, the fusiform face area.

Research into visual memory for faces has undergone huge expansion over the past 30 years and is entering a particularly interesting phase, as neural interactions between different strands of face processing are increasingly the focus of investigation.

6. REFERENCES

Assal, G., Favre, C., & Anderes, J. P. (1984). Non-reconnaissance d'animaux familiers chez un paysan. *Revue Neurologique, 140,* 580–584.

Avidan, G., Hasson, U., Malach, R., & Behrmann, M. (2005). Detailed exploration of face-related processing in congenital prosopagnosia: 2. Functional neuroimaging findings. *Journal of Cognitive Neuroscience, 17,* 1150–1167.

Behrmann, M., & Avidan, G. (2005). Congenital prosopagnosia: Face-blind from birth. *Trends in Cognitive Sciences, 9,* 180–187.

Behrmann, M., Avidan, G., Marotta, J. J., & Kimchi, R. (2005). Detailed exploration of face-related processing in congenital prosopagnosia: 1. Behavioural findings. *Journal of Cognitive Neuroscience, 17,* 1130–1149.

Biederman, I. (1987). Recognition-by-components; A theory of human image understanding. *Psychological Review, 94,* 115–147.

Bodamer, J. (1947). Die Prosopagnosie. *Archiv Fur Psychiatrie and Nervenkrankheiten, 179,* 6–53.

Bornstein, B. (1963). Prosopagnosia. In L. Hapern (Ed.), *Problems of dynamic neurology* (pp. 283–318). Jerusalem, Israel: Hadassah Medical Organisation.

Braje, W. L. (2003). Illumination encoding in face recognition: Effect of position shift. *Journal of Vision, 3,* 161–170.

Bruce, V. (1982). Changing faces—visual and non-visual coding processes in face recognition. *British Journal of Psychology, 73,* 105–116.

Bruce, V., Burton, A. M., Hanna, E., Healey, P., Mason, O., Coombes, A., et al. (1993). Sex discrimination: How do we tell the difference between male and female faces? *Perception, 22,* 131–152.

Bruce, V., Henderson, Z., Greenwood, K., Hancock, P. J. B., Burton, A. M., & Miller, P. (1999). Verification of face identities from images captured on video. *Journal of Experimental Psychology: Applied, 5,* 339–360.

Bruce, V., & Langton, S. (1994). The use of pigmentation and shading information in recognising the sex and identities of faces. *Perception, 23,* 803–822.

Bruce, V., Ness, H., Hancock, P. J. B., Newman, C., & Rarity, J. (2002). Four heads are better than one. . . . *Journal of Applied Psychology, 87,* 894–902.

Bruce, V., & Young, A. W. (1986). Understanding face recognition. *British Journal of Psychology, 77,* 305–328.

Bruyer, R., Laterre, C., Seron, X., Feyereisen, P., Strypstein, E., Pierrard, E., & Rectem, D. (1983). A case of prosopagnosia with some preserved covert remembrance of familiar faces. *Brain and Cognition, 2,* 257–284.

Burton, A. M., Bruce, V., & Dench, N. (1993). What's the difference between men and women? Evidence from facial measurement. *Perception, 22,* 153–176.

Burton, A. M., Wilson, S., Cowan, M., & Bruce, V. (1999). Face recognition from poor quality video: Evidence from security surveillance. *Psychological Science, 10,* 243–248.

Campbell, R., Landis, T., & Regard, M. (1986), Face recognition and lipreading: A neurological dissociation. *Brain, 109,* 509–521.

Christie, F., & Bruce, V. (1998). The role of dynamic information in the recognition of unfamiliar faces. *Memory & Cognition, 26,* 780–790.

Davies, G., Ellis, H. D., & Shepherd, J. (1978a). Face recognition accuracy as a function of mode of presentation. *Journal of Applied Psychology, 63,* 180–187.

Davies, G., Ellis, H. D., & Shepherd, J. (1978b). Face identification: The influence of delay upon accuracy of Photofit construction. *Journal of Police Science and Administration, 6,* 35–42.

Deregowski, J. B., Ellis, H. D., & Shepherd, J. W. (1973). Cross-cultural study of recognition of pictures of faces and cups. *International Journal of Psychology, 8,* 269–273.

De Renzi, E. (1986). Current issues on prosopagnosia. In H. D. Ellis, M. Jeeves, F. Newcombe, & A. W. Young (Eds.), *Aspects of face processing* (pp. 243–252). Dordrecht: Martinus Nijhoff.

Diamond, R., & Carey, S. (1986). Why faces are and are not special: An effect of expertise. *Journal of Experimental Psychology: General, 115,* 107–117.

Ellis, H. D. (1988). The Tichborne Claimant. *Journal of Applied Cognitive Psychology, 2,* 257–264.

Ellis, H. D., Davies G. M., & Shepherd, J. (1978). A critical examination of the Photofit system for recalling faces. *Ergonomics, 21,* 297–307.

Ellis, H. D., Shepherd, J. W., & Davies, G. M. (1979). Identification of familiar and unfamiliar faces from internal and external features: Some implications for theories of face recognition. *Perception, 8,* 119–124.

Ellis, H. D., & Young, A. W. (1989). Faces in their social and biological context. In A. W. Young & H. D. Ellis (Eds.), *Handbook of research in face processing* (pp. 1–26). Amsterdam: North-Holland.

Frowd, C., Bruce, V., McIntyre, A., & Hancock, P. (2007). The relative importance of external and internal features of facial composites. *British Journal of Psychology, 98,* 61–77.

Frowd, C., Bruce, V., Ross, D., McIntyre, A., & Hancock, P. J. B. (2007). An application of caricature: How to improve the recognition of facial composites. *Visual Cognition, 15,* 954–984.

Frowd, C. D., Carson, D., Ness, H., McQuiston-Surrett, D., Richardson, J., Baldwin, H., & Hancock, P. (2005a). Contemporary composite techniques: The impact of a forensically-relevant target delay. *Legal and Criminological Psychology, 10,* 63–81.

Frowd, C. D., Carson, D., Ness, H., Richardson, J., Morrison, L., McLanaghan, S., & Hancock, P. (2005b). A forensically valid comparison of facial composite systems. *Psychology, Crime and Law, 11,* 33–52.

Galper, R. E. (1970). Recognition of faces in photographic negative. *Psychonomic Science, 19,* 207–208.

Gauthier, I., Behrmann, M., & Tarr, M. J. (1999). Can face recognition really be dissociated from object recognition? *Journal of Cognitive Neuroscience, 11,* 349–370.

Gauthier, I., Skudlarski, P., Gore, J. C., & Anderson, A. W. (2000). Expertise for cars and birds recruits brain areas involved in face recognition. *Nature Neuroscience, 3,* 191–197.

Gauthier, I., & Tarr, M. J. (1997). Becoming a "Greeble" expert: Exploring the face recognition mechanism. *Vision Research, 37,* 1673–1682.

Gauthier, I., Williams, P., Tarr, M. J., & Tanaka, J. (1998). Training "Greeble" experts: A framework for studying expert object recognition processes. *Vision Research, 38,* 2401–2428.

Gobbini, M. I., & Haxby, J. V. (2007). Neural systems for recognition of familiar faces. *Neuropsychologia, 45,* 32–41.

Goldstein, A. G., & Chance, J. E. (1971). Visual recognition memory for complex configurations. *Perception & Psychophysics, 9,* 237–241.

Gross, C. G., Rocha-Miranda, C. E., & Bender, D. B. (1972). Visual properties of neurons in inferotemporal cortex of the macaque. *Journal of Neurophysiology, 35,* 96–111.

Hancock, P. J. B. (2000). Evolving faces from principal components. *Behaviour Research Methods, Instruments and Computers, 32,* 327–333.

Hancock, P. J. B., & Frowd, C. D. (2002). Evolutionary generation of faces. In P. J. Bentley & D. W. Corne (Eds.), *Creative evolutionary systems* (pp. 409–424). San Francisco: Morgan Kaufman.

Haxby, J. V., Gobbini, M. I., Furey, M. L., Ishai, A., Schouten, J. L., & Pietrini, P. (2001). Distributed and overlapping representations of faces and objects in ventral temporal cortex. *Science, 293,* 2425–2430.

Haxby, J. V., Hoffman, E. A., & Gobbini, M. I. (2000). The distributed human neural system for face perception. *Trends in Cognitive Sciences, 4,* 223–233.

Heywood, C. A., & Cowey, A. (1992). The role of the face-cell area in the discrimination and recognition of faces by monkeys. *Philosophical Transactions of the Royal Society of London, B, 335,* 31–38.

Hill, H., & Bruce, V. (1996). Effects of lighting on the perception of facial surfaces. *Journal of Experimental Psychology: Human Perception and Performance, 22,* 986–1004.

Kanwisher, N., McDermott, J., & Chun, M. M. (1997). The fusiform face area: A module in human extrastriate cortex specialised for face perception. *Journal of Neuroscience, 17,* 4302–4311.

Knight, B., & Johnston, A. (1997). The role of movement in face recognition. *Visual Cognition, 4,* 265–273.

Lander, K., & Bruce, V. (2000). Recognising famous faces: Exploring the benefits of facial motion. *Ecological Psychology, 12,* 259–272.

Lander, K., & Bruce, V. (2003). The role of motion in learning new faces. *Visual Cognition, 10,* 897–912.

Lander, K., Christie, F., & Bruce, V. (1999). The role of movement in the recognition of famous faces. *Memory & Cognition, 27,* 974–985.

Laughery, K., & Fowler, R. (1980). Sketch artist and identifit procedures for generating facial images. *Journal of Applied Psychology, 65,* 307–316.

Leder, H., & Bruce, V. (1998). Local and relational aspects of facial distinctiveness. *Quarterly Journal of Experimental Psychology, 51,* 449–473.

Leder, H., & Bruce, V. (2000). When inverted faces are recognised: The role of configural information in face recognition *Quarterly Journal of Experimental Psychology, 53A,* 513–536.

Liu, C. H., & Chaudhuri, A. (2003). What determines whether faces are special? *Visual Cognition, 10,* 385–408.

McKone, E., Kanwisher, N., & Duchaine, B. C. (2007). Can generic expertise explain special processing for faces? *Trends in Cognitive Sciences, 11,* 8–15.

McNeil, J. E., & Warrington, E. K. (1993). Prosopagnosia: A face specific disorder. *Quarterly Journal of Experimental Psychology, 46A,* 1–10.

Nederhouser, M., & Mangini, M. (2001). A translation between S1 and S2 eliminates costs of changes in the direction of illumination in object matching. *Journal of Vision, 1,* 92a

Patterson, K. E. (1978). Person recognition: More than a pretty face. In M. M. Gruneberg, P. E. Morris, & R. N. Sykes (Eds.), *Practical aspects of memory* (pp. 227–235). London: Academic Press.

Patterson, K. E., & Baddeley, A. D. (1977). When face recognition fails. *Journal of Experimental Psychology: Human Learning and Memory, 3,* 406–417.

Penry, J. (1971). *Looking at faces and remembering them.* London: Elek Books.

Perrett, D. I., Rolls, E. T., & Caan, W. (1982). Visual neurons responsive to faces in the monkey temporal cortex. *Experimental Brain Research, 47,* 329–342.

Perrett, D. I., Smith, P. A., Potter, D. D., Mistlin, A. J., Head, A. S., Milner, A. D., & Jeeves, M. A. (1984). Neurones responsive to faces in the temporal cortex: Studies of functional organisation, sensitivity to identity and relation to perception, *Human Neurobiology, 3,* 197–208.

Pike, G. E., Kemp, R. I., Towell, N. A., & Phillips, K. C. (1997). Recognising moving faces: The relative contribution of motion and perspective view information. *Visual Cognition, 4,* 409–437.

Pilz, K. S., Thornton, I. M., & Bülthoff, H. H. (2006). A search advantage for faces learned in motion, *Experimental Brain Research, 171,* 436–447.

Rakover, S. S. (2002). Featural vs. configurational information in faces: A conceptual and empirical analysis. *British Journal of Psychology, 93,* 1–30.

Rhodes, G., Byatt, G., Michie, P. T., & Puce, A. (2004). Is the fusiform face area specialised for faces, individuation, or expert individuation? *Journal of Cognitive Neuroscience, 16,* 189–203.

Rhodes, G., & McClean, I. (1990). Distinctiveness and expertise effects with homogeneous stimuli: Towards a model of configural coding. *Perception, 19,* 773–794.

Russell, R., Sinha, P., Biederman, I., & Nederhouser, M. (2006). Is pigmentation important for face recognition? Evidence from contrast negation. *Perception, 35,* 749–759.

Scapinello, K. F., & Yarmey, A. D. (1970). The role of familiarity and orientation in immediate and delayed recognition of pictorial stimuli. *Psychonomic Science, 21,* 329–330.

Schwarzlose, R. F., Baker, C. I., & Kanwisher, N. (2005). Separate face and body selectivity on the fusiform gyrus. *Journal of Neuroscience, 25,* 11055–11059

Shepard, R. N. (1967). Recognition memory for words, sentences and pictures. *Journal of Verbal Learning and Verbal Behaviour, 6,* 156–163.

Subramaniam, S., & Biederman, I. (1997). Does contrast reversal affect object identification? *Investigative Ophthalmology and Visual Science, 38,* 4638.

Tarr, M. J., Kersten, D., & Bülthoff, H. H. (1998). Why the visual recognition system might encode the effects of illumination. *Vision Research, 38,* 2259–2275.

Thomson, D. M. (1986). Face recognition: More than a feeling of familiarity? In H. D. Eliis, M. A. Jeeves, F. Newcombe, & A. Young (Eds.), *Aspects of face processing.* Dordrecht: Martinus Nijhoff.

Thompson, P. (1980). Margaret Thatcher: A new illusion. *Perception, 9,* 483–484.

Vuong, Q. C., Peissig, J. J., Harrison, M. C., & Tarr, M. J. (2005). The role of surface pigmentation for recognition revealed by contrast reversal in faces and Greebles. *Vision Research, 45,* 1213–1223.

Wagenaar, W. A. (1988). *Identifying Ivan: A case study in legal psychology.* New York: Harvester.

Yin, R. K. (1969). Looking at upside-down faces. *Journal of Experimental Psychology, 81,* 141–145

Yin, R. K. (1970). Face recognition by brain-injured patients: A dissociable ability? *Neuropsychologia, 8,* 395–402.

Young, A. W. (1998). *Face and mind.* Oxford: Oxford University Press.

Young, A. W., Hellawell, D. J., & Hay, D. C. (1987). Configural information in face perception. *Perception, 16,* 747–759.

Young , A. W., Newcombe, F., De Haan, E. H. F., Small, M., & Hay, D. C. (1993). Face perception after brain injury: Selective impairments affecting identity and expression. *Brain, 116,* 941–959.

Yovel, G., & Kanwisher, N. (2005). The neural basis of the behavioural face-inversion effect. *Current Biology, 15,* 256–2262.

4   Memory for real-world scenes

Andrew Hollingworth
University of Iowa

1. INTRODUCTION

Humans spend most of their waking lives in complex visual environments that often consist of scores of individual objects. For example, a quick scan of the office in which this chapter was written generates a count of at least 150 objects. How do people perceive and remember environments of such complexity? The growing field of scene perception and memory is built upon a commitment to understanding how perception, attention, and memory operate under conditions of complexity and information oversaturation. For most of the history of vision research, experiments have been conducted using highly simplified stimuli, often presented for very brief durations. Such approaches are necessary to isolate component operations of vision and memory (such as color perception or object recognition). However, relatively little work has been conducted to understand how component operations of vision and memory are coordinated to support real-world perception, memory, and behavior. The present chapter reviews work on this topic, most of which has been conducted in the last 10–15 years. Although this research area is still relatively young, significant strides have been made, and it is now possible to provide a broad account of the means by which visual scene information is perceived and remembered.

Before continuing, it is important to provide a working definition of the term "visual scene". Henderson and Hollingworth (1999a) used the following definition, which will be adopted here:

> the concept of scene is typically defined (though often implicitly) as a semantically coherent (and often nameable) view of a real-world environment comprising background elements and multiple discrete objects arranged in a spatially licensed manner. Background elements are taken to be larger-scale, immovable surfaces and structures, such as ground, walls, floors, and mountains, whereas objects are smaller-scale discrete entities that are manipulable (e.g., can be moved) within the scene. (p. 244)

One of the organizing assumptions of this chapter is that scene perception and memory are dynamic operations that require the serial selection of local scene regions. Complex scenes contain too much information to be perceived in a single glance. Therefore, attention and the eyes are sequentially directed to goal-relevant scene regions and objects as viewing unfolds. Figure 4.1 [in color plate section] shows a typical eye-movement scan path over a complex natural scene. Eye movements enable us to obtain high-resolution visual information from objects but also serve to specify objects in the world as the targets of actions, such as grasping (see chapter 5). During eye movements, vision is suppressed (Matin, 1974), and perceptual input is also disrupted by blinks and occlusion. Memory is required to span these disruptions, and memory is required to accumulate information from local scene regions that is obtained sequentially. Furthermore, if experience within scenes is to influence our subsequent behavior (e.g., remembering where the phone is located so as to reach for it without searching), information about the structure and content of a scene must be stored robustly over the sometimes extended delays between encounters with a particular scene. Thus, visual memory plays an important role not only within our online perceptual interactions with a scene but also over much longer time scales that allow perceptual learning to guide behavior.

The present chapter is divided into two sections. The first concerns the nature of the visual representation constructed as participants view a natural scene. The second concerns the functional role of visual memory in scene perception.

2. THE REPRESENTATION OF NATURAL SCENES

2.1. Memory systems potentially contributing to scene representation

Visual memory appears to be composed of four different memory stores, each of which could potentially contribute to the representation of a natural scene: visible persistence, informational persistence, visual short-term memory (VSTM), and visual long-term memory (VLTM).

Visible and informational persistence are often grouped together as *iconic memory* or *sensory persistence* (Coltheart, 1980). Both maintain a high-capacity, retinotopically organized sensory trace that is generated across the visual field but is highly volatile. Visible persistence is phenomenologically visible and persists for approximately 80–100 ms after the onset of a stimulus (Di Lollo, 1980). Informational persistence is a nonvisible sensory memory that persists for approximately 150–300 ms after stimulus offset (Irwin & Yeomans, 1986). Both visible persistence and informational persistence are susceptible to interference from new sensory processing (i.e., susceptible to backward masking).

Early theories proposed that as attention and the eyes are directed to local scene regions, low-level sensory memory is integrated so as to create a global image of a natural scene (Davidson, Fox, & Dick, 1973; Jonides, Irwin, & Yantis, 1982; McConkie & Rayner, 1975). In particular, high-resolution foveal information from local regions could be combined to create a global image of a scene that contained high-resolution sensory information across much of the visual field. Such integration was thought to be necessary to support our phenomenology of seeing a complete and detailed visual world across the visual field.

However, a large body of research demonstrates conclusively that that is false: participants cannot integrate sensory information presented on separate fixations (Irwin, Yantis, & Jonides, 1983; O'Regan & Lévy-Schoen, 1983; Rayner & Pollatsek, 1983). Recent work using naturalistic scene stimuli has arrived at a similar conclusion. Relatively large changes to a natural scene can go undetected if the change occurs during a saccadic eye movement or other visual disruption (Grimes, 1996; Henderson & Hollingworth, 1999b, 2003b; Rensink, O'Regan, & Clark, 1997; Simons & Levin, 1998), an effect that has been termed *change blindness*. For example, Henderson and Hollingworth (2003b) had participants view scene images that were partially occluded by a set of vertical gray bars (as if viewing the scene from behind a picket fence). During eye movements, the bars were shifted so that the occluded portions of the scene became visible and the visible portions became occluded. Despite the fact that every pixel in the image changed, subjects were almost entirely insensitive to these changes, demonstrating that low-level sensory information is not preserved from one fixation to the next. Because sensory persistence does not to appear to play any *memorial* role in scene representation, these systems will not be considered further. If scene representations are constructed from the incomplete, shifting, and frequently disrupted input that characterizes natural vision, then that construction must depend on more robust, higher-level visual memory systems of VSTM and VLTM.

VSTM maintains a small number of higher-level visual representations abstracted away from precise sensory information. It has a capacity of 3–4 objects (Irwin, 1992; Luck & Vogel, 1997) and lacks the metric precision of sensory persistence (Irwin, 1991; Phillips, 1974). However, VSTM is not significantly disrupted by subsequent perceptual input (Pashler, 1988; Phillips, 1974) and can be maintained over durations on the order of seconds (Phillips, 1974) and across saccades (Hollingworth, Richard, & Luck, 2008). VLTM maintains abstracted visual representations similar to those maintained in VSTM but has the capability to accumulate visual information from scores of individual objects (Hollingworth, 2004, 2005).

2.2. The online representation of scenes

Theoretical accounts of scene representation have been shaped by the phenomenon of change blindness. In change blindness experiments, participants often fail to detect otherwise salient changes when the change occurs across some form of perceptual disruption, such as a blank ISI (Rensink et al., 1997), an eye movement (Grimes, 1996; Henderson & Hollingworth, 1999b, 2003b), or occlusion (Simons & Levin, 1998). The sometimes remarkable insensitivity to changes across perceptual disruptions provides further evidence that the visual system does not construct a complete, low-level sensory representation of a scene. But what *is* represented during online scene perception? Proposals have spanned a wide range of possibilities.

O'Regan (1992; O'Regan & Noë, 2001) has argued that there is essentially no role for visual memory in scene representation, because the world itself acts as an "outside memory". In this view, visual memory is unnecessary, because information in the world can be acquired whenever needed by a shift of attention to the relevant object. In a similar vein, Ballard, Hayhoe, and colleagues (Ballard, Hayhoe, & Pelz, 1995; Ballard, Hayhoe, Pook, & Rao, 1997; Hayhoe, 2000; see also chapter 5) have argued that visual scene memory during common real-world tasks is typically limited to the attended information necessary to support moment-to-moment actions. That is, the visual system minimizes memory demands by representing only the immediately task-relevant information, with eye movements used to acquire this information when it is needed. Rensink (Rensink, 2000, 2002; Rensink et al., 1997) and others (Becker & Pashler, 2002; M. E. Wheeler & Treisman, 2002) also have argued that the visual representation of scenes is minimal, with the visual representation of a scene limited, at any moment, to the currently attended object. In this view, attention is necessary to form a coherent representation of an object that binds together the features of that object (Treisman, 1988). Attention is also necessary to maintain that binding in VSTM (Rensink, 2000; M. E. Wheeler & Treisman, 2002). Once attention is removed from an object, the coherent object representation comes unbound, and the object dissolves back into its constituent features, leaving no lasting visual memory. Irwin (Irwin & Andrews, 1996; Irwin & Zelinsky, 2002) has proposed that more than just the currently attended object is represented during scene viewing. Higher-level visual representations (abstracted away from precise sensory features) of previously attended objects accumulate in VSTM as the eyes and attention are oriented from object to object within a scene. However, this accumulation is limited to the capacity of VSTM: 5–6 objects at the most (Irwin & Zelinsky, 2002). Finally, Hollingworth and Henderson (2002) proposed that both VSTM and VLTM are used to accumulate higher-level visual representations of objects during scene viewing, enabling the construction of scene representations that maintain visual information from many individual objects.

The nonrepresentationalist approach of O'Regan finds little support in the literature. It is certainly true that eye movements are used to acquire visual information when it is needed (Hayhoe, 2000; Land, Mennie, & Rusted, 1999), but the proposal that the visual system relies entirely on the external world for access to visual information fails to account for the clear benefits of having a visual memory. Visual memory allows us to classify objects and scenes as belonging to particular categories, allows us recognize individual objects on the basis of their perceptual features (my dog is the brown one, not the white one), and allows us to remember the locations of objects so that they can be quickly found when needed. Moreover, research reviewed below demonstrates that humans are highly adept at remembering the visual properties of scenes. Thus, the nonrepresentationalist position can be eliminated from further consideration.

The next step in evaluating competing theories of online scene representation is to determine whether the visual representation of a scene is limited to the currently attended object (Rensink, 2000; M. E. Wheeler & Treisman, 2002). The principal evidence cited in support of this idea comes from the original experiments by Rensink et al. (1997). In those studies, changes to objects classified as "central interest" were detected more quickly than changes to objects classified as "marginal interest". Rensink et al. reasoned that because central-interest items were more likely to be attended than marginal-interest items, evidence of faster detection of changes to central-interest items indicated that attention was necessary for change detection and, furthermore, that change detection was limited to the currently attended object. However, with no means to measure or control where attention was allocated in this task, any conclusions about the role of attention in scene memory and change detection must be considered tentative (for a similar criticism, see Scholl, 2000). In particular, one cannot conclude from these data that object representations in VSTM disintegrate upon the withdrawal of attention or that visual scene representation is limited to the currently attended object.

Wheeler and Treisman (2002) sought to examine whether attention is necessary to maintain coherent visual object representations in VSTM. Participants saw an array of simple colored shapes in a change detection task. They either had to remember the individual features (colors and shapes) or the binding of features (which particular shapes were paired with which particular colors). Wheeler and Treisman found that memory for the binding of features was impaired relative to memory for individual features, but only when the entire array was presented again at test; when a single item was presented at test, there was no binding deficit. Wheeler and Treisman argued that the presentation of the entire array at test led to attentional distraction and the withdrawal of attention from the items in VSTM, causing the bound object representations to disintegrate into their constituent features and generating a deficit in binding memory. However, attention was not directly manipulated in this study, and there is no compelling reason to think that presentation of the full array at test led to attentional distraction (Hollingworth, 2006; Jiang, Olson, & Chun, 2000; Johnson, Hollingworth, & Luck, 2008).

Johnson et al. (2008) attempted to replicate the Wheeler and Treisman (2002) result, but found no decrement in binding memory when comparing a full array test with single-object test. More importantly, Johnson et al. directly manipulated attention in a similar change detection task. During the delay between presentation of the study array and test array, participants completed a demanding visual search task that required serial shifts of attention to search array elements. The introduction of this search task lowered memory performance overall, but there was no specific decrement in memory for feature binding, indicating no special role for attention in maintaining feature bindings in VSTM. In addition, Gajewski and Brockmole (2006) found that the recall of objects in a VSTM task did not exhibit any significant loss of binding information when attention was engaged by a peripheral cue. Finally, Allen, Baddeley, and Hitch (2006) found that memory for feature binding in VSTM was not specifically impaired by a secondary task that required central attentional resources. Thus, sustained attention is not required to maintain feature binding in visual memory, and scene representation need not be limited to the currently attended object.

To examine visual memory for previously attended objects during the viewing of real-world scenes, Hollingworth and Henderson (2002) tested visual memory for objects in scenes after attention had been withdrawn from the object. Eye movements were monitored as participants viewed depictions of real-world scenes. The computer waited until the participant had fixated a target object in the scene (to ensure it had been attended). Subsequently, the target object was masked during a saccade to a different object in the scene. Because visual attention is automatically and exclusively allocated to the goal of a saccade prior to an eye movement (e.g., Deubel & Schneider, 1996; Hoffman & Subramaniam, 1995), the target object was no longer attended when it was masked; attention had shifted to the nontarget object that was the goal of the saccade. Two object alternatives were then displayed within the scene. One was the original target object, and the other was either a different token from the same basic-level category (e.g., if the target was a watering can, the token was a different example of a watering can) or the target object rotated 90° in depth. Participants performed this discrimination task at rates above 80% correct. Furthermore, accurate discrimination performance was observed even when many fixations on other objects intervened between target fixation and test. When more than 9 fixations on other objects intervened between target fixation and test, token discrimination performance was 85% correct, and orientation discrimination performance was 92% correct. Memory for the visual details of previously attended objects was clearly robust across shifts of attention and of the eyes, and therefore the online visual representation of a scene is not limited to the currently attended object. Tatler and colleagues have provided complementary evidence that memory for the visual details of objects accumulates over multiple seconds of scene viewing (Tatler, Gilchrist, & Land, 2005; Tatler, Gilchrist, & Rusted, 2003).

In contrast with the studies reviewed above, Wolfe, Reinecke, and Brawn (2006) recently reported data they interpreted as evidence for minimal visual accumulation during scene viewing. On each trial of this experiment, 12 photographs of common objects were superimposed over a scene background. Participants shifted their attention covertly to individual objects in the scene, following a visual cue that specified the locations of either three or six of the objects. After the cue sequence, one object was masked. Participants were then shown an array of 36 object photographs, one of which was the masked object. Percentage correct performance on this 36 alternative forced-choice (AFC) task was approximately 50% for objects cued early in the sequence and approximately 85% for the object cued last in the sequence. Wolfe et al. interpreted their results as at variance with the finding of robust visual accumulation in Hollingworth and Henderson (2002).

What accounts for the apparent discrepancy between these studies? First, it is not clear that there is any significant discrepancy at all. In Wolfe et al. (2006), chance performance on the 36-AFC task was 2.8% (1/36). Memory performance for previously attended objects ranged from approximately 40% correct to 65% correct, and memory for the first cued object (which was cued six objects before the test) was approximately 50% correct. Thus, just as in Hollingworth and Henderson (2002), there was significant accumulation of visual object information as attention was oriented serially to objects in the scene. In addition, two aspects of the Wolfe et al. method were likely to have limited memory performance. To perform the 36-AFC task, participants would have needed to inspect a fairly large number of the 36 test objects in the course of finding the target, potentially introducing significant interference with target memory. The 2-AFC task of Hollingworth and Henderson (2002) is to be preferred, because it minimizes interference generated by the test itself. Furthermore, the speed of cueing was exceedingly rapid in the Wolfe et al. study, with consecutive object cues separated by only 150 or 300 ms SOA. Even if one assumes that each object was focally attended for the full SOA duration, the attentional dwell times were far shorter than those observed during free viewing (Hollingworth & Henderson, 2002) and were likely too short for the reliable consolidation of complex real-world objects into visual memory (Eng, Chen, & Jiang, 2005). In sum, the Wolfe et al. data replicated the central Hollingworth and Henderson (2002) finding of visual accumulation for previously attended objects, but encoding limitations and interference at test were likely to have depressed memory performance.

The results of Hollingworth and Henderson (2002) demonstrate that higher-level memory systems (but not sensory memory systems) accumulate visual information to construct a representation of a natural scene. Two candidate memory systems could contribute to online scene memory: VSTM and VLTM. To tease apart their relative contributions, Hollingworth (2004) used a serial position procedure. On each trial, participants followed a green dot with their eyes as it visited a series of objects in a scene (the SOA between consecutive cues was 1,100 ms). The serial position of a target object in the sequence was manipulated. After the sequence was completed, memory for the visual form of the target object was tested in a 2-AFC token or orientation discrimination test. A reliable recency effect was observed (see also Phillips & Christie, 1977). Performance was highest for the last two objects cued in the scene. This recency effect suggests a VSTM contribution to online scene representation that was limited to approximately two objects, an estimate consistent with independent estimates of VSTM capacity for complex natural objects (Alvarez & Cavanagh, 2004). Supporting the proposal that VLTM plays a significant role in online scene representation (Hollingworth & Henderson, 2002), memory performance for objects examined earlier than two objects before the test was quite accurate, and it did not decline further; performance was equivalent for objects cued three objects before the test and objects cued 10 objects before the test. This robust pre-recency memory easily surpassed VSTM capacity, indicating a large VLTM component to online scene representation (for converging evidence, see Hollingworth, 2005). Similar effects have been found in memory for the identity of objects (Wolfe et al., 2006) and in memory for the binding of objects to locations (Zelinsky & Loschky, 2005). Given that scene viewing often unfolds over the course of minutes and involves serially attending to and fixating scores of objects, it is likely that VLTM carries most of the load in constructing an online representation of a scene.

2.3. Longer-term memory for previously viewed scenes

Having constructed a visual memory representation of a scene during online viewing, how robustly is that representation retained in memory? Initial work on the capacity of picture memory demonstrated that participants have a prodigious ability to remember complex pictures, and such memory can be retained robustly over long delays (Nickerson, 1965, 1968; Shepard, 1967; Standing, 1973; Standing, Conezio, & Haber, 1970). Standing (1973) required participants to view 10,000 photographs of various subject matters for 5 s each over the course of five days of study. On a subsequent 2-AFC recognition task, discrimination performance was approximately 86% correct, which suggested that participants had successfully remembered almost 7,000 pictures. This is quite remarkable, given that the method was single-trial exposure and that each scene was viewed only briefly. Picture memory not only has remarkably large capacity, but visual memory representations of scenes are highly resistant to decay. Nickerson (1968) showed participants 200 grayscale photographs for 5 s each. A unique subset of the pictures was tested at varying intervals in a 2-AFC test. Four retention intervals were tested: one day, one week, one month, and one year. Discrimination performance declined with increasing delay (1 day = 92%; 1 week = 88%; 1 month = 74%; 1 year = 63%). However, forgetting was exceedingly gradual, and discrimination performance remained above chance even a year later, all from a single, 5 s exposure to each scene.

In these early studies on the capacity of visual memory, there was little control of stimulus properties, with pictures chosen from a variety of sources: magazines, travel snapshots, and so on. One possible explanation for prodigious memory capacity is that participants were not remembering perceptual details of the scenes but were instead remembering the abstract gist of the scene (Chun, 2003; Potter, Staub, & O'Connor, 2004; Simons, 1996). However, at least one study from this literature cannot be explained by gist retention. In Standing et al. (1970), participants viewed a set of 120 pictures for 2 s each. After a delay of 30 minutes or 24 hours, their memory for the left–right orientation of the pictures was tested by displaying the original picture or a mirrored-reversed version of that picture. Mirror reversal does not significantly alter scene gist (as long as there is no visible text or other canonically oriented stimuli), and thus accurate memory performance would indicate that participants remembered visual properties of the scenes rather than just semantic gist. Memory performance was approximately 86% correct after a delay of 30 min and approximately 72% correct after a delay of 24 hours. Thus, estimates of very large memory capacity for pictures might draw to some extent on memory for abstract gist, but there is clearly robust retention of visual detail.

To examine the capacity of VLTM for the visual details of individual objects in natural scenes, Hollingworth (2004) had participants view a series of scenes, with individual objects cued by means of a dot onset (described above). Instead of testing memory immediately after scene viewing, the test was delayed until all 48 scenes had been viewed. Memory for the token version of a single object in each scene was tested. More than 400 objects, on average, were examined between target examination and test of that object. Despite these considerable memory demands, participants performed the token change detection task at a rate well above chance (68% correct). For example, participants saw an iron on an ironing board in a laundry scene. This was only one of many objects in that particular scene, and the scene was only one of the 48 scenes viewed. Participants fixated the iron for less than 1 s, on average. Yet, after all scenes had been viewed, participants could report, at rates above chance, that the original iron had been replaced by a different iron. Moreover, memory for object token and orientation in scenes remained above chance even after a delay of 24 hours (Hollingworth, 2005).

This level of specificity in visual memory stands in stark contrast to change blindness effects. For example, in Henderson and Hollingworth (2003b), every pixel in a scene image was changed during a saccade by shifting a set of vertical bars that obscured half of the scene. Such changes were almost completely undetectable (even to those knowledgeable about the change). Yet, in Hollingworth (2004), participants could remember the token version of a single object in a scene viewed 30 minutes earlier. This juxtaposition illustrates the strengths and limitations of visual memory. Low-level sensory memory, which was necessary for the detection of bar shifts in Henderson and Hollingworth (2003b), is so fleeting that it does not even survive a single saccade. Yet, higher-level visual memory, which is abstracted away from precise sensory persistence but retains information about the form and orientation of an object, is highly robust.

2.4. Understanding change blindness

It is important, now, to return to the topic of change blindness so as to reconcile evidence of robust visual memory, reviewed above, with evidence of poor change detection performance in change blindness experiments (for a more extensive discussion, see Hollingworth, 2008). Change blindness has multiple causes. First, there is clearly forgetting in visual memory that causes participants to miss changes. The most dramatic form of forgetting is the loss of visual sensory memory following a stimulus event. There is no doubt that changes would be detected more reliably in change blindness experiments if sensory memory was retained robustly. However, we have known that sensory memory is fleeting ever since the early work by Sperling (1960) and Averbach and Coriell (1961). In higher-level visual memory systems (VSTM and VLTM), there is little subsequent forgetting over the timescales characteristic of change blindness studies (Hollingworth, 2005). A second cause of change blindness is failures of encoding. If the changing region of a scene has not been attended and fixated prior to the change, then the visual system would have minimal ability to detect the change, because the consolidation of perceptual information into VSTM and VLTM depends on focal attention (Averbach & Coriell, 1961; Hollingworth & Henderson, 2002; Schmidt, Vogel, Woodman, & Luck, 2002). A third cause of change blindness is retrieval and comparison failure. Many changes are missed despite the retention of visual information sufficient to detect the change. In these cases, the relevant information is not retrieved from memory and/or is not compared with current perceptual information (Hollingworth, 2003; Simons, Chabris, Schnur, & Levin, 2002; Varakin, Levin, & Collins, 2007). Finally, change blindness occurs when evidence for a change is registered but does not exceed threshold for explicit change detection. In these cases, participants are not consciously aware of a change, but one can observe implicit effects of change detection on sensitive measures (for a review, see Thornton & Fernandez-Duque, 2002), such as fixation duration (Hayhoe, Bensinger, & Ballard, 1998; Henderson & Hollingworth, 2003a; Hollingworth, Williams, & Henderson, 2001; Ryan, Althoff, Whitlow, & Cohen, 2000). As in any complex task, change detection can fail if any component of the task (encoding, maintenance, retrieval, comparison, detection) is compromised. In many cases, participants miss changes despite the retention of information sufficient to detect the change, and thus poor change detection cannot necessarily be interpreted as caused by poor or absent visual memory.

2.5. How are episodic representations of scenes structured?

Having shown that object information accumulates in memory as the eyes are oriented from object to object within a scene, and that scene representations are retained robustly in VLTM, the next question to address is how visual information obtained from individual objects is bound together, episodically, to form a coherent representation of a scene. As a first step in this endeavor, Hollingworth (2006) tested whether memory for the visual form of an object is bound to the scene context in which the object appeared. Prior research in the face perception literature has demonstrated that memory for the features of faces is stored as part of a larger face representation but that memory for the features of houses (a stimulus that more closely resembles a real-world scene) are stored independently of the house context (Tanaka & Farah, 1993) (see chapter 3, section 3.1). Such work suggests that objects might be remembered independently of the scene context in which the object appeared.

To test object-to-scene binding in visual memory, Hollingworth (2006) had participants view a series of complex scenes for 20 s each. Each scene image was followed by a 2-AFC test requiring memory for the perceptual features of a single object in the scene (token or orientation discrimination). The two object alternatives were displayed either within the original scene or in an otherwise empty field. Discrimination performance was reliably superior when the target object was tested within the original scene context, a whole-scene advantage similar to the advantage for the recognition of face features when the features are displayed within the original face context (Tanaka & Farah, 1993). Thus, visual memory for objects is episodically structured via association with the scene context in which the object appeared. Furthermore, faces are not unique in showing such contextual binding.

2.5.1. *Spatial structure in scene memory*

What are the mechanisms of object-to-scene binding? Hollingworth and Henderson (2002) proposed that object memory is organized within a scene through the binding of objects to particular spatial locations within a global spatial representation of the scene. This proposal originated from consideration that spatial information plays a central role in structuring episodic memory (Burgess, Maguire, & O'Keefe, 2002; O'Keefe & Nadel, 1978) and that spatial position structures object information in VSTM (Jiang et al., 2000; Kahneman, Treisman, & Gibbs, 1992).

To test whether memory for objects is indeed bound to scene locations, Hollingworth (2006) manipulated object position in a scene memory study. As in previous experiments, participants viewed a scene for 20 s. Each scene was then followed by a 2-AFC or change detection test probing memory for the visual form of a single object. The test objects were presented either at the original location where the target had appeared or at a different location within the scene (local contextual information was obscured in both conditions). Discrimination accuracy was higher when the test objects appeared at the same location as the target had appeared originally within the scene, a *same-position advantage*, indicating that memory for the visual form of the object was associated with the scene location where the object had appeared.

Hollingworth (2007) used the same-position advantage as a means to understand the spatial properties of a scene that serve to structure memory for objects. The experiments depended on the following logic. If a particular property of a scene is functional in defining object position, and if that property is disrupted, then the same-position advantage for target discrimination should be reduced or eliminated. First, Hollingworth examined whether the spatial position of an object is defined relative to the particular scene context in which the object appeared. Again, participants viewed full scenes, each followed by a 2-AFC discrimination test in which the test object alternatives appeared either in the same scene position as the target object had appeared at study or in a different position. In the full-scene condition, the test objects were displayed within the original scene. In the background-absent condition, the test objects were presented in the same absolute locations but against a blank background. This manipulation is illustrated in Figure 4.2 [in color plate section]. The advantage for presenting the target object in the same position at study and test was replicated in the full-scene condition, but that advantage was all but eliminated in the background-absent condition, indicating that object position was defined relative to the scene context in which it appeared.

Hollingworth (2007) further probed the nature of spatial contextual representations using arrays of common objects that allowed spatial manipulations not possible with scene stimuli. Scrambling the spatial locations of contextual objects at test significantly reduced the same-position benefit, demonstrating that object position is defined relative to the configuration of contextual objects (Jiang et al., 2000). In addition, a background-binding manipulation (in which the contextual objects traded locations) also reduced the same-position advantage. In this latter case, the contextual objects formed the same abstract spatial configuration at study and test. Only the binding of contextual objects to locations changed. Thus, the positions of individual objects appear to be defined relative to a contextual representation that maintains not only the abstract spatial configuration of objects, but also information about which objects appear in which locations in that configuration. Finally, the same-position advantage was preserved after translation of the array context, which did not disrupt object-to-object spatial relationships, demonstrating that object position is defined in scene-relative, rather than absolute, coordinates.

In summary, memory for a visual scene appears to be constructed, at least in part, through the binding of local object representations to locations within a spatial representation of the scene layout (Hollingworth & Henderson, 2002). This contextual representation is specific to the particular viewed scene, maintains the spatial configuration of objects, preserves the binding of contextual objects to locations, and codes individual object position in array-relative coordinates.

2.5.2. *Schema approaches to scene structure*

Historically, a central theoretical construct in the field of picture and scene memory has been the scene schema (Biederman, Mezzanotte, & Rabinowitz, 1982; Brewer & Treyens, 1981; Friedman, 1979; Intraub, 1997; Mandler & Ritchey, 1977; Pedzek, Whetstone, Reynolds, Askari, & Dougherty, 1989). The basic claim of schema theories is that episodic representations of scenes are structured according to prior experience with scenes of that type. For example, one's memory for a particular kitchen scene will be strongly influenced by one's memory for kitchens in general, a *kitchen schema*, which will govern the types of information retained in memory from that scene (see chapter 7 for the influence of schemas on memory for visual events). The standard description of a scene schema is an abstract representation of a particular scene category specifying the objects that are typically found in that type of scene and the typical locations of those objects (Mandler & Parker, 1976).

Two components are consistently present in schema accounts of scene memory: abstraction and distortion (for a critical review, see Alba & Hasher, 1983). First, scene memory is proposed to be highly abstract and conceptual in nature—that is, limited to the gist of the scene (Mandler & Ritchey, 1977; Potter et al., 2004). Scene details are initially activated during perceptual processing of the scene, but the details are quickly forgotten. In this claim, schema theories are quite similar to claims of gist-based representations in the change blindness literature (O'Regan, 1992; Rensink, 2000; Simons & Levin, 1997). The evidence that scene representations preserve significant visual detail, and are not limited to gist, has been reviewed exhaustively above. Thus, the schema theory claim of gist abstraction is not well supported by experimental evidence.

Second, the schema approach holds that memory for scene properties will be distorted by prior knowledge. Objects frequently found within a scene of that type (such as a dresser in a bedroom) will be remembered most frequently, because they have pre-existing "slots" in the schema. Incongruous or unexpected objects (such as a pig in a bedroom) will be remembered less accurately and will be normalized to default values in the schema. Although common sense would dictate that anomalous objects should be remembered most frequently from a scene (as they would be most salient), normalization is a central feature of schema theory (Bartlett, 1932). Brewer and Treyens (1981) tested the normalization claim by having participants remember the objects in a graduate student office, some of which were semantically consistent (desk) and some inconsistent (skull). On a free-recall test, participants more frequently reported semantically consistent objects than inconsistent objects, supporting the claim of normalization. However, Brewer and Treyens provided no control over guessing, and the advantage for consistent objects could easily have been generated by a bias to guess that consistent objects had been present. For example, if asked to report which objects had been in a kitchen scene, one could guess that there was likely to have been a stove, even if one did not specifically remember a stove.

In contrast to the Brewer and Treyens (1981) result, subsequent studies controlling guessing have found the reverse effect: better memory for semantically inconsistent objects in scenes (Friedman, 1979; Hollingworth & Henderson, 2000, 2003; Pedzek et al., 1989). Although some researchers have proposed schema explanations to account for superior inconsistent-object memory, these have been somewhat ad hoc. For example, Friedman (1979) proposed that inconsistent objects are stored robustly as part of a "weird list" that is appended to the schema representation. This type of modification would render the schema approach all but unfalsifiable. In general, the absence of inconsistent-object normalization argues against the standard schema account of scene memory.

3. THE FUNCTION OF VISUAL MEMORY IN SCENE PERCEPTION

The research reviewed thus far has examined the capabilities of visual memory and the means by which memory is used to construct visual representations of scenes. I turn now to the question of the function of visual memory in scene perception. Given that participants can generate robust internal representations of a scene, how and to what purpose is this information used? I first consider the functional role of VSTM and then consider VLTM function.

3.1. The function of VSTM in scene perception

The literature on VSTM has seen a remarkable surge in research over the last decade (for a review, see Luck, 2008). Most of this research has sought to understand the capacity of VSTM and the format of VSTM representations, but the functional purpose of the VSTM system has received relatively little attention. After discussing two common accounts of VSTM function, I argue that VSTM supports perceptual comparison operations that are required almost constantly during real-world perception and behavior.

3.1.1. *VSTM and conscious awareness*

A common proposal regarding VSTM function is that VSTM forms the substrate of visual awareness (Becker & Pashler, 2002; Rensink, 2000; Rensink et al., 1997). In particular, VSTM is thought to reflect activation of the currently attended portion of a visual scene, with constraints on attentional capacity and VSTM capacity reflecting two sides of the same coin (Cowan, 1995; Rensink, 2000). However, it is highly unlikely that VSTM plays any direct role in visual awareness. VSTM representations are not visible and thus are unlikely to be the substrate of visual awareness; one does not continue to *see* the items held in VSTM once they have been removed. For example, one does not see remembered items as persisting during an ISI between study and test images in a change detection task (as in Luck & Vogel, 1997). It is this very property of VSTM—that it is not visible—that distinguishes VSTM from visible persistence (iconic memory), which *is* visible (Coltheart, 1980).

If VSTM does not form the substrate of visual experience, then the fact that we can only hold 3–4 objects in VSTM does not necessarily mean that our visual awareness of a scene is limited to 3–4 objects. Indeed, Sperling (1960) showed that we see a great deal more than we can hold in VSTM. When participants were shown arrays of 12 letters in Sperling's task, they saw 12 letters in the brief moment that they were visible, but they could only transfer 3–4 letter identities into STM for subsequent report. A quick demonstration proves this point. One tells a naïve participant to view a briefly presented visual display. Then one presents an array of 12 letters for 50 ms (as in Sperling, 1960). What observers report is that there were 12 letters, but they can only report the identity of 3–4 of them. Because it is easy to report that there were 12 letters (and not 6 letters or 3 letters), participants must have seen 12 letters when they were visible. If visual awareness was limited to the capacity of VSTM, then participants should have reported that there were only 3–4 letters present. The issue here is that because the report of what one saw requires memory, limitations on memory can easily be confused with limitations on perceptual experience (Chun & Potter, 1995; Moore & Egeth, 1997; Vogel & Luck, 2002; for a full discussion, see Wolfe, 1999).

3.1.2. *VSTM and perceptual integration*

A second proposal regarding the function of VSTM is that VSTM supports the integration of perceptual information across disruptions in visual input (e.g., Brockmole, Irwin, & Wang, 2002; Irwin, 1992). In particular, VSTM has been proposed to play a central role in the integration of visual information across saccadic eye movements. In this view, as attention and the eyes are directed to objects in scenes, information from the attended target of the next saccade (and perhaps 1–2 additional objects) is consolidated into VSTM. Upon landing, newly acquired perceptual information is integrated with the stored information in VSTM. Support for this proposal has come from evidence that participants can remember properties of the saccade target object in VSTM across a saccade (Irwin, 1992; Irwin & Andrews, 1996) and that a preview of an object prior to a saccade leads to speeded naming of that object when the eyes land (Henderson & Anes, 1994; Henderson, Pollatsek, & Rayner, 1987; Pollatsek, Rayner, & Collins, 1984). Although these effects certainly demonstrate that visual representations can be stored in VSTM across an eye movement, they do not necessarily indicate that VSTM is used to *integrate* perceptual information available on separate fixations into a composite representation. And, given the very limited capacity of VSTM—1 or 2 natural objects during scene viewing (Hollingworth, 2004)—any possible integration would have to be minimal and local; VSTM certainly could not support any large-scale integration of scene information.

A few studies have directly examined the role of VSTM in visual integration. It is well established that visible persistence integrates with a trailing stimulus if the SOA between the two stimuli is very short (< 80 ms). For example, Di Lollo (1980) displayed sequentially two arrays of dots in a grid pattern. In the first array, half of the grid cells contained dots. In the second array, dots filled all but one of the cells that were unfilled in the first array. Between the two arrays, one grid cell did not contain a dot, and the task was to specify the location of the "missing dot". At very short SOAs, the visible persistence of the first array integrates with perceptual processing of the second, and participants see a single array with all but one cell filled (which made the task very easy to perform). However, at slightly longer SOAs, no such integration was observed, likely to due to masking of the first array by the second.

Brockmole et al. (2002) extended this approach to examine integration at SOAs likely to be supported by VSTM. At long SOAs (greater than 1,000 ms), performance on the missing-dot task increased significantly, returning to levels similar to those observed at very short SOAs, when perceptual integration is known to occur. Brockmole et al. concluded that VSTM can indeed support perceptual integration. However, Hollingworth, Hyun, and Zhang (2005) and Jiang, Kumar, and Vickery (2005) found that at long SOAs, the task typically is performed not by integrating information in VSTM but, rather, by comparing memory for the empty cells of the first array with the occupied locations in the second array (the one empty cell from the first array that does not have a dot in the second array is the location of the "missing dot") . This alternative is consistent with a general role for VSTM in perceptual comparison, reviewed subsequently. Although the results of Hollingworth et al. and Jiang et al. do not rule out the possibility that participants can solve the missing-dot task by integration in VSTM, high levels of performance at long ISIs cannot be taken as strong evidence of such integration. In summary, although VSTM could potentially support the integration of scene information, little direct evidence for integration in VSTM has been found, and the highly limited capacity of VSTM dictates that any potential for integration must also be highly limited.

3.1.3. *VSTM and perceptual comparison*

The main thesis of this section is that an important function of VSTM is to enable the comparison of perceptual information obtained from objects divided by space, time, or perceptual disruption. For example, if one is trying to decide whether a pie is ready to come out of the oven, one might encode perceptual information about the pie (how browned it is; whether the filling is bubbling at the edges), store that information in VSTM, shift attention and the eyes to the cookbook, and then compare the stored information about the perceptual properties of the pie to the picture in the cookbook. Note that in order for such perceptual comparison to be possible, one's memory for the pie must be maintained after attention is withdrawn from the pie and shifted to the cookbook (Gajewski & Brockmole, 2006; Hollingworth & Henderson, 2002; Johnson et al., 2008). A VSTM system limited to the currently attended object would be of little practical value in complex multiple-object scenes. Because the comparison of spatially separated objects will almost always require a shift of attention (and likely an eye movement) from one object to the other, VSTM is necessary to store information about the first object entering into the comparison as attention is redirected to acquire perceptual information from the second object entering into the comparison.

In addition to comparing two spatially separated objects, VSTM supports a number of other perceptual comparison operations. One well-studied case arises in visual search. Duncan and Humphreys (1989) proposed that during visual search, VSTM is used to maintain perceptual information about the target of the search. When attending sequentially to objects in the course of search, the search template maintained in VSTM is compared with the perceptual properties of each attended object, allowing one to determine whether the currently attended object is the target or a distractor. In addition, attention is biased during search toward objects that match the perceptual features of the target maintained in VSTM (Chelazzi, Miller, Duncan, & Desimone, 1993; Desimone & Duncan, 1995; Olivers, Meijer, & Theeuwes, 2006; Soto, Heinke, Humphreys, & Blanco, 2005).

Several studies have tested the functional role of VSTM in search using dual-task interference methods. Woodman, Vogel, and Luck (2001) had participants perform a search task either with or without a concurrent VSTM load of colors. If VSTM is required to maintain search-target properties, then filling VSTM with a secondary color load should interfere with comparison operations during search, reducing the efficiency of the search. Woodman et al. found effects of VSTM load on the intercept of the function relating RT to set size, but no effect on the slope of the search function. They interpreted this result as indicating that VSTM was not necessary for efficient search. However, the Woodman et al. search task used the same search target on every trial, raising the possibility that participants encoded the search target into VLTM, thereby minimizing the need to maintain the target in VSTM. In a subsequent study, Woodman, Luck, and Schall (2007) changed the properties of the search target on every trial, which should have placed greater demand on VSTM to maintain the currently relevant target properties. Under these conditions, a concurrent VSTM load of colors did impair search efficiency, providing support for the original Duncan and Humphreys (1989) proposal.

Perhaps the most frequent use of VSTM in scene perception involves the mapping of objects across temporal gaps and disruptions in perceptual input. As we interact perceptually with a complex scene, dynamic properties of the observer (shifts of attention and the eyes, blinks, motion) and of the world (object motion, occlusion) create gaps in perceptual input. One of the central challenges of vision is to establish the correspondence between objects visible before and after a disruption. For example, if I make an eye movement from a coffee cup to a pen, the coffee cup lies at the fovea before the saccade and the pen in the periphery. After the saccade is completed, the pen lies at the fovea and the cup in the periphery. The retinal locations of all other visible objects change as well. How does the visual system establish the mapping of objects visible before and after the saccade? One solution is that properties of objects visible before the saccade are stored in VSTM across the saccade and compared with perceptual information available after the saccade (Currie, McConkie, Carlson-Radvansky, & Irwin, 2000; Henderson & Hollingworth, 2003a; Irwin, 1992). In this manner, VSTM could support the perception of scene continuity (i.e., that objects visible now correspond to objects visible a moment ago) despite gaps, disruptions, and changes in perceptual input.

The use of VSTM to establish correspondence across perceptual disruption is particularly important when there is ambiguity in object mapping. This circumstance arises frequently during natural-scene viewing. Saccadic eye movements occur almost constantly, but they are highly prone to error, with the eyes often missing the target of the saccade. Such saccade errors are likely to occur thousands of times each day during normal activities. When the eyes miss the saccade target in a complex scene, there are likely to be multiple objects near the landing position of that saccade. Hollingworth et al. (2008) hypothesized that VSTM is used to remember visual properties of the saccade target object, so that after an inaccurate saccade the target can be found among other nearby objects and gaze efficiently corrected (via a rapid corrective saccade). To test this hypothesis, Hollingworth et al. developed a paradigm that simulated object ambiguity after an inaccurate eye movement. Participants fixated the center of a circular array of colored disks. One disk was cued, and the participant generated a saccade to that object. During the saccade (when vision is suppressed) the entire array was rotated by one half of the distance between adjacent objects. This typically caused the eyes to land between two objects: the target object and a distractor object. To accurately correct gaze to the target, perceptual information from before the saccade (such as the target's color) must be retained across the saccade in VSTM and then compared with objects near the landing position.

Hollingworth et al. (2008) found that VSTM-based gaze correction in this paradigm was highly accurate and efficient. The use of VSTM to correct gaze added only 40 ms to the latency of the corrective saccade (compared with a single-object control condition in which memory was not needed to correct gaze). Similar results were observed using novel objects of similar complexity to objects found in the world. In addition, the accuracy and speed of gaze correction was impaired by a concurrent VSTM load but not by a concurrent verbal WM load, demonstrating that VSTM is indeed functional in establishing object correspondence across saccades. Finally, VSTM-based corrective saccades were generated even when participants were instructed to avoid making them, suggesting that VSTM-based correction is a largely automatized skill. Given that we make hundreds of thousands of saccades each day and many of these fail to land on the saccade target, the use of VSTM to correct gaze is likely to be a central function of the VSTM system.

3.2. The function of VLTM in scene perception

In what manner does VLTM for a scene influence perceptual processing of that scene? First of all, VLTM for scenes allows us to recognize scenes and categorize them. However, there has been surprisingly little research examining the mechanisms of scene identification. Initial evidence suggests that scene identification depends on global scene properties rather than local analysis of constituent objects (Oliva & Torralba, 2006). In addition, scene identification is extraordinarily rapid (Potter & Levy, 1969; Thorpe, Fize, & Marlot, 1996). Efficient scene identification raises the possibility that scene memory might influence even fairly early perceptual operations over a scene. I shall first consider whether scene identification influences the perceptual recognition of objects in a scene. I then examine the role of scene knowledge in guiding attention to task-relevant areas of a scene.

3.2.1. *Effects of scene memory on object recognition*

Hollingworth and Henderson (1998) identified three possible means by which one's knowledge about a particular scene type (e.g., that kitchens tend to contain stoves but not motorcycles) could influence the identification of constituent objects. First, scene knowledge could interact with early visual processing to enhance the perceptual description of scene-consistent objects (*description enhancement*). Second, scene knowledge could influence the comparison of perceptual object representations to stored category representations, lowering goodness-of-fit thresholds for consistent object categories (*criterion modulation*). Third, scene knowledge could be isolated from object recognition operations, influencing only postperceptual reasoning (*functional isolation*).

When examining the influence of scene knowledge on the perceptual recognition of objects, it is critical to ensure that participants cannot use their knowledge of scenes to make an educated guess. For example, if one is blindfolded, taken into a kitchen, and asked to name the large appliance in the corner, one could reason that the probed object is likely to be a stove or a refrigerator (rather than a washing machine or an air conditioner) in the absence of any visual input at all. Early studies examining the effects of scene context on object recognition found that semantically consistent objects (e.g., a computer in an office) were recognize more accurately than inconsistent objects (e.g., a computer in a bathroom) (Biederman et al., 1982; Palmer, 1975). However, educated guessing was not adequately controlled in these studies. The consistent-object advantage could have derived from the fact that participants were biased to report consistent objects, without any direct effect of scene context on the perceptual mechanisms of object recognition.

To provide a better measure of scene context effects on perceptual object recognition, Hollingworth and Henderson (1998) used a 2-AFC method similar to that developed by Reicher (1969; see also D. D. Wheeler, 1970) to examine the effects of word context on letter identification. On each trial, participants saw a brief display of a scene containing either a semantically consistent target object or an inconsistent target object. The scene was followed by two object labels of equivalent consistency. For example, a kitchen scene (or, in the inconsistent condition, a farm scene) contained a mixer target object followed by the labels "mixer" and "coffee maker". Because the two alternatives were both either consistent or inconsistent with the scene, educated guessing on the basis of scene knowledge could not influence performance. With this control over guessing, no advantage for the detection of consistent objects was observed, supporting the functional isolation hypothesis. The Hollingworth and Henderson (1998) results indicate that we accurately see what is present in a scene and not necessarily what we expect to see. Given the opportunity to guess, however, biases generated by scene knowledge will influence report.

Recently, Davenport and Potter (2004; see also Davenport, 2007) revisited the issue of scene context effects. In their paradigm, participants viewed stimuli consisting of a background scene and a prominent foreground object, with the consistency between the two manipulated. After brief presentation of each scene, participants named the foreground object. Davenport and Potter observed more accurate naming of consistent versus inconsistent objects. However, these experiments represent something of a methodological step backward, because Davenport and Potter did not adequately control educated guessing. In this naming paradigm, when an object was not fully identified, participants could use their knowledge of the scene to bias the naming response toward consistent objects (see Palmer, 1975), as the target was more likely to be one of the relatively small set of objects consistent with the scene than one of the large set of objects inconsistent with the scene. Davenport and Potter did include a guessing correction that involved subtracting incorrect reports of consistent objects from correct reports, but simple subtraction is not sufficient when bias could be influencing report (Green & Swets, 1966). In general, any paradigm with an unbound set of alternatives (as in naming) is subject to selection biases that can be very difficult to eliminate. It was precisely for this reason that Reicher (1969) developed the 2-AFC method used by Hollingworth and Henderson (1998).

In summary, current evidence indicates that when educated guessing is adequately controlled, consistent objects are detected no more efficiently than are inconsistent objects. This does not imply, however, that there are no effects of scene knowledge on the perceptual processing of objects. Scene knowledge can guide attention to particular objects in a scene that are relevant to the current task, reviewed below. In addition, context influences the extent of perceptual and cognitive processing devoted to an object. For example, inconsistent objects, once identified, are fixated longer in a scene than are consistent objects (Henderson, Weeks, & Hollingworth, 1999).

3.2.2. *Effects of scene memory on knowing where to look*

One of the principal functions of VLTM for scenes is to store information about the locations of objects so that they can be found efficiently later (for additional discussion of the role of memory in search, see chapter 2, section 4). We know where most of the objects in our own homes are located, and when we search for an object, we tend to look first in those locations where memory tells us it is likely to be found. In addition, even without any knowledge of a particular environment (e.g., in the kitchen of a new acquaintance), we still know roughly where different types of objects are likely to be located.

Hollingworth (in press) examined two forms of scene memory that are likely to control the allocation of attention in a scene during visual search: memory for the remembered location of a specific object (which could guide attention directly to the target location), and memory for the spatial layout of a scene (which could guide attention to the locations where the target object was likely to be found). On each trial, participants viewed a preview display of a complex real-world scene for 10 s. Then a single object was presented in isolation at the center of the screen. This was the search target. Finally, the scene was displayed again, and participants found the search target as quickly as possible. To ensure that participants had to find the target object in each scene, the left–right orientation of the target was randomly varied in the search scene, and participants had to report whether its orientation matched the orientation of the search target displayed before the search. There were three principal conditions. In the *preview-with-target* condition, the target object was present in the preview scene. In the *preview-without-target* condition, the target was not present in the preview scene. In the *no-preview* condition, no preview scene was displayed before the search. This final condition served as a baseline measure of search efficiency, when no memory for the scene was available to aid search.

First of all, memory for the general layout of the scene significantly facilitated search. Search efficiency, as measured both by RT and the elapsed time to the first fixation on the target, was significantly faster in the preview-without-target condition than in the no-preview condition. Memory for the specific location of the target further facilitated search, with faster search in the preview-with-target condition than in the preview-without-target condition. In the preview-with-target condition, participants fixated the target almost immediately after the onset of the search scene, with the very first saccade in the scene typically directed to the target. Thus, both forms of memory (general layout and specific object locations) efficiently guide search within complex scenes (see also Castelhano & Henderson, 2007).

Similar facilitation is observed when participants conduct repeated search through a natural scene. Brockmole and Henderson (2006) had participants search for letters embedded within photographs of real-world scenes. Half of the scene items were repeated. Search through repeated scenes became highly efficient, and a single repetition was sufficient to influence search times. As in Hollingworth (in press), participants quickly learned the location of targets in each repeated scene and could use that memory to guide attention during search. Subsequent experiments demonstrated that memory for the locations of objects is coded relative to a global contextual representation of the scene (Brockmole, Castelhano, & Henderson, 2006).

Finally, memory for categories of scenes also influences search in the absence of any prior exposure to a particular scene. Torralba, Oliva, Castelhano, and Henderson (2006) had participants view scenes with the task of counting the number of people, paintings, or mugs within a scene. Almost immediately upon the onset of search, gaze was directed to locations within the scene where the target object would have been likely to occur (e.g., the walls of a room when participants were searching for paintings).

These results using search in real-world scenes contrast with traditional search experiments using random arrays of simple stimuli. Although memory does influence search over random arrays (Chun & Jiang, 1998), such learning emerges only after multiple repetitions of a particular array, target location is coded relative to local array elements, and learning is typically implicit (for details, see chapter 2, section 4.2). In contrast, a single exposure to a real-world scene can reduce search time by as much as 35% (Hollingworth, in press), memory for scene types guides search even within scenes that have never been viewed before (Torralba et al., 2006), target position is coded relative to global scene elements (Brockmole et al., 2006), and the learning of object locations in scenes is explicitly available rather than implicit (Brockmole & Henderson, 2006). As the literature on visual search moves further toward understanding how search occurs under real-world conditions, researchers will need to use more complex real-world scene stimuli for which visual search mechanisms (and visual memory) are optimized.

4. CONCLUSIONS

Scene perception is a dynamic process in which attention and the eyes are deployed serially to objects of interest. Visual memory is used to retain information from previously attended objects in support of basic perceptual operations, such as mapping objects across frequent perceptual disruptions and ensuring that the eyes are efficiently directed to goal-relevant objects. In addition, object information accumulates in VLTM as attention is directed from object to object in a scene. Over the course of viewing, participants are able to construct an internal visual representation of the scene that is composed of higher-level visual object representations bound to locations within a spatial representation of the scene. These scene representations are then stored robustly over long periods of time and with minimal interference. Upon re-examination of a scene, long-term scene representations are retrieved efficiently and can be used to guide attention and the eyes to task-relevant regions of the scene.

5. REFERENCES

Alba, J., & Hasher, L. (1983). Is memory schematic? *Psychological Bulletin, 93,* 203–231.

Allen, R. J., Baddeley, A. D., & Hitch, G. J. (2006). Is the binding of visual features in working memory resource-demanding? *Journal of Experimental Psychology: General, 135,* 298–313.

Alvarez, G. A., & Cavanagh, P. (2004). The capacity of visual short-term memory is set both by visual information load and by number of objects. *Psychological Science, 15,* 106–111.

Averbach, E., & Coriell, A. S. (1961). Short-term memory in vision. *The Bell System Technical Journal, 40,* 309–328.

Ballard, D. H., Hayhoe, M. M., & Pelz, J. B. (1995). Memory representations in natural tasks. *Journal of Cognitive Neuroscience, 7,* 66–80.

Ballard, D. H., Hayhoe, M. M., Pook, P. K., & Rao, R. P. (1997). Deictic codes for the embodiment of cognition. *Behavioral & Brain Sciences, 20,* 723–767.

Bartlett, F. C. (1932). *Remembering: An experimental and social study.* Cambridge, UK: Cambridge University Press.

Becker, M. W., & Pashler, H. (2002). Volatile visual representations: Failing to detect changes in recently processed information. *Psychonomic Bulletin & Review, 9,* 744–750.

Biederman, I., Mezzanotte, R. J., & Rabinowitz, J. C. (1982). Scene perception: Detecting and judging objects undergoing relational violations. *Cognitive Psychology, 14,* 143–177.

Brewer, W. F., & Treyens, J. C. (1981). Role of schemata in memory for places. *Cognitive Psychology, 13,* 207–230.

Brockmole, J. R., Castelhano, M. S., & Henderson, J. M. (2006). Contextual cueing in naturalistic scenes: Global and local contexts. *Journal of Experimental Psychology: Learning, Memory, and Cognition, 32,* 699–706.

Brockmole, J. R., & Henderson, J. M. (2006). Using real-world scenes as contextual cues for search. *Visual Cognition, 13,* 99–108.

Brockmole, J. R., Irwin, D. E., & Wang, R. F. (2002). Temporal integration of visual images and visual percepts. *Journal of Experimental Psychology: Human Perception and Performance, 28,* 315–334.

Burgess, N., Maguire, E. A., & O'Keefe, J. (2002). The human hippocampus and spatial and episodic memory. *Neuron, 35,* 625–641.

Castelhano, M. S., & Henderson, J. M. (2007). Initial scene representations facilitate eye movement guidance in visual search. *Journal of Experimental Psychology: Human Perception and Performance, 33,* 753–763.

Chelazzi, L., Miller, E. K., Duncan, J., & Desimone, R. (1993). A neural basis for visual-search in inferior temporal cortex. *Nature, 363,* 345–347.

Chun, M. M. (2003). Scene perception and memory. *Psychology of Learning and Motivation, 42,* 79–108.

Chun, M. M., & Jiang, Y. (1998). Contextual cueing: Implicit learning and memory of visual context guides spatial attention. *Cognitive Psychology, 36,* 28–71.

Chun, M. M., & Potter, M. C. (1995). A two-stage model for multiple target detection in rapid serial visual presentation. *Journal of Experimental Psychology: Human Perception and Performance, 21,* 109–127.

Coltheart, M. (1980). The persistences of vision. *Philosophical Transactions of the Royal Society of London, Series B, 290,* 269–294.

Cowan, N. (1995). *Attention and memory: An integrated framework.* New York: Oxford University Press.

Currie, C., McConkie, G., Carlson-Radvansky, L. A., & Irwin, D. E. (2000). The role of the saccade target object in the perception of a visually stable world. *Perception & Psychophysics, 62,* 673–683.

Davenport, J. L. (2007). Consistency effects between objects in scenes. *Memory & Cognition, 35,* 393–401.

Davenport, J. L., & Potter, M. C. (2004). Scene consistency in object and background perception. *Psychological Science, 15,* 559–564.

Davidson, M. L., Fox, M. J., & Dick, A. O. (1973). Effect of eye movements on backward masking and perceived location. *Perception & Psychophysics, 14,* 110–116.

Desimone, R., & Duncan, J. (1995). Neural mechanisms of selective visual attention. *Annual Review of Neuroscience, 18,* 193–222.

Deubel, H., & Schneider, W. X. (1996). Saccade target selection and object recognition: Evidence for a common attentional mechanism. *Vision Research, 36,* 1827–1837.

Di Lollo, V. (1980). Temporal integration in visual memory. *Journal of Experimental Psychology: General, 109,* 75–97.

Duncan, J., & Humphreys, G. (1989). Visual search and stimulus similarity. *Psychological Review, 96,* 433–458.

Eng, H. Y., Chen, D. Y., & Jiang, Y. H. (2005). Visual working memory for simple and complex visual stimuli. *Psychonomic Bulletin & Review, 12,* 1127–1133.

Friedman, A. (1979). Framing pictures: The role of knowledge in automatized encoding and memory for gist. *Journal of Experimental Psychology: General, 108,* 316–355.

Gajewski, D. A., & Brockmole, J. R. (2006). Feature bindings endure without attention: Evidence from an explicit recall task. *Psychonomic Bulletin & Review, 13,* 581–587.

Green, D. M., & Swets, J. A. (1966). *Signal detection theory and psychophysics.* New York: Wiley.

Grimes, J. (1996). On the failure to detect changes in scenes across saccades. In K. Akins (Ed.), *Perception: Vancouver studies in cognitive science, Vol. 5* (pp. 89–110). Oxford, UK: Oxford University Press.

Hayhoe, M. M. (2000). Vision using routines: A functional account of vision. *Visual Cognition, 7,* 43–64.

Hayhoe, M. M., Bensinger, D. G., & Ballard, D. H. (1998). Task constraints in visual working memory. *Vision Research, 38,* 125–137.

Henderson, J. M., & Anes, M. D. (1994). Effects of object-file review and type priming on visual identification within and across eye fixations. *Journal of Experimental Psychology: Human Perception and Performance, 20,* 826–839.

Henderson, J. M., & Hollingworth, A. (1999a). High-level scene perception. *Annual Review of Psychology, 50,* 243–271.

Henderson, J. M., & Hollingworth, A. (1999b). The role of fixation position in detecting scene changes across saccades. *Psychological Science, 10,* 438–443.

Henderson, J. M., & Hollingworth, A. (2003a). Eye movements and visual memory: Detecting changes to saccade targets in scenes. *Perception & Psychophysics, 65,* 58–71.

Henderson, J. M., & Hollingworth, A. (2003b). Global transsaccadic change blindness during scene perception. *Psychological Science, 14,* 493–497.

Henderson, J. M., Pollatsek, A., & Rayner, K. (1987). Effects of foveal priming and extrafoveal preview on object identification. *Journal of Experimental Psychology: Human Perception and Performance, 13,* 449–463.

Henderson, J. M., Weeks, P. A., & Hollingworth, A. (1999). The effects of semantic consistency on eye movements during complex scene viewing. *Journal of Experimental Psychology: Human Perception and Performance, 25,* 210–228.

Hoffman, J. E., & Subramaniam, B. (1995). The role of visual attention in saccadic eye movements. *Perception & Psychophysics, 57,* 787–795.

Hollingworth, A. (2003). Failures of retrieval and comparison constrain change detection in natural scenes. *Journal of Experimental Psychology: Human Perception and Performance, 29,* 388–403.

Hollingworth, A. (2004). Constructing visual representations of natural scenes: The roles of short- and long-term visual memory. *Journal of Experimental Psychology: Human Perception and Performance, 30,* 519–537.

Hollingworth, A. (2005). The relationship between online visual representation of a scene and long-term scene memory. *Journal of Experimental Psychology: Learning, Memory, and Cognition, 31,* 396–411.

Hollingworth, A. (2006). Scene and position specificity in visual memory for objects. *Journal of Experimental Psychology: Learning, Memory, and Cognition, 32,* 58–69.

Hollingworth, A. (2007). Object-position binding in visual memory for natural scenes and object arrays. *Journal of Experimental Psychology: Human Perception and Performance, 33,* 31–47.

Hollingworth, A. (2008). Visual memory for natural scenes. In S. J. Luck & A. Hollingworth (Eds.), *Visual memory* (pp. 123–162). New York: Oxford University Press.

Hollingworth, A. (in press). Two forms of scene memory guide visual search: Memory for scene context and memory for the binding of target object to scene location. *Visual Cognition.*

Hollingworth, A., & Henderson, J. M. (1998). Does consistent scene context facilitate object perception? *Journal of Experimental Psychology: General, 127,* 398–415.

Hollingworth, A., & Henderson, J. M. (2000). Semantic informativeness mediates the detection of changes in natural scenes. *Visual Cognition, 7,* 213–235.

Hollingworth, A., & Henderson, J. M. (2002). Accurate visual memory for previously attended objects in natural scenes. *Journal of Experimental Psychology: Human Perception and Performance, 28,* 113–136.

Hollingworth, A., & Henderson, J. M. (2003). Testing a conceptual locus for the inconsistent object change detection advantage in real-world scenes. *Memory & Cognition, 31,* 930–940.

Hollingworth, A., Hyun, J. S., & Zhang, W. (2005). The role of visual short-term memory in empty cell localization. *Perception & Psychophysics, 67,* 1332–1343.

Hollingworth, A., Richard, A. M., & Luck, S. J. (2008). Understanding the function of visual short-term memory: Transsaccadic memory, object correspondence, and gaze correction. *Journal of Experimental Psychology: General, 137,* 163–181.

Hollingworth, A., Williams, C. C., & Henderson, J. M. (2001). To see and remember: Visually specific information is retained in memory from previously attended objects in natural scenes. *Psychonomic Bulletin & Review, 8,* 761–768.

Intraub, H. (1997). The representation of visual scenes. *Trends in Cognitive Sciences, 1,* 217–222.

Irwin, D. E. (1991). Information integration across saccadic eye movements. *Cognitive Psychology, 23,* 420–456.

Irwin, D. E. (1992). Memory for position and identity across eye movements. *Journal of Experimental Psychology: Learning, Memory, and Cognition, 18,* 307–317.

Irwin, D. E., & Andrews, R. (1996). Integration and accumulation of information across saccadic eye movements. In T. Inui & J. L. McClelland (Eds.), *Attention and performance XVI: Information integration in perception and communication* (pp. 125–155). Cambridge, MA: MIT Press.

Irwin, D. E., Yantis, S., & Jonides, J. (1983). Evidence against visual integration across saccadic eye movements. *Perception & Psychophysics, 34,* 35–46.

Irwin, D. E., & Yeomans, J. M. (1986). Sensory registration and informational persistence. *Journal of Experimental Psychology: Human Perception and Performance, 12,* 343–360.

Irwin, D. E., & Zelinsky, G. J. (2002). Eye movements and scene perception: Memory for things observed. *Perception & Psychophysics, 64,* 882–895.

Jiang, Y., Kumar, A., & Vickery, T. J. (2005). Integrating sequential arrays in visual short-term memory. *Experimental Psychology, 52,* 39–46.

Jiang, Y., Olson, I. R., & Chun, M. M. (2000). Organization of visual short-term memory. *Journal of Experimental Psychology: Learning, Memory, and Cognition, 26,* 683–702.

Johnson, J. S., Hollingworth, A., & Luck, S. J. (2008). The role of attention in the maintenance of feature bindings in visual short-term memory. *Journal of Experimental Psychology: Human Perception and Performance, 34,* 41–55.

Jonides, J., Irwin, D. E., & Yantis, S. (1982). Integrating visual information from successive fixations. *Science, 215,* 192–194.

Kahneman, D., Treisman, A., & Gibbs, B. J. (1992). The reviewing of object files: Object-specific integration of information. *Cognitive Psychology, 24,* 175–219.

Land, M. F., Mennie, N., & Rusted, J. (1999). Eye movements and the roles of vision in activities of daily living: Making a cup of tea. *Perception, 28,* 1311–1328.

Luck, S. J. (2008). Visual short-term memory. In S. J. Luck & A. Hollingworth (Eds.), *Visual Memory* (pp. 43–86). New York: Oxford University Press.

Luck, S. J., & Vogel, E. K. (1997). The capacity of visual working memory for features and conjunctions. *Nature, 390,* 279–281.

Mandler, J. M., & Parker, R. E. (1976). Memory for descriptive and spatial information in complex pictures. *Journal of Experimental Psychology: Human Learning and Memory,* *2,* 38–48.

Mandler, J. M., & Ritchey, G. H. (1977). Long-term memory for pictures. *Journal of Experimental Psychology: Human Learning and Memory, 3,* 386–396.

Matin, E. (1974). Saccadic suppression: A review and an analysis. *Psychological Bulletin,* *81,* 899–917.

McConkie, G. W., & Rayner, K. (1975). The span of the effective stimulus during a fixation in reading. *Perception and Psychophysics,* 578–586.

Moore, C. M., & Egeth, H. (1997). Perception without attention: Evidence of grouping under conditions of inattention. *Journal of Experimental Psychology: Human Perception and Performance, 23,* 339–352.

Nickerson, R. S. (1965). Short-term memory for complex meaningful visual configurations: A demonstration of capacity. *Canadian Journal of Psychology, 19,* 155–160.

Nickerson, R. S. (1968). A note on long-term recognition memory for pictorial material. *Psychonomic Science, 11,* 58.

O'Keefe, J., & Nadel, L. (1978). *The hippocampus as a cognitive map.* Oxford, UK: Clarendon Press.

Oliva, A., & Torralba, A. (2006). Building the gist of a scene: The role of global image features in recognition. *Progress in Brain Research, 155,* 23–36.

Olivers, C. N. L., Meijer, F., & Theeuwes, J. (2006). Feature-based memory-driven attentional capture: Visual working memory content affects visual attention. *Journal of Experimental Psychology: Human Perception and Performance, 32,* 1243–1265.

O'Regan, J. K. (1992). Solving the "real" mysteries of visual perception: The world as an outside memory. *Canadian Journal of Psychology, 46,* 461–488.

O'Regan, J. K., & Lévy-Schoen, A. (1983). Integrating visual information from successive fixations: Does trans-saccadic fusion exist? *Vision Research, 23,* 765–768.

O'Regan, J. K., & Noë, A. (2001). A sensorimotor account of vision and visual consciousness. *Behavioral and Brain Sciences, 24,* 939–1011.

Palmer, S. E. (1975). The effects of contextual scenes on the identification of objects. *Memory & Cognition, 3,* 519–526.

Pashler, H. (1988). Familiarity and the detection of change in visual displays. *Perception & Psychophysics, 44,* 369–378.

Pedzek, K., Whetstone, T., Reynolds, K., Askari, N., & Dougherty, T. (1989). Memory for real-world scenes: The role of consistency with schema expectations. *Journal of Experimental Psychology: Learning, Memory, and Cognition, 15,* 587–595.

Phillips, W. A. (1974). On the distinction between sensory storage and short-term visual memory. *Perception & Psychophysics, 16,* 283–290.

Phillips, W. A., & Christie, D. F. M. (1977). Components of visual memory. *Quarterly Journal of Experimental Psychology, 29,* 117–133.

Pollatsek, A., Rayner, K., & Collins, W. E. (1984). Integrating pictorial information across eye movements. *Journal of Experimental Psychology: General, 113,* 426–442.

Potter, M. C., & Levy, E. I. (1969). Recognition memory for a rapid sequence of pictures. *Journal of Experimental Psychology, 81,* 10–15.

Potter, M. C., Staub, A., & O'Connor, D. H. (2004). Pictorial and conceptual representation of glimpsed pictures. *Journal of Experimental Psychology: Human Perception and Performance, 30,* 478–489.

Rayner, K., & Pollatsek, A. (1983). Is visual information integrated across saccades? *Perception & Psychophysics, 34,* 39–48.

Reicher, G. M. (1969). Perceptual recognition as a function of meaningfulness of stimulus material. *Journal of Experimental Psychology, 81,* 275–280.

Rensink, R. A. (2000). The dynamic representation of scenes. *Visual Cognition, 7,* 17–42.

Rensink, R. A. (2002). Change detection. *Annual Review of Psychology, 53,* 245–277.

Rensink, R. A., O'Regan, J. K., & Clark, J. J. (1997). To see or not to see: The need for attention to perceive changes in scenes. *Psychological Science, 8,* 368–373.

Ryan, J. D., Althoff, R. R., Whitlow, S., & Cohen, N. J. (2000). Amnesia is a deficit in relational memory. *Psychological Science, 8,* 368–373.

Schmidt, B. K., Vogel, E. K., Woodman, G. F., & Luck, S. J. (2002). Voluntary and automatic attentional control of visual working memory. *Perception & Psychophysics, 64,* 754–763.

Scholl, B. J. (2000). Attenuated change blindness for exogenously attended items in a flicker paradigm. *Visual Cognition, 7,* 377–396.

Shepard, R. N. (1967). Recognition memory for words, sentences, and pictures. *Journal of Verbal Learning and Verbal Behavior, 6,* 156–163.

Simons, D. J. (1996). In sight, out of mind: When object representations fail. *Psychological Science, 7,* 301–305.

Simons, D. J., Chabris, C. F., Schnur, T., & Levin, D. T. (2002). Evidence for preserved representations in change blindness. *Consciousness and Cognition, 11,* 78–97.

Simons, D. J., & Levin, D. T. (1997). Change blindness. *Trends in Cognitive Sciences, 1,* 261–267.

Simons, D. J., & Levin, D. T. (1998). Failure to detect changes to people during a real-world interaction. *Psychonomic Bulletin & Review, 5,* 644–649.

Soto, D., Heinke, D., Humphreys, G. W., & Blanco, M. J. (2005). Early, involuntary top-down guidance of attention from working memory. *Journal of Experimental Psychology: Human Perception and Performance, 31,* 248–261.

Sperling, G. (1960). The information available in brief visual presentations. *Psychological Monographs, 74*(11, Whole no. 498).

Standing, L. (1973). Learning 10,000 pictures. *Quarterly Journal of Experimental Psychology, 25,* 207–222.

Standing, L., Conezio, J., & Haber, R. N. (1970). Perception and memory for pictures: Single-trial learning of 2500 visual stimuli. *Psychonomic Science, 19,* 73–74.

Tanaka, J. W., & Farah, M. J. (1993). Parts and wholes in face recognition. *Quarterly Journal of Experimental Psychology, 46A,* 225–245.

Tatler, B. W., Gilchrist, I. D., & Land, M. F. (2005). Visual memory for objects in natural scenes: From fixations to object files. *Quarterly Journal of Experimental Psychology, 58A,* 931–960.

Tatler, B. W., Gilchrist, I. D., & Rusted, J. (2003). The time course of abstract visual representation. *Perception, 32,* 579–592.

Thornton, I. M., & Fernandez-Duque, D. (2002). Converging evidence for the detection of change without awareness. In D. P. Munoz, W. Heide, R. Radach, & J. Hyönä (Eds.), *The brain's eyes: Neurobiological and clinical aspects of occulomotor research* (pp. 99–118). Amsterdam: Elsevier.

Thorpe, S., Fize, D., & Marlot, C. (1996). Speed of processing in the human visual system. *Nature, 381,* 520–522.

Torralba, A., Oliva, A., Castelhano, M. S., & Henderson, J. M. (2006). Contextual guidance of eye movements and attention in real-world scenes: The role of global features in object search. *Psychological Review, 113,* 766–786.

Treisman, A. (1988). Features and objects: The fourteenth Bartlett memorial lecture. *Quarterly Journal of Experimental Psychology, 40A,* 201–237.

Varakin, D. A., Levin, D. T., & Collins, K. M. (2007). Both comparison and representation failures cause real-world change blindness. *Perception, 36,* 737–749.

Vogel, E. K., & Luck, S. J. (2002). Delayed working memory consolidation during the attentional blink. *Psychonomic Bulletin & Review, 9,* 739–743.

Wheeler, D. D. (1970). Process in word recognition. *Cognitive Psychology, 1,* 59–85.

Wheeler, M. E., & Treisman, A. M. (2002). Binding in short-term visual memory. *Journal of Experimental Psychology: General, 131,* 48–64.

Wolfe, J. M. (1999). Inattentional amnesia. In V. Coltheart (Ed.), *Fleeting memories* (pp. 71–94). Cambridge, MA: MIT Press.

Wolfe, J. M., Reinecke, A., & Brawn, P. (2006). Why don't we see changes? The role of attentional bottlenecks and limited visual memory. *Visual Cognition, 14,* 749–780.

Woodman, G. F., Luck, S. J., & Schall, J. D. (2007). The role of working memory representations in the control of attention. *Cerebral Cortex, 17,* 118–124.

Woodman, G. F., Vogel, E. K., & Luck, S. J. (2001). Visual search remains efficient when visual working memory is full. *Psychological Science, 12,* 219–224.

Zelinsky, G. J., & Loschky, L. C. (2005). Eye movements serialize memory for objects in scenes. *Perception & Psychophysics, 67,* 676–690.

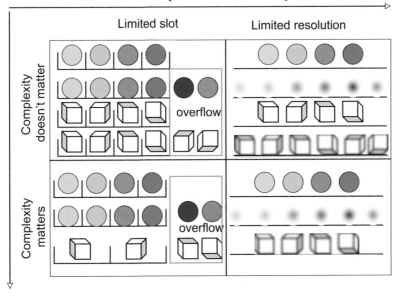

Figure 2.3. Different conceptions of how visual working memory is limited.

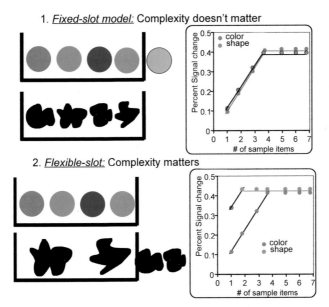

Figure 2.4. Parietal activation as predicted by different models of visual working memory.

Figure 4.1. Eye movement scan path showing the sequence of fixations and saccades during free viewing of a scene for 10 s. Green dots represent fixations and green lines saccades. Note that the eyes typically are directed to discrete objects in the scene and rarely are directed to background regions (such as the sky).

Studied Scene

Test Conditions

	Background Present	Background Absent

Background Present   **Background Absent**

Same Position

Different Position

Figure 4.2. Contextual manipulations in Hollingworth (2007). The top section shows the studied scene. The bottom section shows the target image displayed in the 2-AFC test (in the distractor image, the target was mirror-reversed). When the test objects were displayed within the scene background (background present), there was a reliable discrimination advantage for the same-position condition over the different-position condition. However, when the test objects were displayed against a blank background (background absent), there was no effect of the position of the target object.

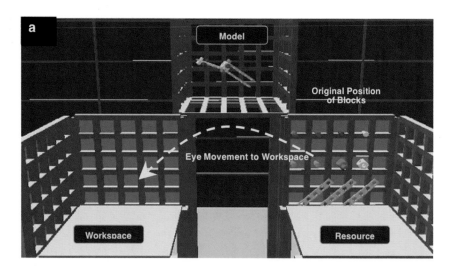

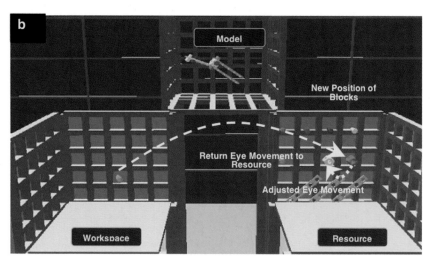

Figure 5.1. (a): View of the virtual environment showing the Model, the Resource area, and the Workspace where the copy is assembled. (b): Illustration of the old–new fixation pattern. The red and yellow pieces change position while the subject is placing the green piece in the Workspace. On the return saccade, shown as the yellow dashed line, the subject lands on the old location of the yellow piece and then makes a corrective saccade to the new location. Adapted by permission from Aivar, M. P., Hayhoe, M. M., Chizk, C. L., & Mruczek, R. E. B. (2005). Spatial memory and saccadic targeting in a natural task. *Journal of Vision, 5*(3), 177–193 (http://www.journalofvision.org/5/3/3/article.aspx). Copyright 2005 The Association for Research in Vision and Opthalmology.

5 Visual memory in motor planning and action

Mary M. Hayhoe
University of Texas, Austin

1. INTRODUCTION

Visual perception is often studied as if our conscious experience were the ultimate end-product of visual processing. However, a major function of visual perception is to control the movements of the body. In the natural world, visual operations are embedded in the context of extended behavioral sequences. For example, a simple action such as picking up an object and placing it somewhere requires visual search to locate the cup, an eye movement to the cup, fixation of the cup during the reaching movement, control of the grasp, locating the target for cup placement, and so on. How do visual processes operate in the service of natural, ongoing behavior such as this? Experiments in vision, described throughout the previous chapters of this book, typically attempt to isolate a single kind of visual process in a brief exposure, or experimental trial, and then examine repeated instances of that process over multiple trials. Natural visual behavior, on the other hand, involves a sequence of different visual operations, the selection and timing of which are under the observer's control. This leads us to question how visual operations operate across time periods of several seconds. For example, to what extent does the current visual operation depend on information obtained in fixations prior to the current one, or are visual operations within a fixation essentially independent? What information in a scene does the observer actually need in order to perform natural visual tasks, and how much of this information was gathered in a prior fixation? That is, how is memory used in natural vision?

Whereas chapter 4 described the memory mechanisms involved in processing a *view of the real world*, in this chapter I focus on memory processes that observers use to guide their natural behavior when they are immersed *in the real world*. Investigation of visual performance in natural tasks is now much more feasible because of the development of complex virtual environments, as well as technical developments in monitoring eye, head, and hand movements in unconstrained observers. This permits some degree of experimental control while allowing relatively natural behavior. In natural behavior, the task structure is evident, and this allows the role of individual fixations to be fairly easily interpreted, because the task provides an external referent for the internal computations (Ballard, Hayhoe, & Pelz, 1995; Droll, Hayhoe, Triesch, & Sullivan, 2006). In contrast, when subjects simply passively view images, the experimenter often has little control of, and no access to what the observer is doing. When viewing pictures, observers may be engaged in object recognition (chapter 4, section 3.2.1), remembering object locations and identity (chapter 4, section 3.2.2), or performing some other visual operation (e.g., chapter 4, section 3.1). Immersion in a real scene calls for different kinds of visual computation. For example, observers need to get information about avoiding obstacles, stepping over curbs, and controlling their direction—information that must be extracted from the dynamic three-dimensional image structure. Additionally, the visual image itself depends on the actions of the observer as he or she moves through the scene, generating a complex spatiotemporal image sequence as a result of eye, head, and body motion. Thus the natural world provides challenges for the visual system that are hard to investigate in simple noninteractive displays. What is the nature of those challenges?

Measurement of gaze location provides important insight into the visual information that is required for natural visually guided behavior. Deployment of gaze during tasks such as driving, walking, playing sports, hand-washing, or making tea or sandwiches has revealed that fixations are tightly linked to the performance of the task (Hayhoe, Shrivastava, Mruczek, & Pelz, 2003; Land & Lee, 1994; Land & Furneaux, 1997; Land, Mennie, & Rusted, 1999; Patla & Vickers, 1997; Pelz & Canosa, 2001; Turano, Geruschat, & Baker, 2003). Subjects exhibit regular, stereotyped fixation sequences as they perform the task. Very few irrelevant areas are fixated, and the fixations are tightly linked, in time, to the actions, such as grasping and placing objects. Fixation moves on to the next object when the needs of the current action have been met (Hayhoe et al., 2003; Johansson, Westling, Backstrom, & Flanagan, 2001; Land et al., 1999). This has been called a "just-in-time" strategy (Ballard et al., 1995). Not only is the sequence of fixations tightly linked to the task, but, in addition, many of the fixations appear to have the purpose of obtaining quite specific information. For example, in driving, Land has shown that drivers reliably fixate the tangent point of the curve to control steering around the curve (Land & Lee, 1994). The angle of gaze with respect to the body then gives the required steering angle. Other work in more controlled tasks has revealed that the information acquired in a particular fixation may be highly specific. For example, when picking up an object, the specific features of the object, such as color or height, that are relevant to the momentary task, are selectively attended and retained in memory, rather than in an integrated representation of the object such as an object file (Droll et al., 2006; Hayhoe, Bensinger & Ballard, 1998; Triesch, Ballard, Hayhoe, & Sullivan, 2003) (for more on feature binding in VWM, see chapter 1, section 5.2, and chapter 2, section 2.3).

Given that the acquisition of information in natural vision is task-specific, we can ask what visual functions require, or benefit from, information that was acquired in previous fixations. That is, what natural visual tasks depend on visual memory? On first consideration, the results described above, where subjects use gaze to acquire information just at the point it is needed in the momentary task, might be thought to point toward a memory-less system. More careful analysis suggests otherwise. While many movements can be controlled by online acquisition of visual information, other aspects of movement control appear to need visual memory representations. For example, when leaving a room we easily orient to the door even if it is outside the field of view when the movement is initiated. Similarly, it is natural to return a book to its previous location on the bookshelf. Loomis and Beall (2004) review evidence that subjects maintain accurate representations of the three-dimensional space around them and use it to control locomotion to previously identified locations (see also chapter 6). Similarly, Chun and colleagues (Chun, 2000; Chun & Jiang, 1998; Chun & Nakayama, 2000; see Chapter 2, Section 4.2) hypothesized that memory may be needed for guiding attention and eye movements around a scene. They argue that such guidance requires continuity of visual representations across different fixation positions. Many natural contexts are stable in time, such as an office, kitchen, or living room (see, e.g., Brockmole & Henderson, 2006a). The reduction in temporal and spatial uncertainty afforded by the continuous presence of visual stimuli in natural scenes allows for the use of information acquired in fixations prior to the current one, to plan both eye and hand movements. Such planning of movements on the basis of spatial memory information may be more efficient than using visual search for image features to locate the target every time an eye or body movement is made. Planning based on spatial memory may also facilitate coordination between eye, head, hands, and body. In natural behavior, eye, head, and hands all need to act with respect to a common coordinate system and remain synchronized in time across multiple actions. An internal stored memory representation of space may facilitate this coordination. What evidence is there for this position?

2. MEMORY AND SACCADIC TARGETING

I will first examine whether memory from prior fixations has a role in saccadic programming. It is well known that observers can make accurate saccades to targets on the basis of memory of stimulus locations when they are required to do so (Gnadt & Andersen, 1988; Hayhoe, Lachter, & Moeller, 1992; Karn, Moeller, & Hayhoe, 1997; Miller, 1980). In structures such as lateral intraparietal cortex (LIP) and the frontal eye fields (FEF), which are involved in saccadic programming, neurons maintain activity over delay periods of several seconds, and this activity presumably serves as the neural substrate for memory-guided saccades (Bruce & Goldberg, 1985; Colby, Duhamel, & Goldberg, 1995). This does not tell us, however, whether memory-guided saccade programming is used in natural vision. Experiments in more natural tasks reveal that visual information from prior fixations has an important role to play in saccadic targeting when locations are outside the field of view. For example, Land et al. (1999) noted instances when subjects appeared to take advantage of spatial memory when making tea. In particular, subjects made a number of very large gaze shifts to locations outside the field of view. These gaze shifts involved a combination of eye, head, and body movements and were remarkably accurate. When objects are within the field of view and the image is present on the retina, it is not strictly necessary to use spatial memory. Subjects have the choice of either searching for a target on the basis of its visual features, or using memory for the target's location, or some combination of the two. What do subjects typically do in this case? Is there any advantage to using memory in this case? Experiments by Epelboim et al. (1995) provide evidence that saccade targeting is facilitated by memory. They found that repeated tapping of a predetermined sequence of lights on a table led to fewer fixations and faster hand movements with each repetition. This demonstration strongly implicates the existence of visual representations that are built up over fixations and used to guide movements in ongoing behavior.

Aivar, Hayhoe, Chizk, and Mruczek (2005) provide further evidence for the role of memory in saccade programming. They performed an experiment where subjects copied a toy model in a thee-dimensional, immersive, virtual environment, by picking up pieces in a resource area and moving them to another area to build a copy of the model. The layout of the environment is shown in Figure 5.1 [in color plate section]. The toy Model is at the top, the Resource area is on the right, and the Workspace where subjects build the copy is on the left. Subjects picked up and moved the pieces, which were used to copy the model, using a 3D position tracker that functioned as a 3D mouse. The display subtended about 50° horizontally, so the eye and hand movements involved in moving the pieces were typically in the range of 20–30°. After subjects had experience with the stable spatial arrangement of the pieces in the Resource area, the layout of the pieces in the Resource area was then changed randomly every time the subject picked up a piece and then looked away to place it in the Workspace to build the copy. When subjects made the next saccade to the Resource area to pick up a piece after the rearrangement, they often made a saccade to the *old location* of the piece to be picked up. Since the desired piece was no longer in that location, they then made a corrective saccade to the *new location* of the piece. This would be expected if subjects had planned the initial saccade on the basis of the memory representation of the position of the desired piece, and then corrected the movement when the piece was no longer there. Figure 5.1 presents an illustration of this pattern. Figure 5.1a shows the initial arrangement of the pieces. Following the movement to the Workspace to place the green piece, the subject returns to pick up the yellow piece, which had been displaced to the left (Figure 5.1b). The subject then makes a saccade to the new location and picks it up. The regular order with which subjects copy the pieces allows us to infer that the yellow piece was indeed the intended target, and that the second movement was corrective, and not just a random change of plan. About 20% of the saccades to the Resource area were of this type (old-to-new), suggesting that subjects frequently use memory to program the saccades, but it is not the only strategy used. In many cases the initial saccades to the old location were made while the incorrect target was visible in that location in the peripheral retina, suggesting that the movement was based exclusively on a memory representation and did not include current visual information from the target location. There was also a significant increase in the total number of fixations required to locate a piece after a change, which was accounted for by the corrective movements that occurred after fixating the (incorrect) old location. Thus it appeared that subjects often planned saccades on the basis of a memory representation, even in the presence of conflicting visual information, and then had to make corrective movements when the scene was no longer consistent with the memory representation.

A related experiment on eye movements in a block-copying task by Karn and Hayhoe (2000) showed that subjects made very accurate saccades to invisible targets that appeared only after the eye was in flight. These targets had been viewed earlier in the task, so a memory representation must have been used to program the saccades. The experimental layout is shown in Figure 5.2A. Subjects picked up blocks with the mouse from the Resource area on the right, and moved them to the Workspace area on the bottom left, in order to make a copy of the Model pattern (top left). After picking up the block, subjects typically

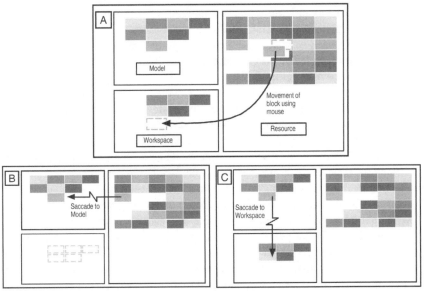

Figure 5.2. A. The block-copying tasks. Subjects pick up blocks from the Resource area with the mouse and make a copy of the Model in the Workspace. B. Sequence of events in Karn and Hayhoe's experiment. After picking up a block, subjects typically saccade to the block in the Model that is being copied, shown by the dashed line. The zig-zag indicates that during the saccade, the partially built copy in the Workspace disappears. C. When the next saccade is made from the Model to Workspace to guide placement of the block, the model reappears and is visible at the end of the saccade. Adapted from Karn and Hayhoe (2000).

made a saccade to the Model to check the location of the block to be copied. During this saccade, the existing partial copy in the Workspace disappeared and then remained invisible during the Model fixation. It then reappeared during the next saccade to the location in the Workspace that the block was to be placed, so that when the eye landed in the Workspace the block could be placed normally. The sequence of events is shown in Figure 5.2B and 5.2C. Thus the saccade from Model to Workspace was launched in the absence of the target. Despite this, saccades landed with high precision at the edge of the copy where the new block was to be placed. This suggests that the saccade was programmed using a memory representation of the workspace layout. Interestingly, subjects were almost entirely unaware that the target block had been invisible before the saccade was launched. This result also supports the claim that a detailed representation of the spatial structure of the environment is typically retained across fixations and used to guide saccadic eye movements.

The need to orient to regions outside the field of view in natural vision (e.g., moving around within a room) provides a rationale for storing information about spatial layout (see chapter 6, section 3). We have observed that individuals with restricted fields of view resulting from damage to early visual cortex (homonymous hemianopia) make accurate saccades into their blind fields when performing real 3D model building tasks analogous to that of Aivar et al. (Martin, Riley, Kelly, Hayhoe, & Huxlin, 2007). Such saccades must be memory-based. Subjects do not need to make a sequence of hunting movements in the general region but, instead, locate targets in the blind field as efficiently as in their normal hemifield. A targeting mechanism that relies heavily on spatial memory does not differentiate between targets inside or outside the current field of view. Consistent with this, many of the memory-guided saccades in Aivar et al.'s (2005) experiment were actually to regions currently visible in the retinal image, and this suggests that spatial memory information is not used exclusively for locations outside the field of view. A strategy that uses both visual and memory information, depending on what is available, would ensure a smooth transition between targeting within and outside the field of view. Consistent with this, Edelman, Cherkasova, and Nakayama (2002) and Kristjánsson and Nakayama (2003) have observed that subjects are able to locate and saccade to targets that are un-resolvable in the peripheral retina, provided that they have been fixated previously. This suggests that spatial memory aids target selection for objects within the field of view, as well as for those outside it. It seems likely that the spatial information from memory, and the visual information from the peripheral retina, are combined in some way to specify the target location. The relative weights of these two sources of information should indicate the strength of the reliance on the memory information. It is possible that the relative weights depend on the constraints in a particular situation. For example, if there is a need to minimize the time to locate the target, or to initiate hand and head movements ahead of the eye, then greater reliance might be found on memory-based targeting. If, however, accuracy is most important, greater weight might be given to the current retinal image.

The spatial precision of memory-guided saccades in both Karn and Hayhoe's and Aivar et al.'s experiments was quite impressive. In Aivar et al.'s experiment, the gaze changes involved were 20–30° in magnitude, and the targeting precision approximately 2°. In Karn and Hayhoe's experiment, the standard deviation of the saccade landing points was about 0.5–0.7° for saccades of about 6°. Thus in both cases the targeting precision is about 10%. This is close to the precision of saccades to visible targets. The precision of memory-guided saccades implies that the memory representations integrated across saccades must include spatial information that is precise enough to support accurate saccade planning. It has often been claimed that the representation of spatial information integrated across saccades is imprecise. The nature of the memory representation from prior fixations has traditionally been addressed in the context of integration of information across saccadic eye movements: whether there is such an integrated representation of a visual scene, and what the contents of that representation might be (Irwin, 1991; Pollatsek & Rayner, 1992). The conclusion from a large body of previous work is that representation of information acquired in prior fixations is very limited. Evidence for limited memory from prior fixations is provided by the finding that observers are extremely insensitive to changes in the visual scene during an eye movement, film cut, or similar masking stimulus (for a review, see, e.g., Simons, 2000), and this insensitivity to changes has been described as "change blindness". Since detection of a change requires a comparison of the information in different fixations, change blindness has been interpreted as evidence that only a small part of the information in the scene is retained across fixations. Irwin suggests that it is limited by the capacity of working memory—that is, to a small number of individual items whose identity is remembered better than their location (Irwin & Andrews, 1996). Thus the change blindness studies suggest that memory from prior fixations is primarily semantic in nature and, by inference, of limited precision (e.g., Irwin, 1991; O'Regan, 1992; for a review, see also Henderson & Hollingworth, 1999). More recently the strength of the conclusions made from change blindness studies has been questioned (Hollingworth & Henderson, 2002; Simons & Rensink, 2005; see also chapter 4, section 2.4), and when eye movements are directly investigated, as in the Aivar et al. study, the evidence reveals that the spatial information cannot be imprecise but, instead, can support high-precision movements. Other evidence also shows that information about the spatial organization of scenes is preserved across fixations. Chun and Jiang (1998) showed that visual search is facilitated (by 60–80 ms) by prior exposure to visual contexts associated with the target. They suggest that this reflects sensitivity to the redundant structure in a scene, which remains invariant across multiple gaze points. It seems likely that observers are sensitive to this invariance. For example, repeated encounters with real-world scenes results in fewer eye movements before a search target is located (Brockmole & Henderson, 2006b). Additionally, De Graef and Verfaille show encoding of precise spatial relationships of "bystander" objects that are not the target of a saccade (de Graef, Verfaille, & Lamote, 2001; Verfaille, De Graef, Germeys, Gysen, & Van Eccelpoel, 2001). Other evidence for an influence of prior views is "priming of popout". This is the reduction of both search latencies and saccade latencies to locations or features that have been recently presented (Maljkovic & Nakayama, 1994, 2000; McPeek, Maljkovic, & Nakayama, 1999). Finally, Hayhoe et al. (1992; see also Brockmole & Irwin, 2005) showed that subjects were able to integrate the spatial location of dots presented at different times during different fixations. Subjects were able to make precise judgments of the angle subtended by the dots. Such judgments must have been made on a memory representation integrated across saccades. The precision of the judgments fell off as the interval between the dot presentations increased from 0 to 800 ms, as might be expected from the temporal decay rate of visual short-term memory. In a subsequent experiment, Lachter and Hayhoe (1995) showed that performance was capacity-limited, as expected if visual short-term memory was the basis for the integrated representation of dot locations. All these findings indicate that visual short-term memory can be spatially very precise when necessary. It is likely that previous experiments that indicated that the spatial precision of working memory was poor (e.g., Irwin, 1991) reflect the particular task demands of the experiment.

3. MEMORY AND JUST-IN-TIME STRATEGIES

An important issue to consider is the relation between the "just-in-time" strategy described by Ballard et al. (1995) and the use of memory to guide movements. Ballard et al. had subjects copy a pattern of 8 colored blocks. Subjects typically fixated a block in the model before picking up a block of the same color and then fixated the block in the model again before placing the selected block in the copy area. Why did subjects choose to look twice at a block in the course of copying it? The suggestion is that subjects acquired color in the first fixation and location in the second fixation. Even though it was easily within the limits of visual short-term memory (VSTM) to remember the color and locations of several blocks, subjects instead appeared to defer acquisition of this information until just at the point it is needed. Subsequent work by Hayhoe et al. (1998), Triesch et al. (2003), and Droll et al. (2006; Droll & Hayhoe, 2007) has confirmed this interpretation. In a task where subjects picked up and sorted virtual bricks on the basis of their features, Droll and Hayhoe (2007) found that subjects made just-in-time fixations more frequently as working memory load increased. Thus subjects select the specific information needed by the task at that moment, and they then flexibly switch between making a fixation or retaining information in working memory depending on the memory load and particular experimental context. The specificity of the information extracted within a fixation suggests a large degree of independence of the visual computations within individual fixations, to the extent that the particular information extracted does not depend on information from prior fixations. This is an essentially memory-less strategy and is consistent with the body of work indicating limited memory across fixation positions. For at least some proportion of the task, observers appear to access the information explicitly at the point of fixation, at the time when it is needed, as opposed to relying on information from prior fixations. This behavior is consistent with O'Regan's suggestion that the scene serves as a kind of external memory that can be quickly accessed when needed (Ballard et al., 1995; O'Regan, 1992).

This does not mean that visually guided behavior is entirely memory-less however. Natural vision presumably reflects some combination of just-in-time acquisition and use of memory representations. There is plenty of evidence that many visual operations in the natural world do not require memory (Warren, 2006). For example, subjects use the instantaneous value of a visual variable to control an action, such as rate of expansion of the image to control braking, or the angle of the tangent point of a curve to control steering angle (Land & Lee, 1994). In making tea or sandwiches, subjects invariably fixate the objects they are about to grasp. During this fixation the subject must compute information to control reach direction and plan the grasp, including the position, orientation, and size of the object, and perhaps information about surface friction and weight to plan the forces. Given the complexity of the information that might be required from the visual scene, it is not too surprising that much of it needs to be extracted on the fly, and it is clearly efficient to compute only task-relevant information (Ballard, Hayhoe, & Pelz, 1997; Warren, 2006). Nor is there any doubt that VSTM is very limited and constrains how much information can be retained from one fixation to the next (Irwin & Andrews, 1996). Just-in-time representations are an elegant way for the brain to deal with those limitations while getting the job done. At the same time, some aspects of natural behavior cannot be accounted for this way. As described in the present chapter, memory across fixations is needed as a basis for motor planning and coordination. The solution, as proposed by Hollingworth and Henderson (2002), and Hollingworth (2004), is in the existence of long-term visual memory, which does not suffer from capacity limitations. Given that humans typically view a given scene, such as their office, for extended periods, and make many thousands of fixations, it is possible to retain quite extensive representations of scenes in longer-term memory. Presumably these long-term memory representations can subserve a variety of natural behaviors. Ballard et al. (1995, 1997) emphasized the "minimal" nature of task-specific representations, consistent with other minimal-representation positions (O'Regan & Noë, 2001; Rensink, 2000). In contrast to the now discredited idea that the function of perception is to reconstruct the entire visual scene in the brain, task-specific representations might indeed be considered minimal. At this point in the development of the field, however, it is important to discover exactly what visual information is actually required by visual tasks. As our understanding of task needs increases, our description of the representations that underlie those tasks is becoming more elaborated. In particular, the current understanding of the role of longer-term memory representations in subserving visually guided behavior makes the "minimal-representations" description somewhat misleading. Thus it seems that the most effective strategy is to examine the informational requirements of natural behavior in order to elucidate exactly what information is represented, and when it is represented (see also chapter 4, section 2.2).

4. MEMORY AND SEARCH

An advantage of a strategy that uses memory information, whether or not the target is within the field of view, is that it may minimize the number of movements (and time) required to locate a search target (cf. Epelboim et al., 1995). All of the results described above, on the role of memory in programming saccades, conflict to some extent with claims that memory plays no role in visual search (e.g., Horowitz & Wolfe, 1998). This issue has been extensively researched and has been reviewed by Woodman and Chun (2006). While there may be some instances where memory provides no clear advantage, there are many demonstrations of the use of visual memory in aiding search, as well as demonstrations that it leads to a reduction in search time. For example, Zelinsky, Rao, Hayhoe, and Ballard (1998) found faster search times and fewer saccades for target objects when subjects were given a preview of the spatial array prior to a search task. Hollingworth (2006) found a similar speeding of search times as a result of a preview. Thus it seems likely that the role of memory in search will depend on the constraints of the particular context. This issue is discussed more fully in chapters 2 and 4.

5. SEQUENCES OF SACCADES

Another way that memory might be important in natural vision is in the planning of sequences of saccades. Hayhoe et al. (2003) showed that natural eye-movement patterns, when subjects made sandwiches, indicated a need for some representation of the spatial structure of the scene that is built up over different fixations and maintained over a period of at least a few seconds. One indication of this was that subjects frequently made sequences of saccades separated by very brief fixations of 100 ms or less. Since the minimum time to program a saccade is 200 ms or more, these saccades must be programmed *as a sequence* in a spatial, not a retinal, reference frame. Zingale and Kowler (1987) have also demonstrated that saccades can be preprogrammed as a sequence. The programming of the second (and subsequent) saccade in a sequence must initially occur in a reference frame that is independent of the eye, and the second saccade must use information acquired prior to the immediately preceding fixation (Becker & Jurgens, 1979). McPeek and Keller (2001) observed that neurons in the superior colliculus show activity related to preparation of the second saccade even while the first saccade is still in progress. Thus neural activity for more than one saccade can be maintained concurrently, even at levels close to the motor output, and the neural activity for the second saccade must be able to take into account the eye displacement by the first saccade. Thus the intrinsic organization of the saccadic system appears to be in spatial, not retinal coordinates.

6. TARGETING HAND MOVEMENTS

Memory representations appear to have a role in programming hand movements as well as eye movements. In Epelboim et al.'s (1995) experiment, where subjects tapped a predetermined sequence of targets on repeated trials, not only were targets located with fewer saccades, but hand movements also were faster with each repetition of the task. In Aivar et al.'s (2005) experiment, we noticed that when an eye movement was incorrectly targeted to the old location of a piece, the hand often accompanied the eye, and it also needed to be redirected to the new location. Brouwer and Knill (2007) have investigated the role of memory in programming hand movements. They devised a task, illustrated in Figure 5.3, where subjects sequentially picked up and moved two virtual "magnetic" target objects into a virtual trash bin with their index fingers. In some of the trials the position of the second target was perturbed while the subject was transporting the first target to the trash. Although the new position of the second target was visible in the peripheral retina, subjects' initial movements to pick up the target were biased to the initial remembered position. For high-contrast targets, the initial part of the reach trajectory reflected a weight of 0.33 for the remembered location of the target, with the visible location weighted by 0.67. Over the course of the movement, the memory weight decreased and the finger ended accurately on the new target position. When the contrast of the target was decreased, the weight given to the remembered location increased substantially (see Figure 5.4). Thus even when the target was visible in the peripheral retina, the remembered location had a role in programming the reaching movement. This result is similar to that of Aivar et al., although the eye movement lands on the target and then corrects, as expected from a ballistic movement, whereas the slower hand movement uses visual feedback to make corrections during the movement.

7. COORDINATION AND PLANNING

An important advantage of the use of memory is that it allows early planning and coordination of head and hand movements with the eye. Typically, in response to a visually presented target, head- and hand-movement initiation lag behind the eye by 100 ms or more (Abrams, Meyer, & Kornblum, 1990). In their observations of sandwich making, Hayhoe et al. (2003) found that hand movements to pick up an object were often initiated as much as a second before or after the corresponding saccade to the object to guide the grasp. These large lags and leads resulted from the interweaving of visual control of the two hands, with some movements starting while the eye was supervising the other hand's action. In one example described in the paper, the movement of one hand to pick up a lid began

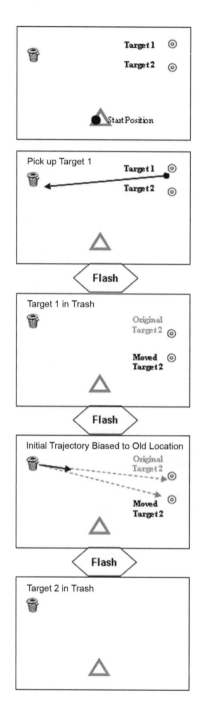

Figure 5.3. Overview of a trial in which the second target is perturbed downwards. Adapted from Brouwer & Knill (2007), Figure 1.

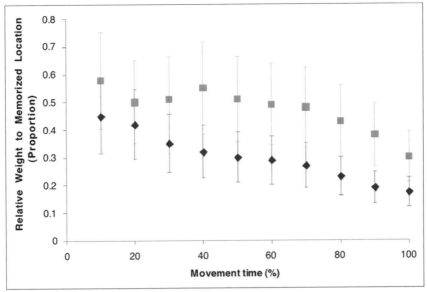

Figure 5.4. Weight of memorized location over time, expressed as the ratio of the weight given to the remembered location to the sum of weights given to the remembered and visually specified locations. Error bars are between-subject standard errors of the mean. Squares represent the low-contrast target; diamonds represent the high-contrast target. Adapted from Brouwer & Knill (2007), Figure 3.

at the same time that the eye and the other hand moved to put down a knife. The eye did not move to the lid until about 600 ms later, after the knife placement by the other hand was complete. Despite this long delay, the eye arrived in time to guide the pickup. These long relative latencies suggest that the next eye or hand movement may be planned as much as a second ahead of time. If fixation of the lid is required for final guidance of the reach, the fixation must be planned when the reach is initiated, so as to be there when needed. This suggests that, in this case, the right hand did indeed "know what the left hand was doing." Because several fixations intervene between the eye and hand movements to the object, this planning must occur in a representation that is independent of eye position—that is, in a spatial coordinate frame.

Further evidence that use of spatial memory allows earlier planning of head and hand movements comes from the experiment described above by Aivar et al. (2005). In that experiment, observers made repetitive head and hand movements from right to left and back, as they picked up the pieces in the Resource area on the right and placed them in the Workspace on the left to build a copy of the model (see Figure 5.1a [in the color plate section]). We measured the relative timing of the eye, head, and hand movements for both leftward and rightward movements (Hayhoe, Aivar, Gaines, & Jovancovic, 2003). These relative latencies are shown in Figure 5.5. For rightward movements to the resource area to

Rightward Movement for Pickup

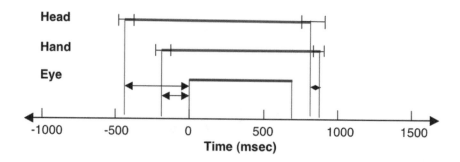

Leftward Movement for Putdown

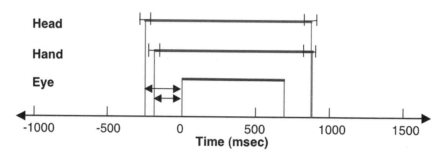

Figure 5.5. Relative timing of eye, head, and hand movements in the three-dimensional
copying task shown in Figure 5.1. Rightward movements in order to pick up
a piece are at the top. Leftward movements in order to drop a piece are on
the bottom. Time is measured relative to the initiation of the eye movement.
The horizontal bars indicate standard error of the mean averaged across 10
subjects.

pick up a piece, subjects initiated the hand movement on average about 400 ms
before the eye movement. The head movement was initiated about 200 ms before
the eye. The early initiation of the movements had the consequence that the head
and hand both arrived close in time to the arrival of the eye in the Resource area.
A similar pattern was found for leftward movements to the Workspace for placement of the piece. In this case the hand movement was initiated about 300 ms
before the eye. As before, head and hand arrived at about the same time, shortly
after the eye. This almost simultaneous arrival of eye, head, and hand suggests
that coordination patterns were orchestrated in order to facilitate the action following the movement. Thus the eye was centered in the orbit and the hand was
on the target at the end of the movement, presumably facilitating pickup. (It has
been shown that reaches are more accurate when the head is pointing toward the

target—Biguer, Jeannerod, & Prablanc, 1985). A memory representation of the spatial layout, independent of eye position, is presumably necessary to plan the hand and head movements to the target, ahead of the saccade. Thus a significant role for memory for the spatial layout of a scene was probably to allow early planning and coordination of the eye, head, and hand movements.

7.1 Looking ahead

Another observation that suggests that subjects might be planning movements several seconds ahead in natural behavior is the occurrence of what has been termed "look-ahead fixations." In a study of gaze during a hand-washing task, as subjects approached the wash basin they fixated the tap, soap, and paper towels in sequence, before returning to fixate the tap to guide contact with the hand (Pelz & Canosa, 2001). These fixations on objects that were not being manipulated, but would be grasped a few seconds later, were called "look-aheads". Since subjects did not look back at objects once they had finished with them (even though the objects remained in full view), it seems likely that these fixations were not random. The timing of the look-aheads, which cluster around 3 sec before the subsequent reach, is also suggestive of a specific role for the fixations (Mennie, Hayhoe, & Sullivan, 2007). Look-ahead fixations have also been observed in tea making (Land et al., 1999) and in sandwich making (Hayhoe et al., 2003), where about a third of the reaching and grasping movements were preceded by a fixation on the object a few seconds earlier. It seems likely that fixating the location of a future reach target provides an accurate spatial memory representation that may facilitate the programming of the next saccade, the next reach, or both. Such facilitation by a prior fixation is suggested by evidence that pointing accuracy to remembered locations are improved by prior fixations on the target (Terao, Andersson, Flanagan, & Johansson, 2002). In an investigation of the role of look-ahead fixations, Mennie et al. (2007) found increased accuracy for the next saccade to the target, as well as earlier fixation on the target. However, they were not able to demonstrate any direct facilitation of the reach, such as reduced reach latencies or increased velocities. This deserves further investigation, as the frequency with which looking ahead is observed certainly reveals some kind of advance planning of the action. What the nature of that planning is, and whether it confers an advantage on the reaching movement, is not clear at this point.

7.2 Internal models

Another way in which memory may be important in visually guided control of natural behavior is that observers must learn the dynamic properties of the world in order to allocate gaze and to orient the body where it is needed. When making tea or sandwiches, for the most part items remain in stable locations with stable properties. In a familiar room, the observer need only update the locations of items that have been moved, or monitor items that are changing state (e.g., water filling the kettle). In dynamic environments, such as driving, walking, or sports, more complex properties must be learnt. Evidence for such learning is the fact that saccades are often proactive; that is, they are made to a location in a scene in advance of an expected event. For example, in Land and MacLeod's investigation of cricket, batsmen anticipated the bounce point of the ball, with the eye arriving at the bounce point 100–200 ms in advance of the ball (Land & McLeod, 2000). The ability to predict where the ball will bounce depends on previous experience of the cricket ball's trajectory. These saccades were always preceded by a fixation on the ball as it left the bowler's hand, showing that batsmen use current sensory data in combination with prior experience of the ball's motion to predict the location of the bounce. This suggests that observers have stored internal models of the dynamic properties of the world that can be used to position gaze in anticipation of a predicted event.

There is considerable evidence for the role of internal models of the body's dynamics in the control of movement (e.g., Wolpert, Miall, & Kawato, 1998). Such models predict the internal state of the body as a consequence of a planned movement, and they help mitigate the problem of delays in sensory feedback about body posture. Subjects also appear to use internal models of the physical properties of objects in order to plan and control grasping (e.g., Flanagan & Wing, 1997; Johansson, 1996). Delays in processing visual information about events in the world suggest a similar need for models of the *environment,* particularly in dynamic situations. The minimum time for visual information to influence a hand movement is about 150 ms (Saunders & Knill, 2005). However, the need for internal models of the environment is not well established. Indeed, the body of evidence in the past, especially that from change blindness studies, has suggested the contrary—that observers construct only minimal representations of the world (Ballard, Hayhoe, Pook, & Rao, 1997; O'Regan, 1992; Simons, 2000). To build internal models of the visual environment, observers must be able accumulate visual information over the time-varying sequence of visual images resulting from eye and body movements.

Hayhoe, Mennie, Sullivan, and Gorgos (2005) provide evidence of the existence of sophisticated internal models of the structure of the environment. Such models may be used to predict upcoming events and plan movements in anticipation of those events. In this study, eye, head, and hand movements were recorded while subjects caught balls thrown with a bounce. Three participants stood in a triangular formation and threw a ball around the circle. Initially, subjects threw a tennis ball around the circle of three participants. Each throw was performed with a single bounce approximately mid-way between the participants.

Similar to batsmen in cricket, when catching a ball subjects initially fixated the hands of the thrower, then made a saccade to the anticipated bounce point, and then pursued the ball until it was close to the hands. Average departure time of gaze from the hands of the thrower was 61 ms after the ball left the hands. Gaze then arrived at a point a little above the anticipated bounce location an average of 53 ms before the bounce. Subjects maintained gaze at this location until the ball came into the fovea, and then they made a smooth pursuit movement, maintaining gaze on the ball until the catch. Since the minimum time to program a saccadic eye movement is 200–250 ms (in the absence of any kind of anticipation or preparation), the saccade from the hands to the bounce point must be at least partially under way prior to the release of the ball. The landing points of the saccades relative to the actual bounce point clustered within about 5° laterally, and about 15° vertically above the bounce point. Thus subjects appeared to be targeting a region just above the bounce point, rather than the bounce point itself. This presumably facilitates the subsequent tracking movement by allowing time to capture the ball's trajectory after the bounce. The tight lateral clustering of the saccade landing points relative to the bounce point suggested that subjects were using information from the early part of the throw to target the likely location of the bounce.

7.2.1. *Adjusting to the ball's dynamic properties*

Ability to pursue the ball in the above example also depended on experience with the ball's dynamic properties. When the tennis ball was unexpectedly replaced with a bouncier one, subjects were unable to track the ball and, instead, made a series of saccades. Within a few trials, subjects were once again able to accurately pursue the ball. A crude evaluation of pursuit accuracy was made by measuring the proportion of time that gaze was less than two ball diameters away from the ball, in the period between bounce and catch. Improvement in pursuit performance over 6 trials is shown in Figure 5.6 (top), which shows pursuit accuracy improving rapidly over the first three trials, approaching the performance level with the tennis ball. The ability to make accurate pursuit movements in this context therefore depends on knowledge of the dynamic properties of the new ball. The adjustment in performance was quite rapid, and uniform across subjects, suggesting that adjusting to such changes in the environment is an important feature of natural behavior. (The ability to pursue the tennis ball accurately on the first trial presumably reflects either its slower speed or that its motion is closer to subjects' prior expectations.) The latency of the first saccade from hands to bounce point also changed over the course of a few trials. Arrival time at the bounce point advanced by about 100 ms over the first 6 trials following the change from tennis to bouncy ball. This is shown in Figure 5.6 (bottom). The earlier arrival of the eye at the bounce point is accompanied by earlier departure from the hands at the point of release. Thus anticipatory saccades and pursuit movements reveal that acquisition of visual information is planned for a predicted state of the world. Such predictions must be based on a stored memory representation of some kind. The precision of the predictions reveals the quality of the information in the stored memory, or internal model. The spatial and temporal precision of the anticipatory saccades, and the fine-tuning of these movements following a change in the ball's dynamic properties, indicate that subjects have an accurate internal model of the ball's spatiotemporal path, and that they rapidly update this model when errors occur. Rapid adjustment of

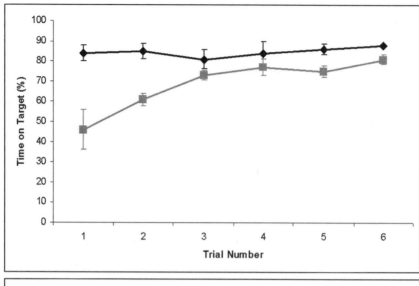

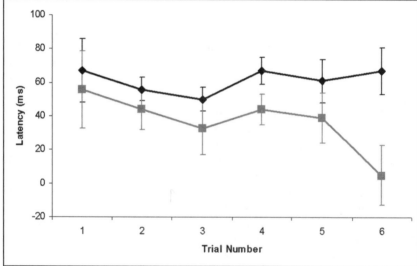

Figure 5.6. Top: Pursuit performance as a function of trial number for the tennis ball (top curve) and more elastic ball (bottom curve). Error bars are ±1 *SEM* between subjects. Bottom: Arrival time of gaze at the bounce point, relative to the time of the bounce, as a function of trial number, for the tennis ball (top curve) and bouncier ball (bottom curve). Error bars are ±1 *SEM* between subjects. Adapted by permission from Hayhoe, M. M., Mennie, N., Sullivan, B., & Gorgos, K. (2005). The role of internal models and prediction in catching balls. *Proceedings of AAAI Fall Symposium Series.* Menlo Park, CA: AAAI.

performance suggests that such prediction is a ubiquitous feature of visually guided behavior.

7.3 Time course

The time course of the memory for spatial structure is difficult to evaluate. The evidence reviewed above does not point to a single kind of memory representation with fixed temporal properties. In the experiment by Epelboim et al. (1995), the number of fixations and the time needed to locate items when subjects repeatedly tapped a sequence of LEDs decreased over a time period of minutes, pointing to the build up of a long-term memory representation across trials. The development of internal models as described above probably occurs over even longer time periods, as a result of extensive practice. On the other hand, look-ahead fixations are made just a few seconds before the reaching movement they are associated with, suggesting that the spatial information gathered in these fixations has a decay constant of seconds, similar to traditional short-term visual memory. In Aivar et al.'s (2005) experiment, some aspects of performance were consistent with a decay constant of seconds, whereas others were consistent with longer-term spatial memory representations. Other work on scene memory also points to long-term memory representations of scenes (Brockmole & Henderson, 2005, 2006b; Hollingworth, 2006; Hollingworth & Henderson, 2002; Karacan & Hayhoe, 2007; Melcher, 2001; Melcher & Kowler, 2001). In terms of movement control, it seems likely that both long-term and short-term memory representations are involved. Spatial information acquired a few seconds prior to the movement is likely to allow a higher-precision movement, but, with continued experience in a familiar environment, long-term representations may eventually acquire comparable precision.

8. SUMMARY

The strict limits set by attention and working memory pose a challenge for visually guided behavior in the natural world. Over the last two decades much has been discovered about the nature of these limitations in the context of studies of change blindness. More recently, there has been an accumulation of evidence that natural behavior draws upon a variety of longer-term memory representations that can compensate, to some extent, for the capacity limitations of working memory. In the domain of motor control and movement planning, there is substantial evidence that observers take advantage of memory representations of the space around them. Such representations seem essential for coordinated movement. Movements are not all reactive. Planning is intrinsic to the motor system, and stored representations are essential for planning. The complexity of these stored representations and the way they are used in planning and control of movements have yet to be fully explored.

9. ACKNOWLEDGMENTS

The author wishes to acknowledge the contribution of her collaborators whose work is discussed in this chapter: Pilar Aivar, Jason Droll, Jelena Jovancevic, Keith Karn, and Neil Mennie. This work was supported by NIH grant EY05729.

10. REFERENCES

Abrams, R., Meyer, D., & Kornblum, S. (1990). Eye–hand coordination: Oculomotor control in rapid aimed limb movements. *Journal of Experimental Psychology: Human Perception and Performance, 15,* 248–267.

Aivar, M. P., Hayhoe, M. M., Chizk, C. L., & Mruczek, R. E. B. (2005). Spatial memory and saccadic targeting in a natural task. *Journal of Vision, 5,* 177–193.

Ballard, D. H., Hayhoe, M., & Pelz, J. B. (1995). Memory representations in natural tasks. *Journal of Cognitive Neuroscience, 7,* 66–80.

Ballard, D. H., Hayhoe, M., Pook, P., & Rao, R. (1997). Deictic codes for the embodiment of cognition. *Behavioral & Brain Sciences, 20,* 723–767.

Becker, W., & Jurgens, R. (1979). An analysis of the saccadic system by means of double-step stimuli. *Vision Research, 19,* 967–983.

Biguer, B., Jeannerod, M., & Prablanc, C. (1985). The role of position of gaze in move-ment accuracy. In M. I. Posner & O. S. Marin (Eds.), *Attention and performance XI: Mechanisms of attention* (pp. 184–204). Hillsdale, NJ: Lawrence Erlbaum Associates.

Brockmole, J. R., & Henderson, J. M. (2005). Attentional prioritization of new objects in real-world scenes: Evidence from eye movements. *Journal of Experimental Psychol-ogy: Human Perception and Performance, 31,* 857–868.

Brockmole, J. R., & Henderson, J. M. (2006a). Using real-world scenes as contextual cues during search. *Visual Cognition, 13,* 99–108.

Brockmole, J. R., & Henderson, J. M. (2006b). Recognition and attention guidance dur-ing contextual cueing in real-world scenes: Evidence from eye movements. *Quarterly Journal of Experimental Psychology, 59,* 1177–1187.

Brockmole, J. R., & Irwin, D. E. (2005). Eye movements and the integration of visual memory and visual perception. *Perception & Psychophysics, 67,* 495–512.

Brouwer, A., & Knill, D. (2007). The role of memory in visually guided reaching. *Journal of Vision, 7*(5), 1–12.

Bruce, C., & Goldberg, M. E. (1985). Primate frontal eye fields I: Single neurons dis-charging before saccades. *Journal of Neurophysiology, 53,* 603–635.

Chun, M. M. (2000). Contextual cueing of visual attention. *Trends in Cognitive Sciences, 4*(5), 170–178.

Chun, M. M., & Jiang, Y. H. (1998). Contextual cueing: Implicit learning and memory of visual context guides spatial attention. *Cognitive Psychology, 36,* 28–71.

Chun, M., & Nakayama, K. (2000). On the functional role of implicit visual memory for the adaptive deployment of attention across scenes. *Visual Cognition, 7,* 65–82.

Colby, C. L., Duhamel, J. R., & Goldberg, M. E. (1995). Oculocentric spatial representa-tion in parietal cortex. *Cerebral Cortex, 5,* 470–481.

De Graef, P., Verfaille, K., & Lamote, C. (2001). Transsaccadic coding of object position: Effects of saccadic status and allocentric reference frame. *Psychologica Belgica, 41,* 29–54.

Droll, J., & Hayhoe, M. (2007). Trade-offs between working memory and gaze. *Journal of Experimental Psychology: Human Perception and Performance, 33*(6), 1352–1365.

Droll, J., Hayhoe, M., Triesch, J., & Sullivan, B. (2006). Task demands control acquisition and maintenance of visual information. *Journal of Experimental Psychology: Human Perception and Performance, 31,* 1416–1438.

Edelman, J. A., Cherkasova, M. V., & Nakayama, K. (2002). A spatial memory system for the guidance of eye movements in crowded visual scenes [Abstract]. *Journal of Vision, 2,* 572a.

Epelboim, J., Steinman, R., Kowler, E., Edwards, M., Pizlo, Z., Erkelens, C., & Collewijn, H. (1995). The function of visual search and memory in sequential looking tasks. *Vision Research, 35,* 3401–3422.

Flanagan, J., & Wing, A. (1997). The role of internal models in motion planning and control: Evidence from grip force adjustments during movements of hand-held loads. *Journal of Neuroscience, 17,* 1519–1528.

Gnadt, J. W., & Andersen, R. A. (1988). Memory related motor planning activity in posterior parietal cortex of macaque. *Experimental Brain Research, 70,* 216–220.

Hayhoe, M. M., Aivar, M. P., Gaines, E., & Jovancovic, J. (2003). Spatial memory use and coordination of eye, head and hand movements. [Abstract]. *Journal of Vision, 3,* 124a.

Hayhoe, M. M., Bensinger, D., & Ballard, D. (1998). Task constraints in visual working memory. *Vision Research, 38,* 125–137.

Hayhoe, M. M., Lachter, J., & Moeller, P. (1992). Spatial memory and integration across saccadic eye movements. In K. Rayner (Ed.), *Eye movements and visual cognition: Scene perception and reading* (pp. 130–145). New York: Springer.

Hayhoe, M. M., Mennie, N., Sullivan, B., & Gorgos, K. (2005). The role of internal models and prediction in catching balls. *Proceedings of AAAI Fall Symposium Series.* Menlo Park, CA: AAAI.

Hayhoe, M. M., Shrivastava, A., Mruczek, R., & Pelz, J. (2003). Visual memory and motor planning in a natural task. *Journal of Vision, 3,* 49–63.

Henderson, J. (2003). Human gaze control during real-world scene perception. *Trends in Cognitive Science, 7,* 498–504.

Henderson, J., & Hollingworth, A. (1999). High-level scene perception. *Annual Review of Psychology, 50,* 243–271.

Hollingworth, A. (2004). Constructing visual representations of natural scenes: The roles of short- and long-term visual memory. *Journal of Experimental Psychology: Human Perception and Performance, 30,* 519–537.

Hollingworth, A. (2006). Visual memory for natural scenes: Evidence from change detection and visual search. *Visual Cognition, 14,* 781–807.

Hollingworth, A., & Henderson, J. (2002). Accurate visual memory for previously attended objects in natural scenes. *Journal of Experimental Psychology: Human Perception and Performance, 28,* 113–136.

Horowitz, T. S., & Wolfe, J. M. (1998). Visual search has no memory. *Nature, 394,* 575–577.

Irwin, D. E. (1991). Information integration across saccadic eye movements. *Cognitive Psychology, 23,* 420–456.

Irwin, D. E., & Andrews, R. V. (Eds.). (1996). Integration and accumulation of information across saccadic eye movements. In T. Inui & J. McClelland (Eds.), *Attention and performance, XVI* (pp. 125–155). Cambridge, MA: MIT Press.

Johansson, R. S. (1996). Sensory control of dextrous manipulation in humans. In A. Wing,

P. Haggard, & J. Flanagan (Eds.), *Hand and brain: the neurophysiology and psychology of hand movements* (pp. 381–414). San Diego, CA: Academic Press.

Johansson, R. S., Westling, G., Backstrom, A., & Flanagan, J. R. (2001). Eye–hand coordination in object manipulation. *Journal of Neuroscience, 21,* 6917–6932.

Karacan, H. (üke), & Hayhoe, M. (2007). Is attention drawn to changes in familiar scenes? *Visual Cognition, 16*(2), 356–374.

Karn, K., Moeller, P., & Hayhoe, M. (1997)   Reference frames in saccade targeting. *Experimental Brain Research, 115,* 267–282.

Karn, K. S., & Hayhoe, M. M. (2000). Memory representations guide targeting eye movements in a natural task. *Visual Cognition, 7,* 673–703.

Kristjánsson, A., & Nakayama, K. (2003). A primitive memory system for the deployment of transient attention. *Perception & Psychophysics, 65,* 711–724.

Lachter, J., & Hayhoe, M. (1995). Capacity limitations in memory for visual locations. *Perception, 24,* 1427–1441.

Land, M. F., & Furneaux, S. (1997). The knowledge base of the oculomotor system. *Philosophical Transactions of the Royal Society of London, Series B, 352,* 1231–1239.

Land, M. F., & Lee, D. N. (1994), Where we look when we steer. *Nature,* 369: 742–744.

Land, M. F., & McLeod, P. (2000). From eye movements to actions: How batsmen hit the ball. *Nature Neuroscience, 3,* 1340–1345.

Land, M. F., Mennie, N., & Rusted, J. (1999). Eye movements and the roles of vision in activities of daily living: Making a cup of tea. *Perception, 28,* 1311–1328.

Loomis, J., & Beall, A. (2004). Model-based control of perception/action. In L. Vaina, S. Beardsley, & S. Rushton (Eds.), *Optic flow and beyond* (pp. 421–441). Boston: Kluwer Academic.

Maljkovic, V., & Nakayama, K. (1994). Priming of pop-out. I. Role of features. *Memory & Cognition, 22,* 657–672.

Maljkovic, V., & Nakayama, K. (2000). Priming of popout. III. A short-term implicit memory system beneficial for rapid target selection. *Visual Cognition, 7,* 571–595.

Martin, T., Riley, M., Kelly, K., Hayhoe, M., & Huxlin, K. (2007). Visually-guided behavior of homonymous hemianopes in a naturalistic task. *Vision Research, 47,* 3434–3446.

McPeek, R. M., & Keller, E. (2001). Short-term priming, concurrent processing, and saccade curvature during a target selection task in the monkey. *Vision Research, 41,* 785–800.

McPeek, R. M., Maljkovic, V., & Nakayama, K. (1999). Saccades require focal attention and are facilitated by a short-term memory system. *Vision Research, 39,* 1555–1566.

Melcher, D. (2001). Persistence of visual memory for scenes. *Nature, 412,* 401.

Melcher, D., & Kowler, E. (2001). Visual scene memory and the guidance of saccadic eye movements. *Vision Research, 41,* 3597–3611.

Mennie, N., Hayhoe, M., & Sullivan, B. (2007). Look-ahead fixations: Anticipatory eye movements in natural tasks. *Experimental Brain Research, 179,* 427–442.

Miller, J. M. (1980). Information used by the perceptual and oculomotor systems regarding the amplitude of saccadic and pursuit eye movements. *Vision Research, 20,* 59–68.

O'Regan, J. K. (1992). Solving the "real" mysteries of visual perception: The world as an outside memory. *Canadian Journal of Psychology, 46,* 461–488.

O'Regan, J. K., & Noë, A. (2001). A sensorimotor account of vision and visual consciousness. *Behavioral & Brain Sciences, 24*(5), 939–973.

Patla, A., & Vickers, J. (1997). Where do we look as we approach and step over an obstacle in the travel path? *NeuroReport, 8,* 3661–3665.

Pelz, J. B., & Canosa, R. (2001). Oculomotor behavior and perceptual strategies in complex tasks. *Vision Research, 41,* 3587–3596.

Pollatsek, A., & Rayner, K. (1992). What is integrated across fixations? In K. Rayner (Ed.), *Eye movements and visual cognition: Scene perception and reading* (pp. 166–191). New York: Springer.

Rensink, R. A. (2000). The dynamic representation of scenes. *Visual Cognition, 7,* 17–42.

Saunders, J., & Knill, D. (2005). Humans use continuous visual feedback from the hand to control both the direction and distance of pointing movements, *Experimental Brain Research, 162,* 458–473.

Simons, D. J. (2000). *Change blindness and visual memory. A special issue of Visual Cognition.* Hove, UK: Psychology Press.

Simons, D. J., & Rensink, R. (2005). Change blindness: Past, present, and future. *Trends in Cognitive Science, 9,* 16–20.

Terao, Y., Andersson, N. E. M., Flanagan, J. R., & Johansson, R. S. (2002). Engagement of gaze in capturing targets for future sequential manual actions. *Journal of Neurophysiology, 88,* 1716–1725.

Triesch, J., Ballard, D., Hayhoe, M., & Sullivan, B. (2003). What you see is what you need. *Journal of Vision, 3,* 86–94.

Turano, K., Geruschat, D., & Baker, F. (2003). Oculomotor strategies for the direction of gaze tested with a real-world activity. *Vision Research, 43,* 333–346.

Verfaille, K., De Graef, P., Germeys, F., Gysen, V., & Van Eccelpoel, C. (2001). Selective transsaccadic coding of object and event-diagnostic information. *Psychologica Belgica, 41,* 89–114.

Warren, W. H. (2006). The dynamics of perception and action. *Psychological Review, 113,* 358–389.

Wolpert, D., Miall, C., & Kawato, M. (1998). Internal models in the cerebellum. *Trends in Cognitive Science, 2,* 338–347.

Woodman, G. F., & Chun, M. M. (2006). The role of working memory and long-term memory in visual search. *Visual Cognition, 14,* 808–830.

Zelinsky, G., Rao, R., Hayhoe, M., & Ballard, D. (1997). Eye movements reveal the spatio-temporal dynamics of visual search. *Psychological Science, 8,* 448–453.

Zingale, C. M., & Kowler, E. (1987). Planning sequences of saccades. *Vision Research, 27,* 1327–1341.

6 Visual memory, spatial representation, and navigation

Amy L. Shelton
Johns Hopkins University

Naohide Yamamoto
George Washington University

1. INTRODUCTION

When asked "Where is the couch located in your living room?" many people would try to imagine the visual scene of the room (much like, in Chapter 8, identifying the shape of a cat's ear). Alternatively, people might conjure up a schematic map of the living room, essentially drawing a mental sketch-map. Some people might use both of these types of images, or some hybrid of the two, to think about the space. The degree to which someone might use any one of these retrieval strategies probably depends on the familiarity of the environment (how recently you rearranged furniture), the scale of the space (can you see it all from a single vantage point?), specific experiences with the space (perhaps you used a schematic to decide where to place the furniture), and individual differences in preferences (e.g., Lawton, 1996; Pazzaglia & De Beni, 2001), but all of these are likely to have the feel of trying to *see* something about the environment (actual scenes or schematics).

For most sighted humans, it is quite natural to think of space as a visual phenomenon. Indeed, many of the core lines of inquiry on the nature of human spatial memory explore the issue in the context of spatial information learned visually (e.g., Easton & Sholl, 1995; Hartley, Maguire, Spiers, & Burgess, 2003; McNamara, 2003; Moeser, 1988; Presson, DeLange, & Hazelrigg, 1989; Rieser, 1989; Shelton & McNamara, 1997, 2001a; Thorndyke & Hayes-Roth, 1982; Waller, 2006; Wraga, Creem, & Proffitt, 2000). The link between space and vision is even stronger in many working memory theories, which posit a *visuo*-spatial working memory component rather than separating spatial from visual (e.g., Baddeley & Hitch, 1974, 1994; Hitch, Brandimonte, & Walker, 1995; but see chapter 1 for an alternative point of view). Even the term "cognitive map" (Tolman, 1948), which has been widely used to identify internal representations of space, conjures up the notion of a map that can be viewed and interrogated.

Despite this strong reliance on vision to study and define spatial representations, few would question that spatial information can come from many sources, both visual and nonvisual—maps, exploratory navigation, text descriptions, haptic exploration, walking without vision, and so forth (e.g., Berthoz et al., 1999; Klatzky, Lippa, Loomis, & Golledge, 2002; Lambrey & Berthoz, 2003; Loomis, 1993; Loomis, Hebert, & Cicinelli, 1990; Shelton & McNamara, 2004a; Yamamoto & Shelton, 2005). Moreover, congenitally blind individuals clearly have the capacity for spatial learning (for review see Golledge, Klatzky, & Loomis, 1996; Millar, 1994; Thinus-Blanc & Gaunet, 1997). As such, the link between spatial memory and visual memory is not inextricable, just pervasive. Here, we attempt to characterize this relationship by considering theoretical and empirical ideas about the role of visual information, visual coding, and visual memory in various aspects of spatial cognition.

2. REPRESENTATIONAL PROPERTIES AND VISION

The nature of spatial memory representations is the subject of many different kinds of debates. Here we present some of the major issues and dichotomies found in the literature and use them to discuss the role that visual processing and visual memory might play. In many of these debates, the evidence is not decisive, but it does speak to the critical questions in the field.

2.1. Vision as the primary spatial modality

Visual mapping theories of spatial memory have suggested the most direct link between vision and spatial representations. According to this type of theory, the human spatial memory system is designed to take information from multiple modalities and create a visual representation of the space—that is, the spatial memory system is one part of a broader visual memory system. In the strong version of the hypothesis, vision or visual experience is a prerequisite for spatial representations because these representations must be coded visually (Hartlage, 1969; Hebb, 1949; Schlaegel, 1953). The wealth of evidence showing that congenitally blind individuals are quite capable of representing spatial information refutes this obligatory dependence on visual experience (e.g., Golledge et al., 1996; Leonard & Newman, 1967; Passini, Delisle, Langlois, & Prouis, 1988; Passini, Proulx, & Rainville, 1990; Tinti, Adenzato, Tamietto, & Cornoldi, 2006). However, several lines of research appear to implicitly support a more moderate version of the hypothesis which gives special status to vision as the primary modality for spatial learning and memory (e.g., Attneave & Benson, 1969; Bertelson & Radeau, 1981; Mastroianni, 1982; Platt & Warren, 1972; Rock, 1966; Vecchi, Tinti, & Cornoldi, 2004; Warren, 1970).

The dominance of vision over other modalities can be seen in studies that put visual and nonvisual information in competition. When visual information and nonvisual information are providing incongruent information about the location of a single stimulus, participants will localize the stimulus to the visual source (Attneave & Benson, 1969; Bertelson & Radeau, 1981; Boring, 1926; Fishbein, Decker, & Wilcox, 1977; Hay, Pick, & Ikeda, 1965; Howard & Templeton,

1966; Jackson, 1953; Rock & Victor, 1964; Thurlow & Kerr, 1970; Welch & Warren, 1980). For example, Hay et al. (1965) had participants judge their own hand position while wearing prism glasses that produced a visual shift. Despite participants' knowledge of the visual shift and the proprioceptive information about hand position, they localized the hand to the (incorrect) visually perceived location—that is, the visual shift led them to feel their limb in a different location from its actual position. A common example of "visual capture" of auditory information is familiar to anyone who has watched a movie in a theater or with a home entertainment system. Even though the speakers are displaced to the left and right (and often throughout a theater), we will perceive an actor's voice as coming directly from his or her location on the screen (Howard & Templeton, 1966).

Visual capture for locations across modalities extends beyond just the immediate resolution of a conflict. After some period of adaptation to the conflict, one can remove the conflict and observe which modality has been adjusted. In such cases, the perceptual adaptation appears to be occurring in the nonvisual modality. That is, the system is recalibrating to make the nonvisual input match the visual input (e.g., Bernier, Chua, Inglis, & Franks, 2007; Botvinik & Cohen, 1998; Ehrsson, 2007; Hay & Pick, 1966; Lenggenhager, Tadi, Metzinger, & Blanke, 2007; Ramachandran, Rogers-Ramachandran, & Cobb, 1995; Redding & Wallace, 1987; Rieser, Pick, Ashmead, & Garing, 1995).

In addition to capturing other modalities, visual reference frames appear to support localization in other modalities (Mastroianni, 1982; Platt & Warren, 1972; Simmering, Peterson, Darling, & Spencer, 2008; Warren, 1970). For example, Warren compared localization of stimuli in three different conditions. In visual localization, participants pointed to visually presented targets. In auditory localization without visual reference, participants pointed to auditory targets with their eyes closed. In auditory localization with visual reference, participants pointed to invisible auditory targets with their eyes open. Not surprisingly, the variability in pointing (i.e., variable error) was smallest in visual localization. However, in the critical comparison of auditory localization with and without vision, there was an advantage for having the visual reference frame available. In other words, performance in auditory localization became more similar to that in visual localization when visual information about physical surroundings was given to the participants, even though this visual information did not provide any direct cues to the auditory stimulus locations. These results have been interpreted to mean that auditory localization in the presence of visual information is carried out by choosing a point corresponding to the auditory target within a visual frame of reference.

The above examples suggest a role for vision in more perceptual processes. In memory, information from nonvisual modalities can produce what appears to be visual memory (Kirasic & Mathes, 1990; Shelton & McNamara, 2001b, 2004a). For example, Shelton and McNamara (2001b) had participants view a display of objects from one perspective and manually reconstruct the display from another perspective without vision (Figure 6.1a). In scene recognition, a

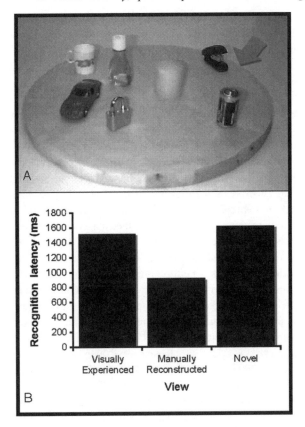

Figure 6.1. A. Sample display from Shelton & McNamara (2001b). B. Summary of response latency data as a function of the to-be-recognized view when participants visually experienced one view and manually reconstructed a different view (without vision). Novel views were not viewed or reconstructed during encoding. Figure 6.1a reproduced by permission from Shelton, A. L., & McNamara, T. P. (2001b). Visual memories from nonvisual experiences. *Psychological Science, 12,* 343–347.

visual task, participants were fastest at recognizing the view that they had manually constructed (Figure 6.1b). Moreover, recognition of the visually perceived view was not different from recognition of novel views of the layout. In follow-up interviews, participants were indeed confused about which view they had actually seen, suggesting that they coded the manually reconstructed view in a manner that confused it with the visually perceived view. Similarly, Kirasic and Mathes found that scene recognition performance was unaffected by the way a space was learned—visually or verbally. Although differences in performance have been noted for scene recognition compared to other spatial tasks (e.g., Shelton & McNamara, 2004a, 2004b), the dependence on visual information in these tasks supports the idea that encoding in nonvisual modalities might be visually mediated.

Returning to the spatial representations of blind individuals, we can consider the primacy of vision for forming and/or coding spatial representation. Although blind individuals form effective spatial representations from nonvisual information, studies have shown that they are often impaired relative to blindfolded sighted individuals (e.g., Fisher, 1964; Gaunet, Martinez, & Thinus-Blanc, 1997; Gaunet & Thinus-Blanc, 1996; Herman, Chatman, & Roth, 1983; McLinden, 1988; Rossano & Warren, 1989). In these and similar studies, early or congenitally blind individuals were comparable to sighted individuals on spatial judgments about environments when tested on a single property of the environment or in simple configurations. However, when the task required more construction among parts of the environment and inferences about abstracted relations, blind individuals showed substantial impairment relative to sighted individuals. Additional work on mental imagery has suggested that inferential processes, and the degree of impairment, can be distinguished based on the degree of visual imagery that might be elicited by the task (Knauff & May, 2006).

In addition to this general difference in task demands, many studies have shown that the degree of impairment on these tasks is correlated with differences in visual experience. That is, the earlier the onset of blindness, the more profound the impairment, suggesting that visual experience may play some critical role in developing the appropriate reference frame for coordinating spatial information from different modalities (e.g., Axelrod, 1959; Cleaves & Royal, 1979; Dodds, Howarth, & Carter, 1982; Hötting, Rösler, & Röder, 2004; Rieser, Hill, Talor, Bradfield, & Rosen, 1992; Rieser, Guth, & Hill, 1986; Rieser, Lockman, & Pick, 1980; Röder, Kusmierek, Spence, & Schicke, 2007; Röder, Rösler, & Spence, 2004; for a more general role visual experience might play for cross-modal interactions, see also Putzar, Goerendt, Lange, Rösler, & Röder, 2007). Additional support for this role of visually mediated integration across modalities comes from work in nonhuman animals. For example, neurons in the superior colliculus of adult cats that had been raised in visual deprivation showed unimodal responses to each modality but failed to show the multimodal response observed in normally reared animals (Wallace, Carriere, Perrault, Vaughan, & Stein, 2006; Wallace, Perrault, Hairston, & Stein, 2004). These results from blindness and visual deprivation studies provide grounding for a privileged and potentially essential role of visual experience in the normal development of the mechanisms that enable the use of multiple modalities to represent space.

Taken together, these and similar lines of evidence support the notion that vision is a dominant, and potentially primary, *source* for spatial information in sighted individuals. Given that humans use vision as a dominant modality for many activities, it is not surprising that they would use visual information when it is available, give greater weight to visual inputs when information is ambiguous, and supplement nonvisual information with visual imagery if possible. However, the question remains as to whether these results should be taken as support for visual coding of spatial information. To address this issue, we now turn to some of the features of spatial memory that have been explored and how they bear on the role of vision and visual memory.

2.2. Egocentric and allocentric information in spatial memory

The very notion of a position in space requires a reference frame, and one of the primary distinctions made among possible reference frames has been between egocentric and allocentric (a.k.a. geocentric, exocentric, environment-centered) reference frames (e.g., Burgess, 2006; Feigenbaum & Rolls, 1991; Howard, 1991; McNamara, Rump, & Werner, 2003; Nardini, Burgess, Breckenridge, & Atkinson, 2006; Neggers, Van der Lubbe, Ramsey, & Postma, 2006; Wang & Spelke, 2000). As the terms suggest, egocentric reference frames code location with respect to the observer, whereas allocentric reference frames code location with respect to something external to the observer (room axes, distal cues, cardinal directions, etc.).

There is substantial evidence for both egocentric and allocentric information coded in the brain from neurophysiology and neuropsychology. In different sub-regions of the parietal cortex, neurons respond to the stimuli in retina-centered, head-centered, and even hand-centered coordinate systems (e.g., Colby & Goldberg, 1999), supporting a system for representing space egocentrically. However, place cells in the medial temporal lobes have been shown to code location with respect to the environmental reference frame (e.g., Burgess, Jeffery, & O'Keefe, 1999). In rats, place cells respond preferentially every time a rat moves to the preferred location in the environment, irrespective of the direction of approach (e.g., O'Keefe, 1976; Wilson & McNaughton, 1993).

A similar type of coding has been identified in nonhuman primates, in the form of spatial view cells (e.g., Feigenbaum & Rolls, 1991; Rolls, 1999; Rolls & O'Mara, 1995). Spatial view cells respond preferentially when the animal is looking at a particular location in the environment (or screen), irrespective of the combination of the animal's location, head direction, and gaze direction from which the preferred location is viewed. Finally, intracranial recordings in humans have demonstrated both place cell and spatial view cell responses in regions of the medial temporal lobe (Ekstrom et al., 2003).

This parietal/medial temporal lobe distinction for egocentric versus allocentric representation is also supported by patient studies (e.g., Abrahams, Pickering, Jarosz, Cox, & Morris, 1999; Abrahams, Pickering, Polkey, & Morris, 1997; Ackerman, 1986; Bisiach & Luzzatti, 1978; Burgess et al., 1999; Holdstock et al., 2000). In the parietal cortex, the strongest evidence for egocentric reference frames has come from work on unilateral neglect (e.g., Bartolomeo, D'Erme, & Gainotti, 1994; Chokron, 2003; Farah, Brunn, Wong, Wallace, & Carpenter, 1990; Halligan & Marshall, 1991; Mennemeier, Chatterjee, & Jeilman, 1994; Rizzolatti & Gallese, 1988). For example, Bisiach and Luzzatti presented a now classic case of unilateral representational neglect in which the neglected information changed as a function of the egocentric location of the patient. When patients with right parietal cortex damage were asked to recall a familiar site—the Piazza del Duomo in Milan, Italy—from one end, they neglected to describe the left half of the piazza. However, when asked to describe it again from the opposite end of the piazza, the previously missing information was readily described. This finding suggested that there was an intact (perhaps allo-centric) representation of the entire Piazza stored in some form, but damage to the parietal cortex impaired the recollection in the egocentric framework.

In contrast, damage to the hippocampus appears to affect more allocentric forms of processing (e.g., Abrahams et al., 1997, 1999; Holdstock et al., 2000; King, Burgess, Hartley, Vargha-Khadem, & O'Keefe, 2002). For example, Hold-stock et al. compared a patient with hippocampal damage to a matched group of controls on a simple location memory task. Participants viewed a single light on an otherwise uniform table and had to recall the location of the light (Figure 6.2). After observing the light, participants had to recall or recognize its location under several different conditions. In a lighted room from the same viewpoint as the learning, both egocentric and allocentric information could be used to retrieve the location information. To test for the use of egocentric information, retrieval was conducted in the dark from the same viewpoint as learning (Figure 6.2a). To test for the use of allocentric information, retrieval was conducted with full visual cues but from a new viewpoint in the room (Figure 6.2b). The hip-pocampal patient was consistently worse than controls in the allocentric condi-tions but had comparable performance to controls in the egocentric conditions, suggesting a specific impairment in representing location in allocentric but not egocentric space.

These results posit a role for both egocentric and allocentric information in the spatial representation(s) that humans use to remember and act within their environments (e.g., Burgess, 2006; McNamara, Rump, & Werner, 2003; Wang & Spelke, 2002). At the perceptual level, all sensory information is initially

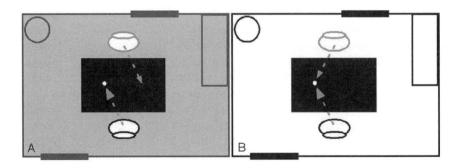

Figure 6.2. Schematic of the type of display used to test contributions of egocentric and allocentric information (e.g., Holdstock et al., 2000). The black chair reflects the learning position, and the gray chair reflects an alternative test position. A. In a darkened room, the response will reflect egocentric pointing from either location because the participant has no allocentric information to indicate a location relative to the distal cues. B. In a lighted room, the response may be guided by allocentric information, allowing the participant to correctly change the response when seated in a new location.

coded in an egocentric reference frame because the location of the perceptual reception is the observer. For example, visual images are retinotopically mapped in the eye, and this retinotopy continues into visual cortex (e.g., Tootell et al., 1998). Similarly, auditory location is coded in a head-centered coordinate frame. An allocentric representation therefore implies some process(es) by which the egocentric information is translated into an allocentric reference frame. As such, any theories that assume an allocentric representation are not consonant with the claim that spatial information is visually coded in spatial memory. In particular, several researchers have suggested that this translation from egocentric to allocentric "coding" occurs at a level independent of any particular modality, giving rise to a single supramodal (also called amodal) representation of space (e.g., Hill & Best, 1981; Milner & Goodale, 1995; Nadel, 1999, 2004; O'Keefe & Nadel, 1978). The hippocampus plays a central role as the proposed locus of this supramodal representation (O'Keefe, 1976; O'Keefe & Dostrovsky, 1971; O'Keefe & Nadel, 1978) or the resource for building up a more distributed representation elsewhere (e.g., Eichenbaum, Dudchenko, Wood, Shapiro, & Tanila, 1999; McNamara & Shelton, 2003).

2.3. Functional equivalence of different types of encoding

Whereas visual dominance suggests that spatial information might be visually mapped either in the memory representation or en route to it, functional equivalence paints a different role for modality in spatial representation. Functional equivalence refers to the degree to which spatial memories function the same way regardless of the modality in which they were learned, a finding that has been shown for a variety of spatial and navigational tasks (Auerbach & Sperling, 1974; Avraamides, Klatzky, Loomis, & Golledge, 2004a; Klatzky, Lippa, Loomis, & Golledge, 2002, 2003; Loomis, Klatzky, & Lederman, 1991; Loomis, Klatzky, Philbeck, & Golledge, 1998; Loomis, Lippa, Klatzky, & Golledge, 2002; Pasqualotto, Finucane, & Newell, 2005; Wang, 2004). For example, Klatzky et al. (2003) asked participants to learn the locations of visual or auditory stimuli from a stationary position. Subsequent memory tests that required localizing the learned locations—pointing to the remembered locations, verbal report of distance, walking to locations, and so forth—revealed no differences due to the learning modality. Performance on inferential tasks, such as pointing from a novel position in the environment, biased the localization in the same way for visually and auditorily learned spaces. These results together suggest that spatial learning in vision and audition resulted in representations that were comparable in terms of both locative information and sensitivity to updating. Similar results have been found for comparisons across other encoding modalities and in other memory tasks (scene recognition, distance and direction estimation among objects, etc.), suggesting that spatial representations derived from each modality share the same functional properties.

It has also been suggested that functional equivalence extends beyond sensory modalities to sources such as spatial language (Avraamides, Loomis, Klatzky, &

Golledge, 2004b; Loomis et al., 2002). For example, Avraamides et al. (2004b) had participants learn locations of four objects in a room through visual perception or verbal descriptions of those object locations. When the participants were subsequently guided to another position in the room and asked to indicate distances and directions between object pairs, their responses were equivalent (both in accuracy and response latency) in visual perception and verbal description conditions. Such findings have been interpreted to mean that, once formed, spatial representations built from indirect "non-sensory" modalities also function equivalently to those learned through more direct perceptual inputs.

However, it should also be noted that research on the functional equivalence of non-sensory-based spatial representations has yet to yield unequivocal findings. By using spatial tasks similar to the one mentioned above, the same group of researchers showed that spatial representations derived from language had some disadvantage in mediating spatial updating performance (Klatzky et al., 2003). Moreover, studies of spatial language have suggested that the correspondence between spatial language and spatial representations is not direct. Instead, it has been proposed that spatial language is a filtered and imprecise reflection of the underlying spatial representation (e.g., Landau & Jackendoff, 1993). As such, this issue presents an interesting challenge for future investigations.

This functional equivalence is taken as further evidence that spatial representations are supramodal (e.g., Bryant, 1997; Eilan, 1993; Loomis et al., 2002). Like visual mapping theories, supramodal representation theories suggest a unitary spatial representation; however, rather than being visually coded, the supramodal representation (as the name suggests) is independent of the modality in which space is learned. For example, the cognitive map theory suggests that the spatial memory system creates a representation that has been abstracted from information coming in through the senses (e.g., Nadel, 1999, 2004; O'Keefe & Nadel, 1978). The abstract nature of spatial representation draws from the philosophical belief that the capacity for spatial representation is innate and therefore precursory to sensory experience (Descartes, 1993). As such, although vision may be a dominant sensory modality, it is simply one of the ways that information can get into a more general spatial memory system. In addition, functional equivalence suggests that there is no special status for vision, because the representations acquired from nonvisual modalities afford the same behaviors as those acquired from vision.

2.4. Modality specificity and spatial representations

As mentioned above, supramodal spatial representations have often been posited based on functional equivalence of spatial memories acquired through various modalities. However, it is important to note that the supramodal representation is not the only form of spatial representations that is consistent with the functional equivalence. That is, it is possible that multiple modality-specific representations, based on different modalities, mediate spatial behaviors equally well independently of each other. Such modality-specific representations would support modality-specific performance on different tests of spatial memory.

Several studies have provided evidence for modality-specific representations by probing spatial memory with tasks that place differential demands on particular modalities (Ernst & Banks, 2002; Lambrey, Viaud-Delmon, & Berthoz, 2002; Newell, Woods, Mernagh, & Bülthoff, 2005; Newport, Rabb, & Jackson, 2002; Shelton & McNamara, 2004a, 2004b; van Beers, Haggard, & Wolpert, 2002). For example, Shelton and McNamara (2004b) had participants learn tabletop displays like the one shown in Figure 6.1a by experiencing two different views. One view was learned visually and the other was "learned" by having the participant describe that view to another person. Participants were tested on both judgments of relative direction—an amodal task—and scene recognition—a visual task. The results revealed that participants were better at recognizing the visually learned view in scene recognition, but they were better at making relative-position judgments from orientations corresponding to the described view (Figure 6.3). These results suggest that participants could tap into different representations[1] for the two different tests of spatial memory. The sensitivity of scene recognition to direct visual experience has also been shown for experience with multiple orientations (e.g., Shelton & McNamara, 2004a; Valiquette & McNamara, 2007). Despite evidence for a single preferred orientation for accessing spatial information needed for relative judgments, participants tend to

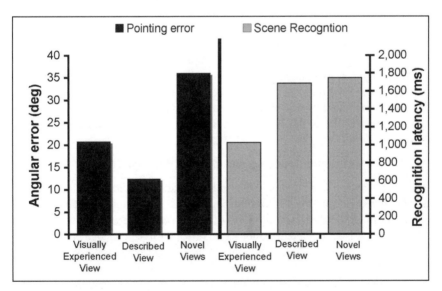

Figure 6.3. Summary data from Shelton & McNamara (2004b), showing the angular error data from judgments of relative direction (JRDs; black bars) and response latency data from scene recognition (gray bars) as a function of the to-be-recognized view when participants experienced one view visually and described a different view (without vision). Novel views were not viewed or described during encoding.

recognize the views from each experienced orientation more quickly than novel views. This finding supports at least two forms of representation, with one being visually sensitive.

These studies have also shown that functional equivalence and modality specificity can co-occur. For example, Newell et al. (2005) had participants learn a tabletop-sized array of seven objects (similar to Figure 6.1a) through either stationary viewing or haptic exploration of the display. After the learning phase, the locations of two objects in the array were switched and participants were asked to identify the change through either stationary viewing or haptic exploration. The learning and test modalities were factorially combined to compare within- and cross-modal performance. In addition, the test displays were shown either from the learned orientation or from a novel orientation. The results revealed both functional equivalence and modality specificity. First, visual and haptic learning in each orientation condition yielded similar accuracy in change detection, supporting functional equivalence. More importantly, however, results also showed that the accuracy was significantly worse when different modalities were used for learning and test, revealing a cost associated with cross-modal (visual-to-haptic or haptic-to-visual) recognition of the display. This pattern of performance is not readily accounted for by supramodal or visually mapped representations. More plausible interpretation would be that the participants formed spatial representations that were still linked to the learning modalities. That is, these modality-specific representations mediated the change detection performance equally well, but when different modalities were used at the time of encoding and retrieval, spatial information in memory had to somehow be translated from learned modality to test modality, with additional cognitive processes incurring a cost in the change detection accuracy.

Taken together, evidence for modality-specific representations suggests that a unitary supramodal representation cannot support empirical findings on its own. Like the supramodal theory, however, multiple modality-specific representations argue against vision as the de facto modality for spatial representation.

2.5. Viewpoint dependence versus orientation dependence

Related to many of the topics above is the debate over viewpoint dependence in spatial representations. Viewpoint dependence was originally debated (and continues to be debated) as a property of visual object representations, and that term has been used interchangeably with "orientation dependence" (Biederman, 1987; Biederman & Gerhardstein, 1993, 1995; Tarr, 1995; Tarr & Pinker, 1989, 1990, 1991). For visual object recognition, viewpoint and orientation have very similar connotations; however, the implications for spatial cognition may be different, particularly with respect to the role of vision and other modalities in the representation.

A viewpoint-dependent representation of space denotes a representation that is specific with regard to both the location and orientation of the observer at the time of encoding. Implicit in this type of representation is the need for visual experience. That is, space is represented with respect to a learned *view*point. Data from scene recognition experiments support this kind of highly visual, view-specific representation of spatial information (Christou & Bülthoff, 1999; Diwadkar & McNamara, 1997; Shelton & McNamara, 2001b, 2004a, 2004b; Shelton & Pippitt, 2007; Waller, 2006). For example, Waller (2006) asked participants to learn scenes of objects and compared recognition for images that were taken from the same viewpoint to those that were translated forward, backward, or laterally. Recognition of forward and lateral translations was slower and less accurate than recognition of the original image, suggesting that participants recognized the specific learned viewpoint better than translated viewpoints. In addition, Shelton and McNamara (2004a) investigated scene recognition following navigational learning from different perspectives. The results suggested that the degree of visual similarity from study to test was associated with the speed of scene recognition, indicating fastest recognition for the exact viewpoint seen during encoding (details of this study are discussed later in section 3.4). Taken together, such results support viewpoint-dependent representations.

Scene recognition is a visual matching task, and viewpoint dependence denotes the capture of spatial information from a specified view—implied to be a visually experienced view of the space. As noted above, however, humans have the capacity to learn and represent spatial information from multiple modalities with equivalent access to that information after learning, raising questions about how viewpoint dependence might be defined in other modalities. Even if we relax the dependence on a visual view, a viewpoint still denotes a stationary position and heading. This necessity for experiencing space from a static position may apply to vision and possibly audition, but it cannot account for other forms of learning. For example, Yamamoto and Shelton (2005) compared visual learning to proprioceptive learning (broadly defined) of room-sized layouts. As shown in Figure 6.4a, viewpoint for the visually learned space is easily defined by the stationary position and heading of the observer. In contrast, for the proprioceptively learned space, the spatial information must be learned from the movements by changing positions along a path, in this case, while maintaining the same heading in space (Figure 6.4b). As a result, the "viewpoint" is constantly changing, and these dynamics make defining the viewpoint in viewpoint dependence complicated for nonvisual modalities.

An alternative to viewpoint dependence for spatial representations is orientation dependence. Orientation dependence refers to a broader concept of accessing a spatial memory from a particular orientation in space. In an orientation-dependent representation, there is greater emphasis placed on the heading in space than on the exact position of the observer. Alignment effects provide strong support for orientation dependence in spatial memory acquired in vision (e.g., Easton & Sholl, 1995; Holmes & Sholl, 2005; McNamara, 2003; McNamara, Rump, & Werner, 2003; Roskos-Ewoldsen, McNamara, Shelton, & Carr, 1998; Shelton & McNamara, 1997, 2001a, 2001b, 2004a, 2004b; Sholl & Nolin, 1997; Yamamoto & Shelton, in press) and other modalities (Shelton & McNamara, 2001b, 2004a, 2004b; Yamamoto & Shelton, 2005, 2007, 2008). For example, Shelton

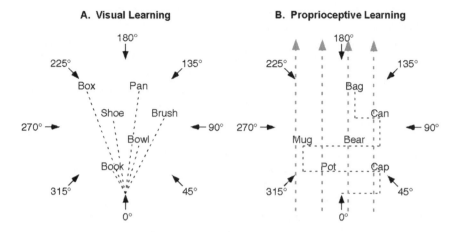

Figure 6.4. Schematics of learning conditions used in Yamamoto & Shelton (2005).
A. Visual learning. 0° is the stationary view, and dashed lines indicate the
direction to each object from the viewpoint. B. Proprioceptive learning
(blindfolded walking) from a single orientation. Dashed line shows the path.
Gray arrows show a vector field corresponding to the common orientation
maintained throughout encoding.

and McNamara (2001a) had participants learn room-sized layouts and tested
memory with judgments of relative direction. Across multiple experiments, the
results revealed that participants had preferential access to one orientation over
all novel orientations and even some previously learned orientations. These
results were taken as an indication that the representation was dependent on a
preferred orientation on the space.

The key difference between viewpoint dependence and orientation dependence
is in flexibility for retrieving information from different positions within a preferred orientation. In both orientation- and viewpoint-dependent representations,
there should be preferential access to the orientation of the representation. Only
in viewpoint-dependent representations, however, would a cost also be expected
for changes in position within the preferred orientation. Although Waller (2006)
showed some evidence for a cost in scene recognition after translations, it was
not clear for all types of translations. For imagined judgments about locations
and directions, the evidence is even less clear. Studies on the role of physical
movement in imagining new locations and headings suggest that rotations but
not translations improve performance relative to a no-movement, imagine-only
baseline (Presson & Montello, 1994; Rieser, 1989). These results indicate the
possibility that mentally translating a viewpoint can be done with very little cost.
However, there has been some limited evidence for a cost in mental translations
(Easton & Sholl, 1995; Tlauka, 2006). For example, Tlauka asked participants
to learn an array of objects that included three possible viewing positions in

addition to the actual learning position. The additional viewing positions were the to-be-imagined positions for the test and reflected different combinations of rotation and translation from the actual learned viewpoint. The results revealed that judgments from positions with imagined rotations were more than 200 ms slower than the original viewpoint or translated views, but the lateral translations (without rotation) also incurred about a 90-ms cost in response latency relative to the original viewpoint. It is notable, however, that there were no differences between the rotational conditions based on whether they included forward translations or forward + lateral translations. Taken together, these findings suggest that rotations are computationally more demanding than translations, as predicted by orientation dependence, but they do not completely discount some degree of viewpoint specificity as well.

Although the evidence is not conclusive with regard to viewpoint versus orientation dependence, positing orientation dependence has certain advantages. First, orientation dependence can more readily accommodate multiple modalities without having to establish different principles across modalities—an important issue given that different modalities can support equivalent performance. As illustrated in Figure 6.4b, for example, while it is difficult to give a strict definition of viewpoint dependence in proprioceptive learning, orientation dependence is readily defined. Even if we accept that viewpoint need not be strictly visual, viewpoint dependence in proprioceptive and haptic learning would still require specifying a mechanism by which a viewpoint might be selected from the many learned positions throughout learning. For haptic learning, one can use the position of learning as a virtual viewpoint on the space. That is, the extension of the arms to each object originates from a particular position, and moving about the space would cause the origin of this proprioceptive information to shift. Such viewpoint dependence for haptic learning accounts for the observation of small but significant translation effects in haptics (Klatzky, 1999). For proprioception from blindfolded walking, this notion of a viewpoint selection may be more akin to finding some canonical position for representing the space. Such canonical positions have already been suggested by Waller (2006) to account for the observation that some translations had an effect when others did not in visual learning.

A second potential advantage of orientation dependence is that it is consonant with theories of spatial representation that posit non-egocentric/environmentally centered reference frames. Unlike viewpoint dependence, which seems to suggest a largely egocentric (learned-position) basis for representation (e.g., Tlauka, 2006), orientation dependence does not require that the preferred orientation be a directly experienced orientation. As such, orientation dependence can more readily accommodate observations of non-egocentric orientations emerging as the preferred orientations in memory (e.g., Mou, Liu, & McNamara, in press; Mou & McNamara, 2002; Mou, Zhao, & McNamara, 2007). For example, Mou and McNamara (2002) asked participants to learn room-sized object displays that had strong intrinsic structure when observed from a view that was 45° away from the learning position. If participants were alerted to the structure, the 45°

view would become the preferred orientation for memory retrieval. Mou and McNamara suggested that this reflected the selection of an intrinsic reference frame that could be based on either egocentric experience or salient structures in the environment.

Returning to visual memory, viewpoint dependence reflects representational constructs that are more analogous to the type of coding one would expect for visual information. That is, we have a point of origin (namely, the eyes) from which we observe the world visually, and viewpoint dependence suggests a similar anchoring position. Orientation dependence is less directly tied to notions of visual coding and may be more commensurate with supramodal theories of spatial information. For example, the principal reference theory (e.g., McNamara & Valiquette, 2004; Shelton & McNamara, 2001a; Werner & Schmidt, 1999), upon which the intrinsic theories have been built, suggests that *any* environmental learning will begin with the selection of a principal orientation, without regard for the degree to which it can be tied to vision. However, the principal reference theory and other supramodal theories are agnostic with regard to how experience might cause this supramodal system to be more tuned for and/or more readily connected to visual inputs. As such, they cannot discount some prominent role for vision as the primary input or as an intermediary for other modalities.

2.6. Summary

In the preceding sections, we have outlined some of the major issues and debates surrounding the properties of spatial representations and how they might be related to vision and visual memory. The jury is still out on a number of these issues, reflecting the lack of a unifying theory in the spatial cognition literature. The balance of the data supports the claim that sighted individuals rely heavily on visual information for spatial learning. However, they also highlight the ability for humans, blind or sighted, to use many other sources of input to acquire spatial information.

3. NAVIGATIONAL PROCESSES AND VISUAL MEMORY

Spatial memory plays a persistent role in many daily activities, perhaps most commonly in our daily navigation—from the bedroom to the kitchen, from home to work, from the office to the vending machine. Navigation itself can also be broken down into the different types of processes we hope to accomplish as we move through space (e.g., Golledge, 1999). At present, there is no unifying theory of the different types of tasks and processes that might engage human spatial memory, but the contribution of visual memory to navigation can be characterized by considering its potential role in these different proposed processes. In the following sections, we discuss some of the known and proposed processes and attempt to draw some preliminary conclusions about the role for visual memory.

3.1. Place and response learning

One of the fundamental distinctions in the processes that guide spatial behavior has been the difference between place- and response-learning mechanisms in rats (e.g., Packard & McGaugh, 1996; Restle, 1957; Tolman, Ritchie, & Kalish, 1946, 1947). In their classic studies, Tolman and colleagues demonstrated this dichotomy using a T-maze learning paradigm. Rats were placed in a maze like the one shown in Figure 6.5a. During training, the rat was placed at the same starting position and the reward was always in the same place. After training, the critical test was conducted by changing the configuration and starting position (Figure 6.5b). From this new position, there are two "correct" responses depending on what the rat has learned. If the rat has learned to use the cues in the environment, it will turn toward the environmental cue, demonstrating place learning. However, if the rat has learned to make a specific response to the T-maze stimulus, it will turn in the same direction that it has been turning throughout the training, demonstrating response learning.

In rats, place and response learning appear to be occurring in parallel, but several factors determine which will guide behavior (e.g., Cook & Kesner, 1988; Morris, Garrud, Rawlins, & O'Keefe, 1982; O'Keefe & Nadel, 1978; Packard & McGaugh, 1996; Tolman, 1948; Tolman et al., 1946, 1947). First, numerous studies indicate that place learning occurs more rapidly with limited learning and over-learning with variable routes, whereas response learning occurs after

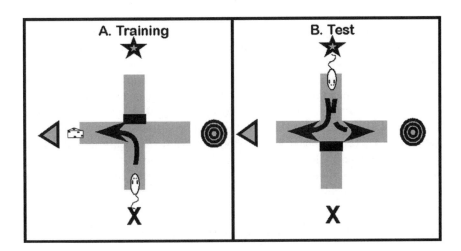

Figure 6.5. Schematics of a typical T-maze setup (e.g., Packard & McGaugh, 1996). Black bar shows a blockade, and shapes represent distal cues. A. During training, the same response (left turn) is required repeatedly to reach the goal. B. During test, the rat enters from the opposite direction. The solid arrow shows the place-learning behavior (turn toward the triangle), and the dashed arrow shows the response-learning behavior (turn left).

extensive training provided that the same route is repeated throughout training. In terms of utility, place learning affords greater flexibility of use, accommodating changes in the environment and the need to find novel routes. However, this flexibility is cognitively demanding. In contrast, response learning lacks flexibility but may allow for accurate performance with limited attention. As such, when attentional resources are limited, it is useful to have a more automated system for navigating familiar environments.

In addition to the behavioral differences, place and response learning have been associated with two different neural systems—hippocampus and caudate, respectively (Cook & Kesner, 1988; Morris et al., 1982; Packard & McGaugh, 1996). For example, using Tolman's T-maze paradigm, Packard and McGaugh demonstrated that lesions of the caudate resulted in solely place-learning performance whereas lesions of the hippocampus resulted in solely response-learning performance.

In humans, there has been a long-standing assumption that these two systems are also operating (e.g., Burgess et al., 1999), and neuroimaging studies have used the known neural correlates to support this contention (e.g., Hartley et al., 2003; Shelton, Marchette, & Yamamoto, 2007). For example, Shelton et al. (2007) used fMRI to scan participants while learning a fictitious environment by watching a repeated route. The results revealed a negative correlation between activation in the right caudate and the bilateral posterior hippocampus—as a given person showed more caudate activation, he or she showed less hippocampal activation. This difference could be attributed to differences in perspective-taking ability, one indicator of flexible spatial reasoning. Hartley et al. (2003) found a similar task-based difference in these regions. Together, these results have been used to suggest that people may differentially rely on place- and response-learning mechanisms based on individual differences and/ or task demands.

In both rats and humans, these relationships have been revealed using largely visual learning conditions. However, there is nothing in the specification of these mechanisms that requires a link to vision (e.g., Hartley, Burgess, Lever, Cacucci, & O'Keefe, 2000). Like the hippocampus (see section 2.2), the caudate nucleus receives inputs from multiple modalities, suggesting that stimuli from different modalities may serve as the signal for engaging the learned response. The role of cues in different modalities is discussed more thoroughly in the next section.

3.2. Cue guidance and landmark-based navigation

Place and response learning provide one way of dichotomizing possible mechanisms for spatial behavior, but the distinction has hard ties to differences between explicit/declarative memories and implicit/habit-based memories (Burgess et al., 1999; Squire & Zola-Morgan, 1988; Squire et al., 1990). In humans, there may be multiple types of explicit spatial mechanisms or strategies for guiding spatial behavior. For example, route knowledge is the result of encoding and representing information about a specific path or route through the environment (Siegel & White, 1975).[2] Learning a route can be viewed as learning a series of landmarks and the corresponding actions that need to be taken in response to the landmarks or cues. This learning of an action plan may be akin to response learning, but it can also clearly take the form of an explicit memory. For example, some people have a strong preference for navigation based on landmarks—that is, they prefer to follow a path of landmarks tied to actions as an explicit strategy (Pazzaglia & De Beni, 2001). Moreover, unlike response learning, route learning has been viewed as an early stage in spatial learning (Siegel & White, 1975; but also see Montello, 1988, for an alternative perspective).

Closely related to the notion of route learning are the processes of cue guidance (e.g., Morris & Parslow, 2004) and landmark-based navigation (e.g., Pazzaglia & De Beni, 2001). In its simplest form, cue guidance is using a cue as the target for locomotion. For example, on a particularly sunny day, I might want to sit under my favorite tree. If there are several trees in sight, I need only to recognize my favorite and walk toward it. Some species are thought to use this kind of targeting in a progressive fashion, relying heavily on proceeding from one target to the next (Collett & Cartwright, 1983). In a slightly more complicated scenario, landmarks serve as cues to the spatial behaviors needed for navigation. For example, the tree I hope to find might not be in my immediate visual scene. If I know that my favorite tree is on the lawn on the right past the art museum, then I can use the art museum as my cue to turn right. To most healthy individuals, either of these cue-driven tasks seems trivial. Even if clouds are casting an unusual shadow or a portion of the museum has unfamiliar scaffolding along one side, our visual recognition of familiar landmarks tends to be pretty effective as a cue to what we know to be the appropriate response (turn right) from previous experience or instructions.

In patients with damage to the lingual gyrus, a ventral region of the brain, this seemingly simple process becomes daunting. These patients are frequently diagnosed more broadly with topographical disorientation because they are unable to orient and navigate in familiar or unfamiliar environments (Aguirre, Zarahn, & D'Esposito, 1998; Landis, Cummings, Benson, & Palmer, 1986). However, upon close examination, they appear to suffer from a specific deficit—landmark agnosia—in which the ability to recognize and use landmarks in the environment is impaired (Aguirre & D'Esposito, 1999). Although these patients can describe what landmark they need to find (e.g., the Art Museum), they do not recognize the landmark when it comes into view.[3] This loss of contact between the spatial information and visual memory for the landmarks, which patients often can describe, severely impairs navigation in these individuals. Many patients report the need to actively compensate for this loss by relying on street names, house numbers, maps, and carefully drawn plans (e.g., Whitely & Warrington, 1978), supporting the intrinsic reliance on visual memory for effective cue-guided navigation.

Landmark-based navigation in sighted humans is likely to have substantial reliance on visual memory. That is, the most obvious landmarks in our environments tend to be visually experienced. However, this reliance on visual cues in most environments does not preclude the use of cues in other modalities to guide navigation. There is clear evidence for the use of patterns of olfactory cues to guide navigation in birds (e.g., Wallraff, 2004) and rats (e.g., Rossier & Schenk, 2003). In humans, blind individuals report using a variety of cues to orient and navigate (e.g., Golledge et al., 1996; Golledge, Marston, Loomis, & Klatzky, 2004; Millar, 1994; Passini et al., 1988), and even sighted individuals can effectively follow auditory cues to navigate (Klatzky, Marston, Giudice, Golledge, & Loomis, 2006). As such, the role of visual information in cue-guided landmark navigation depends on what cues are serving as the landmarks, which, for sighted humans, are more likely to be visual than nonvisual.

3.3. Cognitive maps

Route-based learning is probably the most common way that humans learn about their environments (MacEachren, 1992), but this type of learning does not restrict humans to route knowledge and cue-based navigation. Humans can effectively use this information to build up a flexible spatial representation of the configuration of landmarks in the environment, much like those hypothesized in the place-learning mechanisms described above. Several labels have been used to describe this type of representation—environmental image (Appleyard, 1969, 1970), topographical memory (e.g., Aguirre, Detre, Alsop, & D'Esposito, 1996; Epstein, DeYoe, Press, Rosen, & Kanwisher, 2001; Hartley et al., 2007; Landis et al., 1986; Whitely & Warrington, 1978), spatial model (Franklin, Tversky, & Coon, 1992; Mani & Johnson-Laird, 1982; McGuinness, 1992; Taylor & Tversky, 1992; Tversky, 1991), survey maps/knowledge (Klatzky, Loomis, Golledge, & Cicinelli, 1990; Siegel & White, 1975)—to name but a few. Tolman (1948) introduced the term "cognitive mapping" to describe the establishment of this internal representation of spatial information (for recent discussions see McNamara & Shelton, 2003; Morris & Parslow, 2004),[4] and many psychologists have used "cognitive map" to capture the notion of a representation of information about the configuration of landmarks in the environment (Baird, Merrill, & Tannenbaum, 1979; Downs & Stea, 1973; Foo, Warren, Duchon, & Tarr, 2005; Golledge, 1999; Golledge et al., 1996; Waller, Loomis, Golledge, & Beall, 2000).

Although the term cognitive *map* invokes the notion of a physical map that can be essentially brought to mind and viewed, this literal characterization of a map in the head is not well supported. First, cognitive maps do not appear to be coherent or complete maps of spatial information (e.g., Baird, Wagner, & Noma, 1982; Bryant, Tversky, & Franklin, 1992; Haun, Allen, & Wedell, 2005; McNamara, 1992; McNamara, Hardy, & Hirtle, 1989; Tversky, 1981, 1992). For example, McNamara et al. (1989) found that participants represented large displays of objects by subdividing the display into fragmented spatial categories, even when no physical or perceptual boundaries were available to divide the space. Performance on several tasks reflected faster and more accurate use of within-category relationships compared to between-category relationships. This subjective hierarchical structure in a single large space suggested that the cognitive map of the space was fragmented, and error or distortion occurred when those fragments had to be pieced together at retrieval. Similar chunking and fragmentation into hierarchically organized space has been shown for familiar environments (e.g., Hirtle & Jonides, 1985; Ladd, 1970). The lack of coherence is also found in the asymmetry in distance judgments between two points. For example, people estimated distances from a less salient landmark to a salient landmark to be shorter than the same distance estimate in the opposite direction (McNamara & Diwadkar, 1997), suggesting that one can have a cognitive map in which A to B is shorter than B to A. In a coherent map, these distances would be equal.[5] Finally, recent research has demonstrated that observers are only able to mentally access or spatially update their position within a single chunk of the hierarchical memory structure at a given moment, again challenging the conception of a single cognitive map that describes a known area of space (Brockmole & Wang, 2002, 2003, 2005; Wang & Brockmole, 2003).

A second challenge to the notion of a map-in-the-head is the visual nature that it invokes. Indeed, Tolman's (1948) original conception of cognitive mapping was a representation driven by information from multiple modalities. Again, this harkens back to the supramodal theory of spatial representation described previously. In this context, the cognitive map is viewed as a supramodal abstract representation of the spatial relations among landmarks in the environment. It has been suggested as the primary representation in place learning (Burgess et al., 1999) and is hypothesized to use an allocentric frame of reference (Morris & Parslow, 2004).

Behaviorally, evidence for cognitive maps comes from demonstrating the flexible use of spatial information to solve a number of spatial problems that cannot be solved with ordinal route information alone (for review see Golledge, 1999). For example, to select a direct path between two places that have previously been experienced separately in the same configuration, one needs to be able to represent the relationship between those two places independently of the specific separate paths on which each was previously experienced. The solution to this problem requires that people utilize some sort of allocentric information. One might use local cues to infer a global shape of an environment and locate each place within that framework, essentially creating a complete map. Alternatively, one might make note of the landmarks that appeared in both learned paths and infer the overlap or relationships between those two paths. If the two paths do not overlap, one may need to use a third known path to provide this link. In both of these cases, the learning of the spatial information would augment route-specific information with information about the stable properties of the space.

This process of inference and abstraction of the spatial information, posited as a supramodal representation, would put the cognitive map outside the realm of visual memory. As noted for supramodal representations in general, vision would serve as an input to this type of representation but it need not be the only possible type of input.

3.4. Eidetic memory

Cognitive maps may be the furthest from visual memory in the menagerie of spatial representations for navigation reviewed here, but that does not preclude a more direct role for visual memory in some forms of navigation. In some animals, navigation appears to be primarily driven by the use of visual "snapshots" of the world (e.g., Collett & Cartwright, 1983; Collett, Cartwright, & Smith, 1986). Although it would be difficult to account for all aspects of spatial memory in humans (or most species) with this type of memory, it may play a role in some types of spatial processes. In conjunction with cognitive mapping or place-learning mechanisms, an eidetic memory could explain many of the discrepancies that have arisen in different spatial memory tasks.

Studies have noted that scene recognition and judgments of relative direction can lead to different patterns of performance with learned orientations (Shelton & McNamara, 2004a, 2004b; Valiquette & McNamara, 2007). For example, Shelton and McNamara (2004a) had participants learn an environment in desktop virtual reality from the view of a ground-level observer moving through a space. The encoding required participants to process the spatial information over three turns (4 path legs). The learned orientation was therefore 0°, 90°, 180°, and 270° in legs 1–4, respectively (Figure 6.6a). When participants performed judgments of relative direction for the environment, there was a single preferred orientation based on the initial learned orientation at 0° (Figure 6.6b). These results suggest that participants represented the space in a single reference frame that was determined by the initial view they had of the space, and they tracked information back into this reference as they moved through space (see also Richardson, Montello, & Hegarty, 1999). However, this single coherent reference frame was not evident in scene recognition. When participants had to distinguish target images taken at eight different orientations in each leg of the route from highly similar foils, recognition was fastest and most accurate when the image depicted the orientation that was experienced in a given leg of the route (Figure 6.6c). As such, the "preferred" orientation differed with each leg of the route, suggesting the use of different representations for judgments of relative direction and scene recognition (but, for an alternative interpretation, see Mou, Fan, McNamara, & Owen, 2008).

The scene-recognition data suggest that people may indeed take snapshots of the world as they move through it. These snapshots can then be interrogated to make a comparison to the present sensory inputs. In the case of scene recognition, these snapshots are visual memories—hence, eidetic memories. In the Shelton and McNamara paradigm there appear to be multiple visual memories for different parts of the environment learned in a sequential path through the space. One could also posit "snapshot" memories in other modalities. For example, in a complex environment, the olfactory cues are likely changing as one moves through space. At any given location, one might store the particular combination of odors. These memories are the cues that are described above in cue-based navigation modes, but they also can serve their own role in spatial

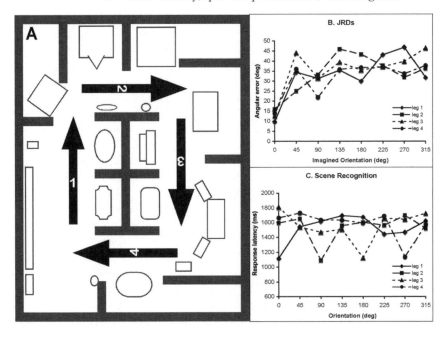

Figure 6.6. Task-specific performance after virtual route encoding. A. Schematic of a large-scale virtual environment, showing the path traversed over four different legs. Arrows show direction and heading on each path leg. Legs 1–4 had orientations corresponding to 0°, 90°, 180°, and 270°, respectively. B. Mean angular error from judgments of relative direction (JRDs) as a function of the imagined orientation and path leg. C. Mean response latency from scene recognition as a function of orientation and path leg. Adapted from Shelton & McNamara (2004a), Experiment 3.

memory performance by serving as templates for matching, as in visual scene recognition. It is likely that this memory interacts with other types of memory for other tasks as well. For example, if a visual scene is used to make a judgment about a location that is out of the range of the visual image, the eidetic memory may serve as a cue to one's orientations within some larger framework, such as a cognitive map. This type of interaction among representation would account for the difference in brain activation observed for appearance versus position judgments cued by the same visual stimuli (Aguirre & D'Esposito, 1997).

3.5. Path integration

As shown in previous sections, landmarks (learned either visually or nonvisually) play integral roles in guiding spatial behaviors in many forms of human navigation. However, in the absence of conspicuous landmarks (and even without any visual inputs), a traveler can still keep track of changes in his/her current position and orientation in the environment with respect to a fixed reference point (e.g., the origin of travel and the known location most recently visited). In this type of navigation, the traveler relies solely on information about velocity and acceleration of his/her own movement, which originates from external (allothetic) sources such as optic and acoustic flow as well as internal (idiothetic) sources such as proprioception, vestibular sense, and efference copies of motor commands. This cognitive process is called path integration, or dead reckoning,[6] and it has been shown that humans and many other animals are capable of carrying out this spatiotemporal computation (for review see Berthoz et al., 1999; Cornell & Heth, 2004; Etienne & Jeffery, 2004; Loomis, Klatzky, Golledge, & Philbeck, 1999; Wehner & Srinivasan, 2003).

There has been a debate over what roles visual information plays in path integration. On the one hand, it has been suggested that idiothetic cues are necessary to accurately perform path integration (e.g., Chance, Gaunet, Beall, & Loomis, 1998; Kearns, Warren, Duchon, & Tarr, 2002; Kirschen, Kahana, Sekuler, & Burack, 2000; Klatzky, Loomis, Beall, Chance, & Golledge, 1998; Péruch, May, & Wartenberg, 1997; Wraga, Creem-Regehr, & Proffitt, 2004), especially when locomotion involves rotational movements. For example, Klatzky et al. (1998) had participants do actual or virtual walking along a 2-leg path containing a single right-angle turn and asked them to face the origin at the endpoint of the path. Results showed that the participants accurately indicated the direction of the origin only when their walking included physical movements (actual walking or optic flow with physical turns). In contrast, when the participants remained stationary and experienced virtual walking only (optic flow alone, imagined walking from a verbal description, and watching another person walking on the path), their performance revealed a systematic pattern of error indicating that they failed to update their heading corresponding to the turn. These results suggest that physical motion (and idiothetic information associated with it) is critical for updating the current position and orientation during locomotion, whereas optic flow cannot elicit the best path integration performance all by itself.

On the other hand, it has also been demonstrated that optic flow alone can be sufficient for path integration (e.g., Bremmer & Lappe, 1999; Ellmore & McNaughton, 2004; Riecke, Cunningham, & Bülthoff, 2007; Riecke, van Veen, & Bülthoff, 2002; Waller, Loomis, & Steck, 2003; Wolbers, Wiener, Mallot, & Büchel, 2007; see also Sun, Campos, & Chan, 2004). For example, Riecke et al. (2007) asked participants to point to various locations in an environment during simulated walking by optic flow, with or without physical rotations corresponding to their trajectory. Results showed that accuracy of pointing response did not vary according to the presence/absence of concomitant physical rotations, both when optic flow information was provided by a familiar, natural scene and when it was replaced with a grayscale fractal texture. These findings have been interpreted as a challenge to the notion that idiothetic cues are critical for path integration. Furthermore, by extending such observations, it has also been proposed that optic flow *is* the essential source of spatial information for path integration (Cornell & Heth, 2004; Rieser, 1999). According to this hypothesis, visually restricted travelers interpret idiothetic cues about their movement by comparing them to previous experience with optic flow under normal viewing conditions. As a result, even when the travelers do not have direct access to distal landmarks, the mere exposure to optic flow during walking (e.g., seeing only a small area around their feet by wearing a vision-restricting device) can enhance their path integration performance compared to walking with no vision at all (e.g., Cornell & Greidanus, 2006). This is reminiscent of the visual mapping theory discussed previously, and certainly presents an interesting possibility. However, evidence supporting this hypothesis is still limited, and, as shown above, the literature provides mixed results.

One potential source of inconsistency in the literature is the variety of methodologies used to investigate vision in path integration. For example, some researchers used a vision-restricting hood that allowed participants to view a small area around their feet (e.g., Presson & Montello, 1994; Sadalla & Montello, 1989), whereas others used complete visual restriction by blindfold (e.g., Farrell & Robertson, 1998; Mittelstaedt & Mittelstaedt, 2001; Rieser, Guth, & Hill, 1986) or carrying out experiments in a dark room (e.g., Böök & Gärling, 1981; Simons & Wang, 1998). When virtual reality was used, sometimes visual stimuli were presented through a head-mounted display (e.g., Kearns, Warren, Duchon, & Tarr, 2002; Klatzky et al., 1998; Wraga, Creem-Regehr, & Proffitt, 2004), and sometimes they were projected onto a screen, either flat (e.g., Ellmore & McNaughton, 2004; Péruch, May, & Wartenberg, 1997) or curved (e.g., Riecke et al., 2002, 2007). To our knowledge, there has been no comprehensive studies of human path integration employing a wide variety of methods, resulting in the difficulty in isolating effects attributable to path integration processes themselves from those simply due to particular methods used for investigation. Initial efforts to address this issue have already been made (e.g., Creem-Regehr, Willemsen, Gooch, & Thompson, 2005; Knapp & Loomis, 2004), and it is expected that this line of research will be further expanded.

3.6. Summary

In the preceding sections we have outlined many of the processes that contribute to spatial navigation in humans and other animals. The use of these different processes and their relationships to visual processing will likely depend on the specific goals of an individual in a given situation. For example, suppose you just asked someone for directions to the new bookstore on a familiar campus, and she said, "Go up to the quad and turn toward the library. Go around the building and down the sidewalk to the right along the driveway. Cross the street, and turn right. Turn left at the corner and the bookstore will be on your left, halfway down the block." To follow these directions, you would likely use cue-based navigation to get to the library and walk around it. To identify the library, you might call upon a previous eidetic memory for its appearance and location on the quad.

The next "cue" might be the sidewalk along the driveway, followed by the street (which you must cross), the corner, and so forth. Once you have traversed this path to the bookstore, you may be able to utilize path integration to retrace your steps without having to explicitly reverse the directions (probably in conjunction with the cues again). Later, you may use your memory for the route (i.e., route knowledge) to return to the bookstore from the quad. Throughout these activities, you may also be formulating a cognitive map that will allow you to find the bookstore from the parking lot, your favorite restaurant, or some other novel direction. Like the properties of spatial representations, the many processes of navigation underscore the range of mechanisms that need to be explained to understand human spatial behaviors and suggest a complexity that has yet to be fully appreciated.

4. CHALLENGE FOR FUTURE INVESTIGATIONS

Throughout this chapter, we have highlighted a number of possible roles for vision and visual memory in spatial learning and memory processes. In some cases, we have suggested a direct role for visual information and visual memory (eidetic memories), whereas other cases seem to suggest that vision is just one of many possible inputs to a largely supramodal or multimodal system (functional equivalence, modality specificity, cognitive maps). It is clear that environmental knowledge comes in many forms and engages many different processes. What is less clear is how these various processes fit together.

The challenge for future research is to come up with a theoretical framework for organizing the many different types of spatial representations and how they might complement, interact, or interfere with one another. This new framework will need to account for different types of experiences, different degrees of familiarity, different goals for spatial learning and memory, and individual differences in spatial skills. Clearly, visual representations in perception and memory will play a critical role in many of the processes and representations. We began this chapter by making the case that the relationship between vision and spatial representation is pervasive but not inextricable. We end on the same basic premise in reverse: although we can clearly establish aspects of spatial representation that are not strictly visually dependent, it is clear that vision and visual memory play a significant role in many different aspects of spatial cognition.

NOTES

1   Whether these should be termed different representations or different aspects of a single representation is largely a semantic distinction. If multiple modality-specific representations (or any other multiple representations) are linked by the fact that they represent the same physical space, then one could call them components of a larger representation of that space. The critical issue is still whether participants can tap into these representations or components for different purposes.

2   Although related, route knowledge is distinguished from route-based learning (see section 3.3).
3   The first author had an acute experience of this sort in London, when scaffolding on St. Paul's Cathedral was so extensive that it appeared to be a different structure. Looking up and seeing an unexpected lack of familiarity produced a profound, albeit fleeting, feeling of disorientation.
4   Cognitive maps have also been closely tied to the discovery of place cells in the rat hippocampus, described previously (e.g., O'Keefe, 1991; O'Keefe & Nadel, 1978).
5   Certainly, there are cases in which different paths must be taken to, versus from, a place because of one-way streets or other oddities, but these cases are atypical and do not apply to these empirical investigations.
6   In the literature, sometimes path integration is more precisely defined as the process of finding one's position and orientation based only on idiothetic cues (e.g., Morris & Parslow, 2004; Philbeck, Behrmann, Levy, Potolicchio, & Caputy, 2004). In this chapter, however, we adopt the broader definition of path integration as including the use of allothetic cues, in the interest of encompassing a wider body of data related to spatial navigation via self-motion signal processing.

5. REFERENCES

Abrahams, S., Pickering, A., Jarosz, J., Cox, T., & Morris, R. G. (1999). Spatial working memory impairment correlates with hippocampal sclerosis. *Brain and Cognition, 41,* 39–65.

Abrahams, S., Pickering, A., Polkey, C. E., & Morris, R. G. (1997). Spatial memory deficits in patients with unilateral damage to the right hippocampal formation. *Neuropsychologia, 35,* 11–24.

Ackerman, P. L. (1986). Individual differences in information processing: An investigation of intellectual abilities and task performance during practice. *Intelligence, 10,* 101–139.

Aguirre, G. K., & D'Esposito, M. (1997). Environmental knowledge is subserved by separable dorsal/ventral neural areas. *Journal of Neuroscience, 17,* 2512–2518.

Aguirre, G. K., & D'Esposito, M. (1999). Topographical disorientation: A synthesis and taxonomy. *Brain, 122,* 1613–1628.

Aguirre, G. K., Detre, J. A., Alsop, D. C., & D'Esposito, M. (1996). The parahippocampus subserves topographical learning in man. *Cerebral Cortex, 6,* 823–829.

Aguirre, G. K., Zarahn, E., & D'Esposito, M. (1998). Neural components of topographical representation. *Proceedings of the National Academy of Science, U.S.A., 95,* 839–846.

Appleyard, D. (1969). Why buildings are known. *Environment and Behavior, 1,* 131–156.

Appleyard, D. (1970). Styles and methods of structuring a city. *Environment and Behavior, 2,* 100–118.

Attneave, F., & Benson, B. (1969). Spatial coding in tactile stimulation. *Journal of Experimental Psychology, 81,* 216–222.

Auerbach, C., & Sperling, P. (1974). A common auditory-visual space: Evidence for its reality. *Perception & Psychophysics, 16,* 129–135.

Avraamides, M. N., Klatzky, R. L., Loomis, J. M., & Golledge, R. G. (2004a). Use of cognitive versus perceptual heading during imagined locomotion depends on the response mode. *Psychological Science, 15,* 403–408.

Avraamides, M. N., Loomis, J. M., Klatzky, R. L., & Golledge, R. G. (2004b). Functional equivalence of spatial representations derived from vision and language: Evidence from allocentric judgments. *Journal of Experimental Psychology: Learning, Memory, and Cognition, 30,* 801–814.

Axelrod, S. (1959). *Effects of early blindness.* New York: American Foundation for the Blind.

Baddeley, A. D., & Hitch, G. J. (1974). Working memory. In G. Bower (Ed.), *Psychology of Learning and Motivation* (Vol. 8, pp. 47–90). San Diego, CA: Academic Press.

Baddeley, A. D., & Hitch, G. J. (1994). Developments in the concept of working memory. *Neuropsychology, 8,* 485–493.

Baird, J. C., Merrill, A. A., & Tannenbaum, J. (1979). Studies of the cognitive representation of spatial relations: II. A familiar environment. *Journal of Experimental Psychology: General, 108,* 92–98.

Baird, J. C., Wagner, M., & Noma, E. (1982). Impossible cognitive spaces. *Geographical Analysis, 14,* 204–216.

Bartolomeo, P., D'Erme, P., & Gainotti, G. (1994). The relationship between visuospatial and representational neglect. *Neurology, 44,* 1710–1714.

Bernier, P. M., Chua, R., Inglis, J. T., & Franks, I. M. (2007). Sensorimotor adaptation in response to proprioceptive bias. *Experimental Brain Research, 177,* 147–156.

Bertelson, P., & Radeau, M. (1981). Crossmodal bias and perceptual fusion with auditory-visual spatial discordance. *Perception & Psychophysics, 29,* 578–584.

Berthoz, A., Amorim, M.-A., Glasauer, S., Grasso, R., Takei, Y., & Viaud-Delmon, I. (1999). Dissociation between distance and direction during locomotor navigation. In R. G. Golledge (Ed.), *Wayfinding behavior: Cognitive mapping and other spatial processes* (pp. 328–348). Baltimore: Johns Hopkins Press.

Biederman, I. (1987). Recognition-by-components: A theory of human image understanding. *Psychological Review, 94,* 115–147.

Biederman, I., & Gerhardstein, P. C. (1993). Recognizing depth-rotated objects: Evidence and conditions for three-dimensional viewpoint invariance. *Journal of Experimental Psychology: Human Perception and Performance, 19,* 1162–1182.

Biederman, I., & Gerhardstein, P. C. (1995). Viewpoint-dependent mechanisms in visual object recognition: Reply to Tarr and Bulthoff. *Journal of Experimental Psychology: Human Perception and Performance, 21,* 1506–1514.

Bisiach, E., & Luzzatti, C. (1978). Unilateral neglect of representational space. *Cortex, 14,* 129–133.

Böök, A., & Gärling, T. (1981). Maintenance of orientation during locomotion in unfamiliar environments. *Journal of Experimental Psychology: Human Perception and Performance, 7,* 996–1006.

Boring, E. G. (1926). Auditory theory with special reference to intensity, volume, and localization. *American Journal of Psychology, 37,* 157–188.

Botvinik, M., & Cohen, J. (1998). Rubber hands "feel" touch that eyes see. *Nature, 391,* 756.

Bremmer, F., & Lappe, M. (1999). The use of optical velocities for distance discrimination and reproduction during visually simulated self motion. *Experimental Brain Research, 127,* 33–42.

Brockmole, J. R., & Wang, R. F. (2002). Switching between environmental representations in memory. *Cognition, 83,* 295–316.

Brockmole, J. R., & Wang, R. F. (2003). Changing perspective within and across environments. *Cognition, 87,* B59–B67.

Brockmole, J. R., & Wang, R. F. (2005). Spatial processing of environmental representations. In L. Itti, G. Rees, & J. Tsotsos (Eds.), *Neurobiology of attention* (pp. 146–151). Burlington, MA: Academic Press.

Bryant, D. J. (1997). Representing space in language and perception. *Mind & Language, 12*, 239–264.

Bryant, D. J., Tversky, B., & Franklin, N. (1992). Internal and external spatial frameworks for representing described scenes. *Journal of Memory and Language, 31*, 74–98.

Burgess, N. (2006). Spatial memory: How egocentric and allocentric combine. *Trends in Cognitive Sciences, 10*, 551–557.

Burgess, N., Jeffery, K. J., & O'Keefe, J. (Eds.). (1999). *The hippocampal and parietal foundations of spatial cognition.* Oxford, UK: Oxford University Press.

Chance, S. S., Gaunet, F., Beall, A. C., & Loomis, J. M. (1998). Locomotion mode affects the updating of objects encountered during travel: The contribution of vestibular and proprioceptive inputs to path integration. *Presence: Teleoperators and Virtual Environments, 7*, 168–178.

Chokron, S. (2003). Right parietal lesions, unilateral spatial neglect, and the egocentric frame of reference. *NeuroImage, 20*, S75–S81.

Christou, C. G., & Bülthoff, H. H. (1999). View dependence in scene recognition after active learning. *Memory & Cognition, 27*, 996–1007.

Cleaves, W. T., & Royal, R. W. (1979). Spatial memory for configurations by congenitally blind, late blind, and sighted adults. *Journal of Visual Impairment & Blindness, 73*, 13–19.

Colby, C. L., & Goldberg, M. E. (1999). Space and attention in parietal cortex. *Annual Review of Neuroscience, 22*, 319–349.

Collett, T. S., & Cartwright, B. A. (1983). Eidetic images in insects: Their role in navigation. *Trends in Neurosciences, 6*, 101–105.

Collett, T. S., Cartwright, B. A., & Smith, B. A. (1986). Landmark learning and visuo-spatial memories in gerbils. *Journal of Comparative Physiology, 158A*, 835–851.

Cook, D., & Kesner, R. P. (1988). Caudate nucleus and memory for egocentric localization. *Behavioral and Neural Biology, 49*, 332–343.

Cornell, E. H., & Greidanus, E. (2006). Path integration during a neighborhood walk. *Spatial Cognition & Computation, 6*, 203–234.

Cornell, E. H., & Heth, C. D. (2004). Memories of travel: Dead reckoning within the cognitive map. In G. Allen (Ed.), *Human spatial memory: Remembering where* (pp. 191–215). Mahwah, NJ: Lawrence Erlbaum Associates.

Creem-Regehr, S. H., Willemsen, P., Gooch, A. A., & Thompson, W. B. (2005). The influence of restricted viewing conditions on egocentric distance perception: Implications for real and virtual environments. *Perception, 34*, 191–204.

Descartes, R. (1993). *Discourse on method* (D. A. Cress, Trans.). Indianapolis, IN: Hackett.

Diwadkar, V. A., & McNamara, T. P. (1997). Viewpoint dependence in scene recognition. *Psychological Science, 8*, 302–307.

Dodds, A., Howarth, C., & Carter, D. (1982). The mental maps of the blind: The role of previous visual experience. *Journal of Visual Impairment & Blindness, 76*, 5–12.

Downs, R. M., & Stea, D. (Eds.). (1973). *Image and environment.* Chicago: Aldine.

Easton, R. D., & Sholl, M. J. (1995). Object-array structure, frame of reference, and retrieval of spatial knowledge. *Journal of Experimental Psychology: Learning, Memory and Cognition, 21*, 483–500.

Ehrsson, H. H. (2007). The experimental induction of out-of-body experiences. *Science, 317*, 1048.

Eichenbaum, H., Dudchenko, P., Wood, E., Shapiro, M., & Tanila, H. (1999). The hippocampus, memory, and place cells: Is it spatial memory or a memory space? *Neuron, 23*, 209–226.

Eilan, N. (1993). Molyneux's question and the idea of an external world. In N. Eilan, R. McCarthy, & B. Brewer (Eds.), *Spatial representation: Problems in philosophy and psychology* (pp. 236–255). New York: Oxford University Press.

Ekstrom, A. D., Kahana, M. J., Caplan, J. B., Fields, T. A., Isham, E. A., Newman, E. L., & Fried, I. (2003). Cellular networks underlying human spatial navigation. *Nature, 425*, 184–187.

Ellmore, T. M., & McNaughton, B. L. (2004). Human path integration by optic flow. *Spatial Cognition and Computation, 4*, 255–272.

Epstein, R., DeYoe, E. A., Press, D. Z., Rosen, A. C., & Kanwisher, N. (2001). Neuropsychological evidence for a topographical learning mechanism in parahippocampal cortex. *Cognitive Neuropsychology, 18*, 481–508.

Ernst, M. O., & Banks, M. S. (2002). Humans integrate visual and haptic information in a statistically optimal fashion. *Nature, 415*, 429–433.

Etienne, A. S., & Jeffery, K. J. (2004). Path integration in mammals. *Hippocampus, 14*, 180–192.

Farah, M. J., Brunn, J. L., Wong, A. B., Wallace, M. A., & Carpenter, P. A. (1990). Frame of reference for allocating attention to space: Evidence from neglect syndrome. *Neuropsychologia, 28*, 335–347.

Farrell, M. J., & Robertson, I. H. (1998). Mental rotation and the automatic updating of body-centered spatial relationships. *Journal of Experimental Psychology: Learning, Memory, and Cognition, 24*, 227–233.

Feigenbaum, J. D., & Rolls, E. T. (1991). Allocentric and egocentric spatial information processing in the hippocampal formation of the behaving primate. *Psychobiology, 19*, 21–40.

Fishbein, H. D., Decker, J., & Wilcox, P. (1977). Cross-modality transfer of spatial information. *British Journal of Psychology, 68*, 503–508.

Fisher, G. H. (1964). Spatial localization by the blind. *American Journal of Psychology, 77*, 2–14.

Foo, P., Warren, W. H., Duchon, A., & Tarr, M. J. (2005). Do humans integrate routes into a cognitive map? Map- versus landmark-based navigation of novel shortcuts. *Journal of Experimental Psychology: Learning, Memory, and Cognition, 31*, 195–215.

Franklin, N., Tversky, B., & Coon, V. (1992). Switching points of view in spatial mental models. *Memory and Cognition, 20*, 507–518.

Gaunet, F., Martinez, J. L., & Thinus-Blanc, C. (1997). Early-blind subjects' spatial representation of manipulatory space: Exploratory strategies and reaction to change. *Perception, 26*, 345–366.

Gaunet, F., & Thinus-Blanc, C. (1996). Early-blind subjects' spatial abilities in the locomotor space: Exploratory strategies and reaction-to-change performance. *Perception, 25*, 967–981.

Golledge, R. G. (1999). Human wayfinding and cognitive maps. In R. G. Golledge (Ed.), *Wayfinding behavior: Cognitive mapping and other spatial processes.* (pp. 5–45). Baltimore: Johns Hopkins University Press.

Golledge, R. G., Klatzky, R. L., & Loomis, J. M. (1996). Cognitive mapping and wayfinding in adults without vision. In J. Portugali (Ed.), *The construction of cognitive maps* (pp. 215–146). Netherlands: Kluwer Academic.

Golledge, R. G., Marston, J. R., Loomis, J. M., & Klatzky, R. L. (2004). Stated preferences for components of a personal guidance system for nonvisual navigation. *Journal of Visual Impairment & Blindness, 98*, 135–147.

Halligan, P. W., & Marshall, J. C. (1991). Left neglect in near but not far space in man. *Nature, 350*, 498–500.

Hartlage, L. C. (1969). Verbal tests of spatial conceptualization. *Journal of Experimental Psychology, 80*, 180–182.

Hartley, T., Bird, C. M., Chan, D., Cipolotti, L., Husain, M., Vargha-Khadem, F., & Burgess, N. (2007). The hippocampus is required for short-term topographical memory in humans. *Hippocampus, 17*, 34–48.

Hartley, T., Burgess, N., Lever, C., Cacucci, F., & O'Keefe, J. (2000). Modeling place fields in terms of the cortical inputs to the hippocampus. *Hippocampus, 10*, 369–379.

Hartley, T., Maguire, E. A., Spiers, H. J., & Burgess, N. (2003). The well-worn route and the path less traveled: Distinct neural bases of route following and wayfinding in humans. *Neuron, 37*, 877–888.

Haun, D. B. M., Allen, G. L., & Wedell, D. H. (2005). Bias in spatial memory: A categorical endorsement. *Acta Psychologica, 118*, 149–170.

Hay, J. C., & Pick, H. L., Jr. (1966). Visual and proprioceptive adaptation to optical displacement of the visual stimulus. *Journal of Experimental Psychology, 71*, 150–158.

Hay, J. C., Pick, H. L., Jr., & Ikeda, K. (1965). Visual capture produced by prism spectacles. *Psychonomic Science, 2*, 215–216.

Hebb, D. O. (1949). *The organization of behavior.* New York: Wiley.

Herman, J. F., Chatman, S. P., & Roth, S. F. (1983). Cognitive mapping in blind people: Acquisition of spatial relationships in a large-scale environment. *Journal of Visual Impairment & Blindness, 77*, 161–166.

Hill, A. J., & Best, P. J. (1981). Effects of deafness and blindness on the spatial correlates of hippocampal unit activity in the rat. *Experimental Neurology, 74*, 204–217.

Hirtle, S. C., & Jonides, J. (1985). Evidence of hierarchies in cognitive maps. *Memory and Cognition, 3*, 208–217.

Hitch, G. J., Brandimonte, M. A., & Walker, P. (1995). Two types of representations in visual memory: Evidence from the effect of stimulus contrast on an image combination task. *Memory & Cognition, 23*, 147–154.

Holdstock, J. S., Mayes, A. R., Cezayirili, E., Isaac, C. L., Aggleton, J. P., & Roberts, N. (2000). A comparison of egocentric and allocentric spatial memory in a patient with selective hippocampal damage. *Neuropsychologia, 38*, 410–425.

Holmes, M. C., & Sholl, M. J. (2005). Allocentric coding of object-to-object relations in overlearned and novel environments. *Journal of Experimental Psychology: Learning, Memory, and Cognition, 31*, 1069–1087.

Hötting, K., Rösler, F., & Röder, B. (2004). Altered auditory–tactile interactions in congenitally blind humans: An event-related potential study. *Experimental Brain Research, 159*, 370–381.

Howard, I. P. (1991). Spatial vision within egocentric and exocentric frames of reference. In S. R. Ellis (Ed.), *Pictorial communication in virtual and real environments* (pp. 338–358). London: Taylor & Francis.

Howard, I. P., & Templeton, W. B. (1966). *Human spatial orientation.* London: Wiley.

Jackson, C. V. (1953). Visual factors in auditory localization. *Quarterly Journal of Experimental Psychology, 5*, 52–65.

Kearns, M. J., Warren, W. H., Duchon, A. P., & Tarr, M. J. (2002). Path integration from optic flow and body senses in a homing task. *Perception, 31*, 349–374.

King, J. A., Burgess, N., Hartley, T., Vargha-Khadem, F., & O'Keefe, J. (2002). Human hippocampus and viewpoint dependence in spatial memory. *Hippocampus, 12,* 811–820.

Kirasic, K. C., & Mathes, E. A. (1990). Effects of different means for conveying environmental information on elderly adults' spatial cognition and behavior. *Environment and Behavior, 22,* 591–607.

Kirschen, M. P., Kahana, M. J., Sekuler, R., & Burack, B. (2000). Optic flow helps humans learn to navigate through synthetic environments. *Perception, 29,* 801–818.

Klatzky, R. L. (1999). Path completion after haptic exploration without vision: Implications for haptic spatial representations. *Perception & Psychophysics, 61,* 220–235.

Klatzky, R. L., Lippa, Y., Loomis, J. M., & Golledge, R. G. (2002). Learning directions of objects specified by vision, spatial audition, or auditory spatial language. *Learning & Memory, 9,* 364–367.

Klatzky, R. L., Lippa, Y., Loomis, J. M., & Golledge, R. G. (2003). Encoding, learning, and spatial updating of multiple object locations specified by 3-D sound, spatial language, and vision. *Experimental Brain Research, 149,* 48–61.

Klatzky, R. L., Loomis, J. M., Beall, A. C., Chance, S. S., & Golledge, R. G. (1998). Spatial updating of self-position and orientation during real, imagined, and virtual locomotion. *Psychological Science, 9,* 293–298.

Klatzky, R. L., Loomis, J. M., Golledge, R. G., & Cicinelli, J. G. (1990). Acquisition of route and survey knowledge in the absence of vision. *Journal of Motor Behavior, 22,* 19–43.

Klatzky, R. L., Marston, J. R., Giudice, N. A., Golledge, R. G., & Loomis, J. M. (2006). Cognitive load of navigating without vision when guided by virtual sound versus spatial language. *Journal of Experimental Psychology: Applied, 12,* 223–232.

Knapp, J. M., & Loomis, J. M. (2004). Limited field of view of head-mounted displays is not the cause of distance underestimation in virtual environments. *Presence, 13,* 572–577.

Knauff, M., & May, E. (2006). Mental imagery, reasoning, and blindness. *Quarterly Journal of Experimental Psychology, 59,* 161–177.

Ladd, F. C. (1970). Black youths view their environment: Neighborhood maps. *Environment and Behavior, 2,* 64–79.

Lambrey, S., & Berthoz, A. (2003). Combination of conflicting visual and non-visual information for estimating actively performed body turns in virtual reality. *International Journal of Psychophysiology, 50,* 101–115.

Lambrey, S., Viaud-Delmon, I., & Berthoz, A. (2002). Influence of a sensorimotor conflict on the memorization of a path traveled in virtual reality. *Cognitive Brain Research, 14,* 177–186.

Landau, B., & Jackendoff, R. (1993). "What" and "where" in spatial language and cognition. *Behavioral and Brain Sciences, 16,* 217–265.

Landis, T., Cummings, J. L., Benson, D. F., & Palmer, E. P. (1986). Loss of topographical familiarity: An environmental agnosia. *Archives of Neurology, 43,* 132–136.

Lawton, C. A. (1996). Strategies for indoor wayfinding: The role of orientation. *Journal of Environmental Psychology, 16,* 137–145.

Lenggenhager, B., Tadi, T., Metzinger, T., & Blanke, O. (2007). Video ergo sum: Manipulating bodily self-consciousness. *Science, 317,* 1096–1099.

Leonard, J. A., & Newman, R. C. (1967). Spatial orientation in the blind. *Nature, 215,* 1413–1414.

Loomis, J. M. (1993). Counterexample to the hypothesis of functional similarity between tactile and visual pattern perception. *Perception & Psychophysics, 54,* 179–184.

Loomis, J. M., Hebert, C., & Cicinelli, J. G. (1990). Active localization of virtual sounds. *Journal of the Acoustical Society of America, 88*, 1757–1764.

Loomis, J. M., Klatzky, R. L., Golledge, R. G., & Philbeck, J. W. (1999). Human navigation by path integration. In R. G. Golledge (Ed.), *Wayfinding: Cognitive mapping and other spatial processes* (pp. 125–151). Baltimore: Johns Hopkins University Press.

Loomis, J. M., Klatzky, R. L., & Lederman, S. J. (1991). Similarity of tactual and visual picture recognition with limited field of view. *Perception, 20*, 167–177.

Loomis, J. M., Klatzky, R. L., Philbeck, J. W., & Golledge, R. G. (1998). Assessing auditory distance perception using perceptually directed action. *Perception & Psychophysics, 60*, 966–980.

Loomis, J. M., Lippa, Y., Klatzky, R. L., & Golledge, R. G. (2002). Spatial updating of locations specified by 3-D sound and spatial language. *Journal of Experimental Psychology: Learning, Memory, and Cognition, 28*, 335–345.

MacEachren, A. M. (1992). Application of environmental learning theory to spatial knowledge acquisition from maps. *Annals of the Association of American Geographers, 82*, 245–274.

Mani, K., & Johnson-Laird, P. N. (1982). The mental representation of spatial descriptions. *Memory and Cognition, 10*, 181–187.

Mastroianni, G. R. (1982). The influence of eye movements and illumination on auditory localization. *Perception & Psychophysics, 31*, 581–584.

McGuinness, C. (1992). Spatial models in the mind. *Irish Journal of Psychology, 13*, 524–535.

McLinden, D. J. (1988). Spatial task performance: A meta-analysis. *Journal of Visual Impairment & Blindness, 82*, 231–236.

McNamara, T. P. (1992). Spatial representations. *Geoforum, 23*, 139–150.

McNamara, T. P. (2003). How are the locations of objects in the environment represented in memory? In C. Freksa, W. Brauer, C. Habel, & K. F. Wender (Eds.), *Spatial cognition III: Routes and navigation, human memory and learning, spatial representation and spatial reasoning. LNAI 2685* (pp. 174–191). Berlin: Springer-Verlag.

McNamara, T. P., & Diwadkar, V. A. (1997). Symmetry and asymmetry of human spatial memory. *Cognitive Psychology, 34*, 160–190.

McNamara, T. P., Hardy, J. K., & Hirtle, S. C. (1989). Subjective hierarchies in spatial memory. *Journal of Experimental Psychology: Learning, Memory and Cognition, 15*, 211–227.

McNamara, T. P., Rump, B., & Werner, S. (2003). Egocentric and geocentric frames of reference in memory of large-scale space. *Psychonomic Bulletin and Review, 10*, 589–595.

McNamara, T. P., & Shelton, A. L. (2003). Cognitive maps and the hippocampus. *Trends in Cognitive Science, 7*, 333–335.

McNamara, T. P., & Valiquette, C. M. (2004). Remembering where things are. In G. L. Allen (Ed.), *Human spatial memory* (pp. 3–24). Mahwah, NJ: Lawrence Erlbaum Associates.

Mennemeier, M., Chatterjee, A., & Jeilman, K. M. (1994). A comparison of the influence of body and environment centred reference frames on neglect. *Brain, 117*, 1013–1021.

Millar, S. (1994). *Understanding and representing space: Theory and evidence from studies with blind and sighted children.* Oxford, UK: Clarendon Press.

Milner, A. D., & Goodale, M. A. (1995). *The visual brain in action.* Oxford, UK: Oxford University Press.

Mittelstaedt, M.-L., & Mittelstaedt, H. (2001). Idiothetic navigation in humans: Estimation of path length. *Experimental Brain Research, 139*, 318–332.

Moeser, S. D. (1988). Cognitive mapping in a complex building. *Environment and Behavior, 20*, 21–49.

Montello, D. R. (1988). A new framework for understanding the acquisition of spatial knowledge in large-scale environments. In M. J. Egenhofer & R. G. Golledge (Eds.), *Spatial and temporal reasoning in geographic information systems* (pp. 143–154). New York: Oxford University Press.

Morris, R. G., & Parslow, D. M. (2004). Neurocognitive components of spatial memory. In G. L. Allen (Ed.), *Human spatial memory* (pp. 217–247). Mahwah, NJ: Lawrence Erlbaum Associates.

Morris, R. G. M., Garrud, P., Rawlins, J. N., & O'Keefe, J. (1982). Place navigation is impaired in rats with hippocampal lesions. *Nature, 297*, 681–683.

Mou, W., Fan, Y., McNamara, T. P., & Owen, C. B. (2008). Intrinsic frames of reference and egocentric viewpoints in scene recognition. *Cognition, 106*, 750–769.

Mou, W., Liu, X., & McNamara, T. P. (in press). Layout geometry in encoding and retrieval of spatial memory. *Journal of Experimental Psychology: Human Perception and Performance.*

Mou, W., & McNamara, T. P. (2002). Intrinsic frames of reference in spatial memory. *Journal of Experimental Psychology: Learning, Memory, and Cognition, 28*, 162–170.

Mou, W., Zhao, M., & McNamara, T. P. (2007). Layout geometry in the selection of intrinsic frames of reference from multiple viewpoints. *Journal of Experimental Psychology: Learning, Memory, and Cognition, 33*, 145–154.

Nadel, L. (1999). Neural mechanisms of spatial orientation and wayfinding: An overview. In R. G. Golledge (Ed.), *Wayfinding behavior: Cognitive mapping and other spatial processes* (pp. 313–327). Baltimore: Johns Hopkins University Press.

Nadel, L. (2004). The spatial brain. *Neuropsychology, 18*, 473–476.

Nardini, M., Burgess, N., Breckenridge, K., & Atkinson, J. (2006). Differential developmental trajectories for egocentric, environmental and intrinsic frames of reference in spatial memory. *Cognition, 101*, 153–172.

Neggers, S. F. W., Van der Lubbe, R. H. J., Ramsey, N. F., & Postma, A. (2006). Interactions between ego- and allocentric neuronal representations of space. *NeuroImage, 31*, 320–331.

Newell, F. N., Woods, A. T., Mernagh, M., & Bülthoff, H. H. (2005). Visual, haptic and crossmodal recognition of scenes. *Experimental Brain Research, 161*, 233–242.

Newport, R., Rabb, B., & Jackson, S. R. (2002). Noninformative vision improves haptic spatial perception. *Current Biology, 12*, 1661–1664.

O'Keefe, J. (1976). Place units in the hippocampus of the freely moving rat. *Experimental Neurology, 51*, 78–109.

O'Keefe, J. (1991). The hippocampal cognitive map and navigational strategies. In J. Paillard (Ed.), *Brain and space* (pp. 273–295). Oxford, UK: Oxford University Press.

O'Keefe, J., & Dostrovsky, J. (1971). The hippocampus as a spatial map: Preliminary evidence from unit activity in the freely moving rat. *Brain Research, 34*, 171–175.

O'Keefe, J., & Nadel, L. (1978). *The hippocampus as a cognitive map.* Oxford, UK: Oxford University Press

Packard, M. G., & McGaugh, J. L. (1996). Inactivation of hippocampus or caudate nucleus with lidocaine differentially affects expression of place and response learning. *Neurobiology of Learning and Memory, 65*, 65–72.

Pasqualotto, A., Finucane, C. M., & Newell, F. N. (2005). Visual and haptic representations of scenes are updated with observer movement. *Experimental Brain Research, 166*, 481–488.

Passini, R., Delisle, J., Langlois, C., & Prouis, G. (1988). Wayfinding information for congenitally blind individuals. *Journal of Visual Impairment and Blindness, 82*, 425–429.

Passini, R., Proulx, G., & Rainville, C. (1990). The spatio-cognitive abilities of the visually impaired population. *Environment and Behavior, 22*, 91–118.

Pazzaglia, F., & De Beni, R. (2001). Strategies of processing spatial information in survey and landmark-centred individuals. *European Journal of Cognitive Psychology, 13*, 493–508.

Péruch, P., May, M., & Wartenberg, F. (1997). Homing in virtual environments: Effects of field of view and path layout. *Perception, 26*, 301–311.

Philbeck, J. W., Behrmann, M., Levy, L., Potolicchio, S. J., & Caputy, A. J. (2004). Path integration deficits during linear locomotion after human medial temporal lobectomy. *Journal of Cognitive Neuroscience, 16*, 510–520.

Platt, B. B., & Warren, D. H. (1972). Auditory localization: The importance of eye movements and a textured visual environment. *Perception & Psychophysics, 12*, 245–248.

Presson, C. C., DeLange, N., & Hazelrigg, M. D. (1989). Orientation-specificity in spatial memory: What makes a path different from a map of the path? *Journal of Experimental Psychology: Learning, Memory, and Cognition, 15*, 887–897.

Presson, C. C., & Montello, D. R. (1994). Updating after rotational and translational body movements: Coordinate structure of perspective space. *Perception, 23*, 1447–1455.

Putzar, L., Goerendt, I., Lange, K., Rösler, F., & Röder, B. (2007). Early visual deprivation impairs multisensory interactions in humans. *Nature Neuroscience, 10*, 1243–1245.

Ramachandran, V. S., Rogers-Ramachandran, D., & Cobb, S. (1995). Touching the phantom limb. *Nature, 377*, 489–490.

Redding, G. M., & Wallace, B. (1987). Perceptual-motor coordination and prism adaptation during locomotion: A control for head posture contributions. *Perception and Psychophysics, 42*, 269–274.

Restle, F. (1957). Discrimination of cues in mazes: A resolution of the "place-vs.-response" question. *Psychological Review, 64*, 217–228.

Richardson, A. E., Montello, D. R., & Hegarty, M. (1999). Spatial knowledge acquisition from maps and from navigation in real and virtual environments. *Memory and Cognition, 27*, 741–750.

Riecke, B. E., Cunningham, D. W., & Bülthoff, H. H. (2007). Spatial updating in virtual reality: The sufficiency of visual information. *Psychological Research, 71*, 298–313.

Riecke, B. E., van Veen, H. A. H. C., & Bülthoff, H. H. (2002). Visual homing is possible without landmarks: A path integration study in virtual reality. *Presence, 11*, 443–473.

Rieser, J. J. (1989). Access to knowledge of spatial structure at novel points of observation. *Journal of Experimental Psychology: Learning, Memory, and Cognition, 15*, 1157–1165.

Rieser, J. J. (1999). Dynamic spatial orientation and the coupling of representation and action. In R. G. Golledge (Ed.), *Wayfinding behavior: Cognitive mapping and other spatial processes* (pp. 168–190). Baltimore: Johns Hopkins University Press.

Rieser, J. J., Guth, D. A., & Hill, E. W. (1986). Sensitivity to perspective structure while walking without vision. *Perception, 15*, 173–188.

Rieser, J. J., Hill, E. W., Talor, C. R., Bradfield, A., & Rosen, S. (1992). Visual experience, visual field size, and the development of nonvisual sensitivity to the spatial structure of outdoor neighborhoods explored by walking. *Journal of Experimental Psychology: General, 2*, 210–221.

Rieser, J. J., Lockman, J. J., & Pick, H. L., Jr. (1980). The role of visual experience in knowledge of spatial layout. *Perception & Psychophysics, 28*, 185–190.

Rieser, J. J., Pick, H. L., Jr., Ashmead, D. H., & Garing, A. E. (1995). Calibration of human locomotion and models of perceptual-motor organization. *Journal of Experimental Psychology: Human Perception and Performance, 21*, 480–497.

Rizzolatti, G., & Gallese, V. (1988). Mechanisms and theories of spatial neglect. In F. B. J. Grafman (Ed.), *Handbook of neuropsychology* (Vol. 1, pp. 223–246). Amsterdam: Elsevier.

Rock, I. (1966). *The nature of perceptual adaptation*. New York: Basic Books.

Rock, I., & Victor, J. (1964). Vision and touch: Experimentally created conflict between the two senses. *Science, 143*, 594–596.

Röder, B., Kusmierek, A., Spence, C., & Schicke, T. (2007). Developmental vision determines the reference frame for the multisensory control of action. *Proceedings of the National Academy of Sciences, U.S.A., 104*, 4753–4758.

Röder, B., Rösler, F., & Spence, C. (2004). Early vision impairs tactile perception in the blind. *Current Biology, 14*, 121–124.

Rolls, E. T. (1999). Spatial view cells and the representation of place in the primate hippocampus. *Hippocampus, 9*, 467–480.

Rolls, E. T., & O'Mara, S. M. (1995). View-responsive neurons in the primate hippocampal complex. *Hippocampus, 5*, 409–424.

Roskos-Ewoldsen, B., McNamara, T. P., Shelton, A. L., & Carr, W. (1998). Mental representations of large and small spatial layouts are orientation dependent. *Journal of Experimental Psychology: Learning, Memory, and Cognition, 24*, 215–226.

Rossano, M. J., & Warren, D. H. (1989). The importance of alignment in blind subjects' use of tactual maps. *Perception, 18*, 805–816.

Rossier, J., & Schenk, F. (2003). Olfactory and/or visual cues for spatial navigation through ontogeny: Olfactory cues enable the use of visual cues. *Behavioral Neuroscience, 117*, 412–425.

Sadalla, E. K., & Montello, D. R. (1989). Remembering changes in direction. *Environment and Behavior, 21*, 346–363.

Schlaegel, T. F., Jr. (1953). The dominant method of imagery in blind compared to sighted adolescents. *Journal of Genetic Psychology, 83*, 265–277.

Shelton, A. L., Marchette, S. A., & Yamamoto, N. (2007). *Place and response mechanisms in human environmental learning*. Manuscript in preparation.

Shelton, A. L., & McNamara, T. P. (1997). Multiple views of spatial memory. *Psychonomic Bulletin and Review, 4*, 102–106.

Shelton, A. L., & McNamara, T. P. (2001a). Systems of spatial reference in human memory. *Cognitive Psychology, 43*, 274–310.

Shelton, A. L., & McNamara, T. P. (2001b). Visual memories from nonvisual experiences. *Psychological Science, 12*, 343–347.

Shelton, A. L., & McNamara, T. P. (2004a). Orientation and perspective dependence in route and survey learning. *Journal of Experimental Psychology: Learning, Memory, and Cognition, 30*, 158–170.

Shelton, A. L., & McNamara, T. P. (2004b). Spatial memory and perspective taking. *Memory and Cognition, 32*, 416–426.

Shelton, A. L., & Pippitt, H. A. (2007). Fixed versus dynamic orientations in environmental learning from ground-level and aerial perspectives. *Psychological Research, 71,* 333–346.

Sholl, M. J., & Nolin, T. L. (1997). Orientation specificity in representations of place. *Journal of Experimental Psychology: Learning, Memory, and Cognition, 23,* 1494–1507.

Siegel, A. W., & White, S. H. (1975). The development of spatial representations of large-scale environments. In H. W. Reese (Ed.), *Advances in child development and behavior* (Vol. 10, pp. 9–55). New York: Academic Press.

Simmering, V. R., Peterson, C., Darling, W., & Spencer, J. P. (2008). Location memory biases reveal the challenges of coordinating visual and kinesthetic reference frames. *Experimental Brain Research, 184,* 165–178.

Simons, D. J., & Wang, R. F. (1998). Perceiving real-world viewpoint changes. *Psychological Science, 9,* 315–320.

Squire, L. R., & Zola-Morgan, S. (1988). Memory: Brain systems and behavior. *Trends in Neuroscience, 11,* 170–175.

Squire, L. R., Zola-Morgan, S., Cave, C. B., Haist, F., Musen, G., & Suzuki, W. A. (1990). Memory organization of brain systems and cognition. *Cold Spring Harbor Symposia on Quantitative Biology, 55,* 1007–1023.

Sun, H.-J., Campos, J. L., & Chan, G. S. W. (2004). Multisensory integration in the estimation of relative path length. *Experimental Brain Research, 154,* 246–254.

Tarr, M. J. (1995). Rotating objects to recognize them: A case study on the role of viewpoint-dependency in the recognition of three-dimensional objects. *Psychonomic Bulletin and Review, 2,* 55–82.

Tarr, M. J., & Pinker, S. (1989). Mental rotation and orientation-dependence in shape recognition. *Cognitive Psychology, 21,* 233–282.

Tarr, M. J., & Pinker, S. (1990). When does human object recognition use a viewer-centered reference frame? *Psychological Science, 4,* 253–256.

Tarr, M. J., & Pinker, S. (1991). Orientation-dependent mechanisms in shape recognition: Further issues. *Psychological Science, 2,* 207–209.

Taylor, H. A., & Tversky, B. (1992). Spatial mental models derived from survey and route descriptions. *Journal of Memory and Language, 31,* 261–292.

Thinus-Blanc, C., & Gaunet, F. (1997). Representation of space in blind persons: Vision as a spatial sense? *Psychological Bulletin, 121,* 20–42.

Thorndyke, P. W., & Hayes-Roth, B. (1982). Differences in spatial knowledge acquired from maps and navigation. *Cognitive Psychology, 14,* 560–589.

Thurlow, W. R., & Kerr, T. P. (1970). Effect of a moving visual environment on localization of sound. *American Journal of Psychology, 83,* 112–118.

Tinti, C., Adenzato, M., Tamietto, M., & Cornoldi, C. (2006). Visual experience is not necessary for efficient survey spatial cognition: Evidence from blindness. *Quarterly Journal of Experimental Psychology, 59,* 1306–1328.

Tlauka, M. (2006). Updating imagined translational movements. *Scandinavian Journal of Psychology, 47,* 471–475.

Tolman, E. C. (1948). Cognitive maps in rats and men. *Psychological Review, 55,* 189–208.

Tolman, E. C., Ritchie, B. F., & Kalish, D. (1946). Studies in spatial learning: II. Place learning versus response learning. *Journal of Experimental Psychology: General, 36,* 221–229.

Tolman, E. C., Ritchie, B. F., & Kalish, D. (1947). Studies in spatial learning: V. Response versus place learning by the noncorrection method. *Journal of Experimental Psychology: General, 37,* 285–292.

Tootell, R. B. H., Hadjikhani, N. K., Vanduffel, W., Liu, A. K., Mendola, J. D., Sereno, M. I., & Dale, A. M. (1998). Functional analysis of primary visual cortex (V1) in humans. *Proceedings of the National Academy of Sciences, U.S.A., 95,* 811–817.

Tversky, B. (1981). Distortions in memory for maps. *Cognitive Psychology, 13,* 407–433.

Tversky, B. (1991). Spatial mental models. In G. H. Bower (Ed.), *The psychology of learning and motivation* (Vol. 27, pp. 109–145). San Diego, CA: Academic Press.

Tversky, B. (1992). Distortions in cognitive maps. *Geoforum, 23,* 131–138.

Valiquette, C., & McNamara, T. P. (2007). Different mental representations for place recognition and goal localization. *Psychonomic Bulletin & Review, 14,* 676–680.

van Beers, R. J., Haggard, P., & Wolpert, D. M. (2002). When feeling is more important than seeing in sensorimotor adaptation. *Current Biology, 12,* 834–837.

Vecchi, T., Tinti, C., & Cornoldi, C. (2004). Spatial memory and integration processes in congenital blindness. *NeuroReport, 15,* 2787–2790.

Wallace, M. T., Carriere, B. N., Perrault, T. J., Jr., Vaughan, J. W., & Stein, B. E. (2006). The development of cortical multisensory integration. *Journal of Neuroscience, 26,* 11844–11849.

Wallace, M. T., Perrault, T. J., Jr., Hairston, W. D., & Stein, B. E. (2004). Visual experience is necessary for the development of multisensory integration. *Journal of Neuroscience, 24,* 9580–9584.

Waller, D. (2006). Egocentric and nonegocentric coding in memory for spatial layout: Evidence from scene recognition. *Memory & Cognition, 34,* 491–504.

Waller, D., Loomis, J. M., Golledge, R. G., & Beall, A. C. (2000). Place learning in humans: The role of distance and direction information. *Spatial Cognition and Computation, 2,* 333–354.

Waller, D., Loomis, J. M., & Steck, S. D. (2003). Inertial cues do not enhance knowledge of environmental layout. *Psychonomic Bulletin & Review, 10,* 987–993.

Wallraff, H. G. (2004). Avian olfactory navigation: Its empirical foundation and conceptual state. *Animal Behaviour, 67,* 189–204.

Wang, R. F. (2004). Between reality and imagination; When is spatial updating automatic? *Perception & Psychophysics, 66,* 68–76.

Wang, R. F., & Brockmole, J. R. (2003). Human navigation in nested environments. *Journal of Experimental Psychology: Learning, Memory, and Cognition, 29,* 398–404.

Wang, R. F., & Spelke, E. S. (2000). Updating egocentric representations in human navigation. *Cognition, 77,* 215–250.

Wang, R. F., & Spelke, E. S. (2002). Human spatial representation: Insights from animals. *Trends in Cognitive Sciences, 6,* 376–382.

Warren, D. H. (1970). Intermodality interactions in spatial localization. *Cognitive Psychology, 1,* 114–133.

Wehner, R., & Srinivasan, M. V. (2003). Path integration in insects. In K. J. Jeffery (Ed.), *The neurobiology of spatial behaviour* (pp. 9–30). New York: Oxford University Press.

Welch, R. B., & Warren, D. H. (1980). Immediate perceptual response to intersensory discrepancy. *Psychological Bulletin, 88,* 638–667.

Werner, S., & Schmidt, K. (1999). Environmental reference systems for large-scale spaces. *Spatial Cognition and Computation, 1,* 447–473.

Whitely, A. M., & Warrington, E. K. (1978). Selective impairment of topographical memory: A case study. *Journal of Neurology, Neurosurgery, and Psychiatry, 41,* 575–578.

Wilson, M. A., & McNaughton, B. L. (1993). Dynamics of the hippocampal ensemble code for space. *Science, 261*, 1055–1058.

Wolbers, T., Wiener, J. M., Mallot, H. A., & Büchel, C. (2007). Differential recruitment of the hippocampus, medial prefrontal cortex, and the human motion complex during path integration in humans. *Journal of Neuroscience, 27*, 9408–9416.

Wraga, M. J., Creem, S. H., & Proffitt, D. R. (2000). Updating scenes after object- and viewer-rotations. *Journal of Experimental Psychology: Learning, Memory, and Cognition, 26*, 151–168.

Wraga, M. J., Creem-Regehr, S. H., & Proffitt, D. R. (2004). Spatial updating of virtual displays during self- and display-rotation. *Memory & Cognition, 32*, 399–415.

Yamamoto, N., & Shelton, A. L. (2005). Visual and proprioceptive representations in spatial memory. *Memory & Cognition, 33*, 140–150.

Yamamoto, N., & Shelton, A. L. (2007). Path information effects in visual and proprioceptive spatial learning. *Acta Psychologica, 125*, 346–360.

Yamamoto, N., & Shelton, A. L. (2008). *Orientation dependence of spatial memory acquired from auditory experience.* Manuscript submitted for publication.

Yamamoto, N., & Shelton, A. L. (in press). Sequential versus simultaneous viewing of an environment: Effects of focal attention to individual object locations on visual spatial learning. *Visual Cognition.*

7 Expectancies, emotion, and memory reports for visual events

Deborah Davis
University of Nevada, Reno

Elizabeth F. Loftus
University of California, Irvine

1. INTRODUCTION

Previous chapters in this volume have considered memory for objects, faces, and scenes, as well as consequences of those memories for visually guided action and behavior. In this chapter, we consider the quality of memory for objects, faces, and scenes when they must be interpreted and remembered in the context of real-life events. Centering our discussion on eyewitness memory for emotionally charged, crime-related events, we focus on *systematic predictable distortions* affecting memory at all stages, from encoding through retrieval.

Eyewitness testimony can be distorted at the earliest stages of perception by strong emotions and existing beliefs and expectations that guide processing and interpretation of unfolding events—and therefore *what* is originally encoded into memory. But this belief- and emotion-generated distortion does not stop at the point of original encoding. Instead, it pervades memory at all stages, from encoding and storage through multiple efforts to retrieve and report on the original events. Therefore, in this chapter we consider the myriad ways in which beliefs, expectations, and emotions can cause predictable distortions at these sequential stages of the memory process. Although relevant to memory for a variety of visual and autobiographical events, here we focus our illustrations specifically on memory for visual *objects* (including persons).

We begin with a discussion of the impact of beliefs at encoding. We focus much of our discussion of encoding processes on the causal role of racial stereotypes in memory errors, because the stereotype literature has provided a wealth of relevant research illustrations, because it has been the source of some of the more creative and promising new methods for studying relevant processes, and because many relevant stereotype studies involve crime-related stimuli. We then turn to discussion of the influence of such factors as emotion and stress on memory. Finally, we consider a variety of postevent influences on memory for what was previously observed.

2. INFLUENCE OF BELIEFS AND EXPECTATIONS DURING EVENT ENCODING

Eyewitness memory errors begin with mistakes in *what* is encoded during the original witnessed event. Encoding mistakes may be the result of such factors as inadequate or misdirected attention or personal or contextually based perceptual difficulties that generally impair accuracy. But beliefs, expectations, and emotion can cause *specific* kinds of errors—as illustrated in a series of studies using a novel method referred to as the "weapons false alarm" paradigm (WFA).

The "weapons false alarm" research was inspired by the 1999 case of an unarmed Black man—Amidou Diallo—who died after being shot 41 times by NYC police officers who believed he was armed, brandishing a weapon instead of showing his wallet. Shortly after the Diallo incident, psychologists began to address the issue of whether racial stereotypes associating Blacks with violence might cause such misidentifications of weapons in the hands of Blacks—a phenomenon dubbed the "weapons false alarm." Efforts to understand the phenomenon soon began to address specific effects of beliefs and expectations on four levels of processing at encoding: (a) deployment of attention, (b) ease of categorization, (c) criteria for categorization, and (d) the content of categorizations or interpretations of unfolding events—all factors affecting the accuracy of *what* is encoded. Here we consider the further possibility that activation of particular concepts, expectations, or beliefs at encoding may generate automatic emotional or behavioral responses that reciprocally influence the preceding processes. A person may automatically react to thoughts activated by a stereotype with fear or defensive behaviors that themselves reciprocally reinforce activation of the thoughts that generated them, along with related material in memory. And, in the process of making attributions for the cause of these reactions, a person may be prone to biased interpretations consistent with the activated schemas (e.g., "I shot him because he was acting strangely and appeared dangerous").

Some readers may recognize such effects as widely investigated features of schematic processing and as consistent with more recently documented automatic behavioral and other sequelae of activated thoughts and emotions (such as direct links between perception and action). Here we review demonstrations of these familiar effects to document the processing effects of beliefs, expectations, and emotion on object identification (i.e., on *what* is encoded into memory). Specifically, for the sake of coherence in our examples, we focus on illustrations of the effects of stereotypes associating Blacks with crime on misidentification of weapons and on distortions in facial perception (for broader reviews of the effects of schematic processing on witness memory see Davis & Follette, 2001; Davis & Loftus, 2007).

2.1. Deployment of attention

A large body of literature has shown that activation of specific schemas is associated with selective attention to schema-relevant information. In part, selective-attention effects have been inferred from the fact that, given activation of a specific schema, schema-relevant information is remembered better than schema-irrelevant information (e.g., Wyer, 2004). But recent research has turned to more direct measures of attention. For example, Eberhardt, Goff, Purdie, and Davies (2004) used such direct measures to show that when specific schemas are activated, visual attention is selectively directed toward schema-relevant stimuli. Specifically, reflecting stereotypes associating Blacks with crime, just as crime-related primes induced selective attention to Black faces, so priming Black faces selectively induced attention to crime-related objects.

To illustrate the former association, Eberhardt et al. (2004) used a modification of the dot-probe task used extensively in the personality disorders literature (e.g., MacLeod, Mathews, & Tata, 1986). In a first step, described as a vigilance task, half of the participants were subliminally primed with crime-relevant objects (such as weapons). Immediately afterward, participants began the dot-probe task. A Black and a White face were simultaneously displayed on the computer screen. When they disappeared, a dot probe appeared in the previous visual location of either the Black face or the White face. Theoretically, the Black face would be more likely to capture the attention of participants previously primed with crime-relevant stimuli, since the activated crime schemas would selectively direct attention to crime-relevant stimuli (i.e., the Black rather than the White face). Indeed, the dot presented in the location of the Black face was detected more rapidly for crime-primed participants, and the dot presented in the location of the White face was detected more slowly. This effect was replicated using police officers as participants and also in a conceptually similar study using positive primes stereotypically associated with Blacks (e.g., basketball-related stimuli).

To the extent that schemas selectively direct attention to relevant objects and events, one might expect that memory would be more accurate for those stimuli. After all, memory follows the focus of attention! However, as subsequent sections illustrate, while attention provides the *opportunity* to encode *at all*, and potentially to encode more accurately, under some conditions it may actually facilitate errors.

2.2. Ease of categorization

Another well-documented effect of schematic processing is greater ease in the identification of stimuli and events (e.g., Bransford & Johnson, 1972) (for detailed discussion of schemas in scene memory, see chapter 4, section 2.5.2). When a schema is activated, comparison and categorization of incoming stimuli is more rapid and efficient. Indeed, without schemas, we would have no concept categories with which to identify stimuli. Hence, it follows that schema activation will facilitate the speed at which relevant stimuli are identified. This may mean the difference between whether a briefly observed stimulus can be encoded or not, and therefore whether a witness can report at all on certain features of a rapidly unfolding event. Or (as illustrated in subsequent sections), if the stimulus cannot be confidently categorized within the available time, the witness may adopt less strict criteria for categorization, leading to errors in what is encoded and therefore included in later memory reports.

In the first study published in the wake of the Amidou Diallo incident, Keith Payne (2001) used a sequential priming paradigm to test the speed of categorization hypothesis with respect to the activation of race-related stereotypes and identification of weapons. After first priming participants with either a Black or a White face on a computer screen, he then presented either a gun or a tool, requiring participants to indicate as rapidly as possible which was displayed. As expected, those primed with a Black face were quicker to identify the gun. However, since Payne presented the primes overtly, it is difficult to know whether participants responded more rapidly after a Black face prime because they identified the gun more easily or because their expectations led them to react in anticipation of clearly seeing one. Hence, Eberhardt et al. (2004) examined the point at which participants would identify an object that began as severely degraded and was progressively clarified over time. Participants subliminally primed with Black, White, or no male faces were to indicate the moment when they could identify crime-relevant (e.g., gun or knife) or crime-irrelevant (e.g., camera, book) objects, and then to name the object. Primes did not affect the identification of crime-irrelevant objects, but crime-relevant objects were detected most quickly following subliminally presented Black faces and least quickly following White faces.

Other studies used computer programs presenting Black or White persons holding weapons or neutral objects to examine the effect of racial primes on speed in the identification of weapons. Participants had to decide as rapidly as possible whether to shoot. Consistent with earlier findings, these studies revealed that participants were quicker to shoot Black than White figures holding weapons (e.g., Correll, Park, Judd, & Wittenbrink, 2002; Greenwald, Oakes, & Hoffman, 2003). Racial stereotypes also appear to facilitate speed of classification of positive stimuli associated with race, such as sports objects (see Judd, Blair, & Chapleau, 2004).

The reverse effect—quicker classification of faces following primes with stereotype-related objects—has also been demonstrated in several studies not specifically related to weapons. For example, participants are quicker to classify faces as male or female following presentation of gender-related primes such as "flower" or "diet" (e.g., Blair & Banaji, 1996), and speed of racial categorization of faces is facilitated by the presentation of race-related primes (e.g., Kawakami & Dovidio, 2001; Kawakami, Dovidio, Moll, Hermsen, & Russin, 2000).

2.3. Criteria for categorization

Although activation of stereotypes or other beliefs and expectations may sometimes facilitate ease of recognition, their effects may also derive from changes in the criteria for categorization. For example, if expectations for violence are sufficiently high, the perceiver may adopt a mentality whereby the weakest or most subtle cues are sufficient to lead him or her to classify and react to an object or person as dangerous. In such a case, a speedier response would not necessarily reflect ease of classification but, rather, the weaker criterion for categorization.

To illustrate this point, imagine a situation in which an observer views a figure cloaked in a hooded robe, from behind. Were he to encounter the figure in a sauna area of an all-male club, he could reasonably classify the figure as "male" without waiting to see its face; in the context of an integrated club, however, he would be more likely to require additional cues such as size, gait, body shape, or a full-face view before being willing to identify the figure's gender. In the former instance, the expectation that only males would be in the sauna of the all-male club would serve to lower criteria for identifying gender, causing the person to feel no need for gender-specific cues to make the presumptive classification. In other words, the observer would require a less comprehensive comparison of the features of the observed object to the features of the category to determine a match. Consistent with this reasoning, those with stronger race-based expectations—such as more negative biases against Blacks (e.g., Payne, 2001), stronger race-based stereotypes (Correll et al., 2002), and more negative implicit biases against Blacks as measured by the Implicit Attitudes Test (e.g., Payne, 2005)—show enhanced racial bias in the WFA paradigm.

Finally, it should be noted that strong emotions may affect encoding in part through selectively lowering identification thresholds for emotion-related stimuli. For example, fear and the resulting activation of self-protection goals may lower thresholds for identification of threatening stimuli such as weapons. Such selective lowering of identification criteria could serve evolutionary survival functions, as suggested by research on the amygdala (the brain's center of "emotional" processing) and perception of emotional stimuli (see later sections).

In fact, Amidou Diallo may have been victimized by such lowered criteria. The officers had stopped Diallo because he matched the description of a suspect. When Diallo reached for his pocket, one officer shouted "Gun!" and the rest opened fire, not waiting to see that the "gun" was really only a wallet. Expectations associated with suspicion that Diallo was the suspect they were searching for, along with racial stereotypes associating Blacks with violence and strong emotions such as fear of harm to themselves or others, may have led them to adopt looser criteria for classifying the object in his hand as a gun. In this case the shooters were confronted with their mistakes, in that no weapons were found. But in many instances, interpretations or classifications made on the basis of emotion- or expectation-weakened identification criteria, unchecked by disconfirming evidence, enter long-term memory uncorrected and become the basis of distorted witness reports. This very possibility has been explored in the body of research on "change blindness."

2.3.1. *"Change blindness" and weakened criteria for stimulus classification*

In 1998 Daniel Simons and Daniel Levin began a rather startling series of demonstrations of observers' failures to detect surreptitious substitutions of one person for another during apparently continuous real-world interactions. Across a number of studies, participants failed to notice that persons with whom they were directly conversing had been replaced by another person, or that a person they were watching in a video had been replaced by another (for review, see Simons & Ambinder, 2005) (for further analysis, see also chapter 4, section 2.4). A common feature in these studies was that participants would *expect* the person to remain the same.

For example, in one study, while participants were giving directions to a pedestrian who had stopped them on campus, two confederates passed between them carrying a large door. As the door passed, the person receiving directions changed places with another who emerged to continue the conversation (Simons & Levin, 1998). In another, a clerk interacting with a student bent down behind the counter, whereupon another person emerged to continue the interaction (Levin, Simons, Angelone, & Chabris, 2002). And in a video, a person working in one room appeared to hear a phone ring and get up to answer it, whereupon the camera cut to the hallway where a different person answered (Levin & Simons, 1997). In each of these studies, large proportions of participants failed to detect the change between people. Presumably, superficial processing prevented observers from engaging in the specific-feature comparisons that would help them distinguish one person from another. This tendency to engage in superficial processing would likely be enhanced when the person's expectations of continuous identity led them to adopt very loose criteria (or none at all) for categorizing the person as the same.

Davis, Loftus, Vanous, and Cucciare (2008) illustrated this problem in the context of studying mistaken eyewitness identifications. Participants watched a video involving the theft of a bottle of liquor in a grocery store. In addition to the perpetrator, two innocent people were shown in immediate contiguity to the perpetrator. One (the continuous innocent, or CI) walked down the liquor aisle and passed behind a stack of boxes, whereupon the perpetrator emerged and stole the liquor. The other (the discontinuous innocent, or DI) appeared immediately after the theft, shopping in the vegetable section. The authors argued that expectations for continuous identity would be strongest when the innocent and perpetrator were shown in the apparently continuous-action sequence in which the CI walked down the liquor aisle and disappeared behind the boxes and the perpetrator emerged. Therefore, they expected participants to be less likely to notice the difference between the CI and perpetrator than that between the DI (the innocent shown in the discontinuous location of the vegetable aisle) and the perpetrator. Distracted participants were expected to be less likely to notice these differences than undistracted participants, and failure to notice the difference was, in turn, expected to lead to more misidentifications of the CI as the perpetrator.

Indeed, this is what Davis et al. (2008) found. Distracted participants were less likely to notice the difference between the actors. In turn, participants who failed to notice the difference between the CI and perpetrator were more likely to misidentify her as the perpetrator than to identify either the DI or others who had not been in the video. In contrast, those who did notice the difference were more likely to misidentify the DI than either the CI or others who had not been in the video. Just being in the video increased the likelihood of being misidentified as the perpetrator. However, the greatest likelihood of misidentification was for the CI, among participants who never realized that two different people had been in the liquor aisle.

Similar results were obtained by Davies and Hine (2007), who found that 61% of participants failed to detect the substitution of one burglar for another in a film of a burglary, and that detection of the change was related to accuracy in identification of both burglars. Furthermore, relevant to "earwitness" identification, Vitevitch (2003) found that more than 40% of participants failed to detect a change in speakers.

The change blindness research has provided very compelling illustrations of processes underlying mistakes in real-life eyewitness identifications. If, after a few seconds, one cannot remember the person with whom one was interacting well enough to know that he or she has been replaced by someone new, what can we expect from eyewitnesses after days, weeks, or months have elapsed?

2.3.2. *Speeded judgments and classification criteria*

Central to real-life situations is pressure to identify dangerous objects or situations quickly enough to react and avoid injury. Such time pressure and speeded judgments appear to enhance expectation-based errors such as the racial bias in "weapons false alarms" (e.g., Payne, 2001, 2005)—that is, the greater tendency to misclassify harmless objects as weapons in the hands of Black targets (discussed below). In the absence of sufficient time, the observer may be unable to engage in the comprehensive feature matching necessary for enforcing strict identification criteria.

2.3.3. *Automatic versus controlled processing*

Payne and his associates (Payne, 2005; Payne, Jacoby & Lambert, 2005; Payne, Shimizu, & Jacoby, 2005) suggested that the racially biased WFA effect should be greatest when controlled processing is limited by time pressures or by failures of executive functioning. Arguably, both factors can inhibit enforcement of stricter, reality-based criteria for classification and interpretation (facilitating misclassifications) as well as impair the ability to override automatic-response tendencies generated by racial stereotypes (facilitating known but uncontrollable errors). Supporting this reasoning, depletion of self-regulatory resources (Muraven & Baumeister, 2000) through several hundred trials in the Stroop color-naming task induced greater race-biased WFAs (Govorun & Payne, 2006). Furthermore, working memory capacity (an index of executive functioning; Govorun & Payne, 2006), measures of attentional control (e.g., Payne, 2005), and neurological activity consistent with detection of conflict between current and intended states (necessary for controlled processes) are negatively related to the magnitude of the race bias. Furthermore, activity consistent with stronger emotional reactions to threatening stimuli (reflecting automatic negative race-based reactions) is positively related to the magnitude of the bias (Amodio et al., 2004; Correll, Urland, & Ito, 2006).

2.4. Interpretation

As the previous discussion of lowered criteria implied, lax identification criteria can both speed identification and create errors such as a WFA or mistaken identifications of innocent bystanders, as illustrated in the change blindness research. But the specific nature of errors is not random. Instead, errors in perception or interpretation of unfolding events tend toward consistency with activated schemata (for review, see Wyer, 2004). Not surprisingly, the WFA research has repeatedly shown that in addition to directing attention to stereotype-related objects, which lowers identification criteria and/or speeds their identification, activation of racial stereotypes also leads to their misclassification—specifically, to the misclassification of neutral objects as weapons. That is, priming with a Black face led to more misclassifications of neutral objects as weapons than did priming with a White face, whereas the reverse was true for classification of tools (e.g., Payne, 2001; regarding errors in classification of both positive and negative stereotype-relevant objects, see also Judd et al., 2004); and the likelihood of erroneously "shooting" a Black person holding a neutral object was greater than that of "shooting" a White person holding a neutral object (Correll et al., 2002; Greenwald et al., 2003).

These biases appear to be strong, uncontrollable, and pervasive. Even Black persons are susceptible (Correll et al., 2002), and it occurs whether participants act without instructions, are told specifically to use race as a cue, or are instructed about the potential of race to bias responses and are told to avoid it (Payne, Lambert, & Jacoby, 2002). In fact, when race is made salient, either by instructions to use it or to avoid using it as a cue, its effects are enhanced, indicating that regardless of intentions or the reason for activation of racial stereotypes, once activated, they still exert their automatic effects. Though focused on racial stereotypes, such results are consistent with the wider literature illustrating schema-consistent errors in memory (for review, see Wyer, 2004), including eyewitness memory (see Davis & Loftus, 2007).

2.4.1. *Automatic activation of behavioral responses*

The race-biased WFA effect has commonly been discussed as the result of the *misclassification* of neutral objects as threatening, which leads the person to shoot (the *illusory perception* explanation; see Correll et al., 2002; Greenwald et al., 2003; Payne, 2001). More recent evidence has shown, however, that some participants are well aware of their errors in response and can correct them if given time (even without the stimulus still in view; e.g., Payne,

Shimizu, & Jacoby, 2005). They seem to fail to override automatic reactions to salient race-related stereotypes when responding to an accurately perceived object (the *executive failure* hypothesis). However, such a view assumes two things: (a) that the object *can be* accurately perceived, and (b) that conscious classification precedes response (however well- or ill-controlled). But, in situations where accurate perception can be difficult, where racial stereotypes or situational scripts may lead the perceiver to feel threatened, and where response time can affect survival, an additional mechanism may come into play, involving direct links to behavior—independent of conscious classification.

Expectations that a particular person or situation poses a threat to oneself or others may directly activate such goal-related scripts as "protection" or "defense" involving shooting or otherwise disabling the threat (for discussion of cognitive and behavioral effects of goal activation, and for evidence of automatic cognitive and behavioral links between goals and means of attaining them, see, e.g., Bargh, 2005, 2006; Chartrand & Bargh, 2002; Shah, 2005). Similar behavioral scripts may also be directly activated by emotions such as fear, or directly by situational cues associated with danger (with or without conscious awareness or expectations of danger). Subliminally presented Black faces, for example, produce greater activation of the amygdala than do White faces, a difference that is reduced when the faces are presented more slowly (Cunningham et al., 2004). In turn, the amygdala can drive automatic fight-or-flight responses prior to conscious intention (see below). As is often the case in criminal incidents, alcohol can impair executive functions (including control of automatic race-based response tendencies; e.g., Bartholow, Dickter, & Sestir, 2006), leaving automatic effects on behavior unchecked.

The concept "shoot" is likely to be among activated self-protective behaviors, particularly among police officers trained to use weapons in response to such threats or among laboratory participants set on choosing only between "shoot" and "don't shoot." Once activated, such concepts or scripts may directly potentiate associated behaviors such as shooting, evading, or yelling threats (for a review of links between subliminal activation of emotions and overt emotion-driven behaviors, see Winkielman & Berridge, 2004). These cognitive and behavioral responses may occur before the person becomes consciously aware of either their triggers or their existence.

Interestingly, self-protection goals can reciprocally influence perception of the stimulus that triggered them, as illustrated by recent findings that activation of self-protection goals led to perception of greater anger in Black and Arab male faces (a tendency that was greater among those with stronger stereotype associations of the target's race with threat). Such reciprocal influences possess great potential to bias subsequent eyewitness identifications (see section 4.1; for illustration and for a review of a variety of effects of goals on social perception and memory, see Maner et al., 2005).

In addition to automatic behavioral reactions to goal activation, research on unconscious mimicry (see Bargh, 2005; Dijksterhuis & Bargh, 2001; Jonas &

Sassenberg, 2006) has shown that priming a social category can lead targets to behave consistently with stereotyped behavior for that category (as, for example, when activation of *elderly* stereotypes leads to slower walking speed). Furthermore, observations of specific behaviors can automatically activate mimicry of the behavior (for review, see Chartrand, Maddux, & Lakin, 2005). A mechanism for such automatic mimicry of behavior is suggested by studies of "mirror neurons" (Buccino et al., 2001; Rizzolatti & Arbib, 1998) found in the premotor cortex of animals and humans. Mirror neurons are activated in the same functionally specific regions of the premotor cortex when watching others engaging in a behavior and when performing it oneself—suggesting a direct connection between seeing and doing. Thus, seeing a person apparently reaching for a gun might well automatically activate the urge to shoot.

Police with extensive weapons training are less susceptible than less trained police or citizens to racially biased WFAs (Correll et al., 2006). This may be the result of better discrimination between weapons and nonweapons, which is what those authors suggest, or it may be that trained officers are simply better able to override automatic impulses to shoot when feeling threatened or fearful, which in turn provides them with time to adopt stricter criteria for identification of situations in which shooting is appropriate. Generally, the racially biased WFA effect is greater among people with stronger automatic racial feelings and attitudes, and weaker among those with stronger executive-control functions (e.g., Payne, 2005). Presumably, police training enhances the latter, although training (through exposure to many trials in which race is unrelated to possession of a weapon) can also reduce race-biased WFA among police officers through modification of automatic associations (e.g., Plant & Peruche, 2005; Plant, Peruche, & Butz, 2005; see also, for more general examples of reduction of automatic biases, Kawakami et al., 2000).

Once a person has reacted in a dramatic and unusual way—such as shooting another human being—the reaction itself also has great potential to reciprocally influence the preceding processes of encoding. That is, by virtue of the response itself (shooting the person), or in the process of interpreting or explaining strong emotional and behavioral responses, the person may enhance or maintain the activation of the original expectations (e.g., Blacks are dangerous) or emotions (e.g., fear) that triggered these responses. In doing so, the person will be susceptible to biased conclusions concerning the causes of these reactions. For example, in thinking about why he felt fear, the person may mistakenly assume it must have been because the target looked or acted dangerous, rather than because his racial stereotypes cause him to fear all Blacks. Imagine the following sequence, for example:

A White policeman responding to a report of a prowler sees a young Black male in a dark alley near the source of the report. The young man turns as he hears the policeman approach, and as the man's right shoulder and arm follow his body's movement toward the officer, the latter feels threatened, shoots, and, *then*, labeling and attribution processes catch up with automatic behavioral responses to emotion and he mistakenly perceives the cell phone in the young man's hand as a weapon as he falls to the street. Memory for sequence being susceptible to error, and with expectations associating Blacks with violence activated by the young man's race, the situation, and his own reactions, he mistakenly "remembers" seeing the "gun" before he shot.

Although it is difficult to test this explanation with the WFA paradigm, there is substantial evidence that activation of specific cognitions, emotions, or goals can directly promote affective, semantic, or motive-consistent judgments and behaviors—with or without awareness of the specific stimuli that triggered them (as discussed earlier). One has only to look at the vast and diverse research literature using subliminal priming to illustrate this point. Our review of the WFA research has clearly shown this with respect to subliminal priming of Black and White faces. However, effects of subliminal primes have been demonstrated across a wide swath of interpersonal behaviors and judgments, health motives and behaviors, consumer behaviors (as reflected in research on subliminal persuasion), and many others (for examples of the effects of subliminal priming on interpersonal goals, judgments, and behaviors, see reviews in Forgas, 2006; Mikulincer & Shaver, 2007; for a variety of reviews of unconscious influences on thoughts and behavior, see Hassin, Uleman, & Bargh, 2005).

Recent neuroscience research has also used subliminal primes to study activation within specific processing areas of the brain that precedes conscious awareness—for example, research showing amygdala activation in response to subliminally presented fearful faces. In turn, this early preconscious activation of the amygdala has two effects that, in combination, enhance processing of threat-relevant stimuli: (a) modulation of attention toward threatening stimuli, and (b) activation of the visual cortex, resulting in greater perceptual sensitivity and enhanced potentiation of the perceptual benefits of attention (see review by Phelps, 2006). Phelps reviewed evidence that signals of emotion are processed and reacted to automatically by the amygdala, irrespective of attention or awareness. Also included was some evidence of the existence of specialized subcortical pathways allowing the amygdala to perceive and drive reactions to threatening stimuli prior to completion of standard perceptual functions such as explicit recognition (although cognitions activated prior to exposure to the stimuli can also affect the amygdala's reactions). Given that Black faces evoke greater amygdala reactions among White persons (Cunningham et al., 2004; but for evidence that this race-specific activation is dependent upon currently activated processing goals, see Wheeler & Fiske, 2005), such findings are compatible with the possibility that defensive reactions such as shooting can occur prior to conscious interpretive and controlled processes.

When such preconscious (and/or conscious) cognitive and behavioral reactions occur, they can become part of the context in which the original threat is identified and interpreted once brought fully into awareness. The tendency to engage in attributions concerning causes of behavior is enhanced for unusual, unexpected, or unfamiliar behaviors (e.g., Weiner, 1985)—such as shooting someone. Moreover, in the aftermath of shooting a person holding an ambiguous object, labeling and attribution processes have great potential to affect "memory" for the object, particularly in the context of self-justification motives demanding just cause for the action (on self-justification and memory distortion, see Tavris & Aronson, 2007).

One's own emotional reactions and behaviors may also exert more direct effects through activation of relevant knowledge structures—as, for example, when shooting a person might reciprocally activate concepts related to threat and danger, including "gun." In fact, behavior itself is tied to associated affective and cognitive structures, as illustrated by the growing literature on *"embodied cognition"* (for reviews, see Anderson, 2003; Garbarini & Adenzato, 2004; Markman & Brendl, 2005; Niedenthal, Barsalou, Winkielman, Krauth-Gruber, & Ric, 2005). That is, overt body positions and behaviors—such as facial expressions, posture, or specific movements or actions—have been shown to directly activate associated cognition, affect, or behavior and, conversely, to inhibit inconsistent reactions. Similar effects have been predicted by "common-coding theory" (Hommel, Musseler, Aschersleben, & Prinz, 2001) and the theory of internal models (e.g., Wolpert & Kawato, 1998), and tests of these theories have shown that overt actions can affect visual and auditory perception (see Repp & Knoblich, 2007).

Generally, these literatures would suggest that the action of shooting would indeed activate (or feed already activated) goals, schemas, and affect triggered consciously or preconsciously by a potentially dangerous object, as well as objects associated with the action. This, in turn, would enhance the likelihood of labeling the object as "gun" and of "remembering" associated contextual features and characteristics of the target and his behavior as "aggressive" or "dangerous."

Essentially, the embodied cognition literature suggests that *"sensory and motor processes, perception, and action are fundamentally inseparable in lived cognition"* (Garbarini & Adenzato, 2004, p. 101; emphasis added). Of particular interest, actions (e.g., shooting) are associated with specific objects or types of objects one uses to perform the action (e.g., guns). This is shown in part by the fact that if a canonical neuron (bimodal neurons responsive to motor and visual stimuli) fires while performing a particular action, it also fires when one sees an object with which this action can be performed (see Garbarini & Adenzato, 2004). Such findings are interpreted to mean that the actions that can be performed with the object are part of the cognitive representation of the object itself—and, therefore, activation of one entails activation of the other. Furthermore, "mirror neurons" fire when performing or seeing an action and even when hearing a sound associated with the action (such as when hearing a gunshot evokes the concept of "gun," i.e., as part of the action of shooting; see Garbarini & Adenzato, 2004), again suggesting that all three embody the concept of the action in question.

3. A NEW LOOK AT EMOTION AND MEMORY FOR VISUAL EVENTS

The foregoing discussion provokes a reexamination of the way eyewitness researchers have thought about the role of emotion in eyewitness memory. One of the current party lines—particularly in regard to the role of emotion in later eyewitness identifications of criminal perpetrators—goes as follows (Reisberg & Heuer, 2007): Memory for emotional events is often superior to that for more mundane events; however, although memory for central features, or the *gist,* of the event is enhanced, memory for peripheral features is generally impaired. This "tunnel memory" (e.g., Safer, Christianson, Autry, & Osterlund, 1998) is presumably caused by narrowing attention to central event features at the expense of peripheral features. Since memory follows the focus of attention, memory will be superior for the better-attended central stimuli.

This narrowing of attention can be due to two processes. First, emotional properties of the stimulus itself, such as threatening behavior or objects, may "capture" attention—a phenomenon that is enhanced among those who fear the specific stimulus (Lipp & Waters, 2007). This process is considered responsible for the "weapons-focus" effect—that is, the tendency of weapons to draw attention at the expense of attention to the perpetrator or to other details. Research has documented the attention-capturing effects of weapons by, for example, tracking eye fixation during encoding (e.g., Loftus, Loftus, & Messo, 1987; Stanny & Johnson, 2000) and has generally shown that the weapon itself (and the hand that holds it) may be well remembered, but witnesses are less accurate in identifications of perpetrators for events involving weapons, and the strength of this effect increases as arousal increases (e.g., Peters, 1988; for a meta-analysis, see Steblay, 1992; for recent review, see Reisberg & Heuer, 2007).

Second, attention may narrow as a result of arousal itself. As originally proposed by Easterbrook (1959), arousal causes a decrease in the "range of stimulus cues" that an organism can attend to. Attention thus narrows to aspects of the environment of most interest or importance. That is, arousal might be viewed as enhancing the already present stimulus-driven tendencies for selected stimuli to capture attention at the expense of others. Such a view is consistent with the previously noted role of the amygdala in modulating attention and perceptual sensitivity toward important or threatening stimuli.

This picture is complicated by findings indicating that whereas important, threatening, or emotion-provoking stimuli may affect processing through attentional capture, *high stress* may generally impair memory (e.g., Deffenbacher, 1994; Deffenbacher, Bornstein, Penrod, & McGorty, 2004; Lupien, Maheu, Tu, Fiocco, & Schramek, 2007; Morgan et al., 2004). Stress in this context is described as consisting of high levels of physiological arousal and associated biological reactions—such as activation of the HPA (hypothalamic-pituitary-adrenal) axis and hormonal effects following from this activation—along with associated psychological reactions such as perceived threat and acute anxiety (e.g., Payne, Nadel, Britton, & Jacobs, 2004). These authors argue that whereas *emotion* serves to activate the amygdala—and hence facilitates memory for the gist of an event (regarding the amygdala and memory, see also Adolphs, Tranel, & Buchanan, 2005; LaBar, 2007; LaBar & Cabeza, 2006; Phelps, 2006)—*high stress* disrupts the functioning of the hippocampus, impairing spatiotemporal processing and memory for event structure and sensory detail (for evidence that anxiety selectively disrupts visuospatial working memory, see Shackman et al., 2006).

While a full discussion of the role of physiological processes involved in emotion and memory is beyond the scope of this chapter, even without considering such issues, the traditional "tunnel-memory" view of the effects of emotion on memory is overly simplistic. That is, it rests on a very simple, but questionable, chain of logic: First, attention is captured by the most important (e.g., interesting, threatening) features of an event. These stimulus features alone capture attention, but emotion can cause attention to be narrowed such that this already selective attention will become even more so, at the expense of other features of the event or context. Attention leads to more accurate encoding. Therefore, the central features of an emotional event will be remembered better, whereas other features will be remembered more poorly.

We suggest that there are two fundamental flaws in this logic. First, emotion may *not* narrow the focus of attention in all cases, and particularly not to entirely predictable stimuli. Stress impairs the operation of executive functions (see reviews in Baumeister & Vohs, 2004)—including the ability to control attention—with the potential result that stressful emotions could cause attention to be more stimulus-driven (so far consistent with the tunnel-memory view). Laboratory studies typically present a narrow range of event features for attentional capture—perhaps only a single candidate (such as a dangerous weapon or dangerous person) that stands out above the rest. But during real-life stressful events there are often multiple central concerns and therefore multiple pulls for attention, some internal and some external—such as the need to monitor threatening persons, the need to control one's own reactions and plan strategies for survival, concerns regarding vulnerable children or the elderly, searching for and monitoring opportunities for protection or escape, and so on. In essence, negative emotions such as fear may well facilitate detection and monitoring of threat-related stimuli, but they can also lead to activation of automatic fight-or-flight goals that demand wider deployment of external attention, active internal processing and planning, and stronger self-regulation, which can in turn deplete cognitive resources—including attention and processing resources. Attempts to control emotion or suppress emotional expression can themselves impair memory for the events (for illustrations with memory for distressing films and for conflictual conversations, see Richards & Gross, 2006; for demonstrations regarding memory of one's own stressful speech, see Egloff, Schmukle, Burns, & Schwerdtfeger, 2006). Such concerns compromise the ability to make clear-cut predictions concerning what features of real-life stressful events will be remembered better or more poorly.

Moreover, independent of selective stress-related effects on the brain, such wide-ranging processing demands might explain the general decrement in memory observed among participants subject to high levels of stress. That is, whereas memory for more significant or emotion-provoking *stimuli* (such as emotional words, pictures, faces, or films; or important and dangerous objects such as weapons) is generally shown to be superior to that for less important or less emotional stimuli, memory for both central and peripheral features (including identification of persons) has been shown to be poorer when the observer is *experiencing* high levels of stress (e.g., Morgan et al., 2004; see reviews by Deffenbacher et al., 2004; McEwen & Sapolsky, 1995).

The second fundamental problem with "tunnel-memory" logic is the assumption that attention promotes accuracy. In fact, attention has more varied and complicated effects. The tunnel-memory logic suggests that attention promotes encoding, quite correctly assuming that attended stimuli are more likely to be encoded at all, and that greater attention provides the *opportunity* for more complete and accurate encoding of details. Furthermore, "elaborative encoding," whereby the person thinks actively about the stimulus, is assumed to enhance memory (as we tell our students!). But, as we know, stimuli are not simply recorded as they objectively exist. Even the simplest acts of visual perception are inherently constructive and interpretive (for an engaging and accessible account of constructive processes in visual perception, see Hoffman, 1998). Stimuli are not merely seen. They are interpreted and evaluated, and provoke related assumptions, and then are reacted to behaviorally—all affecting *what* is encoded.

At this point, it becomes clear that these *consequences* of attention—the observer's cognitive, affective, and behavioral responses while focusing upon the target—have great potential to determine the exact content encoded into memory. It is at this level that attention and elaborative encoding can, in some cases, promote *inaccurate* encoding, as well as constructive and reconstructive processes over time. The literatures on affect and social thinking (e.g., Forgas, 2006), appraisal processes (e.g., Levine & Pizzarro, 2004), automatic goal activation and pursuit (e.g., Bargh, 2005, 2006; Chartrand & Bargh, 2002; Shah, 2005), and schematic processing (e.g., Wyer, 2004) provide the basis for thinking about how this can occur.

Schematic processing results, for example, in selective attention to schema-relevant stimuli, biased interpretation toward consistency with activated schemata, and constructive and reconstructive processes over time, such that schema-consistent (but unpresented) material may be added to memory, and memory for presented material may shift toward consistency with the schema (for forensically relevant examples, see Davis & Follette, 2001; Davis & Loftus, 2007). Schema-*inconsistent* information may be noticed and processed extensively (to explain the inconsistency) and thus remembered well, but it tends to ultimately be reinterpreted toward consistency with the schema. To the extent that attention to a particular object or event occurs in the context of an already activated schema, processing will be biased in these ways. Hence, greater attention can provide greater opportunity for schema-driven selective processing of details of the attended stimulus, and greater likelihood of engaging in biased elaborative processing and interpretations. And in addition to processing the visible target (such as a criminal perpetrator), the observer may engage in schema-driven interpretations of the target's feelings, intentions, underlying motives, character, and much more—each conclusion with potential to bias other judgments.

Emotion has related, but more complicated, effects. Stress, for example, can promote automatic schema-driven (or heuristic) processing through impairment of executive functions and can, therefore, enhance schema-related biases in encoding (for reviews, see Baumeister & Vohs, 2004). Moreover, emotion itself can have equivalent direct effects. For example, both happiness and anger have been found to enhance schematic processing and, thereby, stereotypic judgments. Likewise, anger has been shown to result in more automatic negative responses to outgroups in the minimal groups paradigm, where no previous basis for prejudice exists (i.e., where in-group versus outgroup membership is established by the flip of a coin; e.g., see DeSteno, Dasgupta, Bartlett, & Cajdric, 2004). This suggests that negative biases in processing may occur among angry witnesses. Generally, both automatic and explicit beliefs and attitudes toward social groups are sensitive to external cues such as social context (as, for example, when a basketball game can trigger different aspects of stereotyped associations with Blacks than can a dark alley; for reviews, see Barden, Maddux, Petty, & Brewer, 2004; Blair, 2002). In this light, it is not surprising that emotion, as a contextual cue, can modulate the activation of selective context-relevant content of social-category stereotypes (see DeSteno et al., 2004).

Second, emotion may provide information that is used to interpret the stimulus (the *affect-as-information* mechanism). The observer fails to process all relevant aspects of the stimulus but instead uses his or her own affective reaction as a basis to *infer* the characteristics of the target. If Mary feels happy in the presence of a target, she assumes that the reaction is due to positive characteristics of the target, whereas fearful emotions may lead the target or observed behaviors to be labeled dangerous. Indeed, emotion-congruent biases in perception, judgment, encoding, and retrieval have been widely demonstrated (for evidence for the "affect-as-information" mechanism, see Clore & Storbeck, 2006; Eich & Forgas, 2003; Lerner & Keltner, 2000; Schwartz & Clore, 1988). This mechanism is most likely to produce affect-consistent judgments when the perceiver has little motivation or ability to engage in more thoughtful processing (see Forgas, Wyland, & Laham, 2006). Furthermore, the nature of bias due to the affect-as-information mechanism is likely to be an overall tendency toward congruity of affective tone between the activated emotion and memories and appraisals of the event.

Third, *affect priming* (e.g., Bower, 1981; Bower & Forgas, 2001; Eich & Macaulay, 2006) occurs when specific emotions selectively activate affect-consistent information and schemas, which then drive processing, judgments, and behavioral reactions. Fear, for example, may directly activate concepts such as crime, shooting, or death and promote defensive overt behaviors. Thus, the nature of the affect-priming-driven bias can be somewhat more complicated that that of the affect-as-information mechanism. That is, the bias would be, in part, simple affect congruence due to the activation of congruent information in memory, but would also manifest as congruence with the *content* of information and schemas activated by the affect.

According to the "affect-infusion model" (AIM, Forgas, 2002), the affect-priming mechanism will affect judgments most strongly when some form of constructive processing is used, therefore leading to the somewhat counterintuitive prediction that the more elaborative processing the person engages in, the more affect will bias judgments. Indeed, more unusual or difficult processing tasks and situations invoking longer processing produce greater affect congruence in judgment (see Forgas, 2002; 2006). Such effects are consistent with the notion that attention, particularly prolonged attention involving elaborative processes, can result in more affect or schema-driven biases in encoding.

The above findings suggest clear situational and stimulus-driven differences in how emotion will affect encoding. Likewise, this reasoning predicts individual differences in reactions to emotion. That is, individuals can differ in (a) the content and elaboration of information and knowledge structures linked to affect in memory, (b) the accessibility of this knowledge, and (c) the tendency to focus attention and to think elaboratively about specific stimuli or situations. The former two will affect the likelihood and extent to which affect will activate associated material in memory (providing greater potential for both the "affect-as-information" and the "affect-priming" mechanisms to affect encoding). The latter will affect the extent to which the primed knowledge will be brought to bear upon processing of the stimulus at hand (i.e., the likelihood that "affect priming" will affect encoding). Consistent with this reasoning, people who tend to engage in more elaborative processing show greater schematic and affect-consistent judgments, as do those with stronger, more elaborate relevant attitudes or knowledge structures (e.g., see Petty, 2001). These processes can also lead to greater constructive and reconstructive distortions over time.

Finally, affect can drive the selection of *processing strategies*. Positive and negative *mood* states, for example, promote differences in specific strategies (see Bless & Fiedler, 2006; Forgas, 2006). Of more pertinence to real-life forensically relevant situations, specific negative emotions, such as anger versus fear, may involve qualitatively different processing strategies. Levine and Pizzarro (2004), for example, have complained in their "grumpy overview" of emotion-memory research that our understanding of how emotion affects memory has been seriously limited by focus on the broad construct of "emotional arousal," rather than on the specific processing effects of discrete emotions. The authors put this colorfully: "Arousal is to emotion what brightness is to color; an essential component to be sure, but one that fails to capture some of the most fundamental properties of the phenomenon" (p. 539).

Rather than focusing on processes of affect-congruent priming or affect-as-information mechanisms, Levine and Pizzarro (2004) focus on the application of cognitive appraisal theories to the effects of emotion on information processing. Emotions are alleged to occur when observers perceive that environmental changes have promoted or interfered with one's well-being or achievement of goals. In turn, emotions are presumed to direct attention to aspects of a situation that are functional or are relevant for responding. Such a viewpoint is consistent with our earlier argument that emotion will not necessarily narrow attention, but may deploy it rather widely as the person attempts to assess the situation, assess and select between potential responses, and plan their execution. Such goals would require researchers to consider broader issues than simply differences in affect congruence, schema consistency, or whether the information is central or peripheral.

For example, fear is presumed to trigger attention to a threat, as well as goal-related processing relevant to means of avoiding the threat. Anger, on the other hand, is presumed to trigger attention to sources blocking one's goals and means of removing them. Consistent with Forgas's (2002) affect-infusion model, negative emotions are presumably associated with analytic, data-driven processing strategies targeted toward the goal of assessing and addressing the threat. Therefore, attention, and hence memory, are focused upon a range of threat-appraisal and threat-management-relevant information.

In contrast, positive emotions occur when goals are unobstructed or satisfied and in the absence of threats of all kinds. Therefore, the person has no immediate problem to solve, attention and processing can be more unconstrained and free-ranging, and hence processing strategies and memory can be broad and inclusive, involving both general knowledge and environmental input, but without being as narrowly targeted (for reviews of the relationship of specific emotions to the types of information recalled, see Forgas, 2002; Levine & Pizzarro, 2004). Broadly, the literature on automatic consequences of goal activation is consistent with this view, in that goal activation results in selective attention to and memory for goal-relevant information and in evaluation and interpretation of incoming information in light of its relationship to the goal (Bargh, 2005; Chartrand & Bargh, 2002; Shah, 2005).

Other perspectives on emotion-specific effects on processing strategies have also been offered. For example, some have distinguished between certainty-versus uncertainty-oriented appraisals and the emotions associated with them, providing evidence that certainty-oriented emotions (such as anger) promote heuristic or schematic processing, whereas uncertainty-oriented emotions (such as fear) promote systematic processing (e.g., Nabi, 2002; Tiedens & Linton, 2001). This and other proposed emotion-specific bases of differences in processing strategies (e.g., Watson & Spence, 2007) suggest complex effects of emotion on biases in processing and memory.

3.1. Summary

Clearly, a rather wide range of processing issues must be considered to reasonably investigate the relationship between emotion and memory for events. Rather than the narrow "tunnel-memory"-based theorizing and investigations that have largely characterized eyewitness research to date, the field might profitably move toward consideration of the broader processing issues involved. Although we did not delve deeply into the rapidly expanding body of neuroscience research on physiological mechanisms affecting memory for emotional events, the way in which such processes promote or impair the mechanisms of attention and processing must be considered along with the issues involving the interaction of emotion and schematic and goal-driven concerns driving attention and processing of emotional events. Additionally, a comprehensive model of the effects of emotion on memory for events must consider individual differences impacting each process involved.

Although such a complete model would be challenging to develop and test, the analysis presented here suggests several new directions for eyewitness researchers to pursue. For example, emotion-driven enhanced schematic processing would be expected to promote specific schema-consistent errors in memory of centrally attended features of events. For example, fear might distort memory for the facial expression of a centrally attended robber toward greater anger or hostility, or for the general appearance of a Black perpetrator toward stereotypically "Black" features (see below). The latter effect should be particularly strong for observers with strong racial stereotypes. We should also expect event characteristics relevant to emotion-driven goals to elicit attention and be more likely to be remembered. For example, among bank patrons held hostage by the armed robber, attention should go to the gun as well as to potential means of achieving escape or help, such as an open door or a potentially available cell phone. In other words, there are a number of hypotheses to be tested that involve (a) the specific kinds of errors that might be enhanced by emotion, as opposed to the overall error rates; (b) the distinctive targets of selective processing that are distinctive to specific emotions; and (c) individual differences relevant to all cognitive and physical bases of these effects.

4. INFLUENCE OF BELIEFS AND EXPECTATION ON STORAGE AND RETRIEVAL

As with encoding, beliefs, expectations, and schematic processing continue to affect memory and memory reports as observers experience their memories through time and begin to retrieve and report their memories to others. These influences occur, in part, as a result of the continuing effects of beliefs and expectations held prior to, and during the encoding of, the original event. However, as the witness proceeds forward from the point of original witnessing, multiple processes add to or alter existing beliefs and thereby affect memory and memory reports.

The act of "remembering" consists of subjective internal representations of an event, combined with judgment criteria for determining whether these representations correspond to a previously experienced index event. Internal representations can consist of verbatim visual images (elaborate visual reproductions, essentially "seeing" the event again) and/or gist traces of the essential semantic meaning or generalized physical form of objects and events. Furthermore, judgment criteria can range from the strict requirement to be able to fully picture and clearly describe the entire object or event to very lax criteria, such as fuzzy unelaborated fragmented gist traces. Generally, the stronger the verbatim and gist traces and the weaker the judgment criterion, the more likely a person is to label the experience as a "memory." All three relevant entities can be affected by postevent processes.

Verbatim traces, for example, decay over time. But they may also be strengthened or altered by activities that reinforce the original images or that substitute new images. This can happen through internal rehearsal processes, active imagining, or exposure to new external representations of the event. Semantic-gist traces tend, instead, to strengthen over time. But they can also be altered by activities that alter the visual verbatim images, as well as through activities serving to develop or alter relevant beliefs and therefore to change semantic-gist memory representations. Finally, the judgment criterion itself can be altered, as, for example, when—based on a strong belief in the person's guilt garnered through suggestive postevent influences—a witness identifies a specific suspect as the perpetrator of a crime in the absence of a clear verbatim "memory" of the perpetrator's face (for review of these processes, see Brainerd & Reyna, 2005; Loftus & Davis, 2006). In this instance, a weaker judgment criterion is applied to the memory representations themselves because additional beliefs support their veracity. In the remainder of the chapter we illustrate these processes of postevent influences on memory representations and judgment criteria as they apply to eyewitness reports.

4.1. Expectation, belief, and eyewitness identification

Over the past century, researchers have produced countless articles documenting the antecedents and consequences of failures in eyewitness identification (for reviews, see the recent *Handbook of Eyewitness Psychology*: Vol. 1, Toglia, Read, Ross & Lindsay, 2007; Vol. 2, Lindsay, Ross, Read, & Toglia, 2007). Although many determinants of eyewitness accuracy have been identified, we focus on postencoding factors that exert their influence via effects on *beliefs* concerning the features or identity of the perpetrator.

4.1.1. *Internal constructive and reconstructive processes and face memory*

There is substantial evidence that schema activation affects encoding of faces such that immediate ratings and later memory of the faces are biased toward congruity with the label (for discussion of additional issues related to face memory, see chapter 3, section 4). Furthermore, goal activation promotes schematic processing. For example, "self-protection" goals led Whites to perceive greater anger in the faces of outgroup minorities such as Blacks or Arabs, and mate-search goals led males to perceive more sexual arousal in attractive targets (for review, see Davis & Loftus, 2007).

Of particular interest for the issue of eyewitness identification is the fact that, once labeled, facial memory shifts over time toward prototypicality for the category. That is, the face is likely to be remembered as looking more "Black" when the person is labeled "Black" (for an illustration of shifts toward prototypicality for ethnicity, see Corneille, Huart, Becquart, & Bredart, 2004). Furthermore, stereotypically Black features are associated with generally negative judgments (Blair, Judd, & Fallman, 2004; Blair, Judd, Sadler, & Henkins, 2002), including judgments of criminality; they are also associated with greater harshness in sentencing (Blair, Judd, & Chapleau, 2004), even to the point that defendants with more stereotypically "Black" features are more likely to be sentenced to death (e.g., Eberhardt, Davies, Purdie-Vaughns, & Johnson, 2006). Being labeled "criminal" as well may fuel the shift in memory toward stereotypically Black features.

Such shifts toward prototypes have several testable implications for errors in eyewitness identification, which have yet to be specifically investigated. Among these is the issue of whether Blacks with the most stereotype-consistent features are at enhanced risk of misidentification. If verbatim memory for Black perpetrators shifts toward prototypicality, lineup members with strongly stereotypical features might be judged as a better fit to the witness's memory of the perpetrator than those less similar to the prototype. Hence, between two innocent people, equally similar to the perpetrator (but in different directions on the dimension of stereotypically Black features), the one with more stereotypical features would be at greater risk of misidentification. Such an effect could be enhanced if, at encoding, the witness had been subject to forces (such as intense negative emotions) that enhance schematic processing or fuel activation of race-based schemas and that thereby distort perception toward negative (criminal) or race-based (Black) labels. Beginning with a schema-based category-consistent bias at original encoding that would become more extreme over time, the witness may well be looking for a very "Black"-looking perpetrator in the lineup.

A related question arises concerning the previously noted convergence of memory with facial emotion labels over time. The faces that witnesses must inspect in a lineup typically do not display the angry or hostile expressions that may have been predominant during the crime and in witnesses' semantic and verbatim representations of the face. To the extent that representations converge toward the labeled emotional expression over time, the witness will be confronted with lineup members more and more discrepant from these representations and, thereby, perhaps more difficult to identify. This suggests that while perpetrators whose faces expressed intense emotion during the crime may be generally more difficult to identify than perpetrators with more neutral expressions, this difference may be enhanced by conditions that encourage schematic processing at encoding or during storage. It should also be noted that these processes can be enhanced by activation of schemata associated with the emotion labels themselves. That is, the display of anger and hostility may directly activate crime-related stereotypes that further distort memory for facial features toward "criminality". Finally, internal schema-driven forces toward prototypicality can be enhanced by external information reinforcing relevant category labels such as "dangerous," "criminal," or "violent."

4.1.2. Memory conformity and the effects of co-witnesses

In addition to internal reconstructive influences, the witness may be subject to external reconstructive influences on both verbatim and semantic memory. Among these is information from other witnesses, which can pervasively affect the target witness at all stages of memory (for review; see Davis & Loftus, 2007). Another witness can induce top-down schematic processing by directing attention toward and labeling objects or events during encoding. For example, looking at a dark-skinned man of ambiguous race holding a woman's arm as he talks intently to her, one witness may say to another "Look, that Black guy is trying to hurt that woman" and may thereby activate racial and situational schematic processing that leads the observer to also label the man as Black and the interaction as hostile. Encoding can also be influenced by the *reactions* of other witnesses, as when the person screams in fear and faints, or perhaps runs, at the sight of a perpetrator or event, leading the target witness to interpret the interaction or events as more hostile or dangerous.

Immediately following the event, co-witnesses can influence each others' accounts as they talk about the event and provide their reports to investigators. Witnesses may actively try to reach consensus before providing even the first report. For example, in one of our cases, a witness asked to provide a description to a 911 operator responded: "Wait a minute, we're getting a consensus on that." Such consultation can affect both verbatim images and semantic labels for perpetrator features. Witnesses who maintain contact—such as family, friends, or those who continue to encounter one another as the case proceeds through the legal system—have multiple opportunities to directly influence one another as they talk about both the original event as well as postevent developments such as their own identification attempts, arrests, court proceedings, or information they have acquired from external sources such as police or media.

Cross-contamination between witnesses can occur directly (when witnesses converse) or indirectly (when witnesses' reports are conveyed by police or others) at any stage, from immediate reports through trial, and tend to have greater impact when confirmed through other sources (as when the co-witness information is confirmed by police, media, or other interviewers; see Davis & Loftus, 2007; Paterson & Kemp, 2006). At specific identification proceedings, reactions of other witnesses can exert significant influence. Knowledge that another witness has or has not identified someone, or has identified a specific person, can affect the likelihood that the target witness will make a similar identification.

Other witness reactions can have an impact as well, such as gasping or other outcries. In one of our cases, for example, a teller who had been robbed fainted immediately upon the sight of a suspect brought before 15 witnesses for a show-up ID. It is for such reasons that the *Eyewitness Guide* published by the National Institute of Justice (NIJ Guide: Technical Working Group for Eyewitness Evidence, 1999) and based on years of eyewitness research specifies that all attempts should be made to avoid cross-contamination between witnesses, in part by instructing witnesses not to do anything to convey to other witnesses their own opinions concerning a specific perpetrator identification or the nature of any identification decisions they make.

In addition to memory for *what happened* or *who did it*, co-witness reports can affect the *confidence* of the target witness in these memories. In turn, inflated confidence in the veracity of a "memory" can lower the judgment criteria applied to the event traces such that the witness is more willing to report his *belief* as a *memory* in front of a jury. Inflated confidence can occur as a result of information that supports the target's memories or beliefs about what happened. This has been demonstrated specifically for information from co-witnesses (for review, see Davis & Loftus, 2007; Skagerberg, 2007) and other sources such as the police (for review, see Douglass & Steblay, 2006). This is among the most dangerous of the effects of co-witness influence, as jurors are known to give great weight to witness confidence in assessing credibility (for review, see Davis & Follette, 2001).

Unfortunately, in addition to affecting witness confidence, confirming information tends to affect other witness reports that jurors would rely on to assess witness accuracy—including encoding conditions such as clarity of view, duration of exposure, and so forth (see section 4.1.3.3 on effects of police feedback). In other words, once witnesses *believe* they are correct, they tend to infer in hindsight that the opportunity to observe *must have been* good and that any verbatim and semantic event representations they have are veridical "memories."

Clearly, co-witnesses have great potential to influence the beliefs of the target witness, and hence the reported memory. However, other overarching beliefs affect how the target witness will respond to such co-witness information. That is, witnesses appear to use "metacognitive knowledge" about how memory works to assess the credibility of information from their co-witnesses. If the co-witness information violates what the target witness believes about how memory works, it will be seen as less credible and will have less impact. For example, if the co-witness claims to have seen something the witness believes she/he *would have remembered if it happened*, she/he is likely to give little credence to the co-witness account. In contrast, a co-witness account may be given more credibility when the witness feels that his or her own accounts may be in error due to poor encoding conditions, or that the others' account is likely to be true (because additional witnesses also agree or because the co-witness had better opportunity to observe or had more expertise). In other words, our memory reports are affected not only by what we believed happened, but also by how we believe we can evaluate and verify our own accounts and those of others (for review, see Davis & Loftus, 2007).

4.1.3. Belief-enhancing effects of police procedures

Based on years of research on the effects on witness accuracy of what eyewitness researchers refer to as "system variables" (factors under the control of the justice system), the previously referenced NIJ Guide offers a variety of specific guidelines for how to interview witnesses and conduct identification procedures that are specifically intended to avoid influencing witnesses to report beliefs regarding what *must be* or *probably is* true, rather than what they specifically remember. Essentially, these recommendations advocate procedures (a) that will not contaminate verbatim or semantic representations of the original event and (b) that encourage reliance on stricter memory-judgment criteria for reporting information or perpetrator identifications (as opposed to inference, assumption, or deference to the interviewer).

4.1.3.1. *Suggestive interviewing and the cognitive interview*

Suggestive interviewing involves procedures during which the interviewer (a) directly or indirectly suggests something is or is not true; and/or (b) selectively reinforces witness reports such that some information is attended to, responded to as if important and true, and followed up on, whereas other information results in lack of attention, nonresponse, disapproval, overt disagreement, or trivialization. Although suggestive interviewing may result in witness errors through additional mechanisms, a primary mechanism involves influence on witness beliefs about what is probably true. That is, assuming that the interviewer must have relevant knowledge—perhaps greater than that of the witness—the witness adopts beliefs about what happened consistent with interviewer suggestion. Or, she or he may simply comply with interviewer suggestions (while still disagreeing) in order to avoid overt disagreement or disapproval.

Suggestion may entail subtle differences in language, such as "Did you see *the* (rather than *a*) broken headlight?" or "How fast was the car going when it *smashed* (versus *hit or bumped*) the other car?" These subtle differences result in witness reports consistent with suggestion, such as more reports of seeing a broken headlight, greater speed estimates, and mistaken reports of broken glass consistent with higher speeds. Suggestion may also be more representational, as in the use of anatomically correct dolls, photographs, or other illustrative props, or more direct, such as when the interviewer directly implies a fact (e.g., "What kind of hat was he wearing?") or tells the witness what she or he believes happened ("The evidence from the crime scene and the other witnesses tells us that Johnny was the shooter"). (For reviews of suggestive interviewing and sources of chronic or acute vulnerability to its effects, see the *Handbook of Eyewitness Memory*, Vol. 1, Toglia et al., 2007; Vol. 2, Lindsay, Ross, Read, & Toglia, 2007.)

In an effort to avoid suggestive influences on eyewitness accounts while maximizing the amount of accurate information elicited, the "Cognitive Interview" was developed in the early 1980s (Geiselman et al., 1984; Geiselman, Fisher, MacKinnon, & Holland, 1985) and later revised (Fisher & Geiselman, 1992). The cognitive interview (CI) is designed both to maximize the motivation and comfort of the witness through effective communication and development of rapport and to effectively use knowledge of cognition and memory processes to enhance the accuracy and completeness of interviewee reports. In part, this entails minimization of suggestion through the use of open-ended, nonleading questions, as well as maximization of retrieval through effective use of multiple contextual cues spanning multiple modes (e.g., visual, olfactory, auditory, emotional, or touch), multiple starting points (e.g., beginning from different points during the events), different perspectives, and so on (see Fisher & Geiselman, 1992). The procedure has proven effective in increasing the amount of correct information generated, but it has sometimes been found to increase the amount of incorrect information (for a recent review, see Wells, Memon, & Penrod, 2006).

4.1.3.2.　*Lineup procedures*

The NIJ guidelines recognized two general processes that can compromise eyewitness identifications: (a) inferential processes in which witness inferences about what *is likely to be true* guide his or her selection of the perpetrator, and (b) social-influence processes with potential to affect the above inferences—and thereby, the witness's choice of perpetrator, confidence in that choice, or the nature of related reports bearing on witness accuracy (such as original viewing conditions).

4.1.3.2.1. Inferential processes.　When a witness is asked to participate in an identification procedure, a natural inference is that police have targeted a suspect they believe may have committed the crime. Some witnesses may conclude that police have caught the actual perpetrator and that they must make the identification to facilitate prosecution of the case. They assume that the perpetrator *must be* in the lineup (or why else were they asked to see it?) and that their job is to pick *which lineup member* is the perpetrator—NOT, *whether any lineup member* is the perpetrator. Hence, they do not enforce strict criteria for matching the suspect's face to a verbatim memory trace of the perpetrator. Instead, they adopt a looser criterion (best match rather than absolute match) and choose someone from the lineup, often guessing on the basis of either which looks most like what they remember (see Steblay, Dysart, Fulero, & Lindsay, 2001; Wells, 1984) or which looks most likely to be the perpetrator for other reasons (looks suspicious or dangerous, or photo characteristics are suggestive).

Wells (1993) demonstrated "relative judgment" by exposing witnesses to a staged crime to a lineup that included either the perpetrator and five foils, or simply the same five foils without the perpetrator. With the perpetrator present, 54% of witnesses correctly identified him, another 25% misidentified a foil, and

21% selected no one. But when the perpetrator was removed, 68% misidentified a foil, with 38% identifying the foil that might be regarded as the "best-fit" match to the original perpetrator. Only 32% failed to make an identification, instead of the 75% that would be expected if all who had originally correctly identified the perpetrator had moved to making no choice when he was not in the lineup. In other words, witnesses appeared to assume that the perpetrator was in the lineup, and when he was actually not there, their choices moved to the foil providing the "best fit" to their memory of the perpetrator. Their inferential processes led them to the belief that the foil *must be* the perpetrator. Since Wells's original demonstration, the relative-judgment effect has been shown to apply to both sequential (see below) and simultaneous lineups, and to be greater when memory is weaker (e.g., Clark & Davey, 2005).

Relative judgment can also apply across different identification procedures, as the witness begins to compare current candidates not only to one another, but to others encountered in previous procedures. For example, a witness who once identifies an innocent is more likely to persist in identifying that same innocent in subsequent identification procedures (for reviews see Behrman & Davey, 2001; Deffenbacher, Bornstein, & Penrod, 2006; Dysart, Lindsay, & Hammond, 2001). A single witness can be exposed to quite a number of different procedures as the case proceeds, beginning with field show-ups or working with a police sketch artist or composite procedures, through to looking through a mugbook, exposure to one or more photo lineups, subsequent live lineups, and in-court identifications at preliminary hearings and trial. At each proceeding, the witness may compare the current candidates to previous selections.

This sequential relative-judgment process can be exacerbated when a particular suspect is the only one to appear in multiple procedures. This can strengthen the inference that the person must be the perpetrator. It can also increase the familiarity of the face and thereby enhance the risk that the person will be identified due to the witness's mistaken attribution that the face is familiar because the person was the perpetrator, rather than because he had been seen in previous identification procedures. Such mistaken *beliefs* about why a face is familiar have been implicated as the cause of mistaken identifications of innocents previously seen in a variety of contexts, including as bystanders to the crime, in previous identification procedures, and in other irrelevant contexts (such as on TV; see review by Deffenbacher et al., 2006).

Recommendations have been offered to minimize relative-judgment processes themselves, as well as their effects (see NIJ Guide; for reviews documenting the effectiveness of these recommendations, see Clark, 2005; Steblay, 1997; Steblay et al., 2001; Wells et al., 1998, 2006). First, one can encourage witnesses to use stricter verbatim absolute-matching criteria by instructing them that the perpetrator may or may not be in the lineup. Such an instruction has been shown to dramatically reduce the incidence of misidentifications in target-absent lineups, while exerting minimal effects on the rate of true identifications in target-present lineups. Second, a lineup member should not either (a) draw attention for irrelevant reasons (such as unique clothing, demeanor, or photograph characteristics) or (b) draw attention because he is most similar to the witness's description. If all members fit the witnesses' gist representations, witnesses will be forced to rely on stricter absolute-match criteria to choose. Third, inferential processes may be reduced by using sequential rather than simultaneous lineups. Theoretically, this should suppress the tendency to use relative judgment in favor of an absolute comparison between the specific candidate and memory for the perpetrator. Laboratory tests of sequential versus simultaneous lineups have shown sequential lineups to suppress the overall rate of identification, but with stronger suppression of mistaken than accurate identifications. Unfortunately, field tests of sequential procedures have suffered serious methodological problems, rendering results uninterpretable (see Wells et al., 2006).

4.1.3.3. *Social-influence processes and police procedure*

If police have identified a suspect and asked eyewitnesses to attempt an identification, they can be highly motivated to obtain confirming identifications, often knowing that the perpetrator cannot be successfully prosecuted without them. Unfortunately, standard practice for administration of lineups is for the detective investigating the case—the very person with the most motivation for the witness to make an ID—to be the one to administer the lineup. In light of the extensive literature on experimenter-expectancy effects, it is not surprising that when lineup administrators know who the suspect is, the chance that the eyewitness will identify that suspect (innocent or not) is increased (e.g., Haw & Fisher, 2004; Phillips, McAuliff, Kovera, & Cutler, 1999), and if that suspect is identified, the witness's confidence in the identification is enhanced (e.g., Garrioch & Brimacombe, 2001).

Although administrators in these experiments did not convey awareness of the suspect's identity blatantly or coercively, in practice, police administrators can convey beliefs about the identity of the perpetrator to witnesses either subtly or blatantly (and sometimes coercively) and thereby affect witnesses' beliefs about the perpetrator's identity—leading them not only to identify the administrator's choice, but also to feel enhanced confidence in that choice. For this reason, the NIJ Guide and eyewitness researchers have recommended that lineups be administered by personnel who are not aware of which member is the suspect, or via a laptop-computer program (McLin, Zimmerman, & Malpass, 2005; Technical Working Group for Eyewitness Evidence, 1999; Wells et al., 1998).

Whether or not police influence the witness's identification of a specific lineup member, they may yet exert considerable effect on the witness's confidence in the identification through reactions that appear to validate his or her choice. Beginning with the early demonstration of Wells and Bradfield (1998), a host of studies have shown that postidentification feedback to the witness (e.g., "Good, you identified our suspect!") can both inflate witness confidence in the identification and profoundly distort reports relevant to the reliability of the identification. Suspects given such feedback report, for example, that their original ability to observe the perpetrator was better—for example, that they paid more attention to the target's face, had a better view of the face, and so forth. The effect occurs across witness populations (young and old laboratory populations and actual witnesses to crimes) and types of witness decisions (positive ID and "not there") and is greater for mistaken than for correct witnesses. Ironically, those who report that they are not affected by the feedback are actually affected more (for meta-analysis and review, see Douglass & Steblay, 2006; Wells et al., 2006).

Beginning with this immediate feedback, witnesses can be subject to a number of additional confidence-enhancing forces prior to any identification made in court before the jury. These can include other witness identifications, media reports, the very fact that the suspect is charged and brought to trial, participation in preliminary hearings and other pretrial activities (many entailing repeated exposure to the suspect), and exposure to other "evidence" of guilt—all serving to solidify the *belief* that the suspect is indeed the perpetrator, to impair the relationship between witness confidence and accuracy, and to encourage the witness to rely on weaker verbatim image or gist-match criteria to make an identification (see Wells et al., 2006).

4.1.3.3.1. Direct influences of emotion during encoding on accuracy at identification. In addition to the many belief-enhancing influences that can impair the relationship between confidence and accuracy, there is evidence to suggest that the intense emotions experienced by many witnesses to real-life criminal events may themselves promote confidence independent of accuracy. That is, evidence from several lines of research has shown that emotions tend to enhance the subjective experience of memory accuracy, even in circumstances where emotion is unrelated or negatively related to accuracy (for reviews, see LaBar & Cabeza, 2006; Phelps, 2006; for evidence of distinctive neural systems reflecting dissociations between confidence and accuracy, see Chua, Rand-Giovannetti, Schacter, Albert, & Sperling, 2004).

Perhaps most directly relevant to the issue of eyewitness identification are studies using the remember/know procedure to study recognition of previously presented stimuli. During the recognition phase of a memory task, participants are asked to indicate whether each candidate is "new" (not previously presented), "known" (familiar, but without specific recollection of details for the encoding context), or "remembered" (recalled *with* details of the encoding context). Emotion enhances the proportion of "remembered" judgments, despite having no effect on overall accuracy (see Phelps, 2006). This suggests that witnesses experiencing strong emotions may be no better at discriminating between innocents and perpetrators, but that they may be more willing to make a positive ID (whether correct or not) and/or express greater confidence in that ID based on the greater subjective sense of "remembering" that the person committed the crime, rather than just "knowing" that they looked familiar.

4.1.3.3.2. Behavioral commitment and dissonance-reduction processes. A witness can also be subject to internal self-justification processes that enhance confidence, reinforce commitment to their identification decisions, and increase the likelihood of sequential confirming identifications across procedures (for discussion of self-justification processes, including in memory and the legal system, see Tavris & Aronson, 2007). Beginning with the first identification of the target, self-justification motivations can become more extreme as the consequences for the target become more serious and, therefore, the idea that one could have been mistaken more aversive.

4.1.3.3.3. Implications for jurors.   These influences on the confidence–accuracy relationship make it difficult for jurors to detect inaccurate witnesses. We know that jurors base their judgments of witness accuracy in large part on witness confidence. Moreover, by the time the witness reaches trial, confidence-inflating forces such as discussed above can eliminate any relationship between confidence and accuracy. Thus, the NIJ Guide adopted eyewitness researchers' recommendations that confidence should be assessed and recorded immediately after the identification, before any form of feedback is encountered (NIJ Guide; see also Wells et al., 2006).

4.1.3.3.4. Summary.   Eyewitness identifications are strongly affected by beliefs about *what must be—or probably is—true,* combined with the strength and nature of verbatim and semantic-gist memories of what actually occurred. Inferential processes such as relative judgment and social influence from other witnesses, interviewers, or administrators of identification procedures exert greater influence on witnesses with weaker memories or on those who for any reason lack confidence in their own memories. These and other factors that compromise accuracy at encoding or retrieval cast doubt on the probative value of eyewitness testimony—that is, the weight it should be given as a predictor of guilt. Essentially, the more potentially compromising influences the witness encounters, during encoding or while progressing through the legal system, the less probative value his or her testimony will have.

5. CONCLUSIONS

Given the many and varied sources of errors in witness memory, eyewitness errors are likely to remain the primary source of wrongful conviction for the foreseeable future. While the legal system has begun processes of reform intended to minimize errors caused by police procedures (as reflected in the recommendations of the NIJ Guide), these reforms are not pervasively enacted, and they cannot prevent the many additional sources of error such as those covered in this review. It remains for eyewitness experts to educate jurors as to the sources of error in eyewitness testimony, with the hope that they will consider such factors when attempting to assess the accuracy of an individual witness. In the absence of such testimony, jurors tend to assume that a confident eyewitness is, indeed, accurate (see Wells et al., 2006)—an assumption unlikely to be diffused through normal trial processes. As John Bargh has put it, "only conscious, controlled processes can 'time-travel'" (Bargh, 2006, p. 1), in that they can be subject to recall and examination. But, unfortunately, as our review has made clear, much of what determines the nature of what is encoded into memory and "remembered" and retrieved over time is determined by unconscious inaccessible processes that cannot be brought to light under cross-examination, viewed by legal scholars as the "greatest legal engine ever invented for the discovery of truth" (Wigmore, 1974, vol. 5, 1367, at 32).

6. REFERENCES

Adolphs, R., Tranel, D., & Buchanan, T. W. (2005). Amygdala damage impairs emotional memory for gist but not details of complex stimuli. *Nature Neuroscience, 8*, 512–518.

Amodio, D. M., Harmon-Jones, E., Devine, P. G., Curtin, J. J., Hartley, S. L., & Covert, A. E. (2004). Neural signals for the detection of unintentional race bias. *Psychological Science, 15*, 88–93.

Anderson, M. L. (2003). Embodied cognition: A field guide. *Artificial Intelligence, 149*, 91–131.

Barden, J., Maddux, W. W., Petty, R. E., & Brewer, M. B. (2004). Contextual moderation of racial bias: The impact of social roles on controlled and automatically activated attitudes. *Journal of Personality & Social Psychology, 87*, 1.

Bargh, J. A. (2005). Bypassing the will: Toward demystifying the nonconscious control of social behaviour. In R. R. Hassin, J. S. Uleman, & J. A. Bargh (Eds.), *The new unconscious* (pp. 37–58). Oxford, UK: Oxford University Press.

Bargh, J. A. (2006). The automaticity of social life. *Current Directions in Psychological Science, 15*, 1–4.

Bartholow, B. D., Dickter, C. L., & Sestir, M. A. (2006). Stereotype activation and control of race bias: Cognitive control of inhibition and its impairment by alcohol. *Journal of Personality and Social Psychology, 90*(2), 272–287.

Baumeister, R. F., & Vohs, K. D. (Eds.). (2004). *Handbook of self-regulation: Research, theory, and applications.* New York: Guilford Press.

Behrman, B. W., & Davey, S. L. (2001). Eyewitness identification in actual criminal cases: An archival analysis. *Law and Human Behavior, 25*(5), 475–491.

Blair, I. V. (2002). The malleability of automatic stereotypes and prejudice. *Personality & Social Psychology Review, 6*, 242–261.

Blair, I. V., & Banaji, M. (1996). Automatic and controlled processes in stereotype priming. *Journal of Personality and Social Psychology, 70*, 1142–1163.

Blair, I. V., Judd, C. M., & Chapleau, K. M. (2004). The influence of Afrocentric facial features in criminal sentencing. *Psychological Science, 15*, 674–679.

Blair, I. V., Judd, C. M., & Fallman, J. L. (2004). The automaticity of race and Afrocentric facial features in social judgments. *Journal of Personality & Social Psychology, 87*(6), 763–778.

Blair, I. V., Judd, C. M., Sadler, M. S., & Henkins, C. (2002). The role of Afrocentric features in person perception: Judging by features and categories. *Journal of Personality and Social Psychology, 83*, 5–25.

Bless, H., & Fiedler, K. (2006). Mood and the regulation of information processing and behavior. In J. P. Forgas (Ed.), *Affect in social thinking and behavior* (pp. 65–84). New York: Psychology Press.

Bower, G. H. (1981). Mood and memory. *American Psychologist, 36*, 129–148.

Bower, G. H., & Forgas, J. P. (2001). Mood and social memory. In J. P. Forgas (Ed.), *Handbook of affect and social cognition.* (pp. 95–120). Mahwah, NJ: Lawrence Erlbaum Associates.

Brainerd, C. J., & Reyna, V. F. (2005). *The science of false memory.* New York: Oxford University Press.

Bransford, J. D., & Johnson, M. K. (1972). Contextual prerequisites for understanding: Some investigations of comprehension and recall. *Journal of Verbal Learning and Verbal Behaviour, 11*, 717–726.

Buccino, G., Binkofski, F., Fink, G. R., Fadiga, L., Fogassi, L., Gallese, V., et al. (2001). Action observation activates premotor and parietal areas in somatotopic manner: An fMRI study. *European Journal of Neuroscience, 13*, 400–404.

Chartrand, T. L., & Bargh, J. A. (2002). Nonconscious motivations: Their activation, operation, and consequences. In A. Tesser, D. A. Stapel, & J. V. Wood (Eds.), *Self and motivation: Emerging psychological perspectives* (pp. 13–41). Washington, DC: American Psychological Association.

Chartrand, T. L., Maddux, W. W., & Lakin, J. L. (2005). Beyond the perception–behaviour link: The ubiquitous utility of motivational moderators of nonconscious mimicry. In R. R. Hassin, J. S. Uleman, & J. A. Bargh (Eds.), *The new unconscious* (pp. 334–361). Oxford, UK: Oxford University Press.

Chua, E. F., Rand-Giovannetti, E., Schacter, D. L., Albert, M. S., & Sperling, R. A. (2004). Dissociating confidence and accuracy: Functional magnetic resonance imaging shows origins of the subjective memory experience. *Journal of Cognitive Neuroscience, 16*, 1131–1142.

Clark, S. E. (2005). A re-examination of the effects of biased lineup instructions in eyewitness identification. *Law and Human Behaviour, 29*, 151–172.

Clark, S. E., & Davey, S. L. (2005). The target-to-fillers shift in simultaneous and sequential lineups. *Law and Human Behaviour, 25*, 151–172.

Clore, G. L., & Storbeck, J. (2006). Affect as information about liking, efficacy, and importance. In J. P. Forgas (Ed.), *Affect in social thinking and behaviour* (pp. 123–142). New York: Psychology Press.

Corneille, O., Huart, J., Becquart, E., & Bredart, S. (2004). When memory shifts toward more typical category exemplars: Accentuation effects in the recollection of ethnically ambiguous faces. *Journal of Personality and Social Psychology, 86*, 236–250.

Correll, J., Park, B., Judd, C. M., & Wittenbrink, B. (2002). The police officer's dilemma: Using ethnicity to disambiguate potentially threatening individuals. *Journal of Personality and Social Psychology, 83*, 1314–1329.

Correll, J., Park, B., Judd, C. M., Wittenbrink, B., Sadler, M. S., & Keesee, T. (2006). Across the thin blue line: Police officers and racial bias in the decision to shoot. *Journal of Personality and Social Psychology, 92*, 1006–1023.

Correll, J., Urland, G. L., & Ito, T. A. (2006). Event-related potentials and the decision to shoot: The role of threat perception and cognitive control. *Journal of Experimental Social Psychology, 42*, 120–128.

Cunningham, W. A., Johnson, M. K., Raye, C. L., Gatenby, J. C., Gore, J. C., & Banaji, M. R. (2004). Separable neural components in the processing of Black and White faces. *Psychological Science, 15*, 806–813.

Davies, G., & Hine, S. (2007). Change blindness and eyewitness testimony. *Journal of Psychology: Interdisciplinary and Applied, 141*(4), 423–434.

Davis, D., & Follette, W. C. (2001). Foibles of witness memory for traumatic/high profile events. *Journal of Air Law and Commerce, 66*(4), 1421–1549.

Davis, D., & Loftus, E. F. (2007). Internal and external sources of distortion in adult witness memory. In M. P. Toglia, J. D. Read, D. R. Ross, & R. C. L. Lindsay (Eds.), *Handbook of eyewitness memory: Vol. 1). Memory for Events* (pp. 195–237). Mahwah, NJ: Lawrence Erlbaum Associates.

Davis, D., Loftus, E. F., Vanous, S., & Cucciare, M. (2008). Unconscious transference can be an instance of "change blindness". *Applied Cognitive Psychology, 22*(5), 605–623.

Deffenbacher, K. A. (1994). Effects of arousal on everyday memory. *Human Performance, 7*(2), 141–161.

Deffenbacher, K. A., Bornstein, B. H., & Penrod, S. D. (2006). Mugshot exposure effects: Retroactive interference, mugshot commitment, source confusion, and unconscious transference. *Law and Human Behaviour, 30*, 287–307.

Deffenbacher, K. A., Bornstein, B. H., Penrod, S. D., & McGorty, E. K. (2004). A meta-analytic review of the effects of high stress on eyewitness memory. *Law and Human Behaviour, 28*, 687–706.

DeSteno, D., Dasgupta, N., Bartlett, M. Y., & Cajdric, A. (2004). Prejudice from thin air: The effect of emotion on automatic intergroup attitudes. *Psychological Science, 15*, 319–324.

Dijksterhuis, A., & Bargh, J. A. (2001). The perception-behaviour expressway: Automatic effects of social perception on social behaviour. In M. P. Zanna (Ed.), *Advances in experimental social psychology* (Vol. 33, pp. 1–40). San Diego, CA: Academic Press.

Douglass, A. B., & Steblay, N. (2006). Memory distortion in eyewitnesses: A meta-analysis of the post-identification feedback effect. *Applied Cognitive Psychology, 20*, 859–869.

Dysart, J. E., Lindsay, R. C. L., & Hammond, R. (2001). Mug shot exposure prior to lineup identification: Interference, transference, and commitment effects. *Journal of Applied Psychology, 86*, 1280–1284.

Easterbrook, J. A. (1959). The effect of emotion on cue utilization and the organization of behaviour. *Psychological Review, 66*, 183–201.

Eberhardt, J. L., Davies, P. G., Purdie-Vaughns, V. J., & Johnson, S. L. (2006). Looking deathworthy: Perceived stereotypicality of black defendants predicts capital-sentencing outcomes. *Psychological Science, 17*(5), 383–386.

Eberhardt, J. L., Goff, P. A., Purdie, V. J., & Davies, P. G. (2004). Seeing black: Race, crime, and visual processing. *Journal of Personality and Social Psychology, 87*, 876–893.

Egloff, B., Schmukle, S. C., Burns, L. R., & Schwerdtfeger, A. (2006). Spontaneous emotion regulation during evaluated speaking tasks: Associations with negative affect, anxiety expression, memory and physiological responding. *Emotion, 6*, 356–366.

Eich, E., & Forgas, J. P. (2003). Mood, cognition, and memory. In A. F. Healy & R. W. Proctor (Eds.), *Handbook of psychology: Vol. 4. Experimental psychology* (pp. 61–83). New York: Wiley.

Eich, E., & Macaulay, D. (2006). Cognitive and clinical perspectives on mood-dependent memory. In J. P. Forgas (Ed.), *Affect in social thinking and behavior* (pp. 105–121). New York: Psychology Press.

Fisher, R. P., & Geiselman, R. E. (Eds.). (1992). *Memory enhancing techniques for investigative interviewing: The cognitive interview.* Springfield, IL: Charles C Thomas.

Forgas, J. P. (2002). Feeling and doing: Affective influences on interpersonal behaviour. *Psychological Inquiry, 13*, 1–28.

Forgas, J. P. (Ed.). (2006). *Affect in social thinking and behaviour.* New York: Psychology Press.

Forgas, J. P., Wyland, C. L., & Laham, S. M. (2006). Hearts and minds: An introduction to the role of affect in social cognition and behaviour. In J. P. Forgas (Ed.), *Affect in social thinking and behaviour* (pp. 3–18). New York: Psychology Press.

Garbarini, F., & Adenzato, M. (2004). At the root of embodied cognition: Cognitive science meets neurophysiology. *Brain & Cognition, 56*, 100–106.

Garrioch, L., & Brimacombe, C. A. E. (2001). Lineup administrators' expectations: Their impact on eyewitness confidence. *Law and Human Behavior, 25*(3), 299–314.

Geiselman, R. E., Fisher, R. P., Firstenberg, I., Hutton, L. A., Sullivan, S. J., Avetissian, I. V., & Prosk, A. L. (1984). Enhancement of eyewitness memory: An empirical evaluation of the cognitive interview. *Journal of Police Science and Administration, 12*, 74–79.

Geiselman, R. E., Fisher, R. P., MacKinnon, D. P., & Holland, H. L. (1985). Eyewitness memory enhancement in the police interview. *Journal of Applied Psychology, 27*, 358–418.

Govorun, O., & Payne, B. K. (2006). Ego depletion and prejudice: Separating automatic and controlled components. *Social Cognition, 24*, 111–136.

Greenwald, A. G., Oakes, M. A., & Hoffman, H. G. (2003). Targets of discrimination: Effects of race on responses to weapons holders. *Journal of Experimental Social Psychology, 39*, 399–405.

Hassin, R. R., Uleman, J. S., & Bargh, J. A. (Eds.). (2005). *The new unconscious.* Oxford, UK: Oxford University Press.

Haw, R. M., & Fisher, R. P. (2004). Effects of administrator-witness contact on eyewitness identification accuracy. *Journal of Applied Psychology, 89*(6), 1106–1112.

Hoffman, D. D. (1998). *Visual intelligence.* New York: W. W. Norton.

Hommel, B., Musseler, J., Aschersleben, G., & Prinz, W. (2001). The Theory of Event Coding (TEC): A framework for perception and action planning. *Behavioral and Brain Sciences, 24*(5), 849–937.

Jonas, K. J., & Sassenberg, K. (2006). Knowing how to react: Automatic response priming from social categories. *Journal of Personality & Social Psychology, 90*, 709–721.

Judd, C. M., Blair, I. V., & Chapleau, K. M. (2004). Automatic stereotypes vs. automatic prejudice: Sorting out the possibilities in the Payne (2001). weapon paradigm. *Journal of Experimental Social Psychology, 40*, 75–81.

Kawakami, K., & Dovidio, J. E. (2001). The reliability of implicit stereotyping. *Personality and Social Psychology Bulletin, 27*, 212–225.

Kawakami, K., Dovidio, J. F., Moll, J., Hermsen, S., & Russin, A. (2000). Just say no (to stereotyping): Effects of training in the negation of stereotypic associations on stereotype activation. *Journal of Personality and Social Psychology, 78*, 871–888.

LaBar, K. S. (2007). Beyond fear: Emotional memory mechanisms in the human brain. *Current Directions in Psychological Science, 16*, 173–177.

LaBar, K. S., & Cabeza, R. (2006). Cognitive neuroscience of emotional memory. *Nature Reviews Neuroscience, 7*, 54–64.

Lerner, J. S., & Keltner, D. (2000). Beyond valence: Toward a model of emotion-specific influences on judgment and choice. *Cognition and Emotion, 14*, 473–493.

Levin, D. T., & Simons, D. J. (1997). Failure to detect changes to attended objects in motion pictures. *Psychonomic Bulletin & Review, 4*, 501–506.

Levin, D. T., Simons, D. J., Angelone, B. L., & Chabris, C. F. (2002). Memory for centrally attended changing objects in an incidental real-world change detection paradigm. *British Journal of Psychology, 93*, 289–302.

Levine, L. J., & Pizzarro, D. A. (2004). Emotion and memory research: A grumpy overview. *Social Cognition, 22*, 530–554.

Lindsay, R. C. L., Ross, D. F., Read, J. D., & Toglia, M. P. (2007). *The handbook of eyewitness psychology, Vol. 2: Memory for people.* Mahwah, NJ: Lawrence Erlbaum Associates.

Lipp, O. V., & Waters, A. M. (2007). When danger lurks in the background: Attentional capture by animal fear-relevant distractors is specific and selectively enhanced by animal fear. *Emotion, 7*(1), 192–200.

Loftus, E. F., & Davis, D. (2006). Recovered memories. *Annual Review of Clinical Psychology, 2*, 469–498.

Loftus, E. F., Loftus, G., & Messo, J. (1987). Some facts about "weapons focus". *Law and Human Behaviour, 11*, 55–62.

Lupien, S. J., Maheu, F., Tu, M., Fiocco, A., & Schramek, T. E. (2007). The effects of stress and stress hormones on human cognition: Implications for the field of brain and cognition. *Brain and Cognition, 65*(3), 209–237.

MacLeod, C., Mathews, A., & Tata, P. (1986). Attentional bias in emotional disorders. *Journal of Abnormal Psychology, 95*(1), 15–20.

Maner, J. K., Kenrick, D. T., Becker, D. V., Robertson, T. E., Hofer, B., Neuberg, S. L., et al. (2005). Functional projection: How fundamental social motives can bias interpersonal perception. *Journal of Personality & Social Psychology, 88*, 63–78.

Markman, A. B., & Brendl, C. M. (2005). Constraining theories of embodied cognition. *Psychological Science, 16*, 6–10.

McEwen, B. S., & Sapolsky, R. M. (1995). Stress and cognitive function. *Current Opinion in Neurobiology, 5*, 205–216.

McLin, O. H., Zimmerman, L. A., & Malpass, R. S. (2005). PC_Eye-witness and the sequential superiority effect: Computer-based lineup administration. *Law and Human Behaviour, 29*, 303–321.

Mikulincer, M., & Shaver, P. R. (2007). *Attachment in adulthood: Structure, dynamics, and change.* New York: Guilford Press.

Morgan, C. A., III, Hazlett, G., Doran, A., Garrett, S., Hoyt, G., Thomas, P., et al. (2004). Accuracy of eyewitness memory for persons encountered during exposure to highly intense stress. *International Journal of Law and Psychiatry, 27*, 265–279.

Muraven, M., & Baumeister, R. F. (2000). Self-regulation and depletion of limited resources: Does self-control resemble a muscle? *Psychological Bulletin, 126*(2), 247–259.

Nabi, R. L. (2002). Anger, fear, uncertainty, and attitudes: A test of the cognitive-functional model. *Communication Monographs, 69*(3), 204–216.

Niedenthal, P. M., Barsalou, L. W., Winkielman, P., Krauth-Gruber, S., & Ric, F. (2005). Embodiment in attitudes, social perception, and emotion. *Personality & Social Psychology Review, 9*, 184–211.

Paterson, H. N., & Kemp, R. I. (2006). Comparing methods of encountering post-event information: The power of co-witness suggestion. *Applied Cognitive Psychology, 20*, 1083–1099.

Payne, B. K. (2001). Prejudice and perception: The role of automatic and controlled processes in misperceiving a weapon. *Journal of Personality and Social Psychology, 81*, 181–192.

Payne, B. K. (2005). Conceptualizing control in social cognition: How executive functioning modulates the expression of automatic stereotyping. *Journal of Personality and Social Psychology, 89,* 488–503.

Payne, B. K., Jacoby, L. L., & Lambert, A. J. (2005). Attitudes as accessibility bias: Dissociating automatic and controlled components. In R. Hassin, J. A. Bargh, & J. Uleman (Eds.), *The new unconscious* (pp. 393–420). Oxford, UK: Oxford University Press.

Payne, B. K., Lambert, A. J., & Jacoby, L. L. (2002). Best laid plans: Effects of goals on accessibility bias and cognitive control in race-based misperceptions of weapons. *Journal of Experimental Social Psychology, 38,* 384–396.

Payne, B. K., Shimizu, Y., & Jacoby, L. L. (2005). Mental control and visual illusions: Toward explaining race-biased weapon misidentifications. *Journal of Experimental Social Psychology, 41,* 36–47.

Payne, H. D., Nadel, L., Britton, W. B., & Jacobs, W. J. (2004). The biopsychology and trauma and memory. In D. Rieisberg & P. Hertel (Eds.), *Memory and emotion* (pp. 76–128). New York: Oxford University Press.

Peters, D. (1988). Eyewitness memory and arousal in a natural setting. In M. Gruneberg, P. Morris & R. Sykes (Eds.), *Practical aspects of memory: Current research and issues* (pp. 89–94). New York: John Wiley & Sons.

Petty, R. E. (2001). Subtle influences on judgment and behavior: Who is most susceptible? In J. P. Forgas & K. D. Williams (Eds.), *Social influence: Direct and indirect processes* (pp. 129–146). New York: Psychology Press.

Phelps, E. A. (2006). Emotion and cognition: Insights from studies of the human amygdala. *Annual Review of Psychology, 57,* 27–53.

Phillips, M. R., McAuliff, B. D., Kovera, M. B., & Cutler, B. L. (1999). Double-blind photoarray administration as a safeguard against investigator bias. *Journal of Applied Psychology, 84*(6), 940–951.

Plant, E. A., & Peruche, B. M. (2005). The consequences of race for police officers' responses to criminal suspects. *Psychological Science, 16,* 180–183.

Plant, E. A., Peruche, B. M., & Butz, D. A. (2005). Eliminating automatic racial bias: Making race non-diagnostic for responses to criminal suspects. *Journal of Experimental Social Psychology, 41,* 141–156.

Repp, B. H., & Knoblich, G. N. (2007). Action can affect auditory perception. *Psychological Science, 18*(1), 6–7.

Reisberg, D., & Heuer, F. (2007). The influence of emotion on memory in forensic settings. In M. P. Toglia, J. D. Read, D. F. Ross, & R. C. L. Lindsay (Eds.), *The handbook of eyewitness psychology: Vol. I: Memory for events* (pp. 81–116). Mahwah, NJ: Lawrence Erlbaum Associates.

Richards, J. M., & Gross, J. J. (2006). Personality and emotional memory: How regulating emotion impairs memory for emotional events. *Journal of Research in Personality, 40,* 631–651.

Rizzolatti, G., & Arbib, M. A. (1998). Language within our grasp. *Trends in Neuroscience, 21,* 188–194.

Safer, M. A., Christianson, S.-Å., Autry, M. W., & Osterlund, K. (1998). Tunnel memory for traumatic events. *Applied Cognitive Psychology, 12*(2), 99–117.

Schwartz, N., & Clore, G. L. (1988). How do I feel about it? The informative function of affective states. In K. Fiedler & J. P. Forgas (Eds.), *Affect, cognition and behaviour* (pp. 44–62). Toronto, Canada: Jogrefe.

Shackman, Z. J., Sarinopoulos, I., Maxwell, J. S., Pizzagalli, D. A., Lavric, A., & Davidson, R. J. (2006). Anxiety selectively disrupts visuospatial working memory. *Emotion, 6*, 40–61.

Shah, J. Y. (2005). The automatic pursuit and management of goals. *Current Directions in Psychological Science, 14*(1), 10–13.

Simons, D. J., & Ambinder, M. S. (2005). Change blindness: Theory and consequences. *Current Directions in Psychological Science, 14*, 44–48.

Simons, D. J., & Levin, D. T. (1998). Failure to detect changes to people during a real-world interaction. *Psychonomic Bulletin and Review, 5*, 644–649.

Skagerberg, E. M. (2007). Co-witness feedback in line-ups. *Applied Cognitive Psychology, 21*(4), 489–497.

Stanny, C. J., & Johnson, T. C. (2000). Effects of stress induced by a simulated shooting on recall by police and citizen witnesses. *American Journal of Psychology, 113*, 359–386.

Steblay, N. M. (1992). A meta-analytic review of the weapon focus effect. *Law and Human Behaviour, 16*, 413–424.

Steblay, N. M. (1997). Social influence in eyewitness recall: A meta-analytic review of lineup instruction effects. *Law and Human Behaviour, 21*, 283–298.

Steblay, N. M., Dysart, J., Fulero, S. M., & Lindsay, R. C. L. (2001). Eyewitness accuracy rates in sequential and simultaneous lineup presentations: A meta-analytic comparison. *Law and Human Behaviour, 25*, 459–474.

Tavris, C., & Aronson, E. (2007). *Mistakes were made (but not by me): Why we justify foolish beliefs, bad decisions, and hurtful acts*. Orlando, FL: Harcourt.

Technical Working Group for Eyewitness Evidence. (1999). *Eyewitness evidence: A guide for law enforcement*. Washington, DC: U.S. Department of Justice, Office of Justice Programs.

Tiedens, L. Z., & Linton, S. (2001). Judgment under emotional certainty and uncertainty: The effects of specific emotions on information processing. *Journal of Personality and Social Psychology, 81*(6), 973–988.

Toglia, M. P., Read, J. D., Ross, D. F., & Lindsay, R. C. L. (2007). *The handbook of eyewitness psychology, Vol. 1: Memory for events*. Mahwah, NJ: Lawrence Erlbaum Associates.

Vitevitch, M. S. (2003). Change deafness: The inability to detect changes between two voices. *Journal of Experimental Psychology: Human Perception and Performance, 29*(2), 333–342.

Watson, L., & Spence, M. T. (2007). Causes and consequences of emotions on consumer behaviour: A review and integrative cognitive appraisal theory. *European Journal of Marketing, 41*(5), 487–511.

Weiner, B. (1985). "Spontaneous" causal thinking. *Psychological Bulletin, 97*(1), 74–84.

Wells, G. L. (1984). The psychology of lineup identifications. *Journal of Applied Social Psychology, 14*, 89–103.

Wells, G. L. (1993). What do we know about eyewitness identification? *American Psychologist, 48*, 553–571.

Wells, G. L., & Bradfield, A. L. (1998). "Good, you identified the suspect": Feedback to eyewitness reports distorts their reports of the witnessing experience. *Journal of Applied Social Psychology, 83*, 360–376.

Wells, G. L., Memon, A., & Penrod, S. D. (2006). Eyewitness evidence: Improving its probative value. *Psychological Science in the Public Interest, 7*, 45–75.

Wells, G. L., Small, M., Penrod, S., Malpass, R. S., Fulero, S. M., & Brimacombe, C. A. E. (1998). Eyewitness identification procedures: Recommendations for lineups and photospreads. *Law and Human Behaviour, 22*, 603–647.

Wheeler, M. E., & Fiske, S. T. (2005). Controlling racial prejudice. *Psychological Science, 16*, 56–63.

Wigmore, J. H. (1974). *Evidence in trials at common law* (Revised by Chadbourn, J. H). Boston: Little/Brown.

Winkielman, P., & Berridge, K. C. (2004). Unconscious emotion. *Current Directions in Psychological Science, 13*, 120–123.

Wolpert, D. M., & Kawato, M. (1998). Multiple paired forward and inverse models for motor control. *Neural Networks, 11*(7), 1317–1329.

Wyer, R. S., Jr. (2004). *Social comprehension and judgment: The role of situation models, narratives, and implicit theories*. Mahwah, NJ: Lawrence Erlbaum Associates.

8   Visual mental imagery: More than "seeing with the mind's eye"

Giorgio Ganis
Harvard Medical School

William L. Thompson and Stephen M. Kosslyn
Harvard University

1. INTRODUCTION

We are able to perceive and understand objects, faces, scenes, and events in the environment because our brains construct internal representations of these entities on the basis of information conveyed by our sensory organs. These internal representations are not only activated by information coming from the sensory organs, during perception, but can also be reactivated endogenously in the absence of any external stimulation, during mental imagery. Although mental imagery can take place in all modalities (visual, auditory, tactile, and so on), here we focus on visual mental imagery, the most studied modality. We also discuss motor imagery, a distinct form of mental imagery that relies on the motor system and that often accompanies visual mental imagery.

In the case of visual mental imagery, to answer a question such as "What shape are a cat's ears?" one usually visualizes a cat and then "zooms in" on parts of the image containing the animal's ears to assess their shape. This process of reactivation and inspection of an internal representation in the absence of any external stimulus is at the core of mental imagery. More formally, during visual mental imagery one activates visual representations in long-term memory and uses them to construct a representation in working memory; this representation can then be processed further, such as by reinterpreting or transforming it (Kosslyn, Ganis, & Thompson, 2001; Kosslyn, Thompson, & Ganis, 2006). From this definition it is already evident that there is a tight link between mental imagery and memory processes. Additional in-depth discussion of the relationship between visual mental imagery and visuospatial working memory is provided in chapter 1, sections 3 and 4.

However, we stress that, just as memory is a constructive process, visual mental imagery goes beyond the mere reactivation of visual representations of specific events that have been actually experienced: One not only must construct an image on the basis of incomplete information stored in memory, but also can use visual mental imagery to extract new information (i.e., information that had not been encoded explicitly) by parsing and reassembling them in new ways (Finke, Pinker, & Farah, 1989). This is one reason why visual mental imagery plays an important role in numerous domains, such as engineering and mathematics, and is important for numerous cognitive skills, such as reasoning (e.g., Blajenkova, Kozhevnikov, & Motes, 2006).

1.1. Historical perspective

Recognition that visual mental imagery is a crucial component of our mental life dates back at least to the Greek philosophers (cf. McMahon, 1973), but in the last 30 years there has been an exponential increase in the amount of knowledge about the cognitive and neural processes underlying visual mental imagery. Although this progress may be taken for granted, it is useful to remember that during the previous 50 years, when behaviorism was the dominant approach in American psychology, and until the cognitive revolution in the 1960s and 1970s, virtually no research on mental imagery was carried out. For example, only five articles on mental imagery were published in the 1940s and 1950s, according to *Psychological Abstracts* (Kessel, 1972), and work on mental imagery in the 1920s and 1930s was similarly sparse (Paivio, 1971). Because mental imagery is essentially a private affair that can unfold without any measurable external behavior, behaviorism had declared unscientific not only the introspective methodologies used up to that point to study imagery, but also the entire topic: J. B. Watson himself, despite having been heavily influenced by Titchener (Larson & Sullivan, 1965), in his behaviorist manifesto argued that imagery did not exist and equated all thought processes to "sensori-motor processes in the larynx" (Watson, 1913).

It was only in the 1970s, with new conceptual and methodological tools, that there was a revival of interest in the study of internal representations and the topic of visual mental imagery again became a legitimate object of study in psychology. Among other factors, such a revival was catalyzed by the work of Paivio, which demonstrated powerful interactions between mental imagery and memory (e.g., Paivio, 1971), and by the work of Shepard and collaborators on mental transformations (e.g., Shepard & Cooper, 1982). This resurgence of interest in internal representations and processes generated numerous empirical studies aimed at understanding the organizational details of such entities, leading to a debate probably as intense as the one on the existence of imageless thought at the beginning of the century (Humphrey, 1951). On one side of the debate (depictive theories), researchers argued and provided empirical evidence that visual mental images are distinct types of mental representations and function to depict visual objects and scenes (Kosslyn, 1980). From this view, visual images make explicit shape and spatial relations by virtue of their internal structure: Distances among parts in the image correspond to distances among parts of the stimulus they represent. On the other side (descriptive theories), researchers argued that visual mental image representations were not different from the type of representation used in linguistic thought, which relies on some sort of "propositional" representation (Pylyshyn, 1973). According to this view, the pictorial aspects of imagery evident to introspection play no role in information processing.

1.2. Visual mental imagery and cognitive neuroscience

After several exchanges during the "imagery debate" of the late 1970s and early 1980s, it became increasingly clear that this issue could not be resolved conclusively, even with the more sophisticated empirical methods of cognitive psychology. In an incisive paper, Anderson (1978) showed that behavioral results from a number of visual imagery studies could be interpreted both within a depictive account of visual imagery and within a propositional account, given suitable processing assumptions. Anderson demonstrated that, for a given theory defined by a set of assumptions about depictive representations and processes that operate on them, one could always design an alternative theory based on a set of assumptions about propositional representations and processes that could mimic the first theory. Thus, Anderson pointed out, the results of behavioral experiments were insufficiently constrained to implicate uniquely the existence of specific representation-process pairs: Issues regarding the details about such representation-process pairs could only be resolved by using other types of evidence, such as neuroscientific evidence. This is one reason why the neural evidence is crucial to constraining and understanding the details of how visual mental imagery works.

Behavioral studies that revealed strong parallels between visual mental imagery and visual perception provided a reasonable starting point for the use of neuroscientific data (cf. Kosslyn, 1980): If visual mental imagery depends on the same processes that are recruited during visual perception, then the neural structures that support vision should also support visual mental imagery (Kosslyn, 1994). This logic made it possible to use the knowledge available on the visual system of nonhuman animals to help devise new hypotheses about the working of visual mental imagery. However, until recently, almost all the information about the neurophysiological organization of the human visual system was indirect and came from studies in nonhuman primates, under the assumption of homology among different species. Advances in noninvasive neuroimaging and stimulation methods have allowed cognitive neuroscience researchers to study the neural basis of vision in humans and to test this assumption directly. Findings using techniques such as positron emission tomography (PET) and, more recently, functional magnetic resonance imaging (fMRI) and transcranial magnetic stimulation (TMS) have complemented observations in brain-damaged patients and confirmed that there is indeed a remarkable similarity between the organization of the visual system in humans and in nonhuman primates, especially with regard to early visual areas (e.g., Sereno & Tootell, 2005). Moreover, these same techniques have allowed researchers to study visual mental imagery noninvasively in humans.

In the following sections, we review and discuss some of the empirical literature on the cognitive neuroscience of visual mental imagery, focusing on two related research topics that have received considerable attention. The first is whether, and to what extent, visual mental imagery and visual perception recruit the same neural resources. The second is whether there are different types of visual mental imagery, each relying on at least partially nonoverlapping brain networks.

2. VISUAL MENTAL IMAGERY AND VISUAL PERCEPTION: SHARED NEURAL SYSTEMS

Are the brain regions and neural processes recruited during visual mental imagery the same as those recruited during visual perception, as cognitive studies have suggested? The few neuroimaging studies that have quantified the similarity between visual mental imagery and visual perception across the entire brain have shown that there is an overlap of at least 90% between brain regions recruited by visual perception and visual mental imagery (e.g., Ganis, Thompson, & Kosslyn, 2004). Most of the neuroimaging literature, however, has focused on the qualitative question of whether, and under what circumstances, visual mental imagery relies on visual areas recruited during visual perception. The results of some of these studies are reviewed and discussed below.

2.1. Visual mental imagery and early visual cortex

Considerable research effort has been devoted to the specific question of whether visual mental imagery recruits the early visual cortical areas used in visual perception. To understand why this question is important, it is useful to review some basic principles of the organization of the primate visual system and to consider how these principles relate to depictive theories of visual mental imagery.

2.1.1. *Organization of the human primate visual system and visual mental imagery*

The primate visual system is organized as a hierarchy composed of parallel processing streams (Felleman & Van Essen, 1991), with early visual areas (Areas 17 and 18, also known as Areas V1 and V2, respectively) occupying the lowest level in the hierarchy. Area 17, in particular, is the first cortical site to receive visual information from subcortical nuclei (the main one being the lateral geniculate nucleus), which in turn receive input from the retina. Early visual areas feed two parallel streams in the hierarchy: the ventral stream, which includes ventrolateral areas in the occipital and temporal lobes, and the dorsal stream, which includes dorsal areas in the occipital and parietal lobes (Desimone & Ungerleider, 1989). These two streams subserve different functions: The ventral stream has been implicated in object vision (Desimone &

Ungerleider, 1989; Haxby et al., 1991; Mishkin, Ungerleider, & Macko, 1983; Ungerleider & Mishkin, 1982), whereas the dorsal stream has been implicated in spatial vision and action (Goodale, Westwood, & Milner, 2004; Ungerleider & Mishkin, 1982).

An important feature of early visual cortical areas is that they are organized retinotopically—that is, nearby points in the visual space (which is projected onto the retina) are mapped onto nearby points on the cortical mantle. This topographic representation of the visual space uses two dimensions in polar coordinates: eccentricity and polar angle. "Eccentricity" is the distance of a point from the fovea (the central, high-resolution, region of the visual field), whereas "polar angle" is the angle between a line connecting a point to the center of the visual field and a horizontal line. Polar angle is represented along a roughly orthogonal direction (Figure 8.1). In addition, as one ascends the visual hierarchy, this retinotopic organization becomes less and less pronounced (Felleman & Van Essen, 1991; Fox et al., 1986; Heeger, 1999; Sereno et al., 1995; Tootell et al., 1998b;

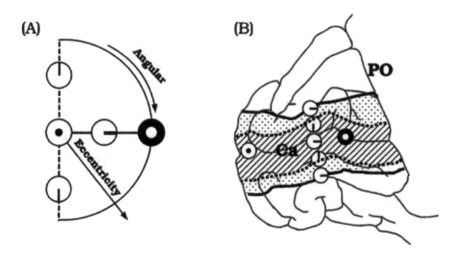

Figure 8.1. A. Key locations in the right visual field are depicted by icons. The central part of the visual field is indicated by a black dot, whereas the peripheral parts of the visual field are indicated by a black ring. The horizontal and vertical meridians are depicted by dipoles oriented in the direction of the region they represent (horizontal right, vertical up, and vertical down. B. Representation of eccentricity and polar angle in Area 17 (hatch-marked area) and Area 18 (dotted area) in the left hemisphere using the icons depicted in (A). Ca indicates the fundus of the calcarine fissure; PO indicates the parieto-occipital sulcus. Reprinted with permission from Wandell (1999, Figure 2, p. 151), from the *Annual Review of Neuroscience, Volume 22* © 1999 by the Annual Review, www.annualreview.org.

Van Essen et al., 2001). The receptive fields—that is, the region of the visual field "seen" by a neuron—become larger and larger as one moves from Area 17 to the inferotemporal cortex. At the same time, the specific visual attributes that drive neurons become more and more complex in later visual areas. Whereas small bars at very specific spatial locations are the optimal stimuli to drive Area 17 neurons, specific combinations of shape, texture, and color appearing almost anywhere in the visual field can drive neurons in the inferotemporal cortex (Fujita, Tanaka, Ito, & Cheng, 1992; Miyashita & Chang, 1988; Tanaka, 1996; Tanaka, Saito, Fukada, & Moriya, 1991). And whereas the topographic code used in Area 17 makes explicit the spatial layout of a stimulus, the distributed code used in the inferotemporal cortex makes explicit the similarities between complex features of object classes (Tanaka, 1996).

In addition, visual areas that are connected via feedforward fibers in the hierarchy are usually also connected via corresponding feedback fibers, although with different distributional properties (Barone, Batardiere, Knoblauch, & Kennedy, 2000; Budd, 1998; Felleman & Van Essen, 1991; Rockland & Pandya, 1979; Salin & Bullier, 1995). This means that later visual areas, such as those in the inferotemporal cortex, can potentially drive neurons in early visual areas.

These characteristics, and others not discussed here, have been used to lay the foundation of neurally inspired depictive theories of visual mental imagery (cf. Kosslyn, 1994). The main idea is that the spatial layout of objects is stored only implicitly in a distributed code in the inferotemporal cortex, and that this layout can be made explicit during visual mental imagery by recreating the corresponding pattern of retinotopic activation in early visual areas via the feedback connections (Kosslyn, 1994).

The observed organization of the visual system is precisely what neurally grounded depictive theories of visual mental imagery would predict. In particular, such theories gain credence because topographically organized areas employ distance on the cortex to represent distance in the visual space. Therefore, evidence that such brain areas are used during visual mental imagery would provide strong support for these theories. In addition, this is also an excellent demonstartion of how neuroscientific evidence can be useful in generating testable predictions from a suitable theory.

2.1.2. *Functional role of retinotopic organization in early visual cortex*

Before we go into the details of specific studies, it is useful to defuse two standard objections by critics of depictive theories of visual mental imagery. The first objection is that the retinotopic organization of early visual cortex is essentially an epiphenomenon when it comes to visual imagery, and possibly even to visual perception. According to this objection, the relationship between retinotopic organization and visual mental imagery is accidental, similar to that between a power LED and the working of an electric appliance (i.e., the power LED plays no functional role in the working of the appliance). According to Pylyshyn (2002):

even if real colored stereo pictures were found on the visual cortex, the problems raised thus far in this article would remain, and would continue to stand as evidence that such cortical pictures were not serving the function attributed to them. For example, the fact that phenomena such as mental scanning are cognitively penetrable [i.e., affected by goals or beliefs] is strong evidence that whatever is displayed on the cortex is not what is responsible for the patterns of behavior observed in mental imagery studies. (p. 179)

This criticism can be refuted by providing evidence that the topographic organization in early visual cortex is not only used but is actually needed during visual processing. Consider two sorts of evidence: First, damage to circumscribed portions of early visual areas produces visual scotomas (i.e., disruption of visual processing) in corresponding parts of the visual field, and the size of the damage is related to the size of the scotoma. For instance, the removal of the left occipital cortex above the calcarine fissure produces blindness in the entire lower-right quadrant (quadrantanopia; e.g., Chiang, Walsh, & Lavidor, 2004). Second, focal stimulation of early visual cortex using TMS can produce faint visual sensations (phosphenes) in the corresponding parts of the visual field. One can ask people to draw the location and shapes of the perceived phosphenes during TMS stimulation, which allows researchers to study the relationship between these parameters and stimulation parameters (e.g., location and intensity). For instance, Kammer and collaborators were able to induce predictable shifts in the perceived location of phosphenes by shifting the TMS coil systematically over the occipital lobe of neurologically normal subjects (e.g., Kammer, Puls, Strasburger, Hill, & Wichmann, 2005b). At higher TMS intensities, they were also able to produce scotomas (identified by asking people to detect small squares at various locations in the visual field) within the same regions of the visual field (e.g., Kammer, Puls, Erb, & Grodd, 2005a; Kammer et al., 2005b).

The second objection is that this retinotopic organization is not a geometrically faithful representation of the visual field, and so it cannot possibly provide useful depictive information about the visual world. For example, visual stimuli falling on the fovea have much larger cortical representations than do identical visual stimuli falling on peripheral regions of the visual field, because of cortical-magnification distortion (Sereno et al., 1995). Furthermore, in addition to deformations due to eccentricity, there are discontinuities in the visual maps—for instance, along the representation of the horizontal meridian in Area 18 and later areas (Felleman & Van Essen, 1991). This is not a serious problem for neurally based depictive theories of visual mental imagery because early visual cortical areas are only one node in a large network (Felleman & Van Essen, 1991): The information they represent is decoded by other brain areas that compensate for these large-scale distortions, similarly to the way they compensate for the fact that the retinal image during perception is "upside-down" (Kosslyn et al., 2006).

2.1.3. *Visual mental imagery and early visual cortex: Brain imaging findings*

Two seminal studies using PET showed that Area 17 is recruited during visual mental imagery and, more importantly, that the pattern of activation is consistent with the known retinotopic organization in this area. In the first study, Kosslyn and collaborators (1993) exploited the systematic representation of eccentricity in Area 17. They monitored blood flow with PET while participants visualized letters at either a very small size (as small as they could visualize them while still being able to distinguish the letters) or at a very large size (as large as they could while still being able to visualize the entire letter). The participants were asked to maintain the image for 4 s and then to make a judgment about the geometric properties of the letter (e.g., whether it had any straight lines). The rationale was that, if visual mental imagery uses topographical representations in Area 17, then large visual images should engage parts of Area 17 that are involved in representing more eccentric regions of the visual field (which are, in the human brain, located in increasingly anterior regions along the calcarine sulcus). Consistent with this prediction and with the topographic organization of Area 17, the results showed stronger activation in posterior parts of Area 17 when participants visualized the letters at a small size and in more anterior parts of Area 17 when they visualized the letters at the larger size. In the second study, Kosslyn, Thompson, Kim, and Alpert (1995) used a similar logic but different stimuli. During the PET session they asked participants to visualize line drawings of objects they had studied in advance within boxes of different size: small, medium, and large. To ensure that people were actually carrying out visual mental imagery, the task asked them to perform various visual judgments on the images (e.g., whether the left side of the pictures they had studied was higher than the right side). The results, again, nicely confirmed the predictions.

However, one limitation of these two studies is the low spatial resolution of PET and the consequent lack of precise localization for Area 17. A single participant study by Tootell, Hadjikani, Mendola, Marrett, and Dale (1998a) with fMRI used stimuli similar to those of Kosslyn et al. (1993) and also used retinotopic mapping to localize Area 17 precisely. These researchers compared two conditions in a blocked design. In the first condition the participant visualized small letters of the alphabet for 32 s (in sequence, starting from the letter "A"), whereas in the second condition the participant visualized a large field of letters, in the same sequence, leaving the center region empty. The results revealed activation consistent with the retinotopic organization in early visual cortical areas, including Area 17, with an especially strong pattern for the small-letter condition.

These results have been replicated and extended in fMRI studies conducted in the last few years. A recent study used event-related fMRI to investigate whether visual mental imagery elicits activation consistent with the retinotopic organization of polar angle in early visual cortex (Klein et al., 2004). In this study the investigators asked a group of six participants either to look at bow-tie stimuli (perception conditions) or to visualize them (visual mental imagery condition) in separate blocks of trials. The stimuli were either vertical or horizontal bow-tie shapes, with each one being associated with a different auditory tone so that participants would know which stimulus to visualize during the visual mental imagery trials. During the perception condition, participants pressed a key as soon as they recognized the orientation of the bow-tie stimuli, whereas during the visual mental imagery condition, participants pressed a key as soon as they had formed a vivid image of the bow-tie stimulus indicated by the auditory tone at the beginning of each trial. The results showed reliable activation in Area 17 in five out of six participants when contrasting visual imagery with a baseline defined by the mean BOLD (blood oxygen level-dependent) signal level for that block. However, this comparison revealed no retinotopic differences between visual mental imagery of horizontal versus vertical bow-tie stimuli.

The researchers argued that the lack of differential activation was brought about by the differences being swamped by a large, nonspecific activation reflecting the overall engagement of early visual cortex in the task, possibly due to visual attention. To eliminate such nonspecific activation, they contrasted activation between the horizontal and vertical bow-tie stimuli directly, and, in fact, this direct comparison revealed differences that followed the retinotopic organization of Area 17 and Area 18. Although the effects were not strong (the significance threshold for the contrast was set at 0.01, uncorrected, with four voxel clusters), four out of six participants showed a significant overlap between voxels active during visual mental imagery and those active during perception of the same shape at the same orientation (relative to voxels during perception of the shape at the other orientation). The fact that only four out of six participants showed the pattern is consistent with findings about individual differences in brain activation during visual mental imagery (e.g., Ganis, Thompson, & Kosslyn, 2005; Kosslyn, Thompson, Kim, Rauch, & Alpert, 1996). Furthermore, there was an interesting asymmetry in the results: The effects were stronger for the vertical meridian representations (vertical bow ties), possibly because the feedback projections to the vertical meridian representation are denser than those to the horizontal meridian (Tootell et al., 1998b).

A follow-up study (Thirion et al., 2006) used more sophisticated analytic methods to extract information from single fMRI trials during visual perception and visual mental imagery. During the perception condition, nine participants looked at simple patterns of rotating Gabor filters (there were a total of six possible patterns) in an event-related design. During the visual mental imagery condition, subjects chose one of the six patterns and visualized it to the left or right of a fixation point, depending on the direction of an arrow that was presented on each trial. These researchers used an approach referred to as "inverse retinotopy" to estimate the actual visual stimulus that would be more likely to have generated a given pattern of activation in early visual cortex, achieved by inverting the mapping between visual space and visual cortex. The results showed an average of over 80% classification rates for the perception conditions (chance was 1/6—i.e., 16.7%—given that there were six possible patterns). All 16 hemispheres examined (one participant was not included for technical reasons) showed robust trial-by-trial classification performance (between 70% and 96%, using a Leave-One-Out classification scheme). Most of the voxels that contributed to successful classification were located in Area 17 (50–60%), followed by Area 18 (20%), which is not surprising, given the topographic characteristics of these areas discussed earlier. For the visual mental imagery condition, the results were much weaker: on a trial-by-trial basis, only 5 hemispheres out of 16 led to above-chance prediction of which stimulus was visualized (min. 38%, max. 67%, using a Leave-One-Out classification scheme).

Another study employed a variant of the standard retinotopic mapping methods (Sereno et al., 1995) to determine whether visual mental imagery elicits activation that is consistent with the representation of polar angle in visual cortex (Slotnick, Thompson, & Kosslyn, 2005). The stimuli consisted of rotating checkerboard bow-tie shapes. During the visual perception condition, six participants fixated the center of the display and pressed a key every time a small red square was flashed inside the revolving bow tie. During the visual mental imagery condition, the stimulus was made up of two thin arcs, outlining the outer edges of the bow tie. The task was to visualize the rest of the pattern and, again, to press a key when a small red square was flashed inside the region that the bow tie (now only visualized) would occupy. There was also an attention condition (using the same participants), during which all parameters were identical to the imagery condition with the difference that participants were not instructed to create visual mental images, only to wait for the red square and to press a key depending on whether it was presented to the left or to the right of fixation. Results for the imagery condition showed small activation foci (the significance threshold was set at 0.01, uncorrected, with four voxel clusters) in Area 17 that were not seen during the control attention conditions in three out of six participants. Activation in extrastriate regions was observed in four out of six participants. Although there was—for some participants—clear topographically organized activation that was not a result of attention, the majority of the imagery-induced activation overlapped with activation induced by visual attention, which might possibly indicate that visuospatial attention functions as a scaffolding upon which at least some forms of visual imagery build.

Overall, the evidence from these studies supports the claim that mental images of shapes sometimes activate topographically organized areas in early visual cortex, although the signals observed are much weaker than those seen during visual perception (and are difficult to detect in single participants).

2.1.4. *Inconsistencies in the brain imaging literature on the involvement of Area 17 in visual mental imagery*

In addition to the many studies that have shown early visual cortex activation during visual mental imagery (for a review, see Kosslyn & Thompson, 2003), a number of studies have not found such activation. Given the large number of studies on this topic, most of them using somewhat different paradigms and techniques, the best way to find meaningful patterns was to carry out a meta-analysis.

Kosslyn and Thompson (2003) conducted such a meta-analysis and looked for factors that were reliably associated with the activation of early visual cortex during visual mental imagery. In this study, three theories first were described that could account for the observed activation in early visual cortex (Area 17 or Area 18) during visual mental imagery. One theory, referred to as "Perceptual Anticipation Theory," was the depictive theory of visual mental imagery developed in Kosslyn (1994). Another theory, "Propositional Theory," the type of descriptive theory put forward by Pylyshyn (1973), specifically predicts no activation in early visual cortex during visual mental imagery, and it postulates that activation in this area, if observed, is solely due to artifacts. The last theory, referred to as "Methodological Factors Theory," postulates that activation in early visual cortex is always present during visual mental imagery but in some studies is not detected because of methodological issues.

Kosslyn and Thompson reviewed and classified 59 neuroimaging studies of visual mental imagery according to six variables relevant for the three theories. The variables employed to characterize the visual imagery tasks were: use of high-resolution details in the task; use of shape judgments (as opposed to spatial judgments); use of exemplars (as opposed to prototypes); the number of participants; the neuroimaging technique utilized; the use of a resting baseline (as opposed to a more controlled baseline). The Perceptual Anticipation Theory was hypothesized to be related to the first three variables, whereas the other two theories were hypothesized to be associated with the remaining three variables but with opposite signs. The Propositional Theory would predict that early visual cortex activation would be observed with small numbers of participants, less powerful techniques, and a resting baseline because these factors would all increase the chance of detecting artifactual activations. The Methodological Factors Theory would predict exactly the opposite—for instance, that (real) activation in early visual cortex would be more likely to be detected by using larger numbers of participants.

A regression analysis on the data revealed that activation in early visual cortex was predicted by four variables, two associated with Perceptual Anticipation Theory (use of high-resolution details and use of shape—as opposed to spatial—judgments) and two associated with Methodological Factors Theory (use of more powerful brain imaging technique and use of a nonresting baseline). Note that the nonresting baseline finding is consistent with the empirical result that resting baselines (e.g., simple fixation) can cause activation increases in early visual cortex, thereby canceling out the usually small increases that may occur during visual mental imagery (Kosslyn et al., 1995).

In addition to this theory-based analysis, the data were also submitted to an exploratory analysis in which the presence or absence of early visual cortex activation across studies was correlated with 15 additional variables (for a total of 21). The results showed that 9 out of these 21 variables were correlated with early visual cortex activation across studies. To understand which of these 9 variables were responsible for the effects, given that some were correlated with each other, they were submitted to a forward stepwise logistic regression. The findings were very similar to the initial theory-based analysis and showed that the use of high-resolution details in the task, the use of shape judgments, and the neuroimaging technique employed reliably predicted activation in early visual cortex.

The importance of visual mental imagery tasks that use high-resolution details for recruiting early visual areas can be understood by keeping in mind the high-resolution topographic organization of these areas. Even though later areas (e.g., Area V4) have a retinotopic organization, this is much coarser than that observed in Area 17 and Area 18—and so these later areas would not be able to support adequate performance on a task that requires the visualization of fine details. In addition, the importance of using shape judgments (as opposed to spatial ones) makes sense because visual memories about shapes are stored in inferotemporal cortex by means of a distributed code (Tanaka, 1996) that does not make their spatial layout explicit; the spatial layout can be made explicit by reconstructing the spatial layout in early visual cortex. In contrast, spatial representations may already be stored in a suitable code in topographically organized areas in the parietal cortex (Sereno, Pitzalis, & Martinez, 2001); early visual cortex may not need to be recruited for spatial judgments to be carried out.

The results of this meta-analysis indicate that the apparent inconsistencies in the brain imaging literature regarding early visual cortex activation during visual mental imagery are due not to random factors, but to systematic variables that can be controlled.

2.1.5. *Visual mental imagery and early visual cortex: Neuropsychological findings*

If early visual cortex is necessary for carrying out at least some forms of visual mental imagery (specifically, when high-resolution images of shapes are required), then at least some types of visual mental imagery should be impaired in patients with damage to these areas. Neuroimaging techniques measure the activity in various brain regions during a given task. This leaves open the possibility that such activation is only *correlated* with the performance of the task, but plays no functional role. For example, Brain Area X may receive neural signals from another region (Brain Area Y) that does play a functional role in a task, but Brain Area X, although activated when the task is performed, may not contribute to the performance of the task—in that sense, its activation is said to be epiphenomenal.

As noted earlier, unilateral focal damage to Area 17 produces scotomas in small parts of the visual field that are represented by the damaged cortical tissue. If the damaged area is large and bilateral (for instance, because of posterior cerebral artery infarct), then the result is cortical blindness. If imagery is also disrupted by such damage, this would indicate that early visual cortex is necessary for visual mental imagery, an inference that cannot be made by using brain imaging data alone.

Before we discuss some of the evidence, we must introduce a few caveats about interpreting evidence obtained in neurological patients. First, although damaged brain tissue can be detected with brain imaging technologies, it is difficult to be sure that brain tissue that looks normal is functioning properly because there could be some abnormalities that are not detectable with the technique used (e.g., for MRI, these abnormalities may be at a scale that is smaller than the voxel size, or they may be undetectable with the sequence parameters used). Furthermore, abnormalities in the white matter connecting brain regions can lead to functional disruption in brain networks that is not easily detectable. Advances in brain imaging technologies (e.g., the more widespread use of diffusion tensor imaging) should reduce, if not eliminate, some of these problems.

Second, there are interpretational problems that are intrinsic to the fact that brain damage is not a variable that can be manipulated experimentally. For instance, we cannot control the location or size of the lesion, and large lesions can affect nearby regions that nonetheless carry out different functions, potentially leading to the incorrect inference that these functions are related (because of the frequent co-occurrence of the resulting functional impairments).

Third, the brain is not a static organ, and damage can trigger compensatory mechanisms at many levels of organization (e.g., Barbay et al., 2006; Dancause et al., 2005). For example, other areas may attempt to take over the lost functions, further complicating the interpretation of the findings. Finally, in most published patient studies, visual mental imagery has not been assessed rigorously. For example, the time patients take to respond is rarely recorded.

Despite these caveats, some of the available evidence has documented visual mental imagery impairments as a result of damage to the occipital cortex. Patients who have hemianopia (i.e., blindness in one-half of the visual field, following damage to one cerebral hemisphere) are particularly worth studying: For these patients, an investigator can administer a visual mental imagery task in the functioning hemifield and compare the results with the same task in the impaired hemifield within the same individual. One of the most solid studies to have used this logic was conducted by Butter, Kosslyn, Mijovic-Prelec, and Riffle (1997). In this study, eight hemianopic patients were assessed on a mental scanning task, an objective test of visual mental imagery (which is rare in the assessment of visual mental imagery in patients). In this paradigm the participants were shown a pattern of four dots and subsequently, after the pattern had disappeared, were asked to decide whether an arrow pointed at a location previously occupied by one of the dots. Compared to healthy controls, patients showed the expected pattern: lower accuracy when the arrow pointed at a dot in the hemifield that was affected compared to when it pointed at a dot in the intact hemifield. A number of control conditions ruled out potential confounds, such as that the patients were unable to see the dot pattern or the arrow to begin with. One weakness of this study is that only CT scans were performed, and only on a subset of the patients, which makes it impossible to know the extent to which the brain damage affected early visual cortex. The findings from this study dovetailed with those obtained in an earlier study in a single patient after removal of the occipital lobe in one hemisphere (Farah, Soso, & Dasheiff, 1992):

In this patient, the horizontal extent of visual images was reduced by half after the surgery, whereas the vertical extent was normal, which is consistent with the fact that the representation of half of the horizontal meridian was lost.

There are also a number of cases in the literature that at first blush appear to contradict neurally inspired depictive theories. In these cases, widespread damage to early visual cortex, including Area 17, results in cortical blindness but does not seem to impair visual mental imagery. Perhaps the most striking case is that of a young woman who had become cortically blind because of a stroke that had damaged her primary visual cortex bilaterally (Chatterjee & Southwood, 1995). Despite her profound blindness, she was able to answer numerous visual mental imagery questions; these questions included judgments about the shape of capital letters and of common animals. She was also able to draw a set of common objects from memory. Finally, she also reported using visual mental imagery during her high-school studies (which she completed after becoming cortically blind). There have been other cases of cortical blindness and apparent sparing of visual mental imagery abilities (e.g., Goldenberg, Müllbacher, & Nowak, 1995), but the tests used to assess visual mental imagery have often been rather crude (see Bartolomeo, 2002).

Cases such as these ones, however, are not strong evidence against the hypothesis that Area 17 is needed to perform at least certain types of visual mental imagery. First, it is very difficult to rule out that there aren't some spared parts of early visual cortex that still function and carry out visual mental imagery, especially with the low-resolution brain scans used in the past. This is an especially important point because activation in only small parts of Area 17 is usually detected during brain imaging studies of visual mental imagery, compared to the corresponding visual perception conditions (e.g., Slotnick et al., 2005). Second, although one would expect to observe at least some drop in performance, many of the tasks used to test visual imagery may not have been sufficiently sensitive—or may not have recruited Area 17 to begin with. For example, imagery questions such as whether the body of a snake has curved parts may tap into semantic memory and not require high-resolution imagery (rather, a verbal strategy may be used); imagery tasks that involve stimuli with an overlearned motor component, such as drawing letters or drawing simple objects, may be carried out using information stored in the motor system (e.g., James & Gauthier, 2006). Third, and related to the previous point, many visual mental imagery tasks may be carried out by using late visual areas or even areas that are not involved in vision per se. For example, as we touched upon in the brain imaging section, if a particular task does not require the discrimination of high-resolution details in the visual image, then Area 17 may be used if available, but later areas may still be able to carry out the task adequately if Area 17 is damaged. In such a task, damage to Area 17 should not disrupt the ability to perform imagery tasks.

Finally, what do we make of the finding that some patients who are cortically blind, such as the patient described by Chatterjee and Southwood, claim to have vivid mental imagery? These types of introspective reports do not prove that these patients can use visual mental images in memory and reasoning: The subjective experience of having a vivid mental image may be the product of processes taking place in other brain areas. The situation is similar to the introspective feeling one has of being able to perceive every detail of a visual scene, which is contradicted by the results of studies of change detection (Rensink, 2002), showing that in fact we perceive relatively few details of a visual scene.

2.1.6. *Visual mental imagery and early visual cortex: Virtual lesion findings*

One technique that is particularly useful for testing the functional role of a brain region (in performing a particular task) is TMS. This technique uses a coil to deliver a magnetic pulse to a targeted brain region, creating slight disruptions to the region for a short period (from milliseconds with single-pulse TMS, to a few minutes with repetitive TMS). The advantages of TMS are that the stimulation can be controlled precisely, the disruption is reversible, the impairment is too short-lived to give rise to compensatory phenomena, and one can easily conduct studies on relatively large groups of people instead of having to rely on single cases. The first TMS study showing that early visual cortex is required for both visual perception and high-resolution visual mental imagery is the one by Kosslyn et al. (1999). This study used low-frequency repetitive TMS, which is known to decrease cortical excitability for several minutes after stimulation (e.g., Muellbacher, Ziemann, Boroojerdi, & Hallett, 2000; Siebner et al., 2000). In the visual perception condition, five participants were asked to compare attributes of four sets of black-and-white stripes, arranged into four quadrants. The stripes varied in length, width, spacing, and orientation. In the visual mental imagery condition the task was identical (e.g., the participants compared the relative lengths of stripes in two specific quadrants), but the same participants had to visualize the visual patterns to make their judgments. Visual mental imagery of these same stimuli had previously been shown to activate early visual areas using PET (in a different group of participants). Stimulation was delivered either to early visual areas by targeting the occipital pole (real-TMS condition) or away from the brain (sham-TMS control condition). Results showed that real TMS (compared to sham TMS) consistently slowed down responses in both the visual perception and visual mental imagery conditions, in support of the idea that early visual cortex is necessary to perform visual mental imagery (Figure 8.2).

2.2. Visual mental imagery and late visual areas in the ventral stream

As discussed previously, early visual areas provide input to later visual areas in the ventral stream (which processes object properties such as shape, texture, and color). Although at a macroscopic level, visual objects are represented in a spatially distributed manner in these cortical areas (Haxby et al., 2001), evidence from both brain imaging and neurological patients has shown that there is also a significant degree of spatial segregation in the representation of at least some

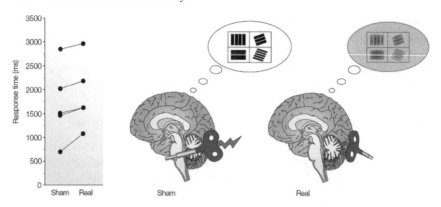

Figure 8.2. Results from the TMS study by Kosslyn et al. (1999). In the visual perception condition, participants compared attributes (e.g., the length of the stripes) of four sets of black-and-white stripes, arranged into four quadrants. As shown, the stripes varied in length, width, spacing, and orientation. The same task was used in the visual mental imagery condition, but the same participants had to visualize the patterns of stripes. Stimulation was delivered either to medial occipital cortex (real-TMS condition, panel on the right) or away from the brain (sham-TMS control condition, panel in the middle). Results (shown in the panel on the left, with a different line for data from each participant) indicated that real TMS (compared to sham TMS) slowed down responses in the visual imagery condition for all participants. Participants were also slowed down by real, but not sham, TMS in the perception condition (data not shown). This result provides support for the idea that early visual cortex is necessary to perform visual mental imagery. Reprinted with permission from Kosslyn, Ganis, and Thompson (2001, Figure 3, p. 640).

object classes (Downing, Chan, Peelen, Dodds, & Kanwisher, 2006; Kanwisher & Yovel, 2006). For example, some patches of cortex in the lateral fusiform gyrus respond more strongly to pictures of faces than to other categories of objects (Kanwisher & Yovel, 2006), and, similarly, patches of cortex in the medial fusiform and parahippocampal gyri respond more strongly to pictures of buildings than to images of other objects (Downing et al., 2006). In this section we review briefly the empirical evidence that this organization also characterizes the system used during visual mental imagery of objects.

2.2.1. *Late visual areas and visual mental imagery: Brain imaging findings*

Regardless of the ultimate reason for the spatial segregation in the ventral stream (Hasson, Harel, Levy, & Malach, 2003; Levy, Hasson, Harel, & Malach, 2004), this organization can be used to probe the similarity between the processes and representations recruited during vision and during visual mental imagery. A number of studies have employed this logic by comparing the spatial pattern of brain activation in ventrotemporal cortex during visual identification of objects and during visual mental imagery of these same objects (Ishai, Haxby, & Ungerleider, 2002; Ishai, Ungerleider, & Haxby, 2000; Mechelli, Price, Friston, & Ishai, 2004; O'Craven & Kanwisher, 2000). In the first of such studies, in independent blocks, eight participants recognized pictures of familiar faces and buildings (from the MIT campus) or they visualized them (O'Craven & Kanwisher, 2000). During the visual perception blocks, a direct comparison between stimulus conditions revealed a clear segregation in ventrotemporal cortex between activation elicited by faces and that elicited by buildings. Critically, the same analysis showed a similar pattern during visual mental imagery, but activation was much less strong than that observed during visual perception (50% weaker, on average) and encompassed much smaller regions (17% for faces, 39% for buildings). Furthermore, almost all the voxels that were active during visual mental imagery were included in the regions that were active during the corresponding visual perception condition (84% for faces, 92% for buildings). Finally, in the visual mental imagery condition, there was considerable individual variability. For instance, only four participants out of eight showed face-specific activation during imagery. Follow-up experiments with the participants who showed the strongest visual mental imagery activations investigated informally the single-trial reliability of the fMRI signals. By looking at the time course of activation in the regions that responded more to faces than to buildings (or vice versa), a blind judge was reported to be able to identify correctly whether the visualized stimulus was a face or a building on 85% of the trials, on average (three participants).

In a study by Ishai et al. (2000), nine participants were tested in visual perception and visual mental imagery conditions. During the main perception condition, participants passively viewed pictures of faces, houses, and chairs in independent blocks. During the main visual mental imagery condition, participants visualized familiar faces, houses, or chairs while looking at a gray background. A perception control condition consisted in having participants passively view scrambled versions of the pictures used during the perception condition, whereas during a visual mental imagery control condition participants passively viewed the same gray background used during the main visual mental imagery condition. After removing the respective baselines and comparing the three conditions, the researchers found a number of regions in the ventral stream that showed differential responses to pictures of faces, houses, and chairs. In these regions, 15% of the voxels showed a similar pattern during visual mental imagery. In fact, no categorical effects were seen during visual mental imagery, after averaging data over the regions that showed categorical effects during visual perception. This confirms the finding by O'Craven & Kanwisher (2000) that only relatively small subsets of voxels in regions that respond differentially during visual perception show the same pattern during visual mental imagery. Interestingly, activation during visual mental imagery (compared to the control condition) was also found in parietal and frontal regions, but no corresponding activation was observed during the perception condition.

A follow-up fMRI study by Ishai et al. (2002) compared visual perception and visual imagery of famous faces. In the perception condition, each of the nine participants was shown pictures of famous faces, whereas in the control perception condition participants were shown scrambled pictures of faces. In the visual mental imagery condition, participants saw names of famous people for 500 ms and then visualized their faces against a blank screen. Participants were trained on half the faces immediately prior to the study, whereas they relied on their preexisting long-term memories for the other half. Furthermore, for half the blocks they made a judgment on a feature of the faces (e.g., whether it had a large nose). During the control imagery condition, participants saw letter strings and passively viewed a blank screen.

As in the previous study, the results showed activation in the lateral fusiform gyrus during face imagery in a subset of voxels (about 25%) within regions that were recruited during visual perception of faces. However, activation in these regions was stronger for faces that the participants had studied just before the study. Activation in late visual cortical areas was not modulated by attention, but visual attention modulated activation in regions outside the ventral stream: the intraparietal sulcus and the inferior frontal gyrus. A more recent study reanalyzed a subset of the data from Ishai et al. (2000), with an eye toward understanding differences in the connectivity of category-specific late visual areas within a large-scale network during visual perception and visual mental imagery (Mechelli et al., 2004). The results showed that during visual perception, functional connections to late visual areas were strongest from early visual areas. Conversely, functional connections were strongest from frontal and parietal regions during visual mental imagery. This indicates that the functional role of the same late visual areas changes depending on whether the task is visual perception or visual mental imagery.

One possible explanation for the much weaker signals and smaller foci of activation during visual mental imagery than during visual perception could be that the feedback signals generated during visual mental imagery are weaker than the feedforward signals generated during visual perception. This account is consistent with the generally more diffuse organization of feedback projections (Budd, 1998), which may suggest that fewer neurons are driven by such signals. After all, introspectively, visual mental images are much "fainter" than percepts, which is probably one way that the visual system can distinguish percepts from visual images. Another possible explanation, not mutually exclusive with the first, is that some of the regions activated in ventral cortex only during the perception conditions may reflect various perceptual processes—such as feature analysis and high-level grouping of visual features—that are not engaged (at least not fully) during visual mental imagery. In addition, other regions may reflect the reactivation of long-term memories that are accessed only during visual perception.

One important question is whether the observed similarities between visual perception and visual mental imagery in late visual cortex hold at the single-neuron level. Although the noninvasive brain imaging approach cannot be used to investigate single neurons, there are a few exceptional circumstances in which other techniques can make this possible. Patients with epilepsy that does not respond to pharmacological treatment may decide to undergo surgical resection of the affected areas. In some cases, chronic electrodes are implanted in their brains to measure brain activity during seizures, which allows the surgeon to determine the location of affected areas. Between seizures, researchers can collect data from these patients in experimental paradigms. One such study compared visual perception and visual mental imagery, recording activity from 276 single neurons (from a total of nine patients) in the medial temporal lobe, including the parahippocampal cortex (Kreiman, Koch, & Fried, 2000). Results showed that a small subset of neurons responded both to visual stimuli and to visual mental imagery of the same stimuli. Furthermore, the pattern of selectivity was very similar in the two cases, which suggests that the similarities seen at the macroscopic level in these regions are also present at the single-neuron level.

2.2.2. *Late visual areas: Neuropsychological findings*

The neuroimaging data are generally consistent with data from patients with damage to late visual areas in the ventral stream (cf. Ganis, Thompson, Mast, & Kosslyn, 2003). Given that visual mental imagery of objects engages different brain regions in the ventral stream depending on the stimuli to be visualized, one would expect to find brain-damaged patients who have problems visualizing certain classes of visual stimuli but not other classes. Furthermore, because visual mental imagery and visual perception tend to engage many of the same late visual areas, patients should tend to exhibit parallels in the patterns of impairments during visual perception and visual mental imagery. In fact, patients have been described with domain-specific deficits in visual perception and with parallel deficits in visual imagery. For example, some patients are impaired at identifying faces (prosopagnosia) but not other objects—and they are also impaired at tasks involving visual imagery of faces (Shuttleworth, Syring, & Allen, 1982; Young, Humphreys, Riddoch, Hellawell, & de Haan, 1994). A single-case study reported a patient who exhibited a selective deficit in identifying animals and showed a parallel deficit when asked to describe animals or to draw them from memory (Sartori & Job, 1988). An early review of the patient literature (Farah, 1984) described 28 cases of object agnosia and reported that, in 14 cases, there was a parallel visual imagery impairment. The remaining cases were either not tested for imagery or the imagery tests were not sufficiently rigorous.

At least some of the cases in which imagery and perception are comparably impaired can be interpreted by assuming damage in brain regions that support long-term visual memories for objects and faces; such areas would be used during both visual perception and visual imagery. Given that the patterns of activation in late visual areas recruited during visual perception are much larger than those in areas recruited during visual mental imagery (and usually include them), dissociations should result from damage to these areas, especially cases with impaired visual perception but spared visual mental imagery. Indeed, some patients with visual agnosia have also been observed with relatively normal visual mental imagery (Bartolomeo et al., 1998; Behrmann, Moscovitch, & Winocur, 1994; Servos & Goodale, 1995). Although some cases can be explained with inadequate visual mental imagery testing (as seen in our discussion on early visual areas), some patients could carry out rather challenging visual mental imagery tasks (e.g., Servos & Goodale, 1995). A likely explanation is that these patients sustained damage to ventral regions that are necessary for visual perception but not for visual mental imagery. These regions may be important for grouping and other perceptual processes that are needed for identifying objects but not for visual mental imagery (Behrmann et al., 1994). Finally, there is sparse data on a few cases with normal visual perception but impaired visual mental imagery (Farah, 1984; Goldenberg, 1993). Damage to inferior frontal and intraparietal regions that modulate activation in the ventral stream during visual mental imagery (Mechelli et al., 2004) may explain some of these cases, but not enough research has been done to draw meaningful conclusions.

3. IMAGERY AND ACTION

Visual imagery is often accompanied and complemented by motor imagery. Motor imagery occurs when one imagines oneself in motion. Such motion may be complex and involve large sections of the body (such as occurs when walking, running, jumping, or playing a sport) or may involve small movements of specific body parts (such as when one simply imagines moving one's fingers or toes). Many neuroimaging studies of motor imagery have revealed that this form of imagery relies on processes that are distinct from visual mental imagery. Unlike visual imagery, motor imagery relies partially on regions of the cortex that implement motor functions. For example, in a pioneering study, Georgopoulos, Lurito, Petrides, Schwartz, and Massey (1989), using single-cell recording, found that neurons in the motor area of monkeys fired in sequence—as they did during the activity—while the animals were preparing to move their arms (before any movement had actually begun).

3.1. Motor imagery and mental transformation

One aspect of visual mental imagery that may partially rely on (or be supplemented by) motor imagery is mental transformation. Mental transformation is a process by which the shape or the position of an imagined object is changed relative to the (imagined) space that it occupies. One form of mental transformation that has been studied extensively is mental rotation, in which an object is visualized rotating on itself.

In one fMRI study, Cohen et al. (1996) asked participants to mentally rotate the classic Shepard and Metzler (1971) three-armed figures (a sample trial is shown in Figure 8.3). They were shown two shapes on a computer screen, which were not oriented in the same way, and were asked to mentally rotate the shape on the right until it was aligned with the one on the left. Participants

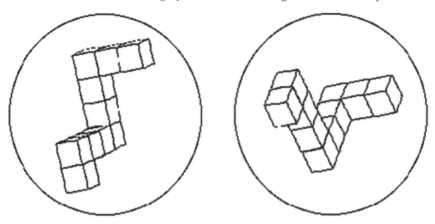

Figure 8.3. An example of a mental rotation trial using the Shepard–Metzler stimuli. Participants are asked to mentally rotate the object on the right into congruence with the object on the left and to decide whether the two objects are the same or are mirror-reversals of each other. In this example, the two figures are the same.

were then asked to judge whether the shapes were identical or mirror reversals of each other. The brain imaging data revealed that motor areas were activated during mental rotation in half the participants (whereas the posterior superior parietal regions, more traditionally associated with spatial transformations, were activated in all the participants). These data suggested that, for some participants, motor regions of the brain might have assisted in the process of mentally rotating the stimuli.

3.2. Different strategies for mental rotation

One might hypothesize from these results that there exists more than one strategy to accomplish mental rotation. It is possible, for example, that in order to mentally rotate an object, one might imagine the object rotating as if moved by an external force, or one might imagine physically rotating the object oneself. In order to test this hypothesis, Kosslyn, Thompson, Wraga, and Alpert (2001) asked participants to perform the Shepard–Metzler mental rotation task (also used by Cohen et al., 1996, described above). However, before performing the task, participants received two different types of instructions. In one condition (external action), participants were asked, as they were mentally rotating the objects, to imagine that the objects were being moved by a motor, whereas in the other condition (internal action), they were asked to imagine that they themselves were physically manipulating the objects to make them rotate. To reinforce these instructions, the two groups received different training prior to the task. Immediately before the external-action condition, the participants viewed a physical model of a Shepard–Metzler figure attached to a motor, and they watched the motor physically rotate the object in different directions. Conversely, before performing the internal-action condition, participants were given a scale model of a figure to hold and manipulate, turning it themselves along different axes of rotation.

The data revealed that the primary motor cortex was activated during the internal-action condition, but not during the external-action condition (although both conditions activated the posterior parietal regions and secondary motor areas). This finding suggests that more than one strategy exists to perform mental rotation, and that mental rotation—which is typically thought of as an aspect of visual imagery—may be aided by motor processes. These results also indicate that each strategy may be adopted voluntarily; the participants were not divided according to their abilities or cognitive styles but, rather, were trained explicitly on a specific strategy before performing the task.

3.2.1. *Implicit adoption of mental rotation strategies*

The results from the study just summarized leave open the question of whether motor-based image transformations may occur spontaneously, or may be adopted without conscious effort. Wraga, Thompson, Kosslyn, and Alpert (2003) designed a study to address this question. Participants were divided into two groups. One group first performed a task where they were asked to mentally rotate drawings of human hands. As in the Shepard–Metzler task, this task involves presenting two drawings—in this case, of hands—side by side; the hands were not presented in the same orientation, and participants were required to rotate one hand into alignment with the other to compare them. The participants were asked to mentally rotate the hand on the right side of the computer display until it had the same orientation as the hand on the left side of the display. They were instructed then to compare the hands and decide whether the two hands were the same (i.e., both left hands or both right hands) or different (one left hand and one right hand). This task had previously been shown to activate motor areas, including the primary motor cortex (Kosslyn, DiGirolamo, Thompson, & Alpert, 1998).

For participants in this hand-rotation group, the hand-rotation task was immediately followed by a mental rotation task with Shepard–Metzler objects, as previously described. Participants in the second group first performed mental rotation with the Shepard–Metzler objects (rather than with drawings of hands) and then repeated that task with another set of Shepard–Metzler objects. Thus, for both groups, the second task required mental rotation of Shepard–Metzler figures. Wraga et al. (2003) hypothesized that for the group that began by mentally rotating drawings of hands, the motor processes involved in that task would implicitly transfer to the Shepard–Metzler rotation task that followed. For the other group, however, there should be no such transfer. Thus, when the second tasks performed by each group (the Shepard–Metzler object-rotation task in both cases) are compared, evidence for motor activations should be present in the group who previously performed mental rotation of hands, but not in the group who previously performed mental rotation of Shepard–Metzler objects.

In fact, when the brain activation maps were examined, this is what was found. The primary-motor area (in addition to the premotor area) was activated in the Shepard–Metzler condition that was preceded by hand rotation, but not in the Shepard–Metzler condition that was preceded by an identical (except for the specific stimulus set) Shepard–Metzler condition (see Figure 8.4). The participants received no specific instruction to use any particular strategy to accomplish the mental rotation. This result demonstrates that not only can different strategies be

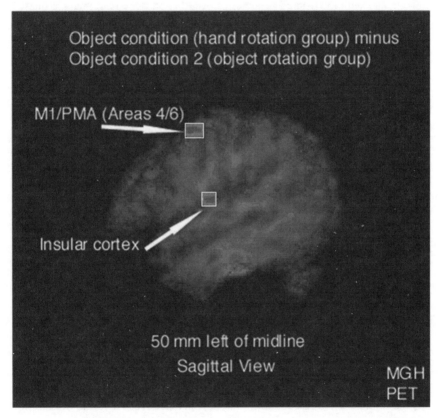

Figure 8.4. An image from the Wraga et al. (2003) PET scanning study. Motor activation in the object-rotation condition following hand rotation can clearly be seen on this sagittal slice 50 mm left of the midline of the brain. Because activation in the object-rotation condition following object rotation has been subtracted out, what remains are those areas that are activated to a greater degree following hand rotation. An average MRI image (Montreal Neurological Institute template) has been fused to the PET data, for better visualization and localization of corresponding brain structures. Figure reprinted from Wraga et al. (2003), copyright 2003, with permission of Elsevier.

employed to reach the same goal, but also that these strategies may be adopted through implicit transfer, without conscious effort by the individual.

3.2.2. *Self- versus object rotations*

The act of rotating an object in space may be considered an egocentric rotation—that is, an object's position is perceived relative to the observer's body, and, as the object rotates, its position changes relative to such egocentric coordinates. In such instances, the external object is always rotated while the position of the observer (self) remains stationary. This is one strategy for visualizing an object from a different perspective—one may imagine the object rotating until it is aligned with the desired perspective. Another strategy is to imagine oneself in a different position relative to the object in question. In such object-centered rotations, one imagines one's body displaced from its original position, now observing the object from a new vantage point (for additional discussion of these issues as they relate to spatial reasoning and navigation, see chapter 6).

In order to investigate whether different mechanisms are used in these two types of mental rotations (object- versus self-rotations), Wraga, Shephard, Church, Inati, and Kosslyn (2005) designed a study in which participants, in separate conditions, were asked either to mentally rotate an object in order to view it from a different perspective or to mentally change their own position in order to view the object from the new perspective. In both the object- and self-rotation conditions, the stimuli consisted of Shepard–Metzler figures depicted inside a sphere. The figures were composed of a series of cubes. Each figure featured one cube that had a different texture than the others. For the object-rotation task, one end-cube of the figure was marked with a T-shaped prompt. Another T-shaped prompt was placed on the periphery of the sphere (see Figure 8.5, panel A). The task consisted of first mentally rotating the entire figure so that the T-prompt on the figure lined up with the T-prompt outside the sphere, and then deciding whether the textured cube would still be visible after the rotation. Note that in this case, the position of the observer does not change.

For the self-rotation task, the stimuli were identical, except that there was no T-prompt placed on the figure itself. Instead, participants were asked to imagine that they were moving around the sphere until their body was aligned with the T, as if looking at the object through the T's horizontal bar (See Figure 8.5, panel B). Participants were then asked to decide whether or not they would be able to see the figure's textured cube from that new perspective. The order of presentation of the conditions was counterbalanced across participants. (There were also control conditions where the participants decided whether the textured cube was visible—no rotation was required in these conditions.)

The brain imaging data revealed that motor areas (including left premotor area, PMA, and extending into Area M1) were more activated in the object-rotation task than in the self-rotation task. Posterior parietal regions, including Areas 7 and 40, the dorsolateral prefrontal cortex (DLFPC), and visual association Areas 18 and 19 were also more activated in the object-rotation than in the

A

B

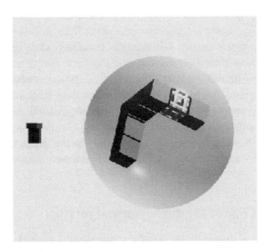

Figure 8.5. Stimuli used in the Wraga et al. (2005) study: A. Object-rotation task: Participants mentally rotate the figure to align the T-prompt on the end-cube with the similar prompt on the periphery of the sphere. They then decide whether the differently textured cube would be visible once the figure has been rotated to its new alignment. In this example, the correct response would be "yes". B. Self-rotation task: Participants mentally rotate themselves to the position of the T-prompt outside the sphere. They then decide whether the differently textured cube would be visible from their new vantage point. In this example, the correct response would be "no". Figure reprinted from Wraga et al. (2005), copyright 2005, with permission of Elsevier.

self-rotation task. The reverse contrast, of self-rotation minus object-rotation, revealed a very different pattern of activation, which did not include Area M1; rather, activation was discovered in the following regions, among others: left supplementary motor area (SMA), the junction of the left middle occipital gyrus and the fusiform gyrus (Area 37), and the right middle temporal gyrus (Area 21). Compared to the control task, the object-rotation task evoked activation in early motor areas (including a swath that extended to M1), whereas the self-rotation condition engendered activation in pre-SMA. The superior parietal lobule, previously demonstrated to be an important site of spatial processing, was activated in both self- and object-rotation conditions, compared to the no-rotation control.

At first glance, these results may seem puzzling: One might intuitively expect that imagining oneself rotating around a sphere would evoke activation in low-level primary-motor areas, whereas imagining the rotation of an object may not. In fact, as we have seen before, people may adopt different strategies to accomplish mental rotation: Even in the object-rotation condition, the participants may have adopted a motor-based strategy. Evidence for this interpretation can be seen in the fact that it was the left early motor areas that were activated, near the region of the motor strip that controls the right hand: All of the participants were strongly right-handed. And regarding the absence of activation of lower-level motor areas in the self-rotation condition, it appears that imagining oneself rotating around a sphere does not necessarily require imagining movement of one's own muscles. Indeed, the behavioral data from this study indicated that participants were faster in the self-rotation condition than in the object-rotation condition. These data also showed that the participants were most efficient at performing self-rotations at an orientation of 100 degrees, which is nearly parallel to one axis of the human body, whereas they were less efficient at 65 and 135 degrees, orientations that are not aligned with the body. This finding suggests that for rotations of the self, it is not always necessary to pass through intermediate points when moving from the origin to the destination—which may partly explain why no low-level motor activations were found in the self-rotation condition.

3.3. Functional role of M1 during mental rotation

Is the activation of motor areas of the brain during mental rotation causally related to performance? Ganis, Keenan, Kosslyn, and Pascual-Leone (2000) examined the performance of participants who were asked to mentally rotate line drawings of human hands and feet. Single-pulse TMS was applied to left M1. In addition to addressing the question of whether early motor areas play a functional role in mental rotation of body parts, the investigators were also interested in when primary-motor areas play their role in this process. Single-pulse TMS was thus delivered at two different time intervals (400 ms and 650 ms after stimulus onset). To control for the fact that TMS to the primary motor cortex causes an overt hand movement (which could affect mental rotation processing), the study included a control condition where peripheral nerve magnetic stimulation (PNMS) was delivered to the right flexor carpi radialis, also eliciting such a movement. The independent variables were response times and error rates.

Ganis et al. (2000) hypothesized that if M1 plays a functional role in mental rotation, participants should be less efficient (i.e., should have longer response times and/or higher error rates) when TMS was delivered to M1 (compared to when PNMS was delivered to the carpi radialis). The results were in line with this prediction: More time was required and more errors were made when TMS disrupted M1. In addition, the results tested the specificity of the effect, in that the part of M1 targeted by the TMS coil was the "hand area," responsible for hand movements. If motor involvement in mental rotation of body parts is mediated by mapping the movement onto one's own body, then mental rotation of hands should have been disrupted to a greater degree than mental rotation of feet. This was shown to be the case: Participants made more errors in the hand-rotation condition than in the foot-rotation condition when TMS was applied to the hand area of M1. Finally, the results demonstrated that M1 involvement occurs at around 650 ms into the processing period. Participants' performance was disrupted to a greater degree when TMS was applied 650 ms (versus 400 ms) following stimulus onset, which suggests that motor involvement begins after initial visual encoding of the stimuli and their spatial relations has taken place in occipital and parietal regions (a summary of these results is presented in Figure 8.6).

However, although TMS caused a general slowdown in performing the mental rotation tasks, the actual rate of rotation was unaffected (TMS affected the intercepts rather than the slopes). It is likely that the effects of TMS were not long-lasting enough to affect the entire process of rotation, and thus TMS may have affected primarily an interface between visual and motor processes just prior to actual rotation (i.e., the preparatory phase preceding rotation per se). (For a discussion of the different phases of mental rotation and their influences on slope and intercept, see Wright, Thompson, Ganis, Newcombe, & Kosslyn, 2008.) Finally, it is important to note that although this study provides evidence for the functional role of M1 in a mental rotation task, the results do not show that processing related to mental rotation takes place in motor cortex—the actual computation may be implemented in other brain regions, and the motor cortex may simply transmit such data between sites, acting as a relay station. These results regarding the involvement of M1 in the mental rotation of hands have been replicated and extended using comparable stimuli and procedures (Tomasino, Borroni, Isaja, & Rumiati, 2005).

3.4. Applications of motor imagery and mental practice

The previous set of results demonstrates that the motor system is engaged by, and plays a functional role in accomplishing, mental rotation. This suggests that mental practice—which consists of visualizing oneself performing an action (such as a sport, or a skilled motor movement)—may actually help to perfect one's abilities when *actually* performing those activities (for addi-

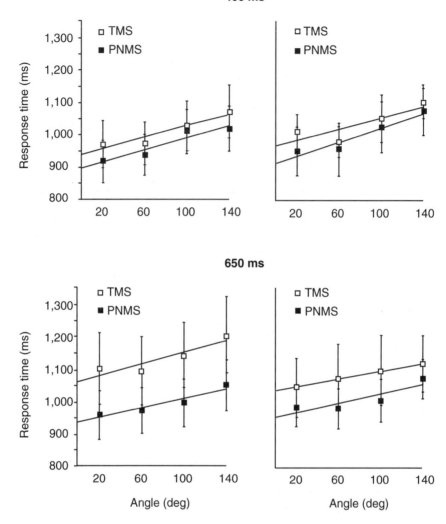

Figure 8.6. Average response times from the Ganis et al. (2000) study, plotted by degree of rotation necessary to make the comparison between left and right images. TMS applied to the primary-motor "hand" area (open squares) disrupted processing more than did PNMS (filled squares). The effect was stronger with hand rotation (left panels) than with foot rotation (right panels) and stronger at 650 ms than at 400 ms following stimulus onset. This result demonstrates that: (1) Area M1 (primary motor cortex) is functionally involved in the mental rotation of hands; (2) the effect is specific, given that hand rotation was disrupted more than foot rotation; and (3) motor involvement probably occurs later in processing, after initial occipital (visual) and parietal (spatial) areas have been recruited. Note that the rotation slopes themselves are unaffected. Figure reprinted with permission from Ganis et al. (2000, Figure 2, p. 177).

tional discussion of how memory is involved in such natural tasks, see chapter 5). In fact, there is evidence for just such mental-practice effects (e.g., Denis, 1985; Driskell, Copper, & Moran, 1994; Feltz & Landers, 1983; MacIntyre, Moran, & Jennings, 2002). Mental rotation, in this sense, may be thought of as part of a broader category of mental transformations, where objects, including parts of the body, are not only rotated in space, but also shifted in location in various ways (relative to their original positions or to other nearby objects). If mental practice exercises the relevant brain regions, and solidifies associations between mental processes and true motor movements, then mental practice may be an invaluable tool for improving one's skills when extensive physical practice is not possible (if one wants to improve one's skiing ability through practice, for example, it helps be located near a snowy mountain—in the absence of which, mental practice may provide a useful substitute between intervals of actual physical practice). In addition to findings that mental practice may improve motor performance (e.g., Denis, 1985; Driskell et al., 1994; Feltz & Landers, 1983), MacIntyre et al. (2002), for example, have shown that mental rotation ability, as measured by standard tests, correlates positively with performance in canoe-slalom racing.

Another potential application of motor imagery is in the rehabilitation of patients who have lost motor abilities, following a stroke, for example. Page, Levine, Sisto, and Johnston (2001) compared two groups of stroke patients. Both groups received physical therapy three times per week. The experimental group also received motor-imagery training after each therapy session, as well as instructions to practice imagery at home. The control group did not receive any imagery training or practice but was simply given information about stroke. At the end of the six-week therapy period, the experimental group had improved significantly more than the control group, as measured by standard recovery tests. The investigators concluded that motor imagery and mental practice may be an effective, low-cost addition to a more comprehensive therapy regimen after stroke.

Other researchers have focused on the specific circumstances under which mental practice may be most effective in speeding the recovery of stroke patients. Malouin , Belleville, Richards, Desrosiers, and Doyon (2004) found that mental practice is most effective with patients who have stronger working memory capacity, particularly in the visuospatial domain. Given the potential therapeutic value of motor imagery, some researchers have focused on techniques for enhancing the capacity of this form of imagery to improve the lives of patients. For example, Morganti et al. (2003) proposed that virtual-reality depictions of motor movements with increasing realism may guide patients in their use of motor imagery until the patient is able to perform the motor movements him/herself. Promising new clinical research and treatments using motor imagery have often been inspired by, and have built upon, earlier research that first demonstrated the common neural substrates underlying mental imagery for motor movements and the actual execution of those movements. Many scientists now seek to understand the mechanisms that lead to such improvement (e.g., Butler & Page, 2006).

4. CONCLUSIONS

The study of mental imagery has benefited enormously from three prior developments. First, research on the nature of perceptual and motor systems has not only made explicit the functional characteristics of those systems, but also revealed key facts about the underlying neural mechanisms. Thus, theories of imagery could be built upon such prior knowledge. Second, new methods—both behavioral and neural—allowed researchers to avoid relying on introspection when studying imagery. These new methods put to rest, once and for all, the central concerns of the behaviorists: Imagery can be studied objectively, like any other object of study in science. The fact that mental images are not directly observable by all is no different from the fact that electrons are not directly observable by all; in both cases, the objects of study have consequences that can be objectively assessed. Third, the advent of artificial intelligence, and computer science more generally, has provided new conceptual tools. These constructs allowed researchers to begin to characterize imagery—and mental representations in general—rigorously. And the emerging theories that relied on such concepts were sufficiently clear that they could not only be mapped into the brain, but could also be tested. Thus, the three sorts of developments have come together in happy synergy.

Nevertheless, we clearly are only in the early stages of understanding mental imagery. As this brief review has made clear, there are many unanswered questions and many open issues. We have suggested accounts for several conundrums, but our suggestions cannot be considered as more than that; these speculations need to be tested directly. And we will not be surprised if some of these tests produce unexpected results, taking researchers in new directions. But the present findings and theories provide a springboard for further investigations, and the existing data will need to be explained by all future theories. Given the enormous progress made in a very brief period (when viewed through the lens of the history of science), we have every reason to be encouraged and to believe that effort spent in studying imagery will be an investment worth making.

5. REFERENCES

Anderson, J. R. (1978). Arguments concerning representations for mental imagery. *Psychological Review, 85*, 249–277.

Barbay, S., Plautz, E. J., Friel, K. M., Frost, S. B., Dancause, N., Stowe, A. M., et al. (2006). Behavioral and neurophysiological effects of delayed training following a small ischemic infarct in primary motor cortex of squirrel monkeys. *Experimental Brain Research, 169*, 106–116.

Barone, P., Batardiere, A., Knoblauch, K., & Kennedy, H. (2000). Laminar distribution of neurons in extrastriate areas projecting to visual areas V1 and V4 correlates with the hierarchical rank and indicates the operation of a distance rule. *Journal of Neuroscience, 20*, 3263–3281.

Bartolomeo, P. (2002). The relationship between visual perception and visual mental imagery: A reappraisal of the neuropsychological evidence. *Cortex, 38*, 357–378.

Bartolomeo, P., Bachoud-Levi, A. C., De Gelder, B., Denes, G., Dalla Barba, G., Brugieres, P., et al. (1998). Multiple-domain dissociation between impaired visual perception and preserved mental imagery in a patient with bilateral extrastriate lesions. *Neuropsychologia, 36*, 239–249.

Behrmann, M., Moscovitch, M., & Winocur, G. (1994). Intact visual imagery and impaired visual perception in a patient with visual agnosia. *Journal of Experimental Psychology: Human Perception and Performance, 20*, 1068–1087.

Blajenkova, O., Kozhevnikov, M., & Motes, M. A. (2006). Object and spatial imagery: Distinctions between members of different professions. *Cognitive Processing, 7*(Suppl. 1), 20–21.

Budd, J. M. (1998). Extrastriate feedback to primary visual cortex in primates: A quantitative analysis of connectivity. *Proceedings. Biological Sciences, 265*, 1037–1044.

Butler, A. J., & Page, S. J. (2006). Mental practice with motor imagery: Evidence for motor recovery and cortical reorganization after stroke. *Archives of Physical Medicine and Rehabilitation, 87*(Suppl. 2), S2–S11.

Butter, C. M., Kosslyn, S. M., Mijovic-Prelec, D., & Riffle, A. (1997). Field-specific deficits in visual imagery following hemianopia due to unilateral occipital infarcts. *Brain and Cognition, 120*, 217–228.

Chatterjee, A., & Southwood, M. H. (1995). Cortical blindness and visual imagery. *Neurology, 45*, 2189–2195.

Chiang, T. C., Walsh, V., & Lavidor, M. (2004). The cortical representation of foveal stimuli: Evidence from quadrantanopia and TMS-induced suppression. *Brain Research. Cognitive Brain Research, 21*, 309–316.

Cohen, M. S., Kosslyn, S. M., Breiter, H. C., DiGirolamo, G., Thompson, W. L., Anderson, A. K., et al. (1996). Changes in cortical activity during mental rotation: A mapping study using functional MRI. *Brain, 119*, 89–100.

Dancause, N., Barbay, S., Frost, S. B., Plautz, E. J., Chen, D., Zoubina, E. V., et al. (2005). Extensive cortical rewiring after brain injury. *Journal of Neuroscience, 25*, 10167–10179.

Denis, M. (1985). Visual imagery and the use of mental practice in the development of motor skills. *Canadian Journal of Applied Sport Sciences, 10*, 4S–16S.

Desimone, R., & Ungerleider, L. G. (1989). Neural mechanisms of visual processing in monkeys. In F. Boller & J. Grafman (Eds.), *Handbook of neuropsychology* (pp. 267–299). Amsterdam: Elsevier.

Downing, P. E., Chan, A. W., Peelen, M. V., Dodds, C. M., & Kanwisher, N. (2006). Domain specificity in visual cortex. *Cerebral Cortex, 16*, 1453–1461.

Driskell, J. E., Copper, C., & Moran, A. (1994). Does mental practice enhance performance? *Journal of Applied Psychology, 79*, 481–492.

Farah, M. J. (1984). The neurological basis of mental imagery: A componential analysis. *Cognition, 18*, 245–272.

Farah, M. J., Soso, M. J., & Dasheiff, R. M. (1992). Visual angle of the mind's eye before and after unilateral occipital lobectomy. *Journal of Experimental Psychology: Human Perception and Performance, 18*, 241–246.

Felleman, D. J., & Van Essen, D. C. (1991). Distributed hierarchical processing in the primate cerebral cortex. *Cerebral Cortex, 1*, 1–47.

Feltz, D., & Landers, D. (1983). The effects of mental practice on motor skill learning and performance: An article. *Journal of Sports Psychology, 5*, 25–57.

Finke, R. A., Pinker, S., & Farah, M. J. (1989). Reinterpreting visual patterns in mental imagery. *Cognitive Science, 13*, 62–78.

Fox, P. T., Mintun, M. A., Raichle, M. E., Miezin, F. M., Allman, J. M., & Van Essen, D. C. (1986). Mapping human visual cortex with positron emission tomography. *Nature, 323*, 806–809.

Fujita, I., Tanaka, K., Ito, M., & Cheng, K. (1992). Columns for visual features of objects in monkey inferotemporal cortex. *Nature, 360*, 343–346.

Ganis, G., Keenan, J. P., Kosslyn, S. M., & Pascual-Leone, A. (2000). Transcranial magnetic stimulation of primary motor cortex affects mental rotation. *Cerebral Cortex, 10*, 175–180.

Ganis, G., Thompson, W. L., & Kosslyn, S. M. (2004). Brain areas underlying visual mental imagery and visual perception: An fMRI study. *Brain Research. Cognitive Brain Research, 20*, 226–241.

Ganis, G., Thompson, W. L., & Kosslyn, S. M. (2005). Understanding the effects of task-specific practice in the brain: Insights from individual-differences analyses. *Cognitive, Affective & Behavioral Neuroscience, 5*, 235–245.

Ganis, G., Thompson, W. L., Mast, F. W., & Kosslyn, S. M. (2003). Visual imagery in cerebral visual dysfunction. *Neurologic Clinics, 21*), 631–646.

Georgopoulos, A. P., Lurito, J. T., Petrides, M., Schwartz, A. B., & Massey, J. T. (1989). Mental rotation of the neuronal population vector. *Science, 243*, 234–236.

Goldenberg, G. (1993). The neural basis of mental imagery. *Baillières Clinical Neurology, 2*, 265–286.

Goldenberg, G., Müllbacher, W., & Nowak, A. (1995). Imagery without perception—a case study of anosognosia for cortical blindness. *Neuropsychologia, 33*, 1373–1382.

Goodale, M. A., Westwood, D. A., & Milner, A. D. (2004). Two distinct modes of control for object-directed action. *Progress in Brain Research, 144*, 131–144.

Hasson, U., Harel, M., Levy, I., & Malach, R. (2003). Large-scale mirror-symmetry organization of human occipito-temporal object areas. *Neuron, 37*, 1027–1041.

Haxby, J. V., Gobbini, M. I., Furey, M. L., Ishai, A., Schouten, J. L., & Pietrini, P. (2001). Distributed and overlapping representations of faces and objects in ventral temporal cortex. *Science, 293*, 2425–2430.

Haxby, J. V., Grady, C. L., Horwitz, B., Ungerleider, L. G., Mishkin, M., Carson, R. E., et al. (1991). Dissociation of object and spatial visual processing pathways in human extrastriate cortex. *Proceedings of the National Academy of Sciences, U.S.A., 88*, 1621–1625.

Heeger, D. J. (1999). Linking visual perception with human brain activity. *Current Opinion in Neurobiology, 9*, 474–479.

Humphrey, G. (1951). *Thinking: An introduction to its experimental psychology*. London: Methuen.

Ishai, A., Haxby, J. V., & Ungerleider, L. G. (2002). Visual imagery of famous faces: Effects of memory and attention revealed by fMRI. *NeuroImage, 17*, 1729–1741.

Ishai, A., Ungerleider, L. G., & Haxby, J. V. (2000). Distributed neural systems for the generation of visual images. *Neuron, 28*, 979–990.

James, K. H., & Gauthier, I. (2006). Letter processing automatically recruits a sensory-motor brain network. *Neuropsychologia, 44*, 2937–2949.

Kammer, T., Puls, K., Erb, M., & Grodd, W. (2005a). Transcranial magnetic stimulation in the visual system. II. Characterization of induced phosphenes and scotomas. *Experimental Brain Research, 160*, 129–140.

Kammer, T., Puls, K., Strasburger, H., Hill, N. J., & Wichmann, F. A. (2005b). Transcranial magnetic stimulation in the visual system. I. The psychophysics of visual suppression. *Experimental Brain Research, 160*, 118–128.

Kanwisher, N., & Yovel, G. (2006). The fusiform face area: A cortical region specialized for the perception of faces. *Philosophical Transactions of the Royal Society London. Series B, Biological Sciences, 361*, 2109–2128.

Kessel, K. S. (1972). Imagery: A dimension of mind rediscovered. *British Journal of Psychology, 63*, 149–162.

Klein, I., Dubois, J., Mangin, J. F., Kherif, F., Flandin, G., Poline, J. B., et al. (2004). Retinotopic organization of visual mental images as revealed by functional magnetic resonance imaging. *Brain Research. Cognitive Brain Research, 22*, 26–31.

Kosslyn, S. M. (1980). *Image and mind*. Cambridge, MA: Harvard University Press.

Kosslyn, S. M. (1994). *Image and brain*. Cambridge, MA: Harvard University Press.

Kosslyn, S. M., Alpert, N. M., Thompson, W. L., Maljkovic, V., Weise, S. B., Chabris, et al. (1993). Visual mental imagery activates topographically organized visual cortex: PET investigations. *Journal of Cognitive Neuroscience, 5*, 263–287.

Kosslyn, S. M., DiGirolamo, G., Thompson, W. L., & Alpert, N. M. (1998). Mental rotation of objects versus hands: Neural mechanisms revealed by positron emission tomography. *Psychophysiology, 35*, 151–161.

Kosslyn, S. M., Ganis, G., & Thompson, W. L. (2001). Neural foundations of imagery. *Nature Reviews Neuroscience, 2*, 635–642.

Kosslyn, S. M., Pascual-Leone, A., Felician, O., Camposano, S., Keenan, J. P., Thompson, W. L., et al. (1999). The role of Area 17 in visual imagery: Convergent evidence from PET and rTMS. *Science, 284*, 167–170.

Kosslyn, S. M., & Thompson, W. L. (2003). When is early visual cortex activated during visual mental imagery? *Psychological Bulletin, 129*, 723–746.

Kosslyn, S. M., Thompson, W. L., & Ganis, G. (2006). *The case for mental imagery*. New York: Oxford University Press.

Kosslyn, S. M., Thompson, W. L., Kim, I. J., & Alpert, N. M. (1995). Topographical representations of mental images in primary visual cortex. *Nature, 378*, 496–498.

Kosslyn, S. M., Thompson, W. L., Kim, I. J., Rauch, S. L., & Alpert, N. M. (1996). Individual differences in cerebral blood flow in Area 17 predict the time to evaluate visualized letters. *Journal of Cognitive Neuroscience, 8*, 78–82.

Kosslyn, S. M., Thompson, W. L., Wraga, M., & Alpert, N. M. (2001). Imagining rotation by endogenous versus exogenous forces: Distinct neural mechanisms. *NeuroReport, 12*, 2519–2525.

Kreiman, G., Koch, C., & Fried, I. (2000). Imagery neurons in the human brain. *Nature, 408*, 357–361.

Larson, C., & Sullivan, J. (1965). Watson's relation to Titchener. *Journal of the History of the Behavioral Sciences, 1*, 338–354.

Levy, I., Hasson, U., Harel, M., & Malach, R. (2004). Functional analysis of the periphery effect in human building related areas. *Human Brain Mapping, 22*, 15–26.

MacIntyre, T., Moran, A., & Jennings, D. J. (2002). Are mental imagery abilities related to canoe-slalom performance? *Perceptual and Motor Skills, 94*, 1245–1250.

Malouin, F., Belleville, S., Richards, C. L., Desrosiers, J., & Doyon, J. (2004). Working memory and mental practice outcomes after stroke. *Archives of Physical Medicine and Rehabilitation, 85*, 177–183.

McMahon, C. E. (1973). Images as motives and motivators: A historical perspective. *American Journal of Psychology, 86*, 465–490.

Mechelli, A., Price, C. J., Friston, K. J., & Ishai, A. (2004). Where bottom-up meets top-down: Neuronal interactions during perception and imagery. *Cerebral Cortex, 14,* 1256–1265.

Mishkin, M., Ungerleider, L. G., & Macko, K. A. (1983). Object vision and spatial vision: Two cortical pathways. *Trends in Neurosciences, 6,* 414–417.

Miyashita, Y., & Chang, H. S. (1988). Neuronal correlate of pictorial short-term memory in the primate temporal cortex. *Nature, 331,* 68–70.

Morganti, F., Gaggioli, A., Castelnuovo, G., Bulla, D., Vettorello, M., & Riva, G. (2003). The use of technology-supported mental imagery in neurological rehabilitation: A research protocol. *Cyberpsychology & Behavior, 6,* 421–427.

Muellbacher, W., Ziemann, U., Boroojerdi, B., & Hallett, M. (2000). Effects of low-frequency transcranial magnetic stimulation on motor excitability and basic motor behavior. *Clinical Neurophysiology, 111,* 1002–1007.

O'Craven, K. M., & Kanwisher, N. (2000). Mental imagery of faces and places activates corresponding stimulus-specific brain regions. *Journal of Cognitive Neuroscience, 12,* 1013–1023.

Page, S. J., Levine, P., Sisto, S. A., & Johnston, M. V. (2001). Mental practice combined with physical practice for upper-limb motor deficit in subacute stroke. *Physical Therapy, 81,* 1455–1462.

Paivio, A. (1971). *Imagery and verbal processes.* New York: Holt, Rinehart & Winston.

Pylyshyn, Z. W. (1973) What the mind's eye tells the mind's brain: A critique of mental imagery. *Psychological Bulletin, 80,* 1–24.

Pylyshyn, Z. W. (2002). Mental imagery: In search of a theory. *Behavioral and Brain Sciences, 25,* 157–238.

Rensink, R. A. (2002). Change detection. *Annual Review of Psychology, 53,* 245–277.

Rockland, K. S., & Pandya, D. N. (1979). Laminar origins and terminations of cortical connections of the occipital lobe in the rhesus monkey. *Brain Research, 179,* 3–20.

Salin, P. A., & Bullier, J. (1995). Corticocortical connections in the visual system: Structure and function. *Physiological Reviews, 75,* 107–154.

Sartori, G., & Job, R. (1988). The oyster with four legs: A neuropsychological study on the interaction of visual and semantic information. *Cognitive Neuropsychology, 5,* 105–132.

Sereno, M. I., Dale, A. M., Reppas, J. B., Kwong, K. K., Belliveau, J. W., Brady, T. J., et al. (1995). Borders of multiple visual areas in humans revealed by functional magnetic resonance imaging. *Science, 268,* 889–893.

Sereno, M. I., Pitzalis, S., & Martinez, A. (2001). Mapping of contralateral space in retinotopic coordinates by a parietal cortical area in humans. *Science, 294,* 1350–1354.

Sereno, M. I., & Tootell, R. B. H. (2005). From monkeys to humans: What do we now know about brain homologies? *Current Opinion in Neurobiology, 15,* 135–144.

Servos, P., & Goodale, M. A. (1995). Preserved visual imagery in visual form agnosia. *Neuropsychologia, 33,* 1383–1394.

Shepard, R. N., & Cooper, L. A. (1982). *Mental images and their transformations.* Cambridge, MA: MIT Press.

Shepard, R. N., & Metzler, J. (1971). Mental rotation of three-dimensional objects. *Science, 171,* 701–703.

Shuttleworth, E. C., Jr., Syring, V., & Allen, N. (1982). Further observations on the nature of prosopagnosia. *Brain and Cognition, 1,* 307–322.

Siebner, H. R., Peller, M., Willoch, F., Minoshima, S., Boecker, H., Auer, C., et al. (2000). Lasting cortical activation after repetitive TMS of the motor cortex: A glucose metabolic study. *Neurology, 54,* 956–963.

Slotnick, S. D., Thompson, W. L., & Kosslyn, S. M. (2005). Visual mental imagery induces retinotopically organized activation of early visual areas. *Cerebral Cortex, 15,* 1570–1583.

Tanaka, K. (1996). Inferotemporal cortex and object vision. *Annual Review of Neuroscience, 19,* 109–139.

Tanaka, K., Saito, H., Fukada, Y., & Moriya, M. (1991). Coding visual images of objects in the inferotemporal cortex of the macaque monkey. *Journal of Neurophysiology, 66,* 170–189.

Thirion, B., Duchesnay, E., Hubbard, E., Dubois, J., Poline, J. B., Le Bihan, D., et al. (2006). Inverse retinotopy: Inferring the visual content of images from brain activation patterns. *NeuroImage, 33,* 1104–1116.

Tomasino, B., Borroni, P., Isaja, A., & Rumiati, R. I. (2005). The role of the primary motor cortex in mental rotation: A TMS study. *Cognitive Neuropsychology, 22,* 348–363.

Tootell, R. B. H., Hadjikani, N. K., Mendola, J. D., Marrett, S., & Dale, A. M. (1998a). From retinotopy to recognition: fMRI in human visual cortex. *Trends in Cognitive Science, 2,* 174–183.

Tootell, R. B. H., Hadjikhani, N. K., Vanduffel, W., Liu, A. K., Mendola, J. D., Sereno, M. I., et al. (1998b). Functional analysis of primary visual cortex (V1) in humans. *Proceedings of the National Academy of Sciences, U.S.A., 95,* 811–817.

Ungerleider, L. G., & Mishkin, M. (1982). Two cortical visual systems. In D. J. Ingle, M. A. Goodale, & R. J. W. Mansfield (Eds.), *Analysis of visual behavior* (pp. 549–586). Cambridge, MA: MIT Press.

Van Essen, D. C., Lewis, J. W., Drury, H. A., Hadjikhani, N., Tootell, R. B., Bakircioglu, M., et al. (2001). Mapping visual cortex in monkeys and humans using surface-based atlases. *Vision Research, 41,* 1359–1378.

Wandell, B. A. (1999). Computational neuroimaging of human visual cortex. *Annual Review of Neuroscience, 22,* 145–173.

Watson, J. (1913). Psychology as the behaviorist views it. *Psychological Review, 20,* 158–177.

Wraga, M., Shephard, J. M., Church, J. A., Inati, S., & Kosslyn, S. M. (2005). Imagined rotations of self versus objects: An fMRI study. *Neuropsychologia, 43,* 1351–1361.

Wraga, M., Thompson, W. L., Alpert, N. M., & Kosslyn, S. M. (2003). Implicit transfer of motor strategies in mental rotation. *Brain and Cognition, 52,* 135–143.

Wright, R., Thompson, W. L., Ganis, G., Newcombe, N. S., & Kosslyn, S. M. (2008). Training generalized spatial skills. *Psychonomic Bulletin & Review, 15,* 763–771.

Young, A. W., Humphreys, G. W., Riddoch, M. J., Hellawell, D. J., & de Haan, E. H. (1994). Recognition impairments and face imagery. *Neuropsychologia, 32,* 693–702.

Author index

Subject index

abstraction, 100
AFC task: *see* alternative forced-choice
    task
affect-as-information mechanism, 193–194
affect-infusion model, 194–195
affect priming, 193–194
agnosia, 76
    landmark, 157
    object, 233
    visual, 233
allocentric reference frame, 145–177
alternative forced-choice (AFC) task,
    94–96, 98–99, 107–108
amnesia, topographical, 8
amygdala, 182, 186, 188, 190–191
angioplasty, 9
anti-caricature, 82
articulatory suppression, 3, 6, 16–19
artificial intelligence, 244
associative memory, 12, 15, 22
    long-term, 11, 13
attention:
    selective, 46, 78, 179–180, 191–192, 195
    spatial, 50
    visual, 22, 24, 34, 38, 41, 52, 56, 94, 180,
        223–224, 232
attentional capture, 55, 190–191
attentional guidance, 53–54
    by contents in visual working memory,
        56
auditory information, visual capture of, 142
auditory localization, 142
automatic processing vs. controlled
    processing, 184–185

backward masking, 90
behavioral neuroscience, 48
behavioral responses, automatic activation
    of, 185–189

behaviorism, 216
beliefs and expectations, effect of on event
    encoding, 179–189
Biased Competition Model, 56
blindfolded walking, 152–153
blindness, 77, 122, 154, 158, 221, 227, 231
    change, 91, 97–98, 101, 123, 132, 135,
        185
    and stimulus classification, 182–184
    congenital, 141, 144
    cortical, 226, 228
block-copying task, 121
brain:
    Area 7, 238
    Area 17 (Area V1), 10, 11, 218–220,
        222–226, 228
    Area 18 (Area V2), 218, 219, 221,
        223–226
        visual association, 238
    Area 19, 238
    Area 21, 240
    Area 37, 240
    Area 40, 238
    Area M1 (primary motor cortex), 238,
        242
        functional role of during mental
            rotation, 240–241
    Area V4, 226
    damage, 1–2, 5, 8, 36, 76–78, 217, 227,
        233
    imaging, 4, 6–7, 11, 224–229, 232, 235,
        238
        findings in role of early visual cortex
            in visual mental imagery, 222–
            224
        late visual areas and visual mental
            imagery, 230–233
    regions recruited during visual mental
        imagery, 218–229

265